NCERT EXEMPLAR

Problems-Solutions

Physics

Detailed Explanation to all Objective & Subjective Problems

Atique Hassan
Sonal Sinha

arihant
Arihant Prakashan (School Division Series)

arihant

Arihant Prakashan (School Division Series)

卐 **Administrative & Production Offices**

Regd. Office

'Ramchhaya' 4577/15, Agarwal Road, Darya Ganj, New Delhi -110002
Tele: 011- 47630600, 43518550

卐 **Head Office**

Kalindi, TP Nagar, Meerut (UP) - 250002
Tel: 0121-7156203, 7156204

卐 **Sales & Support Offices**

Agra, Ahmedabad, Bengaluru, Bareilly, Chennai, Delhi, Guwahati, Hyderabad, Jaipur, Jhansi, Kolkata, Lucknow, Nagpur & Pune.

卐 **ISBN** 978-93-27197-41-9

PO No : TXT-XX-XXXXXXX-X-XX

Published by Arihant Publications (India) Ltd.

For further information about the books published by Arihant, log on to www.arihantbooks.com or e-mail at info@arihantbooks.com

Follow us on   

PREFACE

The Department of Education in Science & Mathematics (DESM) & National Council of Educational Research & Training (NCERT) developed **Exemplar Problems** in Science and Mathematics for Secondary and Senior Secondary Classes with the objective to provide the students a large number of quality problems in various forms and format *viz.* Multiple Choice Questions, Short Answer Questions, Long Answer Questions etc., with varying levels of difficulty.

NCERT Exemplar Problems are very important for both; School & Board Examinations as well as competitive examinations like Engineering & Medical Entrances. The questions given in exemplar book are mainly of higher difficulty order by practicing these problems, you will able to manage with the margin between a good score and a very good or an excellent score.

Approx 20% problems asked in any Board Examination or Entrance Examinations are of higher difficulty order, exemplar problems will make you ready to solve these difficult problems.

This book **NCERT Exemplar Problems-Solutions Physics XI** contains Explanatory & Accurate Solutions to all the questions given in NCERT Exemplar Physics book.

For the overall benefit of the students we have made unique this book in such a way that it presents not only hints and solutions but also detailed and authentic explanations. Through these detailed explanations, students can learn the concepts which will enhance their thinking and learning abilities.

We have introduced some additional features with the solutions which are as follows :

- **Thinking Process** Along with the solutions to questions we have given thinking process that tell how to approach to solve a problem. Here, we have tried to cover all the loopholes which may lead to confusion. All formulae and hints are discussed in detail.
- **Note** We have provided notes also to solutions in which special points are mentioned which are of great value for the students.

With the hope that this book will be of great help to the students, we wish great success to our readers.

Author

CONTENTS

1

Units and Measurements

Multiple Choice Questions (MCQs)

Q. 1 The number of significant figures in 0.06900 is

(a) 5 (b) 4 (c) 2 (d) 3

Thinking Process

If the number is less than 1, the zero(s) on the right of decimal point and before the first non-zero digit are not significant.

Ans. *(b)* In 0.06900, the underlined zeroes are not significant. Hence, number of significant figures are **four** (6900).

Q. 2 The sum of the numbers 436.32, 227.2 and 0.301 in appropriate significant figures is

(a) 663.821 (b) 664 (c) 663.8 (d) 663.82

Ans. *(b)* The sum of the numbers can be calculated as 663.821 arithmetically. The number with least decimal places is 227.2 is correct to only one decimal place.

The final result should, therefore be rounded off to one decimal place *i.e.*, 664.

Note *In calculating the sum, we should not confuse with the number of decimal places and significant figures. The result should have least number of decimal places.*

Q. 3 The mass and volume of a body are 4.237 g and 2.5 cm^3, respectively. The density of the material of the body in correct significant figures is

(a) 1.6048 g cm^{-3} (b) 1.69 g cm^{-3} (c) 1.7 g cm^{-3} (d) 1.695 g cm^{-3}

Thinking Process

In multiplication or division, the final result should retain as many significant figures as are there in the original number with the least significant figures.

Ans. *(c)* In this question, density should be reported to two significant figures.

$$\text{Density} = \frac{4.237\text{g}}{2.5\ \text{cm}^3} = 1.6948$$

As rounding off the number, we get density = 1.7

Q. 4 The numbers 2.745 and 2.735 on rounding off to 3 significant figures will give

(a) 2.75 and 2.74 (b) 2.74 and 2.73 (c) 2.75 and 2.73 (d) 2.74 and 2.74

Ans. *(d)* Rounding off 2.745 to 3 significant figures it would be 2.74. Rounding off 2.735 to 3 significant figures it would be 2.74.

Q. 5 The length and breadth of a rectangular sheet are 16.2 cm and 10.1 cm, respectively. The area of the sheet in appropriate significant figures and error is

(a) 164 ± 3 cm^2 (b) 163.62 ± 2.6 cm^2

(c) 163.6 ± 2.6 cm^2 (d) 163.62 ± 3 cm^2

Thinking Process

If Δx is error in a physical quantity, then relative error is calculated as $\frac{\Delta x}{x}$.

Ans. *(a)* Given,

$$\text{length } l = (16.2 \pm 0.1)\text{ cm}$$

$$\text{Breadth } b = (10.1 \pm 0.1)\text{ cm}$$

$$\text{Area } A = l \times b$$

$$= (16.2\text{ cm}) \times (10.1\text{ cm}) = 163.62\text{ cm}^2$$

Rounding off to three significant digits, area $A = 164\text{ cm}^2$

$$\frac{\Delta A}{A} = \frac{\Delta l}{l} + \frac{\Delta b}{b} = \frac{0.1}{16.2} + \frac{0.1}{10.1}$$

$$= \frac{1.01 + 1.62}{16.2 \times 10.1} = \frac{2.63}{163.62}$$

$$\Rightarrow \quad \Delta A = A \times \frac{2.63}{163.62} = 163.62 \times \frac{2.63}{163.62} = 2.63\text{ cm}^2$$

$$\Delta A = 3\text{ cm}^2 \quad \text{(By rounding off to one significant figure)}$$

$$\therefore \quad \text{Area, } A = A \pm \Delta A = (164 \pm 3)\text{ cm}^2.$$

Q. 6 Which of the following pairs of physical quantities does not have same dimensional formula?

(a) Work and torque (b) Angular momentum and Planck's constant

(c) Tension and surface tension (d) Impulse and linear momentum

Ans. *(c)* (a) Work = force × distance = $[MLT^{-2}][L]\,[ML^2T^{-2}]$

Torque = force × distance = $[ML^2T^{-2}]$

(b) Angular momentum = mvr = $[M][LT^{-1}][L] = [ML^2T^{-1}]$

Planck's constant $= \frac{E}{V} = \frac{[ML^2T^{-2}]}{[T^{-1}]} = [ML^2T^{-1}]$

(c) Tension = force = $[MLT^{-2}]$

Surface tension $= \frac{\text{force}}{\text{length}} = \frac{[MLT^{-2}]}{[L]} = [ML^0T^{-2}]$

(d) Impulse = force × time = $[MLT^{-2}][T] = [MLT^{-1}]$

Momentum = mass × velocity = $[M][LT^{-1}] = [MLT^{-1}]$

Note *One should not be confused with the similar form tension in both the physical quantities-surface tension and tension. Dimensional formula for both of them is not same.*

Q. 7 Measure of two quantities along with the precision of respective measuring instrument is
$A = 2.5\,\text{ms}^{-1} \pm 0.5\,\text{ms}^{-1}$, $B = 0.10\,\text{s} \pm 0.01\,\text{s}$. The value of AB will be

(a) (0.25 ± 0.08) m (b) (0.25 ± 0.5) m (c) (0.25 ± 0.05) m (d) (0.25 ± 0.135) m

Ans. *(a)* Given, $A = 2.5\,\text{ms}^{-1} \pm 0.5\,\text{ms}^{-1}, B = 0.10\,\text{s} \pm 0.01\,\text{s}$

$$x = AB = (2.5)(0.10) = 0.25\text{m}$$

$$\frac{\Delta x}{x} = \frac{\Delta A}{A} + \frac{\Delta B}{B}$$

$$= \frac{0.5}{2.5} + \frac{0.01}{0.10} = \frac{0.05 + 0.025}{0.25} = \frac{0.075}{0.25}$$

$\Delta x = 0.075 = 0.08$ m, rounding off to two significant figures.

$AB = (0.25 \pm 0.08)$ m

Q. 8 You measure two quantities as $A = 1.0\text{ m} \pm 0.2\text{ m}$, $B = 2.0\text{ m} \pm 0.2\text{ m}$. We should report correct value for $\sqrt{AB}$ as

(a) $1.4\text{ m} \pm 0.4\text{ m}$ (b) $1.41\text{ m} \pm 0.15\text{ m}$ (c) $1.4\text{ m} \pm 0.3\text{ m}$ (d) $1.4\text{ m} \pm 0.2\text{ m}$

Ans. *(d)* Given, $A = 1.0\text{m} \pm 0.2\text{ m}, B = 2.0\text{m} \pm 0.2\text{ m}$

Let, $Y = \sqrt{AB} = \sqrt{(1.0)(2.0)} = 1.414\text{m}$

Rounding off to two significant digit $Y = 1.4$ m

$$\frac{\Delta Y}{Y} = \frac{1}{2}\left[\frac{\Delta A}{A} + \frac{\Delta B}{B}\right] = \frac{1}{2}\left[\frac{0.2}{1.0} + \frac{0.2}{2.0}\right] = \frac{0.6}{2 \times 2.0}$$

$$\Rightarrow \quad \Delta Y = \frac{0.6Y}{2 \times 2.0} = \frac{0.6 \times 1.4}{2 \times 2.0} = 0.212$$

Rounding off to one significant digit $\Delta Y = 0.2$ m

Thus, correct value for $\sqrt{AB} = r + \Delta r = 1.4 \pm 0.2$m

Q. 9 Which of the following measurement is most precise?

(a) 5.00 mm (b) 5.00 cm (c) 5.00 m (d) 5.00 km

Ans. *(a)* All given measurements are correct upto two decimal places. As here 5.00 mm has the smallest unit and the error in 5.00 mm is least (commonly taken as 0.01 mm if not specified), hence, 5.00 mm is most precise.

Note *In solving these type of questions, we should be careful about units although their magnitude is same.*

Q. 10 The mean length of an object is 5 cm. Which of the following measurements is most accurate?

(a) 4.9 cm (b) 4.805 cm (c) 5.25 cm (d) 5.4 cm

Ans. *(a)* Given length $l = 5\,\text{cm}$

Now, checking the errors with each options one by one, we get

$$\Delta l_1 = 5 - 4.9 = 0.1\,\text{cm}$$

$$\Delta l_2 = 5 - 4.805 = 0.195\,\text{cm}$$

$$\Delta l_3 = 5.25 - 5 = 0.25\,\text{cm}$$

$$\Delta l_4 = 5.4 - 5 = 0.4\,\text{cm}$$

Error Δl_1 is least.

Hence, 4.9 cm is most precise.

Q. 11 **Young's modulus of steel is 1.9×10^{11} N / m^2. When expressed in CGS units of dyne/cm^2, it will be equal to ($1\text{N} = 10^5$ dyne, $1\text{ m}^2 = 10^4\text{ cm}^2$)**

(a) 1.9×10^{10} (b) 1.9×10^{11} (c) 1.9×10^{12} (d) 1.9×10^{13}

Ans. *(c)* Given, Young's modulus $Y = 1.9\times 10^{11}\text{ N/m}^2$

$$1\text{N} = 10^5 \text{ dyne}$$

Hence, $Y = 1.9\times 10^{11}\times 10^5 \text{ dyne/m}^2$

We know that $1\text{m} = 100\text{cm}$

$\therefore$
$$Y = 1.9\times 10^{11}\times 10^5 \text{ dyne/(100)}^2 \text{ cm}^2$$
$$= 1.9\times 10^{16-4}\text{ dyne/cm}^2$$
$$Y = 1.9\times 10^{12}\text{ dyne/cm}^2$$

Note *While we are going through units conversion, we should keep in mind that proper relation between units are mentioned.*

Q. 12 **If momentum (p), area (A) and time (T) are taken to be fundamental quantities, then energy has the dimensional formula**

(a) $[pA^{-1}T^1]$ (b) $[p^2AT]$ (c) $[pA^{-1/2}T]$ (d) $[pA^{1/2}T]$

Ans. *(d)* Given, fundamental quantities are momentum (p), area (A) and time (T).

We can write energy E as

$$E \propto p^a A^b T^c$$
$$E = kp^a A^A T^c$$

where k is dimensionless constant of proportionality.

Dimensions of $E = [E] = [ML^2T^{-2}]$ and $[p] = [MLT^{-1}]$

$$[A] = [L^2]$$
$$[T] = [T]$$
$$[E] = [K][p]^a[A]^b[T]^c$$

Putting all the dimensions, we get

$$ML^2T^{-2} = [MLT^{-1}]^a[L^2]^b[T]^c$$
$$= M^aL^{2b+a}T^{-a+c}$$

By principle of homogeneity of dimensions,

$$a = 1,\ 2b + a = 2$$

$\Rightarrow$ $2b + 1 = 2$

$\Rightarrow$ $b = 1/2 \quad -a + c = -2$

$\Rightarrow$ $c = -2 + a = -2 + 1 = -1$

Hence, $E = pA^{1/2}T^{-1}$

Multiple Choice Questions (More Than One Options)

Q. 13 On the basis of dimensions, decide which of the following relations for the displacement of a particle undergoing simple harmonic motion is not correct?

(a) $y = a \sin 2\pi t/T$
(b) $y = a \sin vt$
(c) $y = \frac{a}{T} \sin\left(\frac{t}{a}\right)$
(d) $y = a\sqrt{2}\left(\sin \frac{2\pi t}{T} - \cos \frac{2\pi t}{T}\right)$

Thinking Process

We know that angle is dimensionless. Here, a is displacement and y is also displacement, hence they are having same dimensions.

Ans. *(b, c)*

Now, by principle of homogeneity of dimensions LHS and RHS of (a) and (d) will be same and is L.

For (c) $[LHS] = L$

$$[RHS] = \frac{L}{T} = LT^{-1}$$

$$[LHS] \neq [RHS]$$

Hence, (c) is not correct option.

In option (b) dimension of angle is $[vt]$ *i.e.*, L

$\Rightarrow$ $RHS = L.L = L^2$ and $LHS = L$

$\Rightarrow$ $LHS \neq RHS$.

So, option (b) is also not correct.

Q. 14 If P, Q, R are physical quantities, having different dimensions, which of the following combinations can never be a meaningful quantity?

(a) $(P - Q)/R$
(b) $PQ - R$
(c) PQ/R
(d) $(PR - Q^2)/R$
(e) $(R + Q)/P$

Thinking Process

We should keep in mind that when two physical quantities are added or subtracted they should have same dimensions.

Ans. *(a, e)*

In this question, it is given that P, Q and R are having different dimensions, hence they cannot be added or subtracted, so we can say that (a) and (e) are not meaningful. We cannot say about the dimension of product of these quantities, hence (b), (c) and (d) may be meaningful.

Note *In this question, we are certain about the quantity which is never meaningful but we should keep in mind that others may or may not be meaningful.*

Q. 15 Photon is quantum of radiation with energy $E = h\nu$, where ν is frequency and h is Planck's constant. The dimensions of h are the same as that of

(a) linear impulse
(b) angular impulse
(c) linear momentum
(d) angular momentum

Ans. *(b, d)*

We know that energy of radiation, $E = h\nu$

$$[h] = \frac{[E]}{[\nu]} = \frac{[ML^2T^{-2}]}{[T^{-1}]} = [ML^2T^{-1}]$$

Dimension of linear impulse = Dimension of momentum = $[MLT^{-1}]$

As we know that linear impulse $J = \Delta P$

$\Rightarrow$ Angular impulse = $\tau dt = \Delta L$ = Change in angular momentum

Hence, dimension of angular impulse

= Dimension of angular momentum

= $[ML^2T^{-1}]$.

This is similar to the dimension of Planck's constant h.

Q. 16 **If Planck's constant (h) and speed of light in vacuum (c) are taken as two fundamental quantities, which one of the following can, in addition, be taken to express length, mass and time in terms of the three chosen fundamental quantities?**

(a) Mass of electron (m_e)
(b) Universal gravitational constant (G)
(c) Charge of electron (e)
(d) Mass of proton (m_p)

Ans. ***(a, b, d)***

We know that dimension of $h = [h] = [ML^2T^{-1}]$

$$[c] = [LT^{-1}], [m_e] = M$$

$$[G] = [M^{-1}L^3T^{-2}]$$

$$[e] = [AT], [m_p] = [M]$$

$$\left[\frac{hc}{G}\right] = \frac{[ML^2T^{-1}][LT^{-1}]}{[M^{-1}L^3T^{-2}]} = [M^2]$$

$$M = \sqrt{\frac{hc}{G}}$$

Similarly, $$\frac{h}{c} = \frac{[ML^2T^{-1}]}{[LT^{-1}]} = [ML]$$

$$L = \frac{h}{cM} = \frac{h}{c}\sqrt{\frac{G}{hc}} = \frac{\sqrt{Gh}}{c^{3/2}}$$

As, $$c = LT^{-1}$$

$\Rightarrow$ $$[T] = \frac{[L]}{[c]} = \frac{\sqrt{Gh}}{c^{3/2} \cdot c} = \frac{\sqrt{Gh}}{c^{5/2}}$$

Hence, (a), (b) or (d) any can be used to express L, M and T in terms of three chosen fundamental quantities.

Q. 17 **Which of the following ratios express pressure?**

(a) Force/Area
(b) Energy/Volume
(c) Energy/Area
(d) Force/Volume

Thinking Process

While solving this type of questions, we should first write an expression and try to express it in terms of quantities given in the option.

Ans. ***(a, b)***

We know that pressure $= \frac{\text{Force}}{\text{Area}}$

$$\text{Pressure} = \frac{\text{Force} \times \text{Distance}}{\text{Area} \times \text{Distance}} = \frac{\text{Work}}{\text{Volume}} = \frac{\text{Energy}}{\text{Volume}}$$

Note *Here, we should keep it in mind that above values are not exactly equal but these are equivalent with respect to their units.*

Q. 18 **Which of the following are not a unit of time?**

(a) Second (b) Parsec (c) Year (d) Light year

Ans. *(b, d)*

We know that 1 light year $= 9.46 \times 10^{11}$ m

$=$ distance that light travels in 1 year with speed 3×10^8 m/s.

1 parsec $= 3.08 \times 10^{16}$ m

$=$ Distance at which average radius of earth's orbit subtends an angle of 1 parsecond

Here, second and year represent time.

Very Short Answer Type Questions

Q. 19 **Why do we have different units for the same physical quantity?**

Ans. The value of any given physical quantity may vary over a wide range, therefore, different units of same physical quantity are required.

e.g., The length of a pen can be easily measured in cm, the height of a tree can be measured in metres, the distance between two cities can be measured in kilometres and distance between two heavenly bodies can be measured in light year.

Q. 20 **The radius of atom is of the order of 1 Å and radius of nucleus is of the order of fermi. How many magnitudes higher is the volume of atom as compared to the volume of nucleus?**

Ans.

Radius of atom $= 1\text{Å} = 10^{-10}$ m

Radius of nucleus $= 1$ fermi $= 10^{-15}$ m

Volume of atom $= V_A = \frac{4}{3}\pi R_A^3$

Volume of nucleus $V_N = \frac{4}{3}\pi R_N^3$

$$\frac{V_A}{V_N} = \frac{\frac{4}{3}\pi R_A^3}{\frac{4}{3}\pi R_N^3} = \left(\frac{R_A}{R_N}\right)^3 = \left(\frac{10^{-10}}{10^{-15}}\right)^3 = 10^{15}$$

Note *In such type of questions, always change the value in same unit.*

Q. 21 **Name the device used for measuring the mass of atoms and molecules.**

Ans. A mass spectrograph is used for measuring the mass of atoms and molecules.

Q. 22 **Express unified atomic mass unit in kg.**

Ans. One atomic mass unit is the $\frac{1}{12}$ of the mass of a $_6C^{12}$ atom.

Mass of one mole of $_6C^{12}$ atom $= 12$ g

Number of atoms in one mole $=$ Avogadro's number

$= 6.023 \times 10^{23}$

$\therefore$ Mass of one ${}_6C^{12}$ atom $= \dfrac{12}{6.023 \times 10^{23}}$ g

$$1 \text{ amu} = \frac{1}{12} \times \text{mass of one } {}_6C^{12} \text{ atom}$$

$$\therefore \quad 1 \text{ amu} = \left(\frac{1}{12} \times \frac{12}{6.023 \times 10^{23}}\right) \text{g} = 1.67 \times 10^{-24} \text{ g}$$

$$= 1.67 \times 10^{-27} \text{ kg} \qquad (\because 1 \text{ g} = 10^{-3} \text{ kg})$$

Q. 23 **A function $f(\theta)$ is defined as $f(\theta) = 1 - \theta + \dfrac{\theta^2}{2!} - \dfrac{\theta^3}{3!} + \dfrac{\theta^4}{4!} + \ldots$**

Why is it necessary for $f(\theta)$ to be a dimensionless quantity?

Ans. Since, $f(\theta)$ is a sum of different powers of θ and it is a dimensionless quantity.

By principle of homogeneity as RHS is dimensionless, hence LHS should also be dimensionless.

Q. 24 **Why length, mass and time are chosen as base quantities in mechanics?**

Ans. *Length, mass and time are chosen as base quantities in mechanics because*

(i) Length, mass and time cannot be derived from one another, that is these quantities are independent.

(ii) All other quantities in mechanics can be expressed in terms of length, mass and time.

Short Answer Type Questions

Q. 25 **(a) The earth-moon distance is about 60 earth radius. What will be the diameter of the earth (approximately in degrees) as seen from the moon?**

(b) Moon is seen to be of (1/2)° diameter from the earth. What must be the relative size compared to the earth?

(c) From parallax measurement, the sun is found to be at a distance of about 400 times the earth-moon distance. Estimate the ratio of sun-earth diameters.

Thinking Process

To solve this question, we have to treat radius of earth as an arc as seen from the moon.

Ans. (a) Angle subtended at distance r due to an arc of length l is

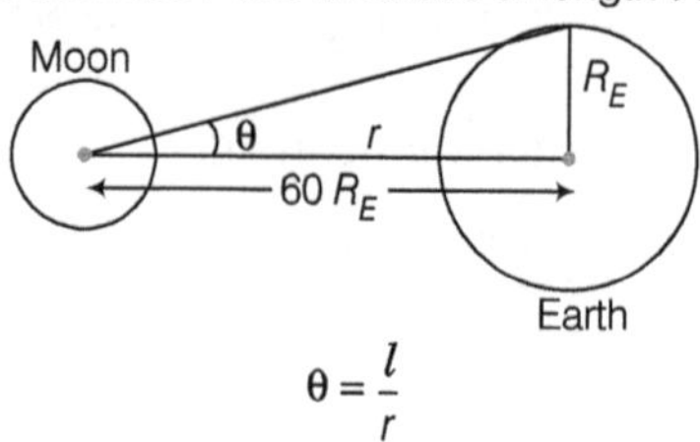

$$\theta = \frac{l}{r}$$

Given, $l = R_E; r = 60R_E$

$$\theta = \frac{R_E}{60R_E} = \frac{1}{60}\text{rad} = \frac{1}{60} \times \frac{180}{\pi}\text{degree}$$
$$= \frac{3}{\pi} \approx 1°$$

Hence, angle subtended by diameter of the earth $= 2\theta = 2°$.

(b) Given that moon is seen as $\left(\frac{1}{2}\right)^{\circ}$ diameter and earth is seen as 2° diameter.

Hence,
$$\frac{\text{Diameter of earth}}{\text{Diameter of moon}} = \frac{(2/\pi)\,\text{rad}}{\left(\frac{1}{2\pi}\right)\text{rad}} = 4$$

(c) From parallax measurement given that sun is at a distance of about 400 times the earth-moon distance, hence, $\frac{r_{sun}}{r_{moon}} = 400$

(Suppose, here r stands for distance and D for diameter)

sun and moon both appear to be of the same angular diameter as seen from the earth.

$$\therefore \quad \frac{D_{sun}}{r_{sun}} = \frac{D_{moon}}{r_{moon}}$$

$$\therefore \quad \frac{D_{sun}}{D_{moon}} = 400$$

But
$$\frac{D_{earth}}{D_{moon}} = 4$$

$$\therefore \quad \frac{D_{sun}}{D_{earth}} = 100$$

Q. 26 Which of the following time measuring devices is most precise?

(a) A wall clock (b) A stop watch

(c) A digital watch (d) An atomic clock

Given reason for your answer.

Ans. A wall clock can measure time correctly upto one second. A stop watch can measure time correctly upto a fraction of a second. A digital watch can measure time up to a fraction of second. An atomic clock can measure time most precisely as its precision is 1s in 10^{13} s.

Q. 27 The distance of a galaxy is of the order of 10^{25} m. Calculate the order of magnitude of time taken by light to reach us from the galaxy.

Ans. Given, distance of the galaxy $= 10^{25}$ m

Speed of light $= 3 \times 10^8$ m/s

Hence, time taken by light to reach us from galaxy is,

$$t = \frac{\text{Distance}}{\text{Speed}} = \frac{10^{25}}{3 \times 10^8} \approx \frac{1}{3} \times 10^{17}$$
$$= \frac{10}{3} \times 10^{16} = 3.33 \times 10^{16}\ \text{s}$$

Q. 28 **The vernier scale of a travelling microscope has 50 divisions which coincide with 49 main scale divisions. If each main scale division is 0.5 mm, calculate the minimum inaccuracy in the measurement of distance.**

Thinking Process

Inaccuracy will be measured by difference of 1MSD and 1VSD, where MSD = main scale division and VSD = verneir scale division.

Ans. By question, it is given that $50\text{VSD} = 49\text{MSD}$

$$1\text{MSD} = \frac{50}{49}\text{VSD}$$

$$1\text{VSD} = \frac{49}{50}\text{MSD}$$

$$\text{Minimum inaccuracy} = 1\text{MSD} - 1\text{VSD}$$

$$= 1\text{MSD} - \frac{49}{50}\text{MSD} = \frac{1}{50}\text{MSD}$$

Given, $1\text{MSD} = 0.5\text{ mm}$

Hence, $$\text{minimum inaccuracy} = \frac{1}{50} \times 0.5\text{ mm} = \frac{1}{100} = 0.01\text{ mm}$$

Q. 29 **During a total solar eclipse the moon almost entirely covers the sphere of the sun. Write the relation between the distances and sizes of the sun and moon.**

Ans. *Consider the diagram given below*

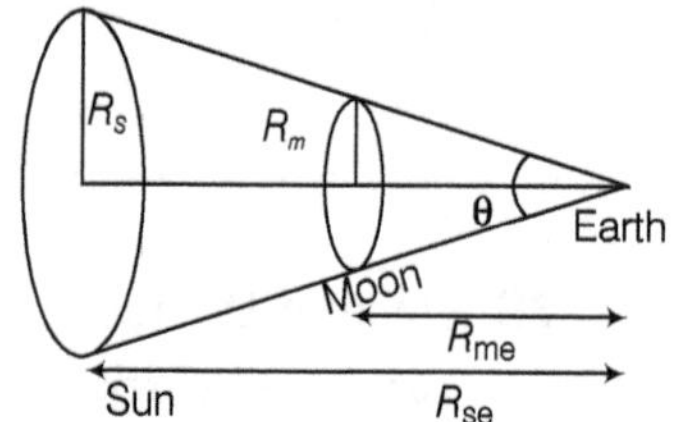

R_{me} = Distance of moon from earth

R_{se} = Distance of sun from earth

Let angle made by sun and moon is θ, we can write

$$\theta = \frac{A_{sun}}{R_{se}^2} = \frac{A_{moon}}{R_{me}^2}$$

Here, A_{sun} = Area of the sun

A_{moon} = Area of the moon

$$\Rightarrow \quad \theta = \frac{\pi R_s^2}{R_{se}^2} = \frac{\pi R_m^2}{R_{me}^2}$$

$$\Rightarrow \quad \left(\frac{R_s}{R_{se}}\right)^2 = \left(\frac{R_m}{R_{me}}\right)^2$$

$$\Rightarrow \quad \frac{R_s}{R_{se}} = \frac{R_m}{R_{me}}$$

$$\Rightarrow \quad \frac{R_s}{R_m} = \frac{R_{se}}{R_{me}}$$

(Here, radius of sun and moon represents their sizes respectively)

Q. 30 **If the unit of force is 100 N, unit of length is 10 m and unit of time is 100 s, what is the unit of mass in this system of units?**

Thinking Process

First write dimension of each quantity and then relate them.

Ans. Dimension of force $F = [\text{MLT}^{-2}] = 100\text{ N}$ ...(i)

Length $(L) = [\text{L}] = 10\text{ m}$ ...(ii)

Time $(t) = [\text{T}] = 100\text{ s}$ ...(iii)

Substituting values of L and T from Eqs. (ii) and (iii) in Eq. (i), we get

$$M \times 10 \times (100)^{-2} = 100$$

$$\Rightarrow \quad \frac{M \times 10}{100 \times 100} = 100$$

$$\Rightarrow \quad M = 100 \times 1000\,\text{kg}$$

$$M = 10^5\ \text{kg}$$

Q. 31 Give an example of

(a) a physical quantity which has a unit but no dimensions

(b) a physical quantity which has neither unit nor dimensions

(c) a constant which has a unit

(d) a constant which has no unit

Ans. **(a)** Plane angle $\theta = \frac{L}{r}$ radian

its unit is radian but has no dimensions

(b) Strain $= \frac{\Delta L}{L} = \frac{\text{Change in length}}{\text{length}}$

It has neither unit nor dimensions

(c) Gravitational constant (G) $= 6.67 \times 10^{-11}\,\text{N-m}^2/\text{kg}^2$

(d) Reynold's number is a constant which has no unit.

Q. 32 Calculate the length of the arc of a circle of radius 31.0 cm which subtends an angle of $\frac{\pi}{6}$ at the centre.

Ans. We know that angle $\theta = \frac{l}{r}$ radian

Given, $\theta = \frac{\pi}{6} = \frac{l}{31}$ cm

Hence, length $= l = 31 \times \frac{\pi}{6}\ \text{cm} = \frac{31 \times 3.14}{6}\ \text{cm} = 16.22\ \text{cm}$

Rounding off to three significant figures it would be 16.2 cm.

Q. 33 Calculate the solid angle subtended by the periphery of an area of $1\,\text{cm}^2$ at a point situated symmetrically at a distance of 5 cm from the area.

Ans. We know that solid angle $\Omega = \frac{\text{Area}}{(\text{Distance})^2}$

$$= \frac{1\ \text{cm}^2}{(5\ \text{cm})^2} = \frac{1}{25} = 4 \times 10^{-2}\ \text{steradian}$$

($\because$ Area $= 1\,\text{cm}^2$, distance = 5 cm)

Note *We should not confuse, solid angle with plane angle* $\theta = \frac{l}{r}$ *radian.*

Q. 34 **The displacement of a progressive wave is represented by $y = A\sin(\omega t - kx)$, where x is distance and t is time. Write the dimensional formula of (i) ω and (ii) k.**

Thinking Process

In solving these type of questions, we should apply principle of homogeneity of dimensions.

Ans. Now, by the principle of homogeneity, *i.e.,* dimensions of LHS and RHS should be equal, hence

$$[\text{LHS}] = [\text{RHS}]$$

$$\Rightarrow \quad [L] = [A] = L$$

As $\omega t - kx$ should be dimensionless, $[\omega t] = [kx] = 1$

$$\Rightarrow \quad [\omega]T = [k]L = 1$$

$$\Rightarrow \quad [\omega] = T^{-1} \text{ and } [k] = L^{-1}$$

Q. 35 **Time for 20 oscillations of a pendulum is measured as $t_1 = 39.6$ s; $t_2 = 39.9$ s and $t_3 = 39.5$ s. What is the precision in the measurements? What is the accuracy of the measurement?**

Thinking Process

We will apply formula for mean value, absolute error as well as mean absolute error.

Ans. Given, $t_1 = 39.6\text{ s}, t_2 = 39.9\text{ s and } t_3 = 39.5\text{ s}$

Least count of measuring instrument = 0.1 s

(As measurements have only one decimal place)

Precision in the measurement = Least count of the measuring instrument = 0.1 s

Mean value of time for 20 oscillations is given by

$$t = \frac{t_1 + t_2 + t_3}{3}$$

$$= \frac{39.6 + 39.9 + 39.5}{3} = 39.7\text{ s}$$

Absolute errors in the measurements

$$\Delta t_1 = t - t_1 = 39.7 - 39.6 = 0.1\text{ s}$$

$$\Delta t_2 = t - t_2 = 39.7 - 39.9 = -0.2\text{ s}$$

$$\Delta t_3 = t - t_3 = 39.7 - 39.5 = 0.2\text{ s}$$

$$\text{Mean absolute error} = \frac{|\Delta t_1| + |\Delta t_2| + |\Delta t_3|}{3}$$

$$= \frac{0.1 + 0.2 + 0.2}{3}$$

$$= \frac{0.5}{3} = 0.17 \approx 0.2$$ (rounding off upto one decimal place)

$\therefore$ Accuracy of measurement = ± 0.2 s

Long Answer Type Questions

Q. 36 A new system of units is proposed in which unit of mass is α kg, unit of length β m and unit of time γ s. How much will 5J measure in this new system?

Thinking Process

For solving this question, we will apply the formula for a system of unit u, nu = constant.

Ans. We know that dimension of energy = $[ML^2T^{-2}]$

Let M_1, L_1, T_1 and M_2, L_2, T_2 are units of mass, length and time in given two systems.

$$\therefore \quad M_1 = 1\,kg, L_1 = 1\,m, T_1 = 1\,s$$
$$M_2 = \alpha\,kg, L_2 = \beta\,m, T_2 = \gamma\,s$$

The magnitude of a physical quantity remains the same, whatever be the system of units of its measurement *i.e.*, $n_1u_1 = n_2u_2$

$$\Rightarrow \quad n_2 = n_1\frac{u_1}{u_2} = n_1\frac{[M_1L_1^2T_1^{-2}]}{[M_2L_2^2T_2^{-2}]} = 5\left[\frac{M_1}{M_2}\right]\times\left[\frac{L_1}{L_2}\right]^2\times\left[\frac{T_1}{T_2}\right]^{-2}$$
$$= 5\left[\frac{1}{\alpha}\,kg\right]\times\left[\frac{1}{\beta}\,m\right]^2\times\left[\frac{1}{\gamma}\,s\right]^{-2}$$
$$= 5\times\frac{1}{\alpha}\times\frac{1}{\beta^2}\times\frac{1}{\gamma^{-2}}$$
$$n_2 = \frac{5\gamma^2}{\alpha\beta^2}$$

Thus, new unit of energy will be $\frac{\gamma^2}{\alpha\beta^2}$.

Q. 37 The volume of a liquid flowing out per second of a pipe of length l and radius r is written by a student as $V = \frac{\pi}{8}\frac{pr^4}{\eta l}$ where p is the pressure difference between the two ends of the pipe and η is coefficent of viscosity of the liquid having dimensional formula $[ML^{-1}T^{-1}]$. Check whether the equation is dimensionally correct.

Thinking Process

If dimensions of LHS of an equation is equal to dimensions of RHS, then equation is said to be dimensionally correct.

Ans. The volume of a liquid flowing out per second of a pipe is given by $V = \frac{\pi}{8}\frac{pr^4}{\eta l}$

Dimension of $V = \frac{\text{Dimension of volume}}{\text{Dimension of time}} = \frac{[L^3]}{[T]} = [L^3T^{-1}]$

($\because$ V is the volume of liquid flowing out per second)

Dimension of $p = [ML^{-1}T^{-2}]$

Dimension of $\eta = [ML^{-1}T^{-1}]$

Dimension of $l = [L]$

Dimension of $r = [L]$

Dimensions of LHS, $[V] = \frac{[L^3]}{[T]} = [L^3T^{-1}]$

Dimensions of RHS, $\frac{[ML^{-1}T^{-2}] \times [L^4]}{[ML^{-1}T^{-1}] \times [L]} = [L^3T^{-1}]$

As dimensions of LHS is equal to the dimensions of RHS.
Therefore, equation is correct dimensionally.

Q. 38 A physical quantity X is related to four measurable quantities a, b, c and d as follows $X = a^2b^3c^{5/2}d^{-2}$. The percentage error in the measurement of a, b, c and d are 1%, 2%, 3% and 4%, respectively. What is the percentage error in quantity X? If the value of X calculated on the basis of the above relation is 2.763, to what value should you round off the result.

Thinking Process

We will apply the formula for percentage error in quantity x, as $\frac{\Delta x}{x} \times 100$.

Ans. Given, physical quantity is $X = a^2b^3c^{5/2}d^{-2}$

Maximum percentage error in X is

$$\frac{\Delta X}{X} \times 100 = \pm\left[2\left(\frac{\Delta a}{a} \times 100\right) + 3\left(\frac{\Delta b}{b} \times 100\right) + \frac{5}{2}\left(\frac{\Delta c}{c} \times 100\right) + 2\left(\frac{\Delta d}{d} \times 100\right)\right]$$

$$= \pm\left[2(1) + 3(2) + \frac{5}{2}(3) + 2(4)\right]\%$$

$$= \pm\left[2 + 6 + \frac{15}{2} + 8\right] = \pm 23.5\%$$

$\therefore$ Percentage error in quantity $X = \pm 23.5\%$

Mean absolute error in $X = \pm 0.235 = \pm 0.24$ (rounding-off upto two significant digits)

The calculated value of x should be round-off upto two significant digits.

$\therefore$ $X = 2.8$

Q. 39 In the expression $P = El^2m^{-5}G^{-2}$, E, m, l and G denote energy, mass, angular momentum and gravitational constant, respectively. Show that P is a dimensionless quantity.

Thinking Process

A dimensionless quantity will have dimensional formula as $[M^0L^0T^0]$.

Ans. Given, expression is $P = EL^2m^{-5}G^{-2}$

where E is energy $[E] = [ML^2T^{-2}]$

m is mass $[m] = [M]$

L is angular momentum $[L] = [ML^2T^{-1}]$

G is gravitational constant $[G] = [M^{-1}L^3T^{-2}]$

Substituting dimensions of each term in the given expression,

$$[P] = [ML^2T^{-2}] \times [ML^2T^{-1}]^2 \times [M]^{-5} \times [M^{-1}L^3T^{-2}]^{-2}$$

$$= [M^{1+2-5+2}L^{2+4-6}T^{-2-2+4}] = [M^0L^0T^0]$$

Therefore, P is a dimensionless quantity.

Q. 40 If velocity of light c, Planck's constant h and gravitational constant G are taken as fundamental quantities, then express mass, length and time in terms of dimensions of these quantities.

Thinking Process

In this problem, we have to apply principle of homogeneity of dimensions that is LHS and RHS of an equation will have same dimensions.

Ans. We know that, dimensions of $(h) = [ML^2T^{-1}]$

Dimensions of $(c) = [LT^{-1}]$

Dimensions of gravitational constant $(G) = [M^{-1}L^3T^{-2}]$

(i) Let $m \propto c^x h^y G^z$

$\Rightarrow \quad m = kc^x h^y G^z \quad$ ...(i)

where, k is a dimensionless constant of proportionality.

Substituting dimensions of each term in Eq. (i), we get

$$[ML^0T^0] = [LT^{-1}]^x \times [ML^2T^{-1}]^y [M^{-1}L^3T^{-2}]^z$$

$$= [M^{y-z}L^{x+2y+3z}T^{-x-y-2z}]$$

Comparing powers of same terms on both sides, we get

$$y - z = 1 \quad \text{...(ii)}$$

$$x + 2y + 3z = 0 \quad \text{...(iii)}$$

$$-x - y - 2z = 0 \quad \text{...(iv)}$$

Adding Eqs. (ii), (iii) and (iv), we get

$$2y = 1 \Rightarrow y = \frac{1}{2}$$

Substituting value of y in Eq. (ii), we get

$$z = -\frac{1}{2}$$

From Eq. (iv)

$$x = -y - 2z$$

Substituting values of y and z, we get

$$x = -\frac{1}{2} - 2\left(-\frac{1}{2}\right) = \frac{1}{2}$$

Putting values of x, y and z in Eq. (i), we get

$$m = kc^{1/2}h^{1/2}G^{-1/2}$$

$$\Rightarrow \quad m = k\sqrt{\frac{ch}{G}}$$

(ii) Let $L \propto c^x h^y G^z$

$\Rightarrow \quad L = kc^x h^y G^z \quad$ ...(v)

where, k is a dimensionless constant.

Substituting dimensions of each term in Eq. (v), we get

$$[M^0LT^0] = [LT^{-1}]^x \times [ML^2T^{-1}]^y \times [M^{-1}L^3T^{-2}]^z$$

$$= [M^{y-z}L^{x+2y+3z}T^{-x-y-2z}]$$

On comparing powers of same terms, we get

$$y - z = 0 \quad \text{...(vi)}$$

$$x + 2y + 3z = 1 \quad \text{...(vii)}$$

$$-x - y - 2z = 0 \quad \text{...(viii)}$$

Adding Eqs. (vi), (vii) and (viii), we get

$$2y = 1$$

$$\Rightarrow \quad y = \frac{1}{2}$$

Substituting value of y in Eq. (vi), we get

$$z = \frac{1}{2}$$

From Eq. (viii),

$$x = -y - 2z$$

Substituting values of y and z, we get

$$x = -\frac{1}{2} - 2\left(\frac{1}{2}\right) = -\frac{3}{2}$$

Putting values of x, y and z in Eq. (v), we get

$$L = kc^{-3/2}h^{1/2}G^{1/2}$$

$$L = k\sqrt{\frac{hG}{c^3}}$$

(iii) Let $T \propto c^x h^y G^z$

$$\Rightarrow \quad T = kc^x h^y G^z \quad \text{...(ix)}$$

where, k is a dimensionless constant.

Substituting dimensions of each term in Eq. (ix), we get

$$[M^0L^0T] = [LT^{-1}]^x \times [ML^2T^{-1}]^y \times [M^{-1}L^3T^{-2}]^z$$

$$= [M^{y-z}L^{x+2y+3z}T^{-x-y-2z}]$$

On comparing powers of same terms, we get

$$y - z = 0 \quad \text{...(x)}$$

$$x + 2y + 3z = 0 \quad \text{...(xi)}$$

$$-x - y - 2z = 1 \quad \text{...(xii)}$$

Adding Eqs. (x), (xi) and (xii), we get

$$2y = 1$$

$$\Rightarrow \quad y = \frac{1}{2}$$

Substituting value of y in Eq. (x), we get

$$z = y = \frac{1}{2}$$

From Eq. (xii),

$$x = -y - 2z - 1$$

Substituting values of y and z, we get

$$x = -\frac{1}{2} - 2\left(\frac{1}{2}\right) - 1 = -\frac{5}{2}$$

Putting values of x, y and z in Eq. (ix), we get

$$T = kc^{-5/2}h^{1/2}G^{1/2}$$

$$T = k\sqrt{\frac{hG}{c^5}}$$

Q. 41 An artificial satellite is revolving around a planet of mass M and radius R, in a circular orbit of radius r. From Kepler's third law about the period of a satellite around a common central body, square of the period of revolution T is proportional to the cube of the radius of the orbit r. Show using dimensional analysis, that $T = \frac{k}{R}\sqrt{\frac{r^3}{g}}$, where k is a dimensionless constant and g is acceleration due to gravity.

Thinking Process

In this problem, we have to apply Kepler's third law, $T^2 \propto a^3$ i.e., square of time period (T^2) of a satellite revolving around a planet, is proportional to cube of the radius of the orbit (a^3).

Ans. By Kepler's third law, $T^2 \propto r^3 \Rightarrow T \propto r^{3/2}$

We know that T is a function of R and g.

Let $$T \propto r^{3/2} R^a g^b$$

$\Rightarrow$ $$T = k r^{3/2} R^a g^b \quad \ldots\text{(i)}$$

where, k is a dimensionless constant of proportionality.

Substituting the dimensions of each term in Eq. (i), we get

$$[M^0L^0T] = k[L]^{3/2}[L]^a[LT^{-2}]^b$$
$$= k[L^{a+b+3/2}T^{-2b}]$$

On comparing the powers of same terms, we get

$$a + b + 3/2 = 0 \quad \ldots\text{(ii)}$$
$$-2b = 1 \Rightarrow b = -1/2 \quad \ldots\text{(iii)}$$

From Eq. (ii), we get

$$a - 1/2 + 3/2 = 0 \Rightarrow a = -1$$

Substituting the values of a and b in Eq. (i), we get

$$T = k r^{3/2} R^{-1} g^{-1/2}$$

$\Rightarrow$ $$T = \frac{k}{R}\sqrt{\frac{r^3}{g}}$$

Note *When we are applying formulae, we should be careful about r (radius of orbit) and R (radius of planet).*

Q. 42 In an experiment to estimate the size of a molecule of oleic acid 1 mL of oleic acid is dissolved in 19 mL of alcohol. Then 1 mL of this solution is diluted to 20 mL by adding alcohol. Now, 1 drop of this diluted solution is placed on water in a shallow trough. The solution spreads over the surface of water forming one molecule thick layer. Now, lycopodium powder is sprinkled evenly over the film and its diameter is measured. Knowing the volume of the drop and area of the film we can calculate the thickness of the film which will give us the size of oleic acid molecule.

Read the passage carefully and answer the following questions

(a) Why do we dissolve oleic acid in alcohol?

(b) What is the role of lycopodium powder?

(c) What would be the volume of oleic acid in each mL of solution prepared?

(d) How will you calculate the volume of n drops of this solution of oleic acid?

(e) What will be the volume of oleic acid in one drop of this solution?

Ans. (a) Oleic acid does not dissolve in water hence, it is dissolved in alcohol.

(b) Lycopodium powder spreads over the entire surface of water when it is sprinkled evenly. When a drop of prepared solution is dropped on water, oleic acid does not dissolve in water. Instead it spreads on the water surface pushing the lycopodium powder away to clear a circular area where the drop falls. We can therefore, measure the area over which oleic acid spreads.

(c) In each mL of solution prepared volume of oleic acid $= \frac{1}{20}\text{ mL} \times \frac{1}{20} = \frac{1}{400}\text{ mL}$

(d) Volume of n drops of this solution of oleic acid can be calculated by means of a burette and measuring cylinder and measuring the number of drops.

(e) If n drops of the solution make 1 mL, the volume of oleic acid in one drop will be $\frac{1}{(400)n}$ mL.

Q. 43 (a) How many astronomical units (AU) make 1 parsec?

(b) Consider a sunlike star at a distance of 2 parsecs. When it is seen through a telescope with 100 magnification, what should be the angular size of the star? Sun appears to be $(1/2)°$ from the earth. Due to atmospheric fluctuations, eye cannot resolve objects smaller than 1 arc minute.

(c) Mars has approximately half of the earth's diameter. When it is closest to the earth it is at about 1/2 AU from the earth. Calculate what size it will appear when seen through the same telescope.

Ans. (a) By definition,

1 parsec = Distance at which 1 AU long arc subtends an angle of 1 s.

$$\therefore \quad 1\text{ parsec} = \left(\frac{1\text{AU}}{1\text{arc sec}}\right)$$

$$1\text{ deg} = 3600\text{ arc sec}$$

$$\therefore \quad 1\text{ parsec} = \frac{\pi}{3600 \times 180}\text{ rad}$$

$$\therefore \quad 1\text{ parsec} = \frac{3600 \times 180}{\pi}\text{ AU} = 206265\text{ AU} \approx 2 \times 10^5\text{ AU}$$

(b) Sun's diameter is $\left(\frac{1}{2}\right)^\circ$ at 1 AU.

Therefore, at 1 parsec, star is $\frac{1/2}{2 \times 10^5}$ degree in diameter $= 15 \times 10^{-5}$ arc min.

With 100 magnification, it should look 15×10^{-3} arcmin. However, due to atmospheric fluctuations, it will still look of about 1 arcmin. It cannot be magnified using telescope.

(c) Given that $$\frac{D_{\text{mars}}}{D_{\text{earth}}} = \frac{1}{2} \quad \text{...(i)}$$

where D represents diameter.

From answer 25(e)

we know that, $$\frac{D_{\text{earth}}}{D_{\text{sun}}} = \frac{1}{100}$$

$\therefore$ $$\frac{D_{\text{mars}}}{D_{\text{sun}}} = \frac{1}{2} \times \frac{1}{100} \quad \text{[from Eq. (i)]}$$

$$\text{At 1 AU sun's diameter} = \left(\frac{1}{2}\right)^{\circ}$$

$\therefore$ $$\text{mar's diameter} = \frac{1}{2} \times \frac{1}{200} = \frac{1}{400}$$

$$\text{At } \frac{1}{2} \text{ AU, mar's diameter} = \frac{1}{400} \times 2^{\circ} = \left(\frac{1}{200}\right)^{\circ}$$

$$\text{With 100 magnification, Mar's diameter} = \frac{1}{200} \times 100^{\circ} = \left(\frac{1}{2}\right)^{\circ} = 30'$$

This is larger than resolution limit due to atmospheric fluctuations. Hence, it looks magnified.

Q. 44 **Einstein's mass-energy relation emerging out of his famous theory of relativity relates mass (m) to energy (E) as $E = mc^2$, where c is speed of light in vacuum. At the nuclear level, the magnitudes of energy are very small. The energy at nuclear level is usually measured in MeV, where 1MeV $= 1.6 \times 10^{-13}$J; the masses are measured in unified atomic mass unit (u) where, 1u $= 1.67 \times 10^{-27}$ kg.**

(a) Show that the energy equivalent of 1u is 931.5 MeV.

(b) A student writes the relation as 1u = 931.5 MeV. The teacher points out that the relation is dimensionally incorrect. Write the correct relation.

Thinking Process

In this problem, we have to apply Einstein's mass-energy relation. $E = mc^2$, to calculate the energy equivalent of the given mass.

Ans. (a) We know that

$$1 \text{ amu} = 1\text{u} = 1.67 \times 10^{-27} \text{kg}$$

Applying $$E = mc^2$$

$$\text{Energy} = E = (1.67 \times 10^{-27})(3 \times 10^8)^2 \text{ J}$$

$$= 1.67 \times 9 \times 10^{-11} \text{J}$$

$$E = \frac{1.67 \times 9 \times 10^{-11}}{1.6 \times 10^{-13}} \text{MeV} = 939.4 \text{ MeV} \approx 931.5 \text{ MeV}$$

(b) The dimensionally correct relation is

$$1 \text{ amu} \times c^2 = 1\text{u} \times c^2 = 931.5 \text{ MeV}$$

2

Motion *in* a Straight Line

Multiple Choice Questions (MCQs)

Q. 1 Among the four graph shown in the figure there is only one graph for which average velocity over the time interval $(0, T)$ can vanish for a suitably chosen T. Which one is it?

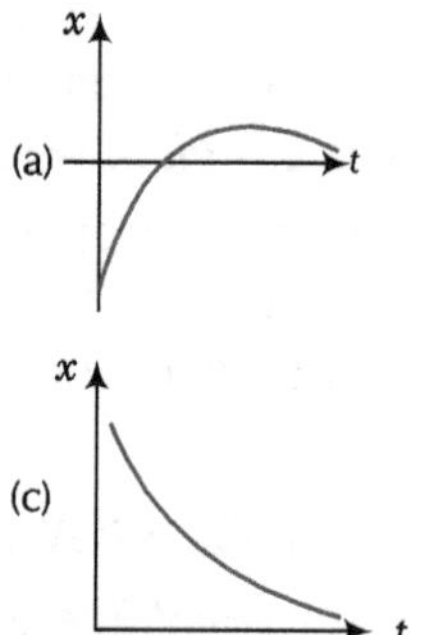

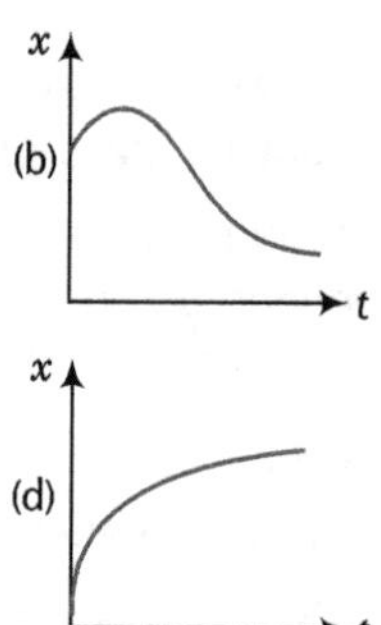

Thinking Process

In this problem, we have to locate the graph which is having same displacement for two timings. When there are two timings for same displacement the corresponding velocities will be in opposite directions.

Ans. ***(b)*** In graph (b) for one value of displacement there are two different points of time. Hence, for one time, the average velocity is positive and for other time is equivalent negative.

As there are opposite velocities in the interval 0 to T hence average velocity can vanish in (b). *This can be seen in the figure given below*

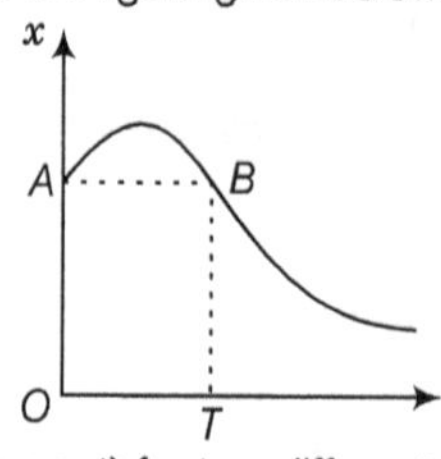

Here, $OA = BT$ (same displacement) for two different points of time.

Q. 2 A lift is coming from 8th floor and is just about to reach 4th floor. Taking ground floor as origin and positive direction upwards for all quantities, which one of the following is correct?

(a) $x < 0, v < 0, a > 0$ (b) $x > 0, v < 0, a < 0$
(c) $x > 0, v < 0, a > 0$ (d) $x > 0, v > 0, a < 0$

Ans. *(a)* As the lift is coming in downward directions displacement will be negative. We have to see whether the motion is accelerating or retarding.

We know that due to downward motion displacement will be negative. When the lift reaches 4th floor is about to stop hence, motion is retarding in nature hence, $x < 0$; $a > 0$.

As displacement is in negative direction, velocity will also be negative *i.e.*, $v < 0$.

This can be shown on the adjacent graph.

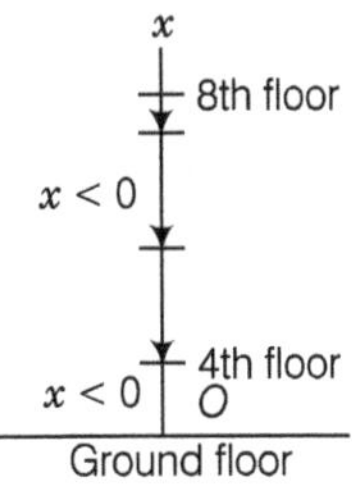

Q. 3 In one dimensional motion, instantaneous speed v satisfies $0 \le v < v_0$.

(a) The displacement in time T must always take non-negative values
(b) The displacement x in time T satisfies $-v_0 T < x < v_0 T$
(c) The acceleration is always a non-negative number
(d) The motion has no turning points

Ans. *(b)* For maximum and minimum displacement we have to keep in mind the magnitude and direction of maximum velocity.

As maximum velocity in positive direction is v_0 maximum velocity in opposite direction is also v_0.

Maximum displacement in one direction $= v_0 T$

Maximum displacement in opposite directions $= -v_0 T$

Hence, $-v_0 T < x < v_0 T$

Note *We should not confuse with direction of velocities i.e., in one direction it is taken as positive and in another direction is taken as negative.*

Q. 4 A vehicle travels half the distance l with speed v_1 and the other half with speed v_2, then its average speed is

(a) $\frac{v_1 + v_2}{2}$ (b) $\frac{2v_1 + v_2}{v_1 + v_2}$ (c) $\frac{2v_1 v_2}{v_1 + v_2}$ (d) $\frac{L(v_1 + v_2)}{v_1 v_2}$

Thinking Process

To calculate average speed we will calculate total distance covered and will divide by total time taken.

Ans. *(c)* Time taken to travel first half distance $t_1 = \frac{l/2}{v_1} = \frac{l}{2v_1}$

Time taken to travel second half distance $t_2 = \frac{l}{2v_2}$

$$\text{Total time} = t_1 + t_2 = \frac{l}{2v_1} + \frac{l}{2v_2} = \frac{l}{2}\left[\frac{1}{v_1} + \frac{1}{v_2}\right]$$

We know that, V_{av} = Average speed = $\dfrac{\text{total distance}}{\text{total time}}$

$$= \frac{l}{\frac{l}{2}\left[\frac{1}{v_1}+\frac{1}{v_2}\right]} = \frac{2v_1v_2}{v_1+v_2}$$

Note *We should not confuse with distance and displacement. Distance ≥ displacement.*

Q. 5 The displacement of a particle is given by $x = (t-2)^2$ where x is in metre and t in second. The distance covered by the particle in first 4 seconds is

(a) 4 m (b) 8 m (c) 12 m (d) 16 m

Thinking Process

In such type of problems we have to see whether the motion is accelerating or retarding. During retarding journey particle will stop in between.

Ans. ***(b)*** Given, $x = (t-2)^2$

Velocity, $v = \dfrac{dx}{dt} = \dfrac{d}{dt}(t-2)^2 = 2(t-2)$ m/s

Acceleration, $a = \dfrac{dv}{dt} = \dfrac{d}{dt}[2(t-2)]$

$= 2[1-0] = 2\,\text{m/s}^2$

When, $t = 0;\ v = -4$ m/s

$t = 2\text{s};\ v = 0$ m/s

$t = 4\text{s};\ v = 4$ m/s

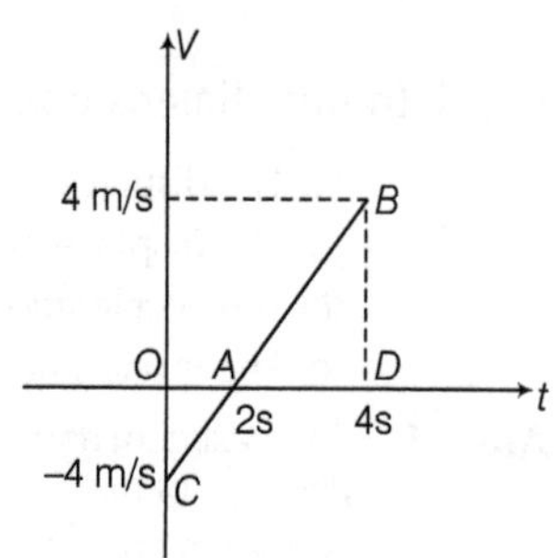

v-t graph is shown in adjacent diagram.

Distance travelled = area of the graph

= area OAC + area ABD

$$= \frac{4\times 2}{2} + \frac{1}{2}\times 2\times 4 = 8\,\text{m}$$

Q. 6 At a metro station, a girl walks up a stationary escalator in time t_1. If she remains stationary on the escalator, then the escalator take her up in time t_2. The time taken by her to walk up on the moving escalator will be

(a) $(t_1+t_2)/2$ (b) $t_1t_2/(t_2-t_1)$ (c) $t_1t_2/(t_2+t_1)$ (d) t_1-t_2

Ans. ***(c)*** In this question, we have to find net velocity with respect to the Earth that will be equal to velocity of the girl plus velocity of escalator.

Let displacement is L, then

velocity of girl $v_g = \dfrac{L}{t_1}$

velocity of escalator $v_e = \dfrac{L}{t_2}$

Net velocity of the girl = $v_g + v_e = \dfrac{L}{t_1} + \dfrac{L}{t_2}$

If t is total time taken in covering distance L, then

$$\frac{L}{t} = \frac{L}{t_1} + \frac{L}{t_2} \Rightarrow t = \frac{t_1t_2}{t_1+t_2}$$

Multiple Choice Questions (More Than One Options)

Q. 7 The variation of quantity A with quantity B, plotted in figure. Describes the motion of a particle in a straight line.

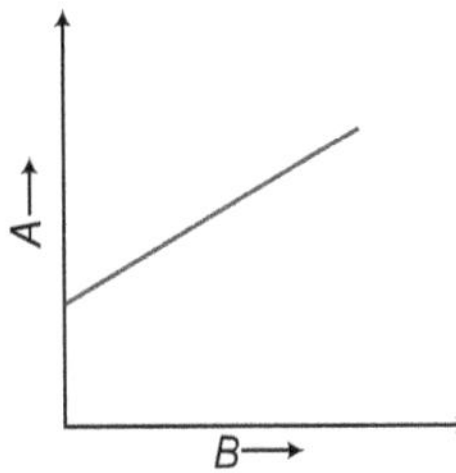

(a) Quantity B may represent time
(b) Quantity A is velocity if motion is uniform
(c) Quantity A is displacement if motion is uniform
(d) Quantity A is velocity if motion is uniformly accelerated

Ans. *(a, c, d)*

When we are calculating velocity of a displacement-time graph we have to take slope similarly we have to take slope of velocity-time graph to calculate acceleration. When slope is constant motion will be uniform.

When we are representing motion by a graph it may be displacement-time, velocity-time or acceleration-time hence, B may represent time. For uniform motion velocity-time graph should be a straight line parallel to time axis. For uniform motion velocity is constant hence, slope will be positive. Hence quantity A is displacement.

For uniformly accelerated motion slope will be positive and A will represent velocity.

Q. 8 A graph of x *versus* t is shown in figure. Choose correct alternatives given below

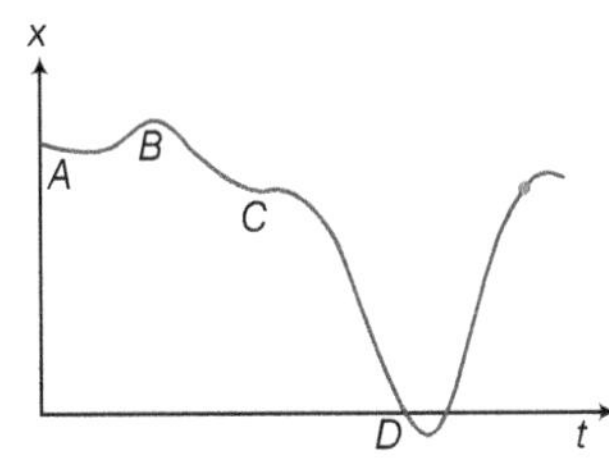

(a) The particle was released from rest at $t = 0$
(b) At B, the acceleration $a > 0$
(c) Average velocity for the motion between A and D is positive
(d) The speed at D exceeds that at E

Thinking Process

In this problem, we have to apply formula for slope $= \frac{dx}{dt}$ *for the graph and velocity* $v = \frac{dx}{dt}$.

Ans. *(a, c, d)*

As per the diagram, at point A the graph is parallel to time axis hence, $v = \frac{dx}{dt} = 0$. As the starting point is A hence, we can say that the particle is starting from rest.

At C, the graph changes slope, hence, velocity also changes. As graph at C is almost parallel to time axis hence, we can say that velocity vanishes.

As direction of acceleration changes hence, we can say that it may be zero in between.

From the graph it is clear that

$$|\text{slope at } D| > |\text{slope at } E|$$

Hence, speed at D will be more than at E.

Note *We should be very clear about magnitude of slope. Negative slope does not mean less value. It represents change in direction of velocity.*

Q. 9 For the one-dimensional motion, described by $x = t - \sin t$

(a) $x(t) > 0$ for all $t > 0$

(b) $v(t) > 0$ for all $t > 0$

(c) $a(t) > 0$ for all $t > 0$

(d) $v(t)$ lies between 0 and 2

Ans. *(a, d)*

Given,

$$x = t - \sin t$$

$$\text{velocity } v = \frac{dx}{dt} = \frac{d}{dt}[t - \sin t]$$

$$= 1 - \cos t$$

$$\text{Acceleration } a = \frac{dv}{dt} = \frac{d}{dt}[1 - \cos t] = \sin t$$

As acceleration $a > 0$ for all $t > 0$

Hence, $x(t) > 0$ for all $t > 0$

$$\text{Velocity } v = 1 - \cos t$$

When, $\cos t = 1$, velocity $v = 0$

$$v_{max} = 1 - (\cos t)_{min} = 1 - (-1) = 2$$

$$v_{min} = 1 - (\cos t)_{max} = 1 - 1 = 0$$

Hence, v lies between 0 and 2.

$$\text{Acceleration } a = \frac{dv}{dt} = -\sin t$$

When $t = 0$; $x = 0$, $x = +1$, $a = 0$

When $t = \frac{\pi}{2}$; $x = 1$, $v = 0$, $a = -1$

When $t = \pi$; $x = 0$, $x = -1$, $a = 1$

When $t = 2\pi$; $x = 0$, $x = 0$, $a = 0$

Note *(i) When sinusoidal function is involved in an expression we should be careful about sine and cosine functions.*

(ii) We should be very careful when calculating maximum and minimum value of velocity because it involves inverse relation with cost in the given expression.

Q. 10 A spring with one end attached to a mass and the other to a rigid support is stretched and released.

(a) Magnitude of acceleration, when just released is maximum

(b) Magnitude of acceleration, when at equilibrium position, is maximum

(c) Speed is maximum when mass is at equilibrium position

(d) Magnitude of displacement is always maximum whenever speed is minimum

Ans. *(a, c)*

When spring is stretched by x, restoring force will be $F = -kx$

Potential energy of the stretched spring = PE = $\frac{1}{2}kx^2$

The restoring force is central hence, when particle released it will execute SHM about equilibrium position.

Acceleration will be $$a = \frac{F}{m} = \frac{-kx}{m}$$

At equilibrium position, $x = 0 \Rightarrow a = 0$

Hence, when just released $x = x_{max}$

Hence, acceleration is maximum. Thus option (a) is correct.

At equilibrium whole PE will be converted to KE hence, KE will be maximum and hence, speed will be maximum.

Q. 11 A ball is bouncing elastically with a speed 1 m/s between walls of a railway compartment of size 10 m in a direction perpendicular to walls. The train is moving at a constant velocity of 10 m/s parallel to the direction of motion of the ball. As seen from the ground.

(a) The direction of motion of the ball changes every 10 .

(b) Speed of ball changes every 10

(c) Average speed of ball over any 20 interval is fixed.

(d) The acceleration of ball is the same as from the train

Ans. *(b, c, d)*

In this problem, we have to keep in mind the frame of the observer. Here we must be clear that we are considering the motion from the ground. Compare to velocity of trains (10 m/s) speed of ball is less (1 m/s).

The speed of the ball before collision with side of train is 10 + 1 = 11 m/s.

Speed after collision with side of train = 10 – 1 = 9 m/s.

As speed is changing after travelling 10 m and speed is 1 m/s hence, time duration of the changing speed is 10.

Since, the collision of the ball is perfectly elastic there is no dissipation of energy hence, total momentum and kinetic energy are conserved.

Since, the train is moving with constant velocity hence, it will act as inertial frame of reference as that of Earth and acceleration will be same in both frames.

We should not confuse with non-inertial and inertial frame of reference. A frame of reference that is not accelerating will be inertial.

Very Short Answer Type Questions

Q. 12 Refer to the graph in figure. Match the following

Graph	Characteristics
(a)	(i) has $v > 0$ and $a < 0$ throughout
(b)	(ii) has $x > 0$ throughout and has a point with $v = 0$ and a point with $a = 0$
(c)	(iii) has a point with zero displacement for $t > 0$
(d)	(iv) has $v < 0$ and $a > 0$

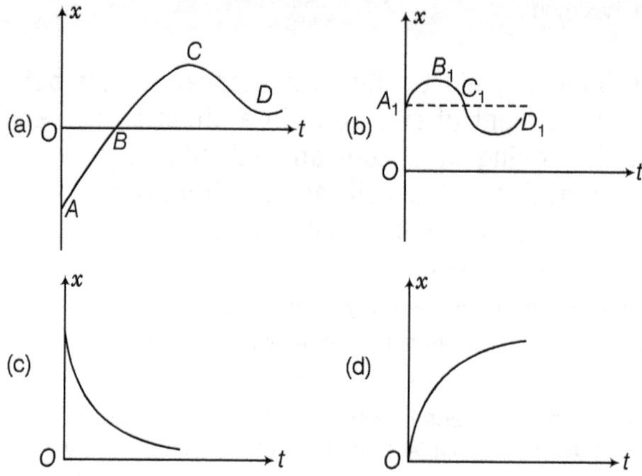

Ans. We have to analyse slope of each curve *i.e.*, $\frac{dx}{dt}$. For peak points $\frac{dx}{dt}$ will be zero as x is maximum at peak points.

For graph (a), there is a point (B) for which displacement is zero. So, a matches with (iii)

In graph (b), x is positive (> 0) throughout and at point B_1, $V = \frac{dx}{dt} = 0$.

since, at point of curvature changes $a = 0$, So b matches with (ii)

In graph (c), slope $V = \frac{dx}{dt}$ is negative hence, velocity will be negative.

so matches wth (iv)

In graph (d), as slope $V = \frac{dx}{dt}$ is positive hence, $V > 0$

Hence, d matches with (i)

Q. 13 A uniformly moving cricket ball is turned back by hitting it with a bat for a very short time interval. Show the variation of its acceleration with time (Take acceleration in the backward direction as positive).

Ans. If gravity effect is neglected then ball moving uniformly turned back with same speed when a bat hit it. Acceleration of the ball is zero just before it strikes the bat. When the ball strikes the bat, it gets accelerated due to the applied impulsive force by the bat.

The variation of acceleration with time is shown in graph

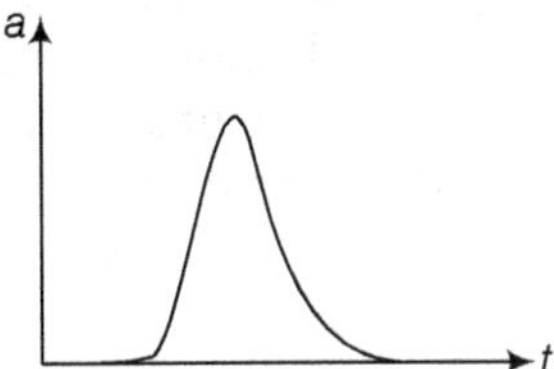

Q. 14 Give examples of a one-dimensional motion where

(a) the particle moving along positive x-direction comes to rest periodically and moves forward.

(b) the particle moving along positive x-direction comes to rest periodically and moves backward.

Ans. When we are writing an equation belonging to periodic nature it will involve sine or cosine function.

(a) The particle will be moving along positive x-direction only if $t > \sin t$

Hence, $$x(t) = 1 - \sin t$$

$$\text{Velocity } v(t) = \frac{dx(1)}{dt} = 1 - \cos t$$

$$\text{Acceleration } a(t) = \frac{dv}{dt} = \sin t$$

When $t = 0;\ x(t) = 0$

When $t = \pi;\ x(t) = \pi > 0$

When $t = 0;\ x(t) = 2\pi > 0$

(b) Equation can be represented by

$$x(t) = \sin t$$

$$v = \frac{d}{dt}x(t) = \cos t$$

As displacement and velocity is involving $\sin t$ and $\cos t$ hence these equations represent periodic.

Q. 15 Give example of a motion where $x > 0,\ v < 0,\ a > 0$ at a particular instant.

Ans. Let the motion is represented by

$$x(t) = A + Be^{-\gamma t} \qquad \text{...(i)}$$

Let $A > B$ and $\gamma > 0$

Now velocity $$x(t) = \frac{dx}{dt} = -B\gamma e^{-\gamma t}$$

Acceleration $$a(t) = \frac{dx}{dt} = B\gamma^2 e^{-\gamma t}$$

Suppose we are considering any instant t, then from Eq. (i), we can say that

$$x(t) > 0;\ v(t) < 0 \quad \text{and} \quad a > 0$$

Q. 16 **An object falling through a fluid is observed to have acceleration given by $a = g - bv$ where g = gravitational acceleration and b is constant. After a long time of release, it is observed to fall with constant speed. What must be the value of constant speed?**

Ans. When speed becomes constant acceleration $a = \frac{dv}{dt} = 0$

Given acceleration $a = g - bv$

where, g = gravitational acceleration

Clearly, from above equation as speed increases acceleration will decrease. At a certain speed say v_0, acceleration will be zero and speed will remain constant.

Hence, $a = g - bv_0 = 0$

$\Rightarrow$ $v_0 = g / b$

Short Answer Type Questions

Q. 17 **A ball is dropped and its displacement *versus* time graph is as shown (Displacement x from ground and all quantities are positive upwards).**

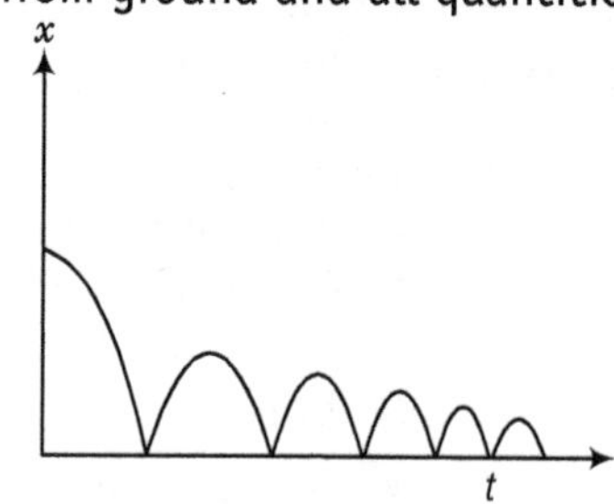

(a) Plot qualitatively velocity *versus* time graph

(b) Plot qualitatively acceleration *versus* time graph

Thinking Process

To calculate velocity we will find slope $\frac{dx}{dt}$ for displacement-time curve and to find acceleration we will find slope $\frac{dV}{dt}$ of velocity-time curve.

Ans. It is clear from the graph that displacement x is positive throughout. Ball is dropped from a height and its velocity increases in downward direction due to gravity pull. In this condition v is negative but acceleration of the ball is equal to acceleration due to gravity *i.e.*, $a = -g$. When ball rebounds in upward direction its velocity is positive but acceleration is $a = -g$.

(a) The velocity-time graph of the ball is shown in fig. (i).

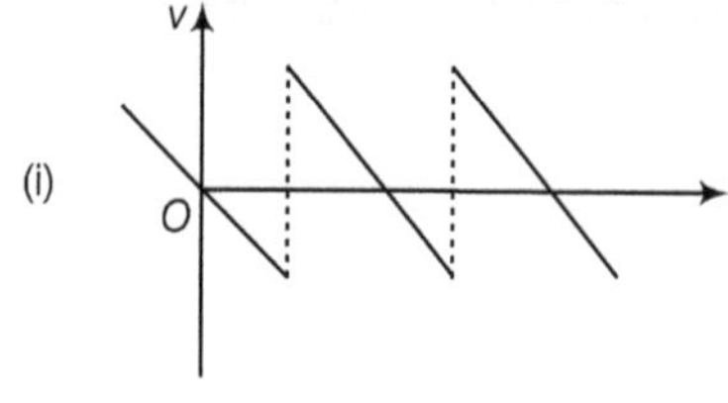

(b) The acceleration-time graph of the ball is shown in fig. (ii).

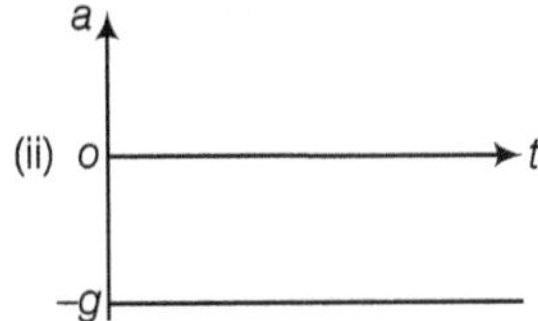

Q. 18 A particle executes the motion described by $x(t) = x_0(1 - e^{-\gamma t}); t \geq 0$, $x_0 > 0$.

(a) Where does the particle start and with what velocity?

(b) Find maximum and minimum values of $x(t)$, $v(t)$, $a(t)$. Show that $x(t)$ and $a(t)$ increase with time and $v(t)$ decreases with time.

Thinking Process

First we have to calculate velocity and acceleration and then we can determine the maximum or minimum value accordingly.

Ans. Given,
$$x(t) = x_0(1 - e^{-\gamma t})$$
$$v(t) = \frac{dx(t)}{dt} = x_0\gamma e^{-\gamma t}$$
$$a(t) = \frac{dv(t)}{dt} = -x_0\gamma^2 e^{-\gamma t}$$

(a) When $t = 0$; $x(t) = x_0(1 - e^{-0}) = x_0(1 - 1) = 0$

$$x(t = 0) = x_0\gamma e^{-0} = x_0\gamma(1) = \gamma x_0$$

(b) $x(t)$ is maximum when $t = \infty$ $\qquad [x(t)]_{max} = x_0$

$x(t)$ is minimum when $t = 0$ $\qquad [x(t)]_{min} = 0$

$v(t)$ is maximum when $t = 0$; $v(0) = x_0\gamma$

$v(t)$ is minimum when $t = \infty$; $v(\infty) = 0$

$a(t)$ is maximum when $t = \infty$; $a(\infty) = 0$

$a(t)$ is minimum when $t = 0$; $a(0) = -x_0\gamma^2$

Note *We should be careful about nature of variation of the curve and maximum and minimum value will be decided accordingly.*

Q. 19 A bird is tossing (flying to and fro) between two cars moving towards each other on a straight road. One car has a speed of 18 km/h while the other has the speed of 27 km/h. The bird starts moving from first car towards the other and is moving with the speed of 36 km/h and when the two cars were separated by 36 km. What is the total distance covered by the bird?

Thinking Process

In this problem we have to use the concept of relative velocity it will be subtracted for velocities in same direction and added for velocities in opposite directions.

Ans. Given, Speed of first car = 18 km/h

Speed of second car = 27 km/h

∴ Relative speed of each car w.r.t. each other

$$= 18 + 27 = 45 \text{ km/h}$$

Distance between the cars = 36 km

$\therefore$ Time of meeting the cars $(t) = \dfrac{\text{Distance between the cars}}{\text{Relative speed of cars}} = \dfrac{36}{45} = \dfrac{4}{5}\text{ h} = 0.8\text{ h}$

Speed of the bird $(v_b) = 36$ km/h

$\therefore$ Distance covered by the bird $= v_b \times t = 36 \times 0.8 = 28.8$ km

Q. 20 **A man runs across the roof, top of a tall building and jumps horizontally with the hope of landing on the roof of the next building which is at a lower height than the first. If his speed is 9 m/s, the (horizontal) distance between the two buildings is 10 m and the height difference is 9 m, will be able to land on the next building? (Take $g = 10\text{ m/s}^2$)**

Thinking Process

When the man runs on the roof-top the velocity will be horizontal. Then, acceleration will be vertically down ward taken as g and then equations of kinematies will be applied.

Ans. Given, horizontal speed of the man $(u_x) = 9$ m/s

Horizontal distance between the two buildings = 10 m

Height difference between the two buildings = 9 m

and $g = 10\text{ m/s}^2$

Let the man jumps from point A and land on the roof of the next building at point B.

Taking motion in vertical direction,

$$y = ut + \frac{1}{2}at^2$$

$$9 = 0 \times t + \frac{1}{2} \times 10 \times t^2$$

$$9 = 5t^2$$

or
$$t = \sqrt{\frac{9}{5}} = \frac{3}{\sqrt{5}}$$

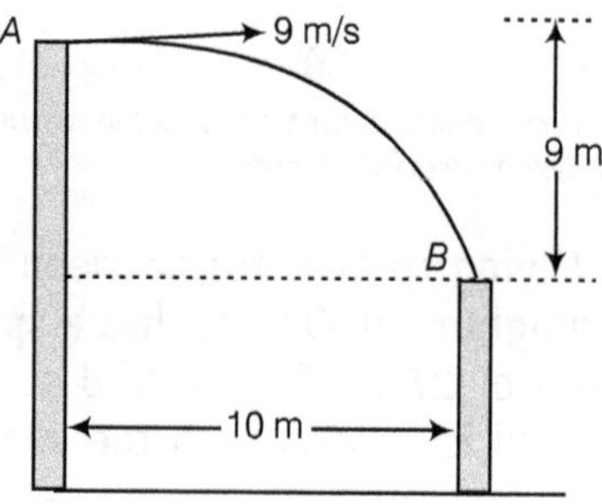

$\therefore$ Horizontal distance travelled $= u_x \times t = 9 \times \dfrac{3}{\sqrt{5}} = \dfrac{27}{\sqrt{5}}$ m

$$\approx 12\text{ m}$$

Horizontal distance travelled by the man is greater than 10 m, therefore, he will land on the next building.

Q. 21 A ball is dropped from a building of height 45 m. Simultaneously another ball is thrown up with a speed 40 m/s. Calculate the relative speed of the balls as a function of time.

Thinking Process

In this problem as ball is dropped, initial velocity will be taken as zero. We will apply equations involving one dimensional motion.

Ans. For the ball dropped from the building, $u_1 = 0, u_2 = 40\text{m/s}$

Velocity of the dropped ball after time t,

$$v_1 = u_1 + gt$$
$$v_1 = gt \qquad \text{(downward)}$$

For the ball thrown up, $u_2 = 40$ m/s

Velocity of the ball after time t

$$v_2 = u_2 - gt$$
$$= (40 - gt) \qquad \text{(upward)}$$

$\therefore$ Relative velocity of one ball w.r.t. another ball

$$= v_1 - v_2$$
$$= gt - [-(40 - gt)] = 40 \text{ m/s}$$

Note *When we are applying equations for rectilinear motion we should carefully put up the signs for the physical quantities.*

Q. 22 The velocity- displacement graph of a particle is shown in figure.

(a) Write the relation between v and x.

(b) Obtain the relation between acceleration and displacement and plot it.

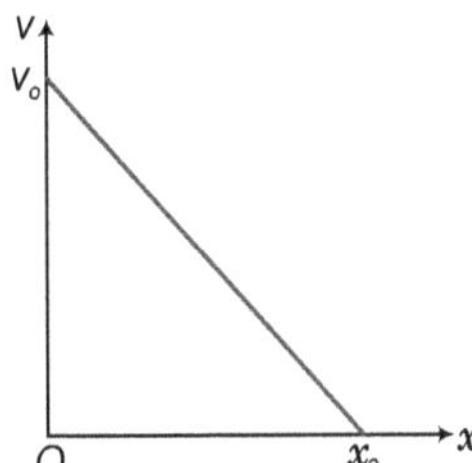

Thinking Process

In this problems we will use the concept of slope. Suppose the slope is m then equation will come out to be y = mx + c.

Ans. Given, initial velocity = v_0

Let the distance travelled in time $t = x_0$.

For the graph $\tan\theta = \dfrac{v_0}{x_0} = \dfrac{v_0 - v}{x}$ ...(i)

where, v is velocity and x is displacement at any instant of time t.

From Eq. (i) $v_0 - v = \dfrac{v_0}{x_0} x$

$\Rightarrow$ $v = \dfrac{-v_0}{x_0} x + v_0$

We know that

$$\text{Acceleration } a = \frac{dv}{dt} = \frac{-v_0}{x_0}\frac{dx}{dt} + 0$$

$$\Rightarrow \quad a = \frac{-v_0}{x_0}(v)$$

$$= \frac{-v_0}{x_0}\left(\frac{-v_0}{x_0}x + v_0\right)$$

$$= \frac{v_0^2}{x_0^2}x - \frac{v_0^2}{x_0}$$

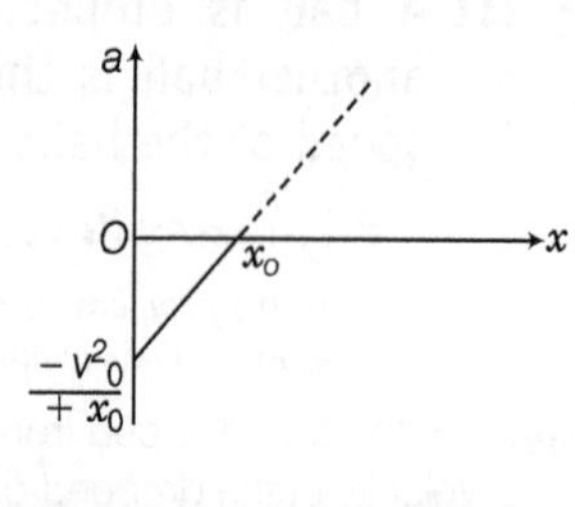

Graph of *a versus x* is given above.

Long Answer Type Questions

Q. 23 It is a common observation that rain clouds can be at about a kilometer altitude above the ground.

(a) If a rain drop falls from such a height freely under gravity, what will be its speed? Also calculate in km/h ($g = 10\ \text{m/s}^2$).

(b) A typical rain drop is about 4 mm diameter. Momentum is mass × speed in magnitude. Estimate its momentum when it hits ground.

(c) Estimate the time required to flatten the drop.

(d) Rate of change of momentum is force. Estimate how much force such a drop would exert on you.

(e) Estimate the order of magnitude force on umbrella. Typical lateral separation between two rain drops is 5 cm.

(Assume that umbrella is circular and has a diameter of 1 m and cloth is not pierced through.)

Thinking Process

In this problem equation of motion and Newton's seconds law that is $F_{ext} = \frac{dp}{dt}$ will be used. where dp is change in momentum over time dt.

Ans. Given, height (h) = 1 km = 1000 m

$$g = 10\ \text{m/s}^2$$

(a) Velocity attained by the rain drop in freely falling through a height *h*.

$$v = \sqrt{2gh} = \sqrt{2 \times 10 \times 1000} = 100\sqrt{2}\ \text{m/s}$$

$$= 100\sqrt{2} \times \frac{60 \times 60}{1000}\ \text{km/h}$$

$$= 360\sqrt{2}\ \text{km/h} \approx 510\ \text{km/h}$$

(b) Diameter of the drop (d) = $2r$ = 4 mm

$\therefore$ Radius of the drop (r) = 2 mm = 2×10^{-3} m

Mass of a rain drop $(m) = V \times \rho$

$$= \frac{4}{3}\pi r^3 \rho$$

$$= \frac{4}{3} \times \frac{22}{7} \times (2 \times 10^{-3})^3 \times 10^3 \quad (\because \text{Density of water} = 10^3 \text{ kg/m}^3)$$

$$\approx 3.4 \times 10^{-5} \text{ kg}$$

Momentum of the rain drop $(p) = mv$

$$= 3.4 \times 10^{-5} \times 100\sqrt{2}$$

$$= 4.7 \times 10^{-3} \text{ kg-m/s}$$

$$\approx 5 \times 10^{-3} \text{kg-m/s}$$

(c) Time required to flatten the drop = time taken by the drop to travel the distance equal to the diameter of the drop near the ground

$$t = \frac{d}{v} = \frac{4 \times 10^{-3}}{100\sqrt{2}} = 0.028 \times 10^{-3} \text{ s}$$

$$= 2.8 \times 10^{-5} \text{ s} \approx 30 \text{ ms}$$

(d) Force exerted by a rain drop

$$F = \frac{\text{Change in momentum}}{\text{Time}} = \frac{p - 0}{t}$$

$$= \frac{4.7 \times 10^{-3}}{2.8 \times 10^{-5}} \approx 168 \text{ N}$$

(e) Radius of the umbrella $(R) = \frac{1}{2}$ m

$\therefore$ Area of the umbrella $(A) = \pi R^2 = \frac{22}{7} \times \left(\frac{1}{2}\right)^2 = \frac{22}{28} = \frac{11}{14} \approx 0.8 \text{m}^2$

Number of drops striking the umbrella simultaneously with average separation of 5 cm $= 5 \times 10^{-2}$ m.

$$= \frac{0.8}{(5 \times 10^{-2})^2} = 320$$

$\therefore$ Net force exerted on umbrella $= 320 \times 168 = 53760 \text{ N} \approx 54000 \text{ N}$

Note *In practice, the velocity of the drops decreases due to air friction.*

Q. 24 A motor car moving at a speed of 72 km/h cannot come to a stop in less than 3.0 s while for a truck this time interval is 5.0 s. On a highway, the car is behind the truck both moving at 72 km/h. The truck gives a signal that it is going to stop at emergency. At what distance the car should be from the truck so that it does not bump onto (collide with) the truck. Human response time is 0.5 s.

Ans. In this problem equations related to one dimensional motion will be applied for acceleration positive sign will be used and for retardation negative sign will be used.

Given, speed of car as well as truck = 72 km/h

$$= 72 \times \frac{5}{18} \text{ m/s} = 20 \text{ m/s}$$

Retarded motion for truck $\quad v = u + a_t t$

$$0 = 20 + a_t \times 5$$

or $\quad a_t = -4 \text{ m/s}^2$

Retarded motion for the car $v = u + a_c t$

$$0 = 20 + a_c \times 3$$

or $$a_c = -\frac{20}{3}\ \text{m/s}^2$$

Let car be at a distance x from truck, when truck gives the signal and t be the time taken to cover this distance.

As human response time is 0.5 s, therefore, time of retarded motion of car is $(t - 0.5)$ s.

Velocity of car after time t,

$$v_c = u - at$$

$$= 20 - \left(\frac{20}{3}\right)(t - 0.5)$$

Velocity of truck after time t,

$$v_t = 20 - 4t$$

To avoid the car bump onto the truck,

$$v_c = v_t$$

$$20 - \frac{20}{3}(t - 0.5) = 20 - 4t$$

$$4t = \frac{20}{3}(t - 0.5)$$

$$t = \frac{5}{3}(t - 0.5)$$

$$3t = 5t - 2.5$$

$\Rightarrow$ $$t = \frac{2.5}{2} = \frac{5}{4}\ \text{s}$$

Distance travelled by the truck in time t,

$$s_t = u_t t + \frac{1}{2}a_t t^2$$

$$= 20 \times \frac{5}{4} + \frac{1}{2} \times (-4) \times \left(\frac{5}{4}\right)^2$$

$$= 21.875\ \text{m}$$

Distance travelled by car in time t = Distance travelled by car in 0.5 s (without retardation) + Distance travelled by car in $(t - 0.5)$ s (with retardation)

$$s_c = (20 \times 0.5) + 20\left(\frac{5}{4} - 0.5\right) - \frac{1}{2}\left(\frac{20}{3}\right)\left(\frac{5}{4} - 0.5\right)^2$$

$$= 23.125\ \text{m}$$

$\therefore$ $$s_c - s_t = 23.125 - 21.875 = 1.250\ \text{m}$$

Therefore, to avoid the bump onto the truck, the car must maintain a distance from the truck more than 1.250 m.

Q. 25 A monkey climbs up a slippery pole for 3 and subsequently slips for 3 . Its velocity at time t is given by $v(t) = 2t(3s - t); 0 < t < 3$ and $v(t) = -(t - 3)(6 - t)$ for $3 < t < 6$ s in m/s. It repeats this cycle till it reaches the height of 20 m.

(a) At what time is its velocity maximum?

(b) At what time is its average velocity maximum?

(c) At what time is its acceleration maximum in magnitude?

(d) How many cycles (counting fractions) are required to reach the top?

Ans. It this problem to calculate maximum velocity we will use $\frac{dv}{dt} = 0$,then the time corresponding to maximum velocity will be obtained.

Given velocity

$$v(t) = 2t(3 - t) = 6t - 2t^2 \quad ...(i)$$

(a) For maximum velocity $\frac{dv(t)}{dt} = 0$

$$\Rightarrow \quad \frac{d}{dt}(6t - 2t^2) = 0$$

$$\Rightarrow \quad 6 - 4t = 0$$

$$\Rightarrow \quad t = \frac{6}{4} = \frac{3}{2}\text{s} = 1.5\,\text{s}$$

(b) From Eq. (i) $v = 6t - 2t^2$

$$\Rightarrow \quad \frac{ds}{dt} = 6t - 2t^2$$

$$\Rightarrow \quad ds = (6t - 2t^2)dt$$

where, s is displacement

∴ Distance travelled in time interval 0 to 3s.

$$s = \int_0^3 (6t - 2t^2)dt$$

$$= \left[\frac{6t^2}{2} - \frac{2t^3}{3}\right]_0^3 = \left[3t^2 - \frac{2}{3}t^3\right]_0^3$$

$$= 3 \times 9 - \frac{2}{3} \times 3 \times 3 \times 3$$

$$= 27 - 18 = 9\,\text{m}.$$

$$\text{Average velocity} = \frac{\text{Distance travelled}}{\text{Time}}$$

$$= \frac{9}{3} = 3\,\text{m/s}$$

Given,

$$x = 6t - 2t^2$$

$$\Rightarrow \quad 3 = 6t - 2t^2$$

$$\Rightarrow \quad 2t^2 - 6t - 3 = 0$$

$$\Rightarrow \quad t = \frac{6 \pm \sqrt{6^2 - 4 \times 2 \times 3}}{2 \times 2} = \frac{6 \pm \sqrt{36 - 24}}{4}$$

$$= \frac{6 \pm \sqrt{12}}{4} = \frac{3 \pm 2\sqrt{3}}{2}$$

Considering positive sign only

$$t = \frac{3 + 2\sqrt{3}}{2} = \frac{3 + 2 \times 1.732}{2} = \frac{9}{4}\,\text{s}$$

(c) In a periodic motion when velocity is zero acceleration will be maximum putting $v = 0$ in Eq. (i)

$$0 = 6t - 2t^2$$

$$\Rightarrow \quad 0 = t(6 - 2t)$$

$$= t \times 2(3 - t) = 0$$

$$\Rightarrow \quad t = 0 \text{ or } 3\text{s}$$

(d) Distance covered in 0 to 3s = 9 m

Distance covered in 3 to 6s = $\int_3^6 (18 - 9t + t^2)\,dt$

$$= \left(18t - \frac{9t^2}{2} + \frac{t^3}{3}\right)_3^6$$

$$= 18 \times 6 - \frac{9}{2} \times 6^2 + \frac{6^3}{3} - \left(18 \times 3 - \frac{9 \times 3^2}{2} + \frac{3^3}{3}\right)$$

$$= 108 - 9 \times 18 + \frac{6^3}{3} - 18 \times 3 + \frac{9}{2} \times 9 - \frac{27}{3}$$

$$= 108 - 18 \times 9 + \frac{216}{3} - 54 + 4.5 \times 9 - 9 = -4.5\text{m}$$

$\therefore$ Total distance travelled in one cycle = $s_1 + s_2 = 9 - 4.5 = 4.5$ m

Number of cycles covered in total distance to be covered = $\frac{20}{4.5} \approx 4.44 \approx 5.$

Q. 26 **A man is standing on top of a building 100m high. He throws two balls vertically, one at $t = 0$ and after a time interval (less than 2 seconds). The later ball is thrown at a velocity of half the first. The vertical gap between first and second ball is + 15 m at $t = 2$s. The gap is found to remain constant. Calculate the velocity with which the balls were thrown and the exact time interval between their throw.**

Thinking Process

In this question equation of kinematics will be applied with proper sign and to calculate time interval we will take difference of displacements.

Ans. Let the speeds of the two balls (1and 2) be v_1 and v_2 where

if $v_1 = 2v, v_2 = v$

if y_1 and y_2 and the distance covered by

the balls 1 and 2 , respectively, before coming to rest, then

$$y_1 = \frac{v_1^2}{2g} = \frac{4v^2}{2g} \text{ and } y_2 = \frac{v_2^2}{2g} = \frac{v^2}{2g}$$

Since, $$y_1 - y_2 = 15\text{m}, \frac{4v^2}{2g} - \frac{v^2}{2g} = 15\text{m or } \frac{3v^2}{2g} = 15\text{m}$$

or $$v^2 = \sqrt{5\text{m} \times (2 \times 10)}\ \text{m/s}^2$$

or $$v = 10\ \text{m/s}$$

Clearly, $v_1 = 20$m/s and $v_2 = 10$ m/s

as $$y_1 = \frac{v_1^2}{2g} = \frac{(20\text{m})^2}{2 \times 10\text{m}15} = 20\text{m},$$

$$y_2 = y_1 - 15\text{m} = 5\text{m}$$

If t_2 is the time taken by the ball 2 toner

a distance of 5m, then from $y_2 = v_2 t - \frac{1}{2} g t_2^2$

$$5 = 10t_2 - 5t_2^2 \text{ or } t_2^2 - 2t_2 + 1 = 0,$$

where $$t_2 = 15$$

Since t_1 (time taken by ball 1 to cover distance of 20m) is 2s, time interval between the two thrvws

$$= t_1 - t_2 = 2\text{s} - 1\text{s} = 1\text{s}$$

Note *We should be very careful, when we are applying the equation of rectilinear motion.*

3

Motion *in* a Plane

Multiple Choice Questions (MCQs)

Q. 1 The angle between $\mathbf{A} = \hat{\mathbf{i}} + \hat{\mathbf{j}}$ and $\mathbf{B} = \hat{\mathbf{i}} - \hat{\mathbf{j}}$ is

(a) 45° (b) 90° (c) – 45° (d) 180°

Thinking Process

To solve such type of questions, we have to use the formula for dot product or cross product.

Ans. *(b)* Given, $\mathbf{A} = \hat{i} + \hat{j}$

$\mathbf{B} = \hat{i} - \hat{j}$

We know that

$$\mathbf{A} \cdot \mathbf{B} = |\mathbf{A}||\mathbf{B}| \cos \theta$$

$$\Rightarrow \quad (\hat{\mathbf{i}} + \hat{\mathbf{j}}) \cdot (\hat{\mathbf{i}} - \hat{\mathbf{j}}) = (\sqrt{1+1})(\sqrt{1+1}) \cos \theta$$

where θ is the angle between **A** and **B**

$$\Rightarrow \quad \cos \theta = \frac{1 - 0 + 0 - 1}{\sqrt{2}\sqrt{2}} = \frac{0}{2} = 0$$

$$\Rightarrow \quad \theta = 90^\circ$$

Q. 2 Which one of the following statements is true?

(a) A scalar quantity is the one that is conserved in a process

(b) A scalar quantity is the one that can never take negative values

(c) A scalar quantity is the one that does not vary from one point to another in space

(d) A scalar quantity has the same value for observers with different orientation of the axes

Ans. *(d)* A scalar quantity is independent of direction hence has the same value for observers with different orientations of the axes.

Q. 3 **Figure shows the orientation of two vectors u and v in the xy-plane.**

If $\mathbf{u} = a\hat{\mathbf{i}} + b\hat{\mathbf{j}}$ and $\mathbf{v} = p\hat{\mathbf{i}} + q\hat{\mathbf{j}}$

Which of the following is correct?

(a) a and p are positive while b and q are negative

(b) a, p and b are positive while q is negative

(c) a, q and b are positive while p is negative

(d) a, b, p and q are all positive

Thinking Process

In this question according to the diagram, we have to decide the components of a given vector.

Ans. *(b)* Clearly from the diagram, $\mathbf{u} = a\hat{\mathbf{i}} + b\hat{\mathbf{j}}$

As $\mathbf{u}$ is in the first quadrant, hence both components a and b will be positive.

For $\mathbf{v} = p\hat{\mathbf{i}} + q\hat{\mathbf{j}}$, as it is in positive x-direction and located downward hence x-component p will be positive and y-component q will be negative.

Q. 4 **The component of a vector r along X-axis will have maximum value if**

(a) **r** is along positive Y-axis

(b) **r** is along positive X-axis

(c) **r** makes an angle of 45° with the X-axis

(d) **r** is along negative Y-axis

Ans. *(b)* Let **r** makes an angle θ with positive x-axis component of **r** along X-axis

$$r_x = |\mathbf{r}| \cos\theta$$

$$(r_x)_{\text{maximum}} = |\mathbf{r}| (\cos\theta)_{\text{maximum}}$$

$$= |\mathbf{r}| \cos 0^\circ = |\mathbf{r}| \qquad (\because \cos\theta \text{ is maximum of } \theta = 0^\circ)$$

As $\theta = 0^\circ$,

r is along positive x-axis.

Q. 5 **The horizontal range of a projectile fired at an angle of 15° is 50 m. If it is fired with the same speed at an angle of 45°, its range will be**

(a) 60 m (b) 71 m

(c) 100 m (d) 141 m

Ans. *(c)* We know that

where θ is angle of projection

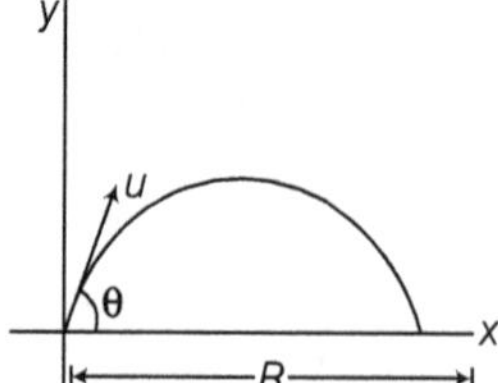

Given, $\theta = 15°$ and $R = 50\,\text{m}$

$$\text{Range, } R = \frac{u^2 \sin 2\theta}{g}$$

Putting all the given values in the formula, we get

$$\Rightarrow \quad R = 50\,\text{m} = \frac{u^2 \sin (2 \times 15^\circ)}{g}$$

$$\Rightarrow \quad 50 \times g = u^2 \sin 30^\circ = u^2 \times \frac{1}{2}$$

$$\Rightarrow \quad 50 \times g \times 2 = u^2$$

$$\Rightarrow \quad u^2 = 50 \times 9.8 \times 2 = 100 \times 9.8 = 980$$

$$\Rightarrow \quad u = \sqrt{980} = \sqrt{49 \times 20} = 7 \times 2 \times \sqrt{5} \text{ m/s}$$

$$= 14 \times 2.23 \text{ m/s} = 31.304 \text{ m/s}$$

For $\theta = 45°; R = \dfrac{u^2 \sin 2 \times 45°}{g} = \dfrac{u^2}{g}$ $(\because \sin 90° = 1)$

$$\Rightarrow \quad R = \frac{(14\sqrt{5})^2}{g} = \frac{14 \times 14 \times 5}{9.8} = 100 \text{ m}$$

Q. 6 Consider the quantities, pressure, power, energy, impulse, gravitational potential, electrical charge, temperature, area. Out of these, the only vector quantities are

(a) impulse, pressure and area (b) impulse and area
(c) area and gravitational potential (d) impulse and pressure

Ans. *(b)* We know that impulse $J = F . \Delta t = \Delta p$, where F is force, Δt is time duration and Δp is change in momentum. As Δp is a vector quantity, hence impulse is also a vector quantity. Sometimes area can also be treated as vector.

Q. 7 In a two dimensional motion, instantaneous speed v_0 is a positive constant. Then, which of the following are necessarily true?

(a) The average velocity is not zero at any time
(b) Average acceleration must always vanish
(c) Displacements in equal time intervals are equal
(d) Equal path lengths are traversed in equal intervals

Thinking Process

As speed is a scalar quantity, hence it will be related with path length (scalar quantity) only.

Ans. *(d)* We know that

$$\text{speed, } v_0 = \frac{\text{total distance travelled}}{\text{time taken}}$$

Hence, total distance travelled = Path length
= (speed) × time taken

Note *We should be very careful with the fact, that speed is related with total distance covered not with displacement.*

Q. 8 In a two dimensional motion, instantaneous speed v_0 is a positive constant. Then, which of the following are necessarily true?

(a) The acceleration of the particle is zero
(b) The acceleration of the particle is bounded
(c) The acceleration of the particle is necessarily in the plane of motion
(d) The particle must be undergoing a uniform circular motion

Ans. *(c)* As given motion is two dimensional motion and given that instantaneous speed v_0 is positive constant. Acceleration is rate of change of velocity (instantaneous speed) hence it will also be in the plane of motion.

Multiple Choice Questions (More Than One Options)

Q. 9 Three vectors A, B and C add upto zero. Find which is false.

(a) $(\mathbf{A}\times \mathbf{B})\times \mathbf{C}$ is not zero unless **B, C** are parallel

(b) $(\mathbf{A}\times \mathbf{B}) . \mathbf{C}$ is not zero unless **B, C** are parallel

(c) If **A, B, C** define a plane, $(\mathbf{A}\times \mathbf{B})\times \mathbf{C}$ is in that plane

(d) $(\mathbf{A}\times \mathbf{B}) . \mathbf{C} = |\mathbf{A}|\,|\mathbf{B}||\mathbf{C}| \rightarrow \mathbf{C}^2 = \mathbf{A}^2 + \mathbf{B}^2$

Thinking Process

This question can solved by checking each options one by one.

Ans. *(b, d)*

Given $\mathbf{A} + \mathbf{B} + \mathbf{C} = 0$

Hence, we can say that **A**, **B** and **C** are in one plane and are represented by the three sides of a triangle taken in one order. Now consider the options one by one.

(a) We can write

$$\mathbf{B}\times(\mathbf{A}+\mathbf{B}+\mathbf{C}) = \mathbf{B}\times 0 = 0$$

$$\Rightarrow \quad \mathbf{B}\times\mathbf{A} + \mathbf{B}\times\mathbf{B} + \mathbf{B}\times\mathbf{C} = 0$$

$$\Rightarrow \quad \mathbf{B}\times\mathbf{A} + 0 + \mathbf{B}\times\mathbf{C} = 0$$

$$\Rightarrow \quad \mathbf{B}\times\mathbf{A} = -\mathbf{B}\times\mathbf{C}$$

$$\Rightarrow \quad \mathbf{A}\times\mathbf{B} = \mathbf{B}\times\mathbf{C}$$

$$\therefore \quad (\mathbf{A}\times\mathbf{B})\times\mathbf{C} = (\mathbf{B}\times\mathbf{C})\times\mathbf{C}$$

It cannot be zero.

If $\mathbf{B} \,||\, \mathbf{C}$, then $\mathbf{B}\times\mathbf{C} = 0$, than $(\mathbf{B}\times\mathbf{C})\times\mathbf{C} = 0$.

(b) $(\mathbf{A}\times\mathbf{B}).\mathbf{C} = (\mathbf{B}\times \mathbf{AC}).\mathbf{C} = 0$ whatever be the positions of **A**, **B** and **C**. If $\mathbf{B} \,||\, \mathbf{C}$, then $\mathbf{B}\times\mathbf{C} = 0$, then $(\mathbf{B}\times\mathbf{C})\times\mathbf{C} = 0$.

(c) $(\mathbf{A}\times\mathbf{B}) = \mathbf{X} = \mathbf{AB}\sin\theta\,\mathbf{X}$. The direction of X is perpendicular to the plane containing **A** and **B**. $(\mathbf{A}\times\mathbf{B})\times\mathbf{C} = \mathbf{X}\times\mathbf{C}$. Its direction is in the plane of **A**, **B and C**.

(d) If $\mathbf{C}^2 = \mathbf{A}^2 + \mathbf{B}^2$, then angle between **A** and **B** is 90°

$$\therefore \quad (\mathbf{A}\times\mathbf{B}).\mathbf{C} = (AB\sin 90^\circ\,\mathbf{X}).\mathbf{C} = AB\,(\mathbf{X}.\mathbf{C})$$

$$= ABC\cos 90^\circ = 0$$

Q. 10 It is found that $|\mathbf{A}+\mathbf{B}| = |\mathbf{A}|$. This necessarily implies.

(a) $\mathbf{B} = 0$

(b) **A, B** are antiparallel

(c) **A, B** are perpendicular

(d) $\mathbf{A}.\mathbf{B} \leq 0$

Ans. *(a, b)*

Given that $\quad |\mathbf{A}+\mathbf{B}| = |\mathbf{A}|$ or $|\mathbf{A}+\mathbf{B}|^2 = |\mathbf{A}|^2$

$$\Rightarrow \quad |\mathbf{A}|^2 + |\mathbf{B}|^2 + 2|\mathbf{A}||\mathbf{B}|\cos\theta = |\mathbf{A}|^2$$

where θ is angle between **A** and **B**.

$$\Rightarrow \quad |\mathbf{B}|(|\mathbf{B}| + 2|\mathbf{A}|\cos\theta) = 0$$

$$\Rightarrow \quad |\mathbf{B}| = 0 \text{ or } |\mathbf{B}| + 2|\mathbf{A}|\cos\theta = 0$$

$$\Rightarrow \quad \cos\theta = -\frac{|\mathbf{B}|}{2|\mathbf{A}|} \qquad \text{...(i)}$$

If **A** and **B** are antiparallel, then $\theta = 180°$
Hence, from Eq. (i)

$$-1 = -\frac{|\mathbf{B}|}{2|\mathbf{A}|} \Rightarrow |\mathbf{B}| = 2|\mathbf{A}|$$

Hence, correct answer will be either $|\mathbf{B}| = 0$ or **A** and **B** are antiparallel provided $|\mathbf{B}| = 2\,|\mathbf{A}|$

Q. 11 Two particles are projected in air with speed v_0 at angles θ_1 and θ_2 (both acute) to the horizontal, respectively. If the height reached by the first particle is greater than that of the second, then tick the right choices.

(a) Angle of projection $q_1 > q_2$
(b) Time of flight $T_1 > T_2$
(c) Horizontal range $R_1 > R_2$
(d) Total energy $U_1 > U_2$

Thinking Process

In this problem, we have to apply equation for maximum height reached $H = \frac{u^2 \sin^2 \theta}{2g}$, *where* θ *is angle of projection and u is speed of projection of a projectile motion.*

Ans. *(a, b, c)*

We know that maximum height reached by a projectile,

$$H = \frac{u^2 \sin^2 \theta}{2g}$$

$$H_1 = \frac{v_0^2 \sin^2 \theta_1}{2g} \quad \text{(for first particle)}$$

$$H_2 = \frac{v_0^2 \sin^2 \theta_2}{2g} \quad \text{(for second particle)}$$

According to question, we know that

$$H_1 > H_2$$

$$\Rightarrow \quad \frac{v_0^2 \sin^2 \theta_1}{2g} > \frac{v_0^2 \sin^2 \theta_2}{2g}$$

$$\Rightarrow \quad \sin^2 \theta_1 > \sin^2 \theta_2$$

$$\Rightarrow \quad \sin^2 \theta_1 - \sin^2 \theta_2 > 0$$

$$\Rightarrow \quad (\sin\theta_1 - \sin\theta_2)(\sin\theta_1 + \sin\theta_2) > 0$$

Thus, either $\quad \sin\theta_1 + \sin\theta_2 > 0$

$$\Rightarrow \quad \sin\theta_1 - \sin\theta_2 > 0$$

$$\Rightarrow \quad \sin\theta_1 > \sin\theta_2 \text{ or } \theta_1 > \theta_2$$

Time of fight, $\quad T = \frac{2u\sin\theta}{g} = \frac{2\,v_0 \sin\theta}{g}$

Thus, $\quad T_1 = \frac{2\,v_0 \sin\theta_1}{g}$

$$T_2 = \frac{2\,v_0 \sin\theta_2}{g}$$

(Here, T_1 = Time of flight of first particle and T_2 = Time of flight of second particle).

As, $\quad \sin\theta_1 > \sin\theta_2$

Hence, $\quad T_1 > T_2$

We know that

$$\text{Range, } R = \frac{u^2 \sin 2\theta}{g} = \frac{v_0^2 \sin 2\theta}{g}$$

$$R_1 = \text{Range of first particle} = \frac{u_0^2 \sin 2\theta_1}{g}$$

$$R_2 = \text{Range of second particle} = \frac{v_0^2 \sin 2\theta_2}{g}$$

Given, $\sin\theta_1 > \sin\theta_2$

$\Rightarrow$ $\sin 2\theta_1 > \sin 2\theta_2$

$\Rightarrow$ $\dfrac{R_1}{R_2} = \dfrac{\sin 2\theta_1}{\sin 2\theta_2} > 1$

$\Rightarrow$ $R_1 > R_2$

Total energy for the first particle,

$$U_1 = \text{KE} + \text{PE} = \frac{1}{2} m_1 v_0^2$$

(This value will be constant throughout the journey)

$$U_2 = \text{KE} + \text{PE} = \frac{1}{2} m_2 v_0^2 \qquad \text{(Total energy for the second particle)}$$

Total energy for the second particle

If $m_1 = m_2$ then $U_1 = U_2$

$m_1 > m_2$ then $U_1 > U_2$

$m_1 < m_2$, then $U_1 < U_2$

Q. 12 **A particle slides down a frictionless parabolic $(y + x^2)$ track $(A - B - C)$ starting from rest at point A (figure). Point B is at the vertex of parabola and point C is at a height less than that of point A. After C, the particle moves freely in air as a projectile. If the particle reaches highest point at P, then**

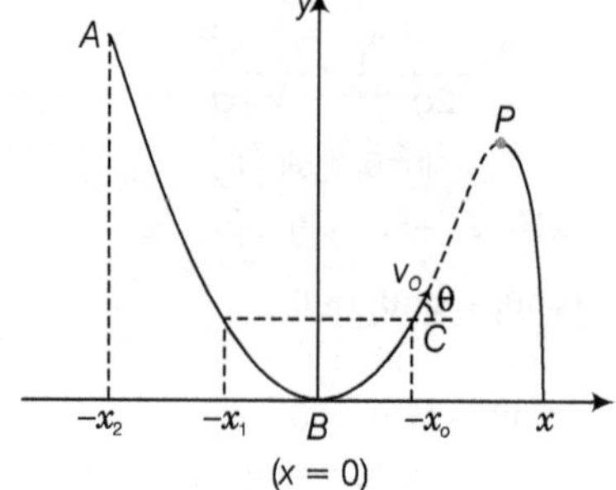

(a) KE at P = KE at B

(b) height at P = height at A

(c) total energy at P = total energy at A

(d) time of travel from A to B = time of travel from B to P

Thinking Process

In this type of question, nature of track is very important of consider, as friction is not in this track, total energy of the particle will remain constant throughout the journey.

Ans. *(c)*

As the given track $y = x^2$ is a frictionless track thus, total energy (KE + PE) will be same throughout the journey.

Hence, total energy at A = Total energy at P. At B, the particle is having only KE but at P some KE is converted to P.

Hence, $$(KE)_B > (KE)_P$$

Total energy at A = PE = Total energy at B = KE

$$= \text{Total energy at } P$$

$$= PE + KE$$

The potential energy at A, is converted to KE and PE at P, hence

$$(PE)\, P < (PE)\, A$$

Hence, $$(\text{Height})\, P < (\text{Height})\, A$$

As, height of P < Height of A

Hence, path length AB > path length BP

Hence, time of travel from A to B ≠ Time of travel from B to P.

Q. 13 **Following are four different relations about displacement, velocity and acceleration for the motion of a particle in general. Choose the incorrect one (s).**

(a) $v_{av} = \frac{1}{2}[v(t_1) + v(t_2)]$

(b) $v_{av} = \frac{r(t_2) - r(t_1)}{t_2 - t_1}$

(c) $r = \frac{1}{2}(v(t_2) - v(t_1)(t_2 - t_1)$

(d) $a_{av} = \frac{v(t_2) - v(t_1)}{t_2 - t_1}$

Ans. *(a, c)*

If an object undergoes a displacement Δr in time Δt, its average velocity is given by

$v = \frac{\Delta r}{\Delta t} = \frac{r_2 - r_1}{t_2 - t_1}$; where r_1 and r_2 are position vectors corresponding to time t_1 and t_2.

It the velocity of an object changes from v_1 to v_2 in time Δt. Average acceleration is given by

$$a_{av} = \frac{\Delta \mathbf{v}}{\Delta t} = \frac{v_2 - v_1}{t_2 - t_2}$$

But, when acceleration is non-uniform

$$v_{av} \neq \frac{v_1 + v_2}{2}$$

We can write $$\Delta v = \frac{\Delta r}{\Delta t}$$

Hence, $$\Delta r = r_2 - r_1 = (v_2 - v_1)(t_2 - t_1)$$

Q. 14 **For a particle performing uniform circular motion, choose the correct statement(s) from the following.**

(a) Magnitude of particle velocity (speed) remains constant

(b) Particle velocity remains directed perpendicular to radius vector

(c) Direction of acceleration keeps changing as particle moves

(d) Angular momentum is constant in magnitude but direction keeps changing

Ans. *(a, b, c)*

For a particle performing uniform circular motion

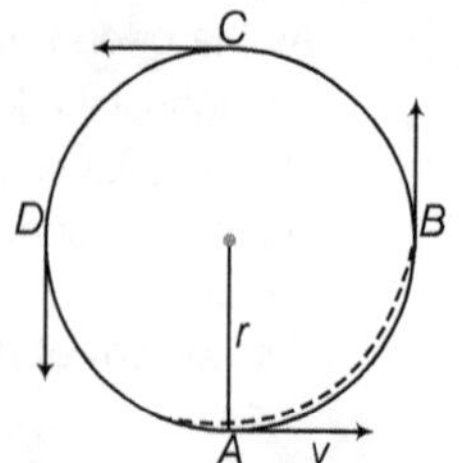

(i) speed will be constant throughout.

(ii) velocity will be tangential in the direction of motion at a particular point.

(iii) acceleration $a = \frac{v^2}{r}$, will always be towards centre of the circular path.

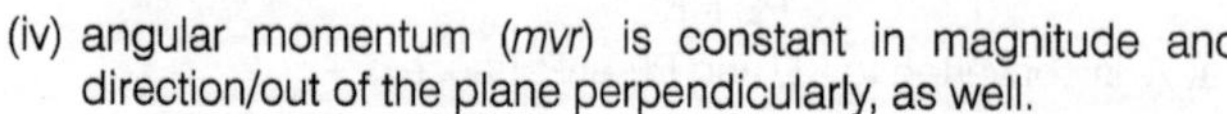

(iv) angular momentum (mvr) is constant in magnitude and direction/out of the plane perpendicularly, as well.

Note *In uniform circular motion, magnitude of velocity and acceleration is constant but direction changes continuously.*

Q. 15 For two vectors **A** and **B**, $|\mathbf{A}+\mathbf{B}| = |\mathbf{A}-\mathbf{B}|$ is always true when

(a) $|\mathbf{A}| = |\mathbf{B}| \neq 0$

(b) $\mathbf{A} \perp \mathbf{B}$

(c) $|\mathbf{A}| = |\mathbf{B}| \neq 0$ and **A** and **B** are parallel or anti-parallel

(d) when either $|\mathbf{A}|$ or $|\mathbf{B}|$ is zero

Ans. *(b, d)*

Given, $|\mathbf{A}+\mathbf{B}| = |\mathbf{A}-\mathbf{B}|$

$$\Rightarrow \sqrt{|\mathbf{A}|^2 + |\mathbf{B}|^2 + 2|\mathbf{A}||\mathbf{B}|\cos\theta} = \sqrt{|\mathbf{A}|^2 + |\mathbf{B}|^2 - 2|\mathbf{A}||\mathbf{B}|\cos\theta}$$

$$\Rightarrow |\mathbf{A}|^2 + |\mathbf{B}|^2 + 2|\mathbf{A}||\mathbf{B}|\cos\theta = |\mathbf{A}|^2 + |\mathbf{B}|^2 - 2|\mathbf{A}||\mathbf{B}|\cos\theta$$

$$\Rightarrow 4|\mathbf{A}||\mathbf{B}|\cos\theta = 0$$

$$\Rightarrow |\mathbf{A}||\mathbf{B}|\cos\theta = 0$$

$$\Rightarrow |\mathbf{A}| = 0 \text{ or } |\mathbf{B}| = 0 \text{ or } \cos\theta = 0$$

$$\Rightarrow \theta = 90^\circ$$

When $\theta = 90^\circ$, we can say that $\mathbf{A} \perp \mathbf{B}$

Very Short Answer Type Questions

Q. 16 A cyclist starts from centre *O* of a circular park of radius 1 km and moves along the path *OPRQO* as shown in figure. If he maintains constant speed of 10 ms^{-1}, what is his acceleration at point *R* in magnitude and direction?

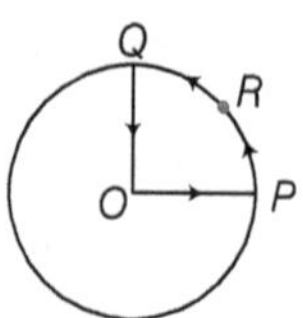

Ans. As shown in the adjacent figure. The cyclist covers the path *OPRQO*.

As we know whenever an object performing circular motion, acceleration is called centripetal acceleration and is always directed towards the centre.

Hence, acceleration at *R* is $a = \frac{v^2}{r}$

$$\Rightarrow a = \frac{(10)^2}{1\,\text{km}} = \frac{100}{10^3} = 0.1\,\text{m/s}^2 \text{ along } RO.$$

Q. 17 **A particle is projected in air at some angle to the horizontal, moves along parabola as shown in figure where x and y indicate horizontal and vertical directions, respectively. Shown in the diagram, direction of velocity and acceleration at points A, B and C.**

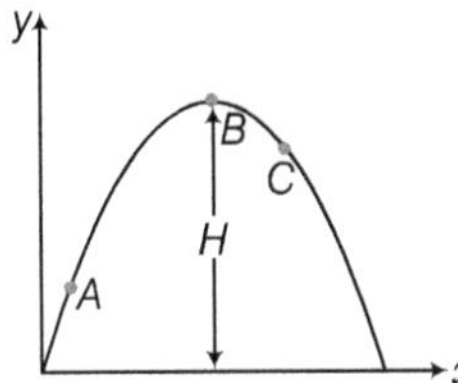

Thinking Process

When a particle is under projectile motion, horizontal component of velocity will always be constant and acceleration is always vertically downward and is equal to g.

Ans. Consider the adjacent diagram in which a particle is projected at an angle θ.

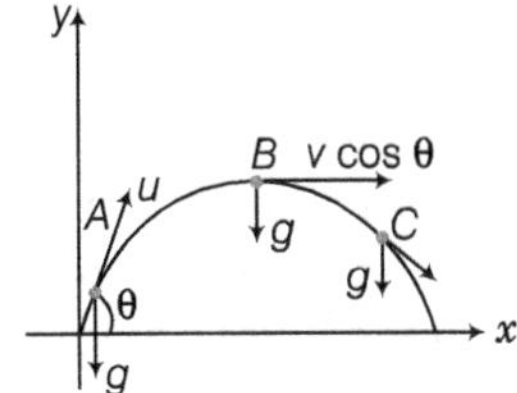

v_x = Horizontal component of velocity = $v \cos\theta$ = constant.
v_y = Vertical component of velocity = $v \sin\theta$
Velocity will always be tangential to the curve in the direction of motion and acceleration is always vertically downward and is equal to g (acceleration due to gravity).

Q. 18 **A ball is thrown from a roof top at an angle of 45° above the horizontal. It hits the ground a few seconds later. At what point during its motion, does the ball have**

(a) greatest speed **(b) smallest speed**

(c) greatest acceleration

Explain.

Ans. Consider the adjacent diagram in which a ball is projected from point O, and covering the path $OABC$.

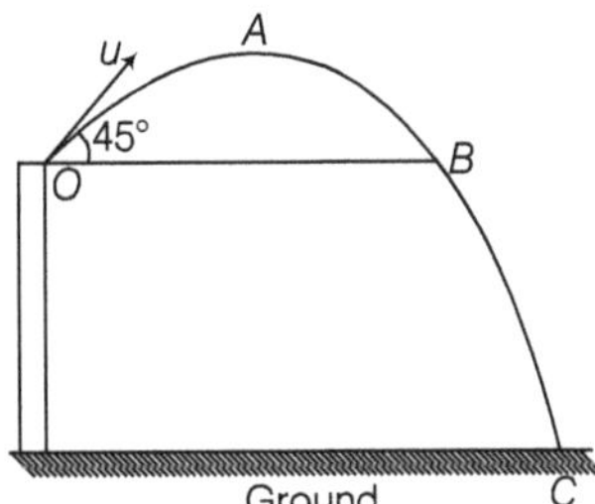

(a) At point B, it will gain the same speed u and after that speed increases and will be maximum just before reaching C.

(b) During upward journey from O to A speed decreases and will be minimum at point A.

(c) Acceleration is always constant throughout the journey and is vertically downward equal to g.

Q. 19 A football is kicked into the air vertically upwards. What is its (a) acceleration and (b) velocity at the highest point?

Ans. (a) Consider the adjacent diagram in which a football is kicked into the air vertically upwards. Acceleration of the football will always be vertical downward and is equal to g.

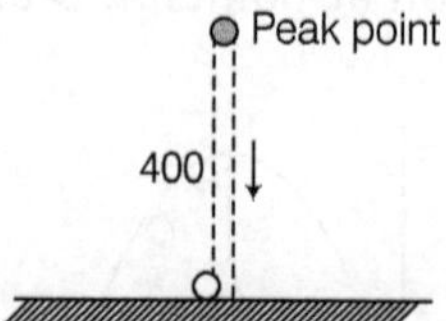

(b) When the football reaches the highest point velocity will be zero as it is continuously retarded by acceleration due to gravity g.

Q. 20 A, B and C are three non-collinear, non co-planar vectors. What can you say about direction of A × (B × C)?

Ans. The direction of (**B** × **C**) will be perpendicular to the plane containing **B** and **B** by right hand rule. **A** × (**B** × **C**) will lie in the plane of **B** and **C** and is perpendicular to vector **A**.

Q. 21 A boy travelling in an open car moving on a levelled road with constant speed tosses a ball vertically up in the air and catches it back. Sketch the motion of the ball as observed by a boy standing on the footpath. Give explanation to support your diagram.

Ans. The path of the ball observed by a boy standing on the footpath is parabolic. The horizontal speed of the ball is same as that of the car, therefore, ball as well car travells equal horizontal distance. Due to its vertical speed, the ball follows a parabolic path.

Note *We must be very clear that we are working with respect to ground. When we observe with respect to the car motion will be along vertical direction only.*

Q. 22 A boy throws a ball in air at 60° to the horizontal along a road with a speed of 10 m/s (36 km/h). Another boy sitting in a passing by car observes the ball. Sketch the motion of the ball as observed by the boy in the car, if car has a speed of (18km/h). Give explanation to support your diagram.

Ans. *Consider the diagram below*

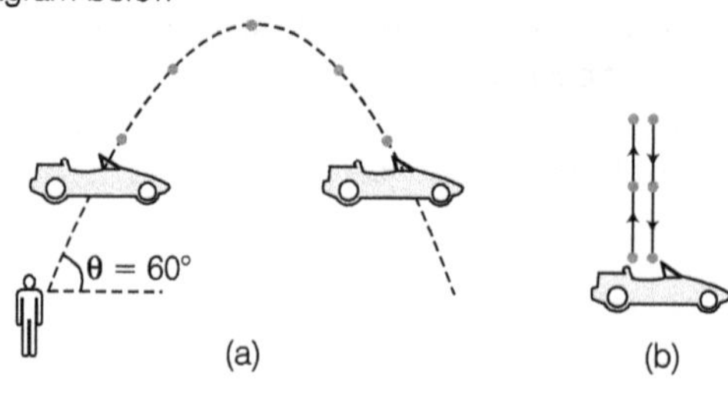

The boy throws the ball at an angle of 60°.

$\therefore$ Horizontal component of velocity $= 4\cos\theta$

$$= (10\text{ m/s})\cos 60^\circ = 10 \times \frac{1}{2} = 5\text{ m/s}.$$

Speed of the car = 18 km/h = 5 m/s.

As horizontal speed of ball and car is same, hence relative velocity of car and ball in the horizontal direction will be zero.

Only vertical motion of the ball will be seen by the boy in the car, as shown in fig. (b)

Q. 23 In dealing with motion of projectile in air, we ignore effect of air resistance on motion. This gives trajectory as a parabola as you have studied. What would the trajectory look like if air resistance tance is include? Sketch such a trajectory and explain why you have drawn it that way.

Thinking Process

When air resistance is included the horizontal component of velocity will not be constant and obviously trajectory will change.

Ans. Due to air resistance, particle energy as well as horizontal component of velocity keep on decreasing making the fall steeper than rise as shown in the figure.

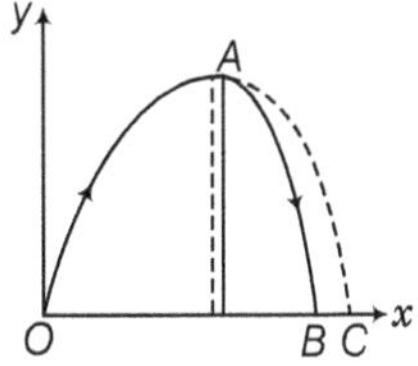

When we are neglecting air resistance path was symmetric parabola (*OAB*). When air resistance is considered path is asymmetric parabola (*OAC*).

Short Answer Type Questions

Q. 24 A fighter plane is flying horizontally at an altitude of 1.5 km with speed 720 km/h. At what angle of sight (w.r.t. horizontal) when the target is seen, should the pilot drop the bomb in order to attack the target?

Thinking Process

When the bomb is dropped from the plane, the bomb will have same velocity as that of plane.

Ans. Consider the adjacent diagram. Let a fighter plane, when it be at position *P*, drops a bomb to hit a target *T*.

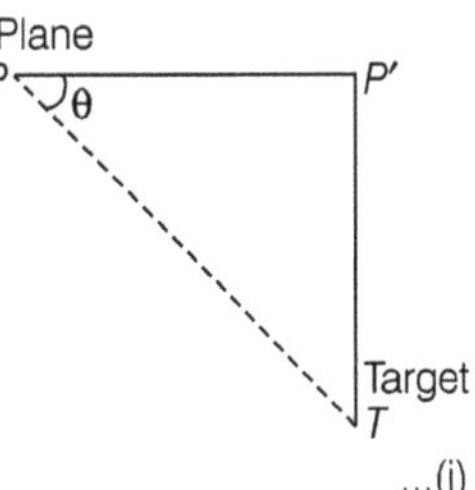

Let $\angle P'PT = \theta$

Speed of the plane $= 720\text{ km/h} = 720 \times \frac{5}{18}\text{ m/s} = 200\text{ m/s}$

Altitude of the plane $(P'T) = 1.5\text{ km} = 1500\text{ m}$

If bomb hits the target after time t, then horizontal distance travelled by the bomb,

$$PP' = u \times t = 200t \quad \text{...(i)}$$

Vertical distance travelled by the bomb,

$$P'T = \frac{1}{2}gt^2 \Rightarrow 1500 = \frac{1}{2} \times 9.8t^2$$

$$\Rightarrow \quad t^2 = \frac{1500}{4.9} \Rightarrow t = \sqrt{\frac{1500}{49}} = 17.49\text{ s}$$

Using value of t in Eq. (i),

$$PP' = 200 \times 17.49 \text{ m}$$

Now,
$$\tan\theta = \frac{P'T}{P'P} = \frac{1500}{200 \times 17.49} = .49287 = \tan 23^\circ 12'$$

$$\theta = 23^\circ 12'$$

Note *Angle is with respect to target. As seen by observer in the plane motion of the bomb will be vertically downward below the plane.*

Q. 25 (a) Earth can be thought of as a sphere of radius 6400 km. Any object (or a person) is performing circular motion around the axis of the earth due to the earth rotation (period 1 day). What is acceleration of object on the surface of the earth (at equator) towards its centre? What is it at latitude θ? How does these accelerations compare with $g = 9.8 \text{ m/s}^2$?

(b) Earth also moves in circular orbit around the sun once every year with an orbital radius of 1.5×10^{11} m. What is the acceleration of the earth (or any object on the surface of the earth) towards the centre of the sun? How does this acceleration compare with $g = 9.8 \text{ m/s}^2$?

Ans. (a) Radius of the earth $(R) = 6400 \text{ km} = 6.4 \times 10^6$ m

Time period $(T) = 1 \text{ day} = 24 \times 60 \times 60 \text{ s} = 86400$ s

$$\text{Centripetal acceleration } (a_c) = \omega^2 R = R\left(\frac{2\pi}{T}\right)^2 = \frac{4\pi^2 R}{T}$$

$$= \frac{4 \times (22/7)^2 \times 6.4 \times 10^6}{(24 \times 60 \times 60)^2}$$

$$= \frac{4 \times 484 \times 64 \times 10^6}{49 \times (24 \times 3600)^2}$$

$$= 0.034 \text{ m/s}^2$$

At equator, latitude $\theta = 0^\circ$

$$\therefore \quad \frac{a_c}{g} = \frac{0.034}{9.8} = \frac{1}{288}$$

(b) Orbital radius of the earth around the sun $(R) = 1.5 \times 10^{11}$ m

Time period = 1 yr = 365 day

$$= 365 \times 24 \times 60 \times 60 \text{ s} = 3.15 \times 10^7 \text{ s}$$

$$\text{Centripetal acceleration } (a_c) = R\omega^2 = \frac{4\pi^2 R}{T^2}$$

$$= \frac{4 \times (22/7)^2 \times 1.5 \times 10^{11}}{(3.15 \times 10^7)^2}$$

$$= 5.97 \times 10^{-3} \text{ m/s}^2$$

$$\therefore \quad \frac{a_c}{g} = \frac{5.97 \times 10^{-3}}{9.8} = \frac{1}{1642}$$

Q. 26 Given below in Column I are the relations between vectors **a**, **b** and **c** and in Column II are the orientations of **a**, **b** and **c** in the *XY*- plane. Match the relation in Column I to correct orientations in Column II.

Column I	Column II
(a) $\mathbf{a}+\mathbf{b}=\mathbf{c}$	(i)
(b) $\mathbf{a}-\mathbf{c}=\mathbf{b}$	(ii)
(c) $\mathbf{b}-\mathbf{a}=\mathbf{c}$	(iii)
(d) $\mathbf{a}+\mathbf{b}+\mathbf{c}=0$	(iv)

Thinking Process

In this problem, triangular law of vector addition will be applied.

Ans. Consider the adjacent diagram in which vectors **A** and **B** are corrected by head and tail.

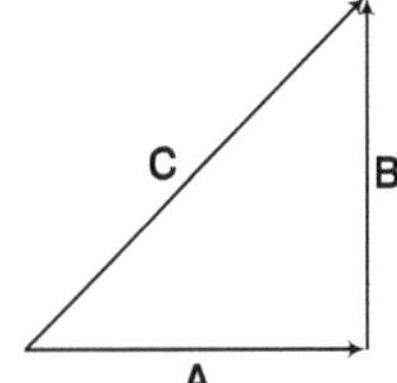

Resultant vector $\mathbf{C}=\mathbf{A}+\mathbf{B}$

(a) from (iv) it is clear that $\mathbf{c}=\mathbf{a}+\mathbf{b}$

(b) from (iii) $\mathbf{c}+\mathbf{b}=\mathbf{a} \Rightarrow \mathbf{a}-\mathbf{c}=\mathbf{b}$

(c) from (i) $\mathbf{b}=\mathbf{a}+\mathbf{c} \Rightarrow \mathbf{b}-\mathbf{a}=\mathbf{c}$

(d) from (ii) $-\mathbf{c}=\mathbf{a}+\mathbf{b} \Rightarrow \mathbf{a}+\mathbf{b}+\mathbf{c}=0$

Q. 27 If $|\mathbf{A}| = 2$ and $|\mathbf{B}| = 4$, then match the relation in Column I with the angle θ between A and B in Column II.

	Column I		Column II
(a)	$\mathbf{A} \cdot \mathbf{B} = 0$	(i)	$\theta = 0$
(b)	$\mathbf{A} \cdot \mathbf{B} = +8$	(ii)	$\theta = 90^\circ$
(c)	$\mathbf{A} \cdot \mathbf{B} = 4$	(iii)	$\theta = 180^\circ$
(d)	$\mathbf{A} \cdot \mathbf{B} = -8$	(iv)	$\theta = 60^\circ$

Ans. Given $|\mathbf{A}| = 2$ and $|\mathbf{B}| = 4$

(a) $\mathbf{A} \cdot \mathbf{B} = AB\cos\theta = 0 \quad \Rightarrow \quad 2 \times 4\cos\theta = 0$

$\Rightarrow \quad \cos\theta = 0 = \cos 90^\circ \quad \Rightarrow \quad \theta = 90^\circ$

$\therefore$ Option (a) matches with option (ii).

(b) $\mathbf{A} \cdot \mathbf{B} = AB\cos\theta = 8 \quad \Rightarrow \quad 2 \times 4\cos\theta = 8$

$\Rightarrow \quad \cos\theta = 1 = \cos 0^\circ \quad \Rightarrow \quad \theta = 0^\circ$

$\therefore$ Option (b) matches with option (i).

(c) $\mathbf{A} \cdot \mathbf{B} = AB\cos\theta = 4 \quad \Rightarrow \quad 2 \times 4\cos\theta = 4$

$\Rightarrow \quad \cos\theta = \frac{1}{2} = \cos 60^\circ \quad \Rightarrow \quad \theta = 60^\circ$

$\therefore$ Option (c) matches with option (iv).

(d) $\mathbf{A} \cdot \mathbf{B} = AB\cos\theta = -8 \quad \Rightarrow \quad 2 \times 4\cos\theta = -8$

$\Rightarrow \quad \cos\theta = -1 = \cos 180^\circ \quad \Rightarrow \quad \theta = 180^\circ$

$\therefore$ Option (d) matches with option (iii).

Q. 28 If $|\mathbf{A}| = 2$ and $|\mathbf{B}| = 4$, then match the relations in Column I with the angle θ between A and B in Column II

	Column I		Column II
(a)	$\lvert\mathbf{A} \times \mathbf{B}\rvert = 0$	(i)	$\theta = 30^\circ$
(b)	$\lvert\mathbf{A} \times \mathbf{B}\rvert = 8$	(ii)	$\theta = 45^\circ$
(c)	$\lvert\mathbf{A} \times \mathbf{B}\rvert = 4$	(iii)	$\theta = 90^\circ$
(d)	$\lvert\mathbf{A} \times \mathbf{B}\rvert = 4\sqrt{2}$	(iv)	$\theta = 0^\circ$

Ans. Given $|\mathbf{A}| = 2$ and $|\mathbf{B}| = 4$

(a) $|\mathbf{A} \times \mathbf{B}| = AB\sin\theta = 0 \quad \Rightarrow \quad 2 \times 4 \times \sin\theta = 0$

$\Rightarrow \quad \sin\theta = 0 = \sin 0^\circ \quad \Rightarrow \quad \theta = 0^\circ$

$\therefore$ Option (a) matches with option (iv).

(b) $|\mathbf{A} \times \mathbf{B}| = AB\sin\theta = 8 \quad \Rightarrow \quad 2 \times 4\sin\theta = 8$

$\Rightarrow \quad \sin\theta = 1 = \sin 90^\circ \quad \Rightarrow \quad \theta = 90^\circ$

$\therefore$ Option (b) matches with option (iii).

(c) $|\mathbf{A} \times \mathbf{B}| = AB\sin\theta = 4 \quad \Rightarrow \quad 2 \times 4\sin\theta = 4$

$\Rightarrow \quad \sin\theta = \frac{1}{2} = \sin 30^\circ \quad \Rightarrow \quad \theta = 30^\circ$

$\therefore$ Option (c) matches with option (i).

(d) $|\mathbf{A} \times \mathbf{B}| = AB\sin\theta = 4\sqrt{2} \quad \Rightarrow \quad 2 \times 4\sin\theta = 4\sqrt{2}$

$\Rightarrow \quad \sin\theta = \frac{1}{\sqrt{2}} = \sin 45^\circ \quad \Rightarrow \quad \theta = 45^\circ$

$\therefore$ Option (d) matches with option (ii).

Long Answer Type Questions

Q. 29 A hill is 500 m high. Supplies are to be sent across the hill using a canon that can hurl packets at a speed of 125 m/s over the hill. The canon is located at a distance of 800 m from the foot of hill and can be moved on the ground at a speed of 2 m/s; so that its distance from the hill can be adjusted. What is the shortest time in which a packet can reach on the ground across the hill? Take, $g = 10 \text{ m/s}^2$.

Ans. Given, speed of packets = 125 m/s

Height of the hill = 500 m.

To cross the hill, the vertical component of the velocity should be sufficient to cross such height.

$$u_y \geq \sqrt{2gh}$$
$$\geq \sqrt{2 \times 10 \times 500}$$
$$\geq 100 \text{m/s}$$

But $$u^2 = u_x^2 + u_y^2$$

∴ Horizontal component of initial velocity,

$$u_x = \sqrt{u^2 - u_y^2} = \sqrt{(125)^2 - (100)^2} = 75 \text{ m/s}$$

Time taken to reach the top of the hill,

$$t = \sqrt{\frac{2h}{g}} = \sqrt{\frac{2 \times 500}{10}} = 10 \text{ s}$$

Time taken to reach the ground from the top of the hill $t' = t = 10$ s. Horizontal distance travelled in 10 s

$$x = u_x \times t = 75 \times 10 = 750 \text{ m}$$

∴ Distance through which canon has to be moved = 800 − 750 = 50 m

Speed with which canon can move = 2 m/s

∴ Time taken by canon $= \frac{50}{2} \Rightarrow t'' = 25$ s

∴ Total time taken by a packet to reach on the ground $= t'' + t + t' = 25 + 10 + 10 = 45$ s

Q. 30 A gun can fire shells with maximum speed v_0 and the maximum horizontal range that can be achieved is $\mathbf{R} = \frac{v_0^2}{g}$. If a target farther away by distance Δx (beyond R) has to be hit with the same gun, show that it could be achieved by raising the gun to a height at least $h = \Delta x \left[1 + \frac{\Delta x}{R}\right]$

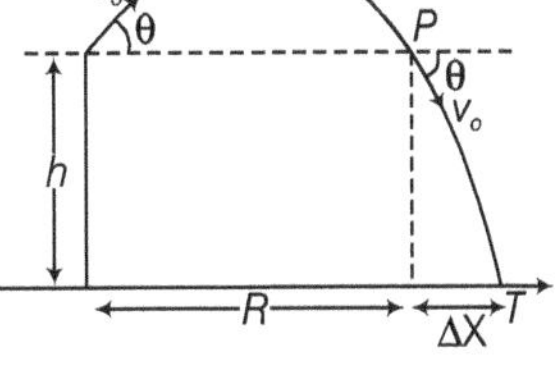

Thinking Process

Horizontal range of a projectile is maximum when it is thrown at an angle 45° from the horizontal and $R_{max} = \frac{u^2}{g}$, *where u is speed of projection of the projectile.*

Ans. *This problem can be approached in two different ways*

(i) Refer to the diagram, target T is at horizontal distance $x = R + \Delta x$ and between point of projection $y = -h$.

(ii) From point P in the diagram projection at speed v_0 at an angle θ below horizontal with height h and horizontal range ΔxA)

Applying method (i)

Maximum horizontal range

$$R = \frac{v_0^2}{g}, \text{ for } \theta = 45° \quad ...(i)$$

Let the gun be raised through a height h from the ground so that it can hit the target. Let vertically downward direction is taken as positive

Horizontal component of initial velocity $= v_0 \cos\theta$

Vertical component of initial velocity $= -v_0 \sin\theta$

Taking motion in vertical direction, $h = (-v_0 \sin\theta)t + \frac{1}{2}gt^2$ ...(ii)

Taking motion in horizontal direction

$$(R + \Delta x) = v_0 \cos\theta \times t$$

$$\Rightarrow \quad t = \frac{(R + \Delta x)}{v_0 \cos\theta} \quad ...(iii)$$

Substituting value of t in Eq. (ii), we get

$$h = (-v_0 \sin\theta) \times \left(\frac{R + \Delta x}{v_0 \cos\theta}\right) + \frac{1}{2}g\left(\frac{R + \Delta x}{v_0 \cos\theta}\right)^2$$

$$h = -(R + \Delta x)\tan\theta + \frac{1}{2}g\frac{(R + \Delta x)^2}{v_0^2 \cos^2\theta}$$

As angle of projection is $\theta = 45°$, therefore

$$h = -(R + \Delta x) + \tan 45° + \frac{1}{2}g\frac{(R + \Delta x)^2}{v_0^2 \cos^2 45°}$$

$$h = -(R + \Delta x) \times 1 + \frac{1}{2}g\frac{(R + \Delta x)^2}{v_0^2 (1/2)}$$

$$\left(\because \tan 45° = 1 \text{ and } \cos 45° = \frac{1}{\sqrt{2}}\right)$$

$$h = -(R + \Delta x) + \frac{(R + \Delta x)^2}{R} \quad \text{[Using Eq. (i), } R = v_0^2/g]$$

$$= -(R + \Delta x) + \frac{1}{R}(R^2 + \Delta x^2 + 2R\Delta x)$$

$$= -R - \Delta x + \left(R + \frac{\Delta x^2}{R} + 2\Delta x\right)$$

$$= \Delta x + \frac{\Delta x^2}{R}$$

$$h = \Delta x\left(1 + \frac{\Delta x}{R}\right)$$

Hence proved.

Note *We should not confuse with the positive direction of motion. May be vertically upward direction or vertically downward direction is taken as positive according to convenience.*

Q. 31 A particle is projected in air at an angle β to a surface which itself is inclined at an angle α to the horizontal (figure).

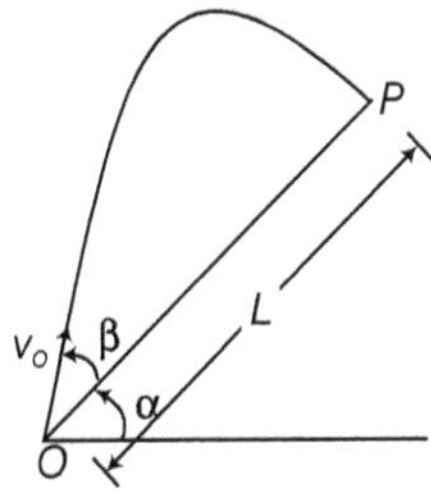

(a) Find an expression of range on the plane surface (distance on the plane from the point of projection at which particle will hit the surface).

(b) Time of flight.

(c) β at which range will be maximum.

Thinking Process

To solve problems involving projectile motion on an inclined plane, we have to choose two mutually perpendicular axes, one along inclined plane and other perpendicular to the inclined plane.

Ans. Consider the adjacent diagram.

Mutually perpendicular x and y-axes are shown in the diagram.

Particle is projected from the point O.

Let time taken in reaching from point O to point P is T.

(b) Considering motion along vertical upward direction perpendicular to OX.

For the journey O to P.

$$y = 0, u_y = v_0 \sin\beta, a_y = -g\cos\alpha, t = T$$

Applying equation,

$$y = u_y t + \frac{1}{2} a_y t^2$$

$$\Rightarrow \quad 0 = v_0 \sin\beta T + \frac{1}{2}(-g\cos\alpha)T^2$$

$$\Rightarrow \quad T\left[v_0 \sin\beta - \frac{g\cos\alpha}{2} T\right] = 0$$

$$\Rightarrow \quad T = 0, T = \frac{2v_0 \sin\beta}{g\cos\alpha}$$

As $T = 0$, corresponding to point O

Hence, $$T = \text{Time of flight} = \frac{2v_0 \sin\beta}{g\cos\alpha}$$

(a) Considering motion along OX.

$$x = L, u_x = v_0 \cos\beta, a_x = -g\sin\alpha$$

$$t = T = \frac{2v_0 \sin\beta}{g\cos\alpha}$$

$$x = u_x t + \frac{1}{2} a_x t^2$$

$$\Rightarrow \quad L = v_0 \cos\beta\, T + \frac{1}{2}(-g \sin\alpha) T^2$$

$$\Rightarrow \quad L = v_0 \cos\beta T - \frac{1}{2} g \sin\alpha T^2$$

$$= T\,[v_0 \cos\beta - \frac{1}{2} g \sin\alpha T]$$

$$= T\left[v_0 \cos\beta - \frac{1}{2} g \sin\alpha \times \frac{2v_0 \sin\beta}{g \cos\alpha}\right]$$

$$= \frac{2\, v_0 \sin\beta}{g \cos\alpha}\left[v_0 \cos\beta - \frac{v_0 \sin\alpha \sin\beta}{\cos\alpha}\right]$$

$$= \frac{2\, v_0^2 \sin\beta}{g \cos^2\alpha}[\cos\beta . \cos\alpha - \sin\alpha \sin\beta]$$

$$\Rightarrow \quad L = \frac{2\, v_0^2 \sin\beta}{g \cos^2\alpha}\cos(\alpha + \beta)$$

(c) For range (L) to be maximum,

$\sin\beta . \cos(\alpha + \beta)$ should be maximum.

Let, $Z = \sin\beta . \cos(\alpha + \beta)$

$$= \sin\beta\, [\cos\alpha . \cos\beta - \sin\alpha . \sin\beta)$$

$$= \frac{1}{2}[\cos\alpha . \sin 2\beta - 2 \sin\alpha . \sin^2\beta]$$

$$= \frac{1}{2}[\sin 2\beta . \cos\alpha - \sin\alpha(1 - \cos 2\beta)]$$

$$\Rightarrow \quad z = \frac{1}{2}[\sin 2\beta . \cos\alpha - \sin\alpha + \sin\alpha . \cos 2\beta]$$

$$= \frac{1}{2}[\sin 2\beta . \cos\alpha + \cos 2\beta . \sin\alpha - \sin\alpha]$$

$$= \frac{1}{2}[\sin(2\beta + \alpha) - \sin\alpha]$$

For z to be maximum,

$$\sin(2 = \beta + \alpha) = \text{maximum} = 1$$

$$\Rightarrow \quad 2\beta + \alpha = \frac{\pi}{2} \text{ or, } \beta = \frac{\pi}{4} - \frac{\alpha}{2}$$

Q. 32 A particle falling vertically from a height hits a plane surface inclined to horizontal at an angle θ with speed v_0 and rebounds elastically. Find the distance along the plane where it will hit second time.

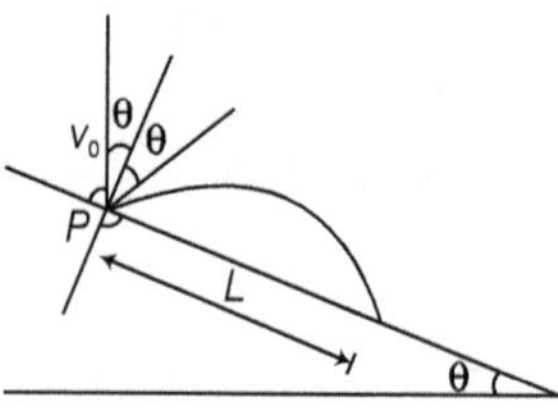

Thinking Process

When particle rebounded elastically speed will remain same.

Ans. Considering x and y-axes as shown in the diagram.

For the motion of the projectile from O to A.

$$y = 0, u_y = v_0 \cos\theta$$
$$a_y = -g\cos\theta, t = T$$

Applying equation of kinematics,

$$y = u_y t + \frac{1}{2} a_y t^2$$

$$\Rightarrow \quad 0 = v_0 \cos\theta\, T + \frac{1}{2}(-g\cos\theta)T^2$$

$$\Rightarrow \quad T, \left[v_0 \cos\theta - \frac{g\cos\theta\, T}{2}\right] = 0$$

$$T = \frac{2\, v_0 \cos\theta}{g\cos\theta}$$

As $T = 0$, corresponds to point O

Hence, $$T = \frac{2v_0}{g}$$

Now considering motion along OX.

$$x = L, u_x = v_0 \sin\theta, a_x = g\sin\theta, t = T = \frac{2\, v_0}{g}$$

Applying equation of kinematics,

$$x = u_x t + \frac{1}{2} a_x t^2$$

$$\Rightarrow \quad L = v_0 \sin\theta t + \frac{1}{2} g \sin\theta t^2 = (v_0 \sin\theta)(T) + \frac{1}{2} g \sin\theta\, T^2$$

$$= (v_0 \sin\theta)\left(\frac{2v_0}{g}\right) + \frac{1}{2} g\sin\theta \times \left(\frac{2\, v_0}{g}\right)^2$$

$$= \frac{2\, v_0^2}{g}\sin\theta + \frac{1}{2} g\sin\theta \times \frac{4v_0^2}{g^2} = \frac{2\, v_0^2}{g}[\sin\theta + \sin\theta]$$

$$\Rightarrow \quad L = \frac{4v_0^2}{g}\sin\theta$$

Q. 33 A girl riding a bicycle with a speed of 5 m/s towards north direction, observes rain falling vertically down. If she increases her speed to 10 m/s, rain appears to meet her at 45° to the vertical. What is the speed of the rain? In what direction does rain fall as observed by a ground based observer?

Thinking Process

Draw the vector diagram is for the information given and find a and b. We may draw all vectors in the reference frame of ground based observer.

Ans. Assume north to be $\hat{\mathbf{i}}$ direction and vertically downward to be $-\hat{\mathbf{j}}$.

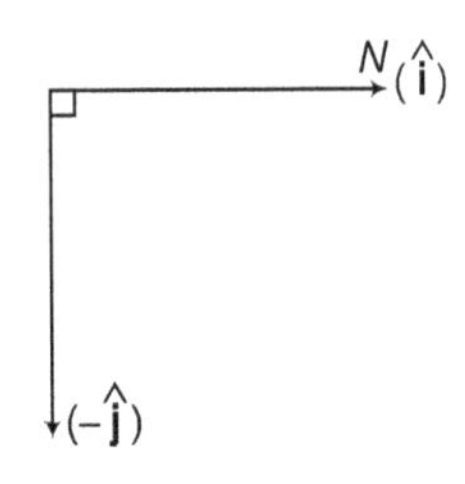

Let the rain velocity v_r be $a\,\hat{\mathbf{i}} + b\,\hat{\mathbf{j}}$.

$$\mathbf{v_r} = a\,\hat{\mathbf{i}} + b\,\hat{\mathbf{j}}$$

***Case* I** Given velocity of girl $= \mathbf{v_g} = (5\,\text{m/s})\,\hat{\mathbf{i}}$

Let $\mathbf{v_{rg}}$ = Velocity of rain w.r.t girl

$$= \mathbf{v_r} - \mathbf{v_g} = (a\hat{\mathbf{i}} + b\hat{\mathbf{j}}) - 5\hat{\mathbf{i}}$$
$$= (a-5)\,\hat{\mathbf{i}} + b\hat{\mathbf{j}}$$

According to question rain, appears to fall vertically downward.

Hence, $a - 5 = 0 \Rightarrow a = 5$

***Case* II** Given velocity of the girl, $\mathbf{v}_g = (10\,\text{m/s})\,\hat{\mathbf{i}}$

$\therefore$
$$\mathbf{v}_{rg} = \mathbf{v}_r - \mathbf{v}_g$$
$$= (a\hat{\mathbf{i}} + b\hat{\mathbf{j}}) - 10\hat{\mathbf{i}} = (a - 10)\,\hat{\mathbf{i}} + b\hat{\mathbf{j}}$$

According to question rain appears to fall at 45° to the vertical hence $\tan 45° = \dfrac{b}{a - 10} = 1$

$\Rightarrow$
$$b = a - 10 = 5 - 10 = -5$$

Hence, velocity of rain $= a\hat{\mathbf{i}} + b\hat{\mathbf{j}}$

$\Rightarrow$
$$\mathbf{v}_r = 5\hat{\mathbf{i}} - 5\hat{\mathbf{j}}$$

Speed of rain $= |\mathbf{v}_r| = \sqrt{(5)^2 + (-5)^2} = \sqrt{50} = 5\sqrt{2}\,\text{m/s}$

Q. 34 A river is flowing due east with a speed 3 m/s. A swimmer can swim in still water at a speed of 4 m/s (figure).

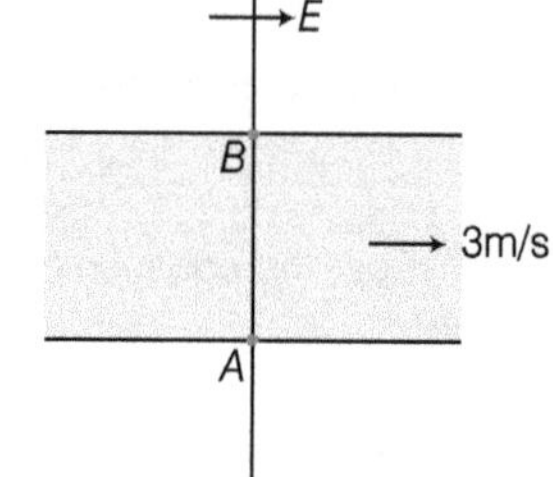

(a) If swimmer starts swimming due north, what will be his resultant velocity (magnitude and direction)?

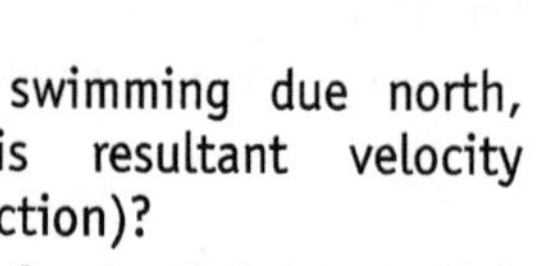

(b) If he wants to start from point *A* on south bank and reach opposite point *B* on north bank,

(i) which direction should he swim?

(ii) what will be his resultant speed?

(c) From two different cases as mentioned in (a) and (b) above, in which case will he reach opposite bank in shorter time?

Ans. Given, Speed of the river $(v_r) = 3$ m/s (east)

Speed of swimmer $(v_s) = 4$ m/s (east)

(a) When swimmer starts swimming due north then his resultant velocity

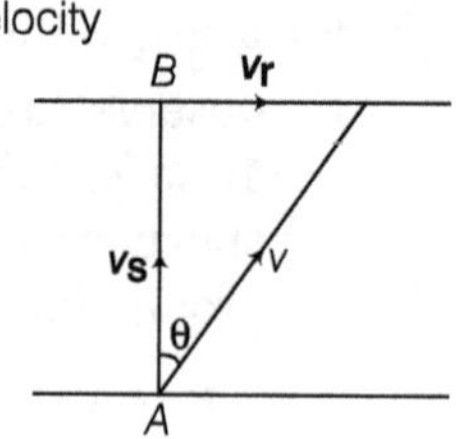

$$v = \sqrt{v_r^2 + v_s^2} = \sqrt{(3)^2 + (4)^2}$$
$$= \sqrt{9 + 16} = \sqrt{25} = 5\,\text{m/s}$$
$$\tan\theta = \frac{v_r}{v_s} = \frac{3}{4}$$
$$= 0.75 = \tan 36°54'$$

Hence,
$$\theta = 36°54'\ \text{N}$$

(b) To reach opposite points *B*, the swimmer should swim at an angle θ of north.

Resultant speed of the swimmer

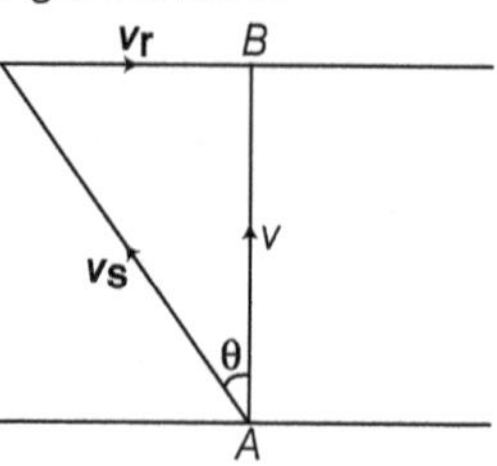

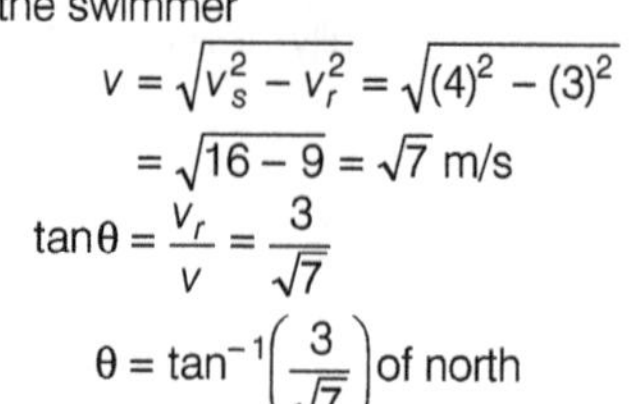

$$v = \sqrt{v_s^2 - v_r^2} = \sqrt{(4)^2 - (3)^2}$$
$$= \sqrt{16 - 9} = \sqrt{7}\ \text{m/s}$$
$$\tan\theta = \frac{v_r}{v} = \frac{3}{\sqrt{7}}$$

$\Rightarrow$
$$\theta = \tan^{-1}\left(\frac{3}{\sqrt{7}}\right) \text{of north}$$

(c) In case (a),

Time taken by the swimmer to cross the river, $t_1 = \frac{d}{v_s} = \frac{d}{4}$ s

In case (b),

Time taken by the swimmer to cross the river

$$t_1 = \frac{d}{v} = \frac{d}{\sqrt{7}}$$

As $\frac{d}{4} < \frac{d}{\sqrt{7}}$, therefore $t_1 < t_2$

Hence, the swimmer will cross the river in shorter time in case (a).

Q. 35 A cricket fielder can throw the cricket ball with a speed v_0. If he throws the ball while running with speed u at an angle θ to the horizontal, find

(a) the effective angle to the horizontal at which the ball is projected in air as seen by a spectator.

(b) what will be time of flight?

(c) what is the distance (horizontal range) from the point of projection at which the ball will land?

(d) find θ at which he should throw the ball that would maximise the horizontal range as found in (iii).

(e) how does θ for maximum range change if $u > u_0$, $u = u_0$, $u < v_0$?

(f) how does θ in (v) compare with that for $u = 0$ (*i.e.*, 45°)?

Ans. Consider the adjacent diagram.

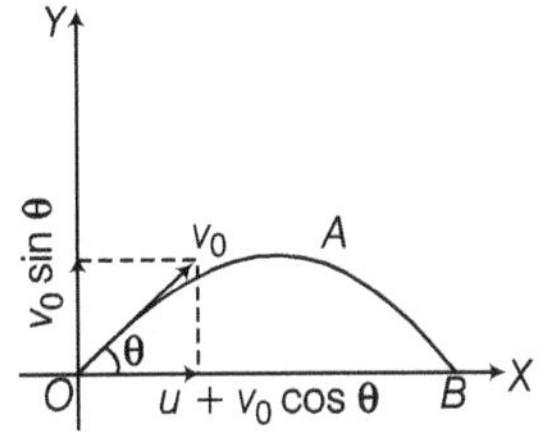

(a) Initial velocity in

x-direction, $u_x = u + v_0 \cos\theta$

u_y = Initial velocity in y-direction

$= v_0 \sin\theta$

where angle of projection is θ.

Now, we can write

$$\tan\theta = \frac{u_y}{u_x} = \frac{u_0 \sin\theta}{u + u_0 \cos\theta}$$

$$\Rightarrow \qquad \theta = \tan^{-1}\left(\frac{v_0 \sin\theta}{u + v_0 \cos\theta}\right)$$

(b) Let T be the time of flight.

As net displacement is zero over time period T.

$$y = 0, u_y = v_0 \sin\theta, a_y = -g, t = T$$

We know that $$y = u_y t + \frac{1}{2} a_y t^2$$

$$\Rightarrow \quad 0 = v_0 \sin\theta\, T + \frac{1}{2}(-g)T^2$$

$$\Rightarrow \quad T\left[v_0 \sin\theta - \frac{g}{2}T\right] = 0 \Rightarrow T = 0, \frac{2v_0 \sin\theta}{g}$$

$T = 0_1$, corresponds to point O.

Hence, $$T = \frac{2u_0 \sin\theta}{g}$$

(c) Horizontal range, $R = (u + v_0 \cos\theta)T = (u + v_0 \cos\theta)\dfrac{2v_0 \sin\theta}{g}$

$$= \frac{v_0}{g}[2u \sin\theta + v_0 \sin 2\theta]$$

(d) For horizontal range to be maximum, $\dfrac{dR}{d\theta} = 0$

$$\Rightarrow \quad \frac{v_0}{g}[2u\cos\theta + v_0 \cos 2\theta \times 2] = 0$$

$$\Rightarrow \quad 2u\cos\theta + 2v_0\,[2\cos^2\theta - 1] = 0$$

$$\Rightarrow \quad 4v_0 \cos^2\theta + 2u\cos\theta - 2v_0 = 0$$

$$\Rightarrow \quad 2v_0 \cos^2\theta + u\cos\theta - v_0 = 0$$

$$\Rightarrow \quad \cos\theta = \frac{-u \pm \sqrt{u^2 + 8v_0^2}}{4v_0}$$

$$\Rightarrow \quad \theta_{max} = \cos^{-1}\left[\frac{-u \pm \sqrt{u^2 + 8v_0^2}}{4v_0}\right]$$

$$= \cos^{-1}\left[\frac{-u + \sqrt{u^2 + 8v_0^2}}{4v_0}\right]$$

(e) If $u = v_0$,

$$\cos\theta = \frac{-v_0 \pm \sqrt{v_0^2 + 8v_0^2}}{4v_0} = \frac{-1+3}{4} = \frac{1}{2}$$

$$\Rightarrow \quad \theta = 60°$$

If $u << v_0$, then $8v_0^2 + u^2 \approx 8v_0^2$

$$\theta_{max} = \cos^{-1}\left[\frac{-u \pm 2\sqrt{2}v_0}{4v_0}\right] = \cos^{-1}\left[\frac{1}{\sqrt{2}} - \frac{u}{4v_0}\right]$$

If $u << v_0$, then $$\theta_{max} = \cos^{-1}\left(\frac{1}{\sqrt{2}}\right) = \frac{\pi}{4}$$

If $u > u_0$ and $$u >> v_0$$

$$\theta_{max} = \cos^{-1}\left[\frac{-u \pm u}{4v_0}\right] = 0 \Rightarrow \theta_{max} = \frac{\pi}{2}$$

(f) If $u = 0$, $\theta_{max} = \cos^{-1}\left[\dfrac{0 \pm \sqrt{8v^2{}_0}}{4v_0}\right] = \cos^{-1}\left(\dfrac{1}{\sqrt{2}}\right) = 45°$

Q. 36 Motion in two dimensions, in a plane can be studied by expressing position, velocity and acceleration as vectors in cartesian coordinates $\mathbf{A} = A_x\hat{\mathbf{i}} + A_y\hat{\mathbf{j}}$, where $\hat{\mathbf{i}}$ and $\hat{\mathbf{j}}$ are unit vector along x and y-directions, respectively and A_x and A_y are corresponding components of A. Motion can also be studied by expressing vectors in circular polar coordinates as $\mathbf{A} = A_r\hat{\mathbf{r}} + A_\theta\hat{\theta}$, where $\hat{\mathbf{r}} = \frac{\mathbf{r}}{r} = \cos\theta\,\hat{\mathbf{i}} + \sin\theta\,\hat{\mathbf{j}}$ and $\hat{\theta} = -\sin\theta\,\hat{\mathbf{i}} + \cos\theta\hat{\mathbf{j}}$ are unit vectors along direction in which r and θ are increasing.

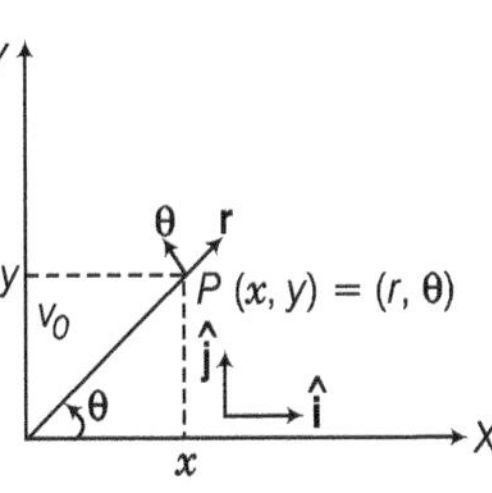

(a) Express $\hat{\mathbf{i}}$ and $\hat{\mathbf{j}}$ in terms of $\hat{\mathbf{r}}$ and $\hat{\theta}$.

(b) Show that both $\hat{\mathbf{r}}$ and $\hat{\theta}$ are unit vectors and are perpendicular to each other.

(c) Show that $\frac{d}{dt}(\hat{\mathbf{r}}) = \omega\,\hat{\theta}$, where $\omega = \frac{d\theta}{dt}$ and $\frac{d}{dt}(\hat{\theta}) = -\theta\hat{\mathbf{r}}$.

(d) For a particle moving along a spiral given by $r = a\theta\hat{\mathbf{r}}$, where $a = 1$ (unit), find dimensions of a.

(e) Find velocity and acceleration in polar vector representation for particle moving along spiral described in (d) above.

Ans. (a) Given, unit vector

$$\hat{\mathbf{r}} = \cos\theta\hat{\mathbf{i}} + \sin\theta\hat{\mathbf{j}} \qquad \text{...(i)}$$

$$\hat{\theta} = -\sin\theta\hat{\mathbf{i}} + \cos\theta\hat{\mathbf{j}} \qquad \text{...(ii)}$$

Multiplying Eq. (i) by $\sin\theta$ and Eq. (ii) with $\cos\theta$ and adding

$$\hat{\mathbf{r}}\sin\theta + \hat{\theta}\cos\theta = \sin\theta.\cos\theta\hat{\mathbf{i}} + \sin^2\theta\hat{\mathbf{j}} + \cos^2\theta\hat{\mathbf{j}} - \sin\theta.\cos\theta\hat{\mathbf{i}}$$

$$= \hat{\mathbf{j}}\,(\cos^2\theta + \sin^2\theta) = \hat{\mathbf{j}}$$

$$\Rightarrow \qquad \hat{\mathbf{r}}\sin\theta + \hat{\theta}\cos\theta = \hat{\mathbf{j}}$$

By Eq. (i) $\times\cos\theta$ – Eq. (ii) $\times\sin\theta$

$$n\,(\hat{\mathbf{r}}\cos\theta - \hat{\theta}\sin\theta) = \hat{\mathbf{i}}$$

(b) $\hat{\mathbf{r}}.\hat{\theta} = (\cos\theta\hat{\mathbf{i}} + \sin\theta\hat{\mathbf{j}}).(-\sin\theta\hat{\mathbf{i}} + \cos\theta\hat{\mathbf{j}}) = -\cos\theta.\sin\theta + \sin\theta.\cos\theta = 0$

$$\Rightarrow \qquad \theta = 90^\circ \text{ Angle between } \hat{\mathbf{r}} \text{ and } \hat{\theta}.$$

(c) Given, $\hat{\mathbf{r}} = \cos\theta\hat{\mathbf{i}} + \sin\theta\hat{\mathbf{j}}$

$$\frac{d\hat{\mathbf{r}}}{dt} = \frac{d}{dt}(\cos\theta\hat{\mathbf{i}} + \sin\theta\hat{\mathbf{j}}) = -\sin\theta.\frac{d\theta}{dt}\hat{\mathbf{i}} + \cos\theta.\frac{d\theta}{dt}\hat{\mathbf{j}}$$

$$= \omega\,[-\sin\theta\hat{\mathbf{i}} + \cos\theta\hat{\mathbf{j}}] \qquad \left[\because \theta = \frac{d\theta}{dt}\right]$$

(d) Given, $\mathbf{r} = a\theta\hat{\mathbf{r}}$, here, writing dimensions $[\mathbf{r}] = [a][\theta][\hat{\mathbf{r}}]$

$$\Rightarrow \qquad L = [a]\,\%1 \;\Rightarrow\; [a] = L = [M^0L^1T^0]$$

(e) Given, $a = 1$ unit $\quad \mathbf{r} = \theta\hat{\mathbf{r}} = \theta[\cos\theta\hat{\mathbf{i}} + \sin\theta\hat{\mathbf{j}}]$

Velocity, $\quad v = \frac{d\mathbf{r}}{dt} = \frac{d\theta}{dt}\hat{\mathbf{r}} + \theta\frac{d}{dt}\hat{\mathbf{r}} = \frac{d\theta}{dt}\hat{\mathbf{r}} + \theta\frac{d}{dt}[(\cos\theta\hat{\mathbf{i}} + \sin\theta\hat{\mathbf{j}})]$

$$= \frac{d\theta}{dt}\hat{\mathbf{r}} + \theta\left[(-\sin\theta\hat{\mathbf{i}} + \cos\theta\hat{\mathbf{j}})\frac{d\theta}{dt}\right]$$

$$= \frac{d\theta}{dt}\hat{\mathbf{r}} + \theta\,\hat{\theta}\,\omega = \omega\hat{\mathbf{r}} + \omega\theta\hat{\theta}$$

Acceleration, $\quad \mathbf{a} = \frac{d}{dt}[\omega\hat{\mathbf{r}} + \omega\theta\hat{\theta}] = \frac{d}{dt}\left[\frac{d\theta}{dt}\hat{\mathbf{r}} + \frac{d\theta}{dt}(\theta\hat{\theta})\right]$

$$= \frac{d^2\theta}{dt^2}\hat{\mathbf{r}} + \frac{d\theta}{dt}\cdot\frac{d\hat{\mathbf{r}}}{dt} + \frac{d^2\theta}{dt^2}\theta\hat{\theta} + \frac{d\theta}{dt}\frac{d}{dt}(\theta\hat{\theta})$$

$$= \frac{d^2\theta}{dt^2}\hat{\mathbf{r}} + \omega[-\sin\theta\hat{\mathbf{i}} + \sin\theta\hat{\mathbf{j}}] + \frac{d^2\theta}{dt^2}\theta\hat{\theta} + \frac{\omega d}{dt}(\theta\hat{\theta})$$

$$= \frac{d^2\theta}{dt^2}\hat{\mathbf{r}} + \omega^2\hat{\theta} + \frac{d^2\theta}{dt^2}\times\theta\hat{\theta} + \omega^2\hat{\theta} + \omega^2\theta(-\hat{\mathbf{r}})$$

$$\left(\frac{d^2\theta}{dtv^2} - \omega^2\right)\hat{\mathbf{r}} + \left(2\omega^2 + \frac{d^2\theta}{dt^2}\theta\right)\theta$$

Q. 37 A man wants to reach from A to the opposite corner of the square C. The sides of the square are 100 m. A central square of 50m × 50m is filled with sand. Outside this square, he can walk at a speed 1 m/s. In the central square, he can walk only at a speed of v m/s ($v < 1$). What is smallest value of v for which he can reach faster *via* a straight path through the sand than any path in the square outside the sand?

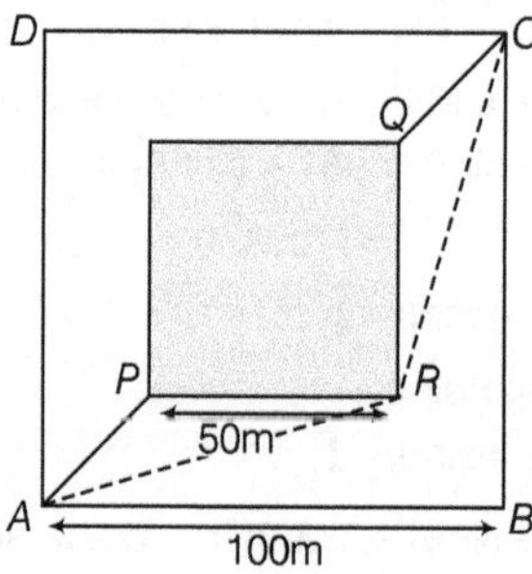

Ans. Consider adjacent diagram.

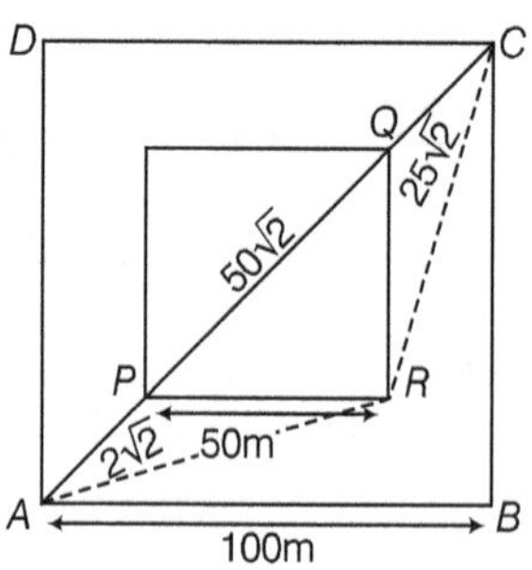

Time taken to go from A to C *via* straight line path $APQC$ through the S and

$$T_{sand} = \frac{AP + QC}{1} + \frac{PQ}{v} = \frac{25\sqrt{2} + 25\sqrt{2}}{1} + \frac{50\sqrt{2}}{v}$$

$$= 50\sqrt{2} + \frac{50\sqrt{2}}{v} = 50\sqrt{2}\left(\frac{1}{v} + 1\right)$$

Clearly from figure the shortest path outside the sand will be ARC.

Time taken to go from A to C *via* this path

$$T_{outside} = \frac{AR + RC}{1} \text{ s}$$

Clearly,

$$AR = \sqrt{75^2 + 25^2} = \sqrt{75 \times 75 + 25 \times 25}$$

$$= 5 \times 5\sqrt{9 + 1} = 25\sqrt{10} \text{ m}$$

$$RC = AR = \sqrt{75^2 + 25^2} = 25\sqrt{10} \text{ m}$$

$$\Rightarrow \quad T_{outside} = 2AR = 2 \times 25\sqrt{10} \text{ s} = 50\sqrt{10} \text{ s}$$

For $\quad T_{sand} < T_{outside}$

$$\Rightarrow \quad 50\sqrt{2}\left(\frac{1}{v} + 1\right) < 2 \times 25\sqrt{10}$$

$$\Rightarrow \quad \frac{2\sqrt{2}}{2}\left(\frac{1}{v} + 1\right) < \sqrt{10}$$

$$\Rightarrow \quad \frac{1}{v} + 1 < \frac{2\sqrt{10}}{2\sqrt{2}} = \frac{\sqrt{5}}{2} \times 2 = \sqrt{5}$$

$$\Rightarrow \quad \frac{1}{v} < \frac{\sqrt{5}}{2} \times 2 - 1 \Rightarrow \frac{1}{v} < \sqrt{5} - 1$$

$$\Rightarrow \quad v > \frac{1}{\sqrt{5} - 1} \approx 0.81 \text{ m/s}$$

$$\Rightarrow \quad v > 0.81 \text{ m/s}$$

4

Laws *of* Motion

Multiple Choice Questions (MCQS)

Q. 1 A ball is travelling with uniform translatory motion. This means that

(a) it is at rest

(b) the path can be a straight line or circular and the ball travels with uniform speed

(c) all parts of the ball have the same velocity (magnitude and direction) and the velocity is constant

(d) the centre of the ball moves with constant velocity and the ball spins about its centre uniformly

Ans. *(c)* In a uniform translatory motion, all parts of the ball have the same velocity in magnitude and direction and this velocity is constant.

The situation is shown in adjacent diagram where a body A is in uniform translatory motion.

Q. 2 A metre scale is moving with uniform velocity. This implies

(a) the force acting on the scale is zero, but a torque about the centre of mass can act on the scale

(b) the force acting on the scale is zero and the torque acting about centre of mass of the scale is also zero

(c) the total force acting on it need not be zero but the torque on it is zero

(d) neither the force nor the torque need to be zero

Ans. *(b)* To solve this question we have to apply Newton's second law of motion, in terms of force and change in momentum.

We known that $$F = \frac{dp}{dt}$$

given that meter scale is moving with uniform velocity, hence, $dp = 0$

$$\text{Force} = F = 0.$$

As all part of the scale is moving with uniform velocity and total force is zero, hence, torque will also be zero.

Q. 3 A cricket ball of mass 150 g has an initial velocity $\mathbf{u} = (3\hat{\mathbf{i}} + 4\hat{\mathbf{j}})\text{ms}^{-1}$ and a final velocity $\mathbf{v} = -(3\hat{\mathbf{i}} + 4\hat{\mathbf{j}})\text{ ms}^{-1}$, after being hit. The change in momentum (final momentum–initial momentum) is (in kgms^{-1})

(a) zero
(b) $-(0.45\hat{\mathbf{i}} + 0.6\hat{\mathbf{j}})$
(c) $-(0.9\hat{\mathbf{j}} + 1.2\hat{\mathbf{j}})$
(d) $-5(\hat{\mathbf{i}} + \hat{\mathbf{j}})\hat{\mathbf{i}}$

Ans. *(c)* Given, $\mathbf{u} = (3\hat{i} + 4\hat{j})\text{ m/s}$

and $\mathbf{v} = -(3\hat{i} + 4\hat{j})\text{m/s}$

Mass of the ball = 150 g = 0.15 kg

Δp = Change in momentum

= Final momentum – Initial momentum

$= m\mathbf{v} - m\mathbf{u}$

$= m(\mathbf{v} - \mathbf{u}) = (0.15)\,[-(3\hat{i} + 4\hat{j}) - (3\hat{i} + 4\hat{j})]$

$= (0.15)\,[-6\hat{i} - 8\hat{j}]$

$= -[0.15 \times 6\hat{i} + 0.15 \times 8\hat{j}]$

$= -[0.9\hat{i} + 1.20\hat{j}]$

Hence, $\Delta\mathbf{p} = -[0.9\hat{i} + 1.2\hat{\mathbf{j}}]$

Q. 4 In the previous problem (3), the magnitude of the momentum transferred during the hit is

(a) zero
(b) 0.75 kg-m s^{-1}
(c) 1.5 kg-m s^{-1}
(d) 14 kg-m s^{-1}

Ans. *(c)* By previous solution $\Delta\mathbf{p} = -(0.9\hat{i} + 1.2\hat{j})$

$$\text{Magnitude} = |\Delta\mathbf{p}| = \sqrt{(0.9)^2 + (1.2)^2}$$

$$= \sqrt{0.81 + 1.44} = 1.5\text{ kg-m s}^{-1}.$$

Q. 5 Conservation of momentum in a collision between particles can be understood from

(a) conservation of energy
(b) Newton's first law only
(c) Newton's second law only
(d) both Newton's second and third law

Thinking Process

For conservation of momentum we have to see whether net external force is acting on a system or not.

Ans. *(d)* We know that for a system $F_{ext} = \dfrac{dp}{dt}$ (from Newton's second law)

If $F_{ext} = 0, dp = 0 \Rightarrow p = \text{constant}$

Hence, momentum of a system will remain conserve if external force on the system is zero.

In case of collision' between particles equal and opposite forces will act on individuel particles by Newtons third law,

Hence total force on the system will be zero.

Note *We should not confuse with system and individual particles. As total force on the system of both particles is zero but force acts on individual particles.*

Q. 6 **A hockey player is moving northward and suddenly turns westward with the same speed to avoid an opponent. The force that acts on the player is**

(a) frictional force along westward
(b) muscle force along southward
(c) frictional force along south-West
(d) muscle force along south-West

Ans. *(c)* Consider the adjacent diagram

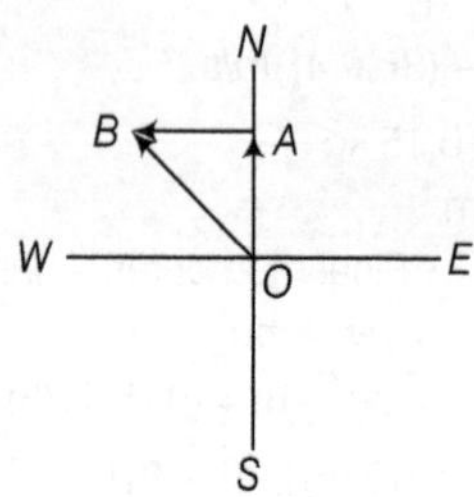

Let $\mathbf{OA} = \mathbf{p}_1$
= Initial momentum of player northward
$\mathbf{AB} = \mathbf{p}_2$ = Final momentum of player towards west.

Clearly $\mathbf{OB} = \mathbf{OA} + \mathbf{AB}$

Change in momentum $= \mathbf{p}_2 - \mathbf{p}_1$

$= \mathbf{AB} - \mathbf{OA} = \mathbf{AB} + (-\mathbf{OA})$

= Clearly resultant **AR** will be along south-west.

Q. 7 **A body of mass 2kg travels according to the law $x(t) = pt + qt^2 + rt^3$ where, $q = 4\text{ms}^{-2}$, $p = 3\text{ms}^{-1}$ and $r = 5\text{ms}^{-3}$. The force acting on the body at $t = 2\text{s}$ is**

(a) 136 N
(b) 134 N
(c) 158 N
(d) 68 N

Thinking Process

We have to apply differentiations to calculate acceleration and then Newton's second law will be applied.

Ans. *(a)* Given, mass = 2 kg

$$x(t) = pt + qt^2 + rt^3$$

$$v = \frac{dx}{dt} = p + 2qt + 3rt^2$$

$$a = \frac{dv}{dt} = 0 + 2q + 6rt$$

$$\text{at } t = 2\text{s}; a = 2q + 6 \times 2 \times r$$

$$= 2q + 12r$$

$$= 2 \times 4 + 12 \times 5$$

$$= 8 + 60 = 68 \text{ m/s}$$

$$\text{Force} = F = ma$$

$$= 2 \times 68 = 136 \text{ N}$$

Q. 8 A body with mass 5 kg is acted upon by a force $\mathbf{F} = (-3\hat{\mathbf{i}} + 4\hat{\mathbf{j}})$ N. If its initial velocity at $t = 0$ is $v = (6\hat{\mathbf{i}} - 12\hat{\mathbf{j}})\text{ms}^{-1}$, the time at which it will just have a velocity along the Y-axis is

(a) never (b) 10 s (c) 2 s (d) 15 s

Ans. *(b)* Given, mass = m = 5 kg

Acting force = $\mathbf{F} = (-3\hat{\mathbf{i}} + 4\hat{\mathbf{j}})$ N

Initial velocity at $t = 0$, $\mathbf{u} = (6\hat{\mathbf{i}} - 12\hat{\mathbf{j}})$ m / s

Retardation, $\hat{\mathbf{a}} = \frac{\mathbf{F}}{m} = \left(-\frac{3\hat{\mathbf{i}}}{\mathbf{5}} + \frac{4\hat{\mathbf{j}}}{5}\right)\text{m/s}^2$

As final velocity is along Y-axis only, its x-component must be zero.

From $v = u + at$, for X-component only, $0 = 6\hat{\mathbf{i}} - \frac{3\hat{\mathbf{i}}}{5}t$

$$t = \frac{5 \times 6}{3} = 10 \text{ s}$$

Q. 9 A car of mass m starts from rest and acquires a velocity along east, $\mathbf{v} = v\hat{\mathbf{i}}$ $(v > 0)$ in two seconds. Assuming the car moves with uniform acceleration, the force exerted on the car is

(a) $\frac{mv}{2}$ eastward and is exerted by the car engine

(b) $\frac{mv}{2}$ eastward and is due to the friction on the tyres exerted by the road

(c) more than $\frac{mv}{2}$ eastward exerted due to the engine and overcomes the friction of the road

(d) $\frac{mv}{2}$ exerted by the engine

Ans. *(b)* Given, mass of the car = m

As car starts from rest, $u = 0$

Velocity acquired along east = $v\hat{\mathbf{i}}$

Duration = t = 2s.

We know that $v = u + at$

$\Rightarrow$ $v\hat{\mathbf{i}} = o + a \times 2$

$\Rightarrow$ $\mathbf{a} = \frac{\mathbf{v}}{2}\hat{\mathbf{i}}$

Force, $\mathbf{F} = m\mathbf{a} = \frac{\mathbf{mv}}{2}\hat{\mathbf{i}}$

Hence, force acting on the car is $\frac{mv}{2}$ towards east. As external force on the system is only friction hence, the force $\frac{mv}{2}$ is by friction. Hence, force by engine is internal force.

Multiple Choice Questions (More Than One Options)

Q. 10 The motion of a particle of mass m is given by $x = 0$ for $t < 0$s, $x(t) = A \sin 4\pi t$ for $0 < t < (1/4)$s $(A > 0)$, and $x = 0$ for $t > (1/4)$ s. Which of the following statements is true?

(a) The force at $t = (1/8)$s on the particle is $-16\pi^2$A-m

(b) The particle is acted upon by on impulse of magnitude $4\pi^2$A-m at $t = 0$ s and $t = (1/4)$ s

(c) The particle is not acted upon by any force

(d) The particle is not acted upon by a constant force

(e) There is no impulse acting on the particle

Thinking Process

Here, position of the particle is given for different time intervals. Hence, we have to find velocity and acceleration corresponding to the intervals.

Ans. *(a, b, d)*

Given,
$$x = 0 \text{ for } t < 0\text{ s.}$$
$$x(t) = A \sin 4\pi t; \text{ for } 0 < t < \frac{1}{4}\text{ s}$$
$$x = 0; \text{ for } t > \frac{1}{4}\text{ s}$$

For, $0 < t < \frac{1}{4}$ s
$$v(t) = \frac{dx}{dt} = 4\pi\, A\cos 4\pi t$$
$$a(t) = \text{acceleration}$$
$$= \frac{dv(t)}{dt} = -16\,\pi^2 A \sin 4\pi t$$
$$\text{At } t = \frac{1}{8}\text{ s, } a(t) = -16\pi^2\, A \sin 4\pi \times \frac{1}{8} = -16\pi^2 A$$
$$F = ma\,(t) = -16\pi^2\, A \times m = -16\pi^2\, mA$$
$$\text{Impulse} = \text{Change in linear momentum}$$
$$= F \times t = (-16\pi^2\, Am) \times \frac{1}{4}$$
$$= -4\pi^2\, Am$$

The impulse (Change in linear momentum)
$$\text{at } t = 0 \text{ is same as, } t = \frac{1}{4}\text{ s.}$$

Clearly, force depends upon A which is not constant. Hence, force is also not constant.

Note *We have to keep in mind that the force is varying for different time intervals. Hence, we should apply differential formulae for each interval separately.*

Q. 11 In figure the coefficient of friction between the floor and the body B is 0.1. The coefficient of friction between the bodies B and A is 0.2. A force **F** is applied as shown on B. The mass of A is $m/2$ and of B is m. Which of the following statements are true?

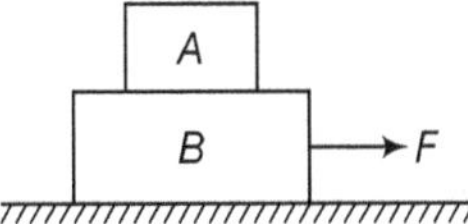

(a) The bodies will move together if $\mathbf{F} = 0.25$ mg
(b) The body A will slip with respect to B if $\mathbf{F} = 0.5$ mg
(c) The bodies will move together if $\mathbf{F} = 0.5$ mg
(d) The bodies will be at rest if $\mathbf{F} = 0.1$ mg
(e) The maximum value of **F** for which the two bodies will move together is 0.45 mg

Thinking Process

In this problem we have to find frictional forces on each surface and accordingly we will decide maximum force.

Ans. *(a, b, d, e)*

Consider the adjacent diagram. Frictional force on $B(f_1)$ and frictional force on A (f_2) will be as shown.

Let A and B are moving together $a_{common} = \dfrac{F - f_1}{m_A + m_B} = \dfrac{F - f_1}{(m/2) + m} = \dfrac{2(F - f_1)}{3m}$

$$\text{Pseudo force on } A = (m_A) \times a_{common}$$

$$= m_A \times \frac{2(F - f_1)}{3m} = \frac{m}{2} \times \frac{2(F - f_1)}{3m} = \frac{(F - f_1)}{3}$$

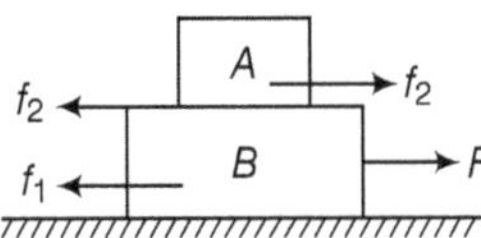

The force (F) will be maximum when

$$\text{Pseudo force on } A = \text{Frictional force on } A$$

$$\Rightarrow \quad \frac{F_{max} - f_1}{3} = \mu\, m_A g$$

$$= 0.2 \times \frac{m}{2} \times g = 0.1 \text{ mg}$$

$$\Rightarrow \quad F_{max} = 0.3 \text{ mg} + f_1$$

$$= 0.3 \text{ mg} + (0.1)\frac{3}{2} \text{ mg} = 0.45 \text{ mg}$$

$\Rightarrow$ Hence, maximum force upto which bodies will move together is $F_{max} = 0.45$ mg

(a) Hence, for $F = 0.25 \text{ mg} < F_{max}$ bodies will move together.

(b) For $F = 0.5 \text{ mg} > F_{max}$, body A will slip with respect to B.

(c) For $F = 0.5 \text{ mg} > F_{max}$, bodies slip.

$$(f_1)_{max} = \mu\, m_B g = (0.1) \times \frac{3}{2} m \times g = 0.15 \text{ mg}$$

$$(f_2)_{max} = \mu\, m_A g = (0.2)\left(\frac{m}{2}\right)(g) = 0.1 \text{ mg}$$

Hence, minimum force required for movement of the system $(A + B)$

$$F_{min} = (f_1)_{max} + (f_2)_{max}$$
$$= 0.15\,mg + 0.1\,mg = 0.25\,mg$$

(d) Given, force $F = 0.1\,mg < F_{min}$.
Hence, the bodies will be at rest.

(e) Maximum force for combined movement $F_{max} = 0.45\,mg$.

Q. 12 **Mass m_1 moves on a slope making an angle θ with the horizontal and is attached to mass m_2 by a string passing over a frictionless pulley as shown in figure. The coefficient of friction between m_1 and the sloping surface is μ. Which of the following statements are true?**

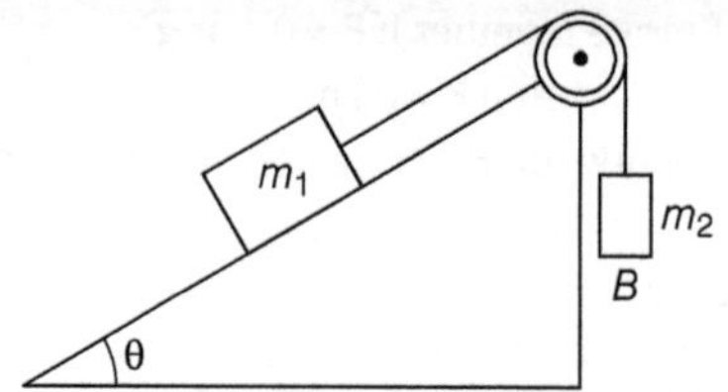

(a) If $m_2 > m_1 \sin\theta$, the body will move up the plane
(b) If $m_2 > m_1 (\sin\theta + \mu\cos\theta)$, the body will move up the plane
(c) If $m_2 < m_1 (\sin\theta + \mu\cos\theta)$, the body will move up the plane
(d) If $m_2 < m_1 (\sin\theta - \mu\cos\theta)$, the body will move down the plane

Thinking Process

The friction force always have tendency to oppose the motion. Consider the adjacent diagram.

Ans. ***(b, d)***

Let m_1, moves up the plane. Different forces involved are shown in the diagram.

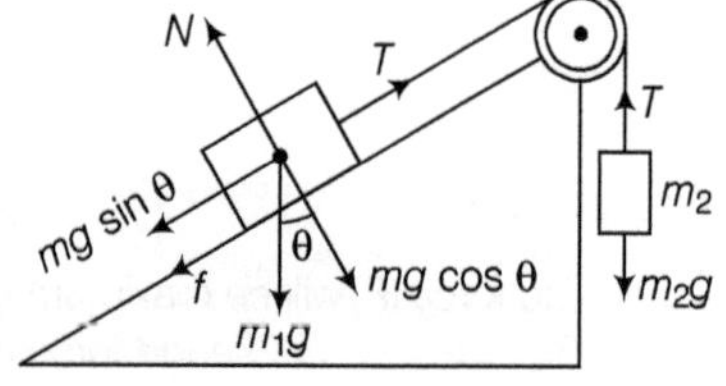

N = Normal reaction
f = Frictional force
T = Tension in the string
$f = \mu N = \mu m_1 g \cos\theta$

For the system $(m_1 + m_2)$ to move up

$$m_2 g - (m_1 g \sin\theta + f) > 0$$
$$\Rightarrow \quad m_2 g - (m_1 g \sin\theta + \mu m_1 g \cos\theta) > 0$$
$$\Rightarrow \quad m_2 > m_1 (\sin\theta + \mu\cos\theta)$$

Hence, option (b) is correct.

Let the body moves down the plane, in this case f acts up the plane.

Hence, $$m_1 g \sin\theta - f > m_2 g$$
$$\Rightarrow \quad m_1 g \sin\theta - \mu m_1 g \cos\theta > m_2 g$$
$$\Rightarrow \quad m_1 (\sin\theta - \mu\cos\theta) > m_2$$
$$\Rightarrow \quad m_2 < m_1(\sin\theta - \mu\cos\theta)$$

Hence, option (d) is correct.

Q. 13 In figure a body A of mass m slides on plane inclined at angle θ_1 to the horizontal and μ is the coefficent of friction between A and the plane. A is connected by a light string passing over a frictionless pulley to another body B, also of mass m, sliding on a frictionless plane inclined at an angle θ_2 to the horizontal. Which of the following statements are true?

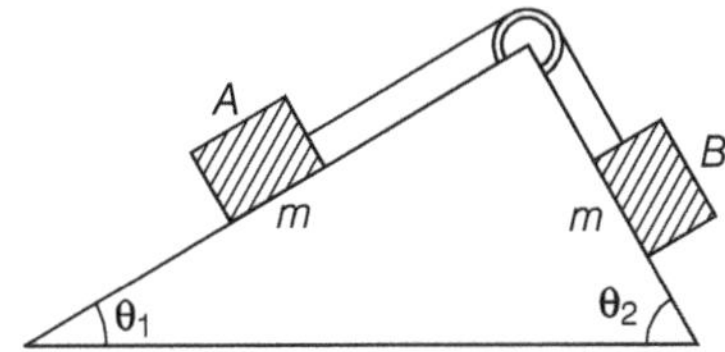

(a) A will never move up the plane

(b) A will just start moving up the plane when $\mu = \dfrac{\sin\theta_2 - \sin\theta_1}{\cos\theta_1}$

(c) For A to move up the plane, θ_2 must always be greater than θ_1

(d) B will always slide down with constant speed

Ans. *(b, c)*

Let A moves up the plane frictional force on A will be downward as shown.

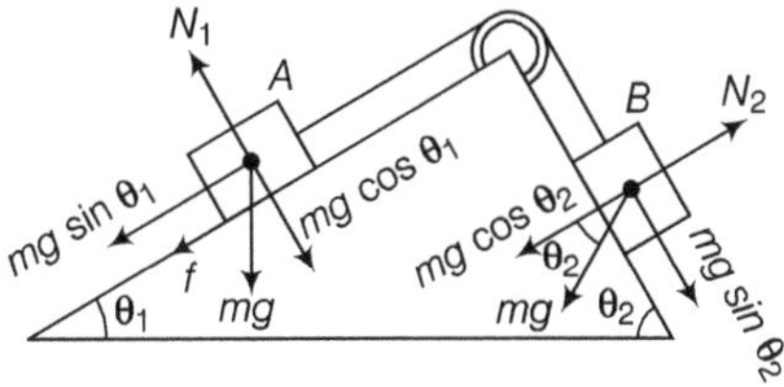

When A just starts moving up

$$mg\sin\theta_1 + f = mg\sin\theta_2$$

$$\Rightarrow \quad mg\sin\theta_1 + \mu\, mg\cos\theta_1 = mg\sin\theta_2$$

$$\Rightarrow \quad \mu = \frac{\sin\theta_2 - \sin\theta_1}{\cos\theta_1}$$

When A moves upwards

$$f = mg\sin\theta_2 - mg\sin\theta_1 > 0$$

$$\Rightarrow \quad \sin\theta_2 > \sin\theta_1 \Rightarrow \theta_2 > \theta_1$$

Q. 14 Two billiard balls A and B, each of mass 50g and moving in opposite directions with speed of 5 m s^{-1} each, collide and rebound with the same speed. If the collision lasts for 10^{-3} s, which of the following statements are true?

(a) The impulse imparted to each ball is 0.25 kg-ms^{-1} and the force on each ball is 250 N

(b) The impulse imparted to each ball is 0.25 kg-ms^{-1} and the force exerted on each ball is 25×10^{-5} N

(c) The impulse imparted to each ball is 0.5 N-s

(d) The impulse and the force on each ball are equal in magnitude and opposite in directions

Ans. *(c, d)*

Given, $m_1 = m_2 = 50(\text{g}) = \frac{50}{1000}\text{ kg} = \frac{1}{20}\text{ kg}$

Initial velocity $(u) = u_1 = u_2 = 5\text{m/s}$

Final velocity $(v) = v_1 = v_2 = -5\text{ m/s}$

Time duration of collision $= 10^{-3}\text{s}$.

Change in linear momentum $= m(v-u)$

$$= \frac{1}{20}[-5-5] = -0.5\text{ N-s.}$$

$$\text{Force} = \frac{\text{Impulse}}{\text{Time}} = \frac{\text{Change in momentum}}{10^{-3}\text{s}}$$

$$= \frac{0.5}{10^{-3}} = 500\text{ N}$$

Impulse and force are opposite in directions.

Q. 15 **A body of mass 10 kg is acted upon by two perpendicular forces, 6N and 8N. The resultant acceleration of the body is**

(a) 1 m s^{-2} at an angle of $\tan^{-1}\left(\frac{4}{3}\right)$ w.r.t. 6N force

(b) 0.2 m s^{-2} at an angle of $\tan^{-1}\left(\frac{4}{3}\right)$ w.r.t. 6N force

(c) 1 m s^{-2} at an angle of $\tan^{-1}\left(\frac{3}{4}\right)$ w.r.t. 8N force

(d) 0.2 m s^{-2} at an angle of $\tan^{-1}\left(\frac{3}{4}\right)$ w.r.t. 8N force

Thinking Process

In this problem, we have to use the concept of resultant of two vectors, when they are perpendicular.

Ans. *(a, c)*

Consider the adjacent diagram

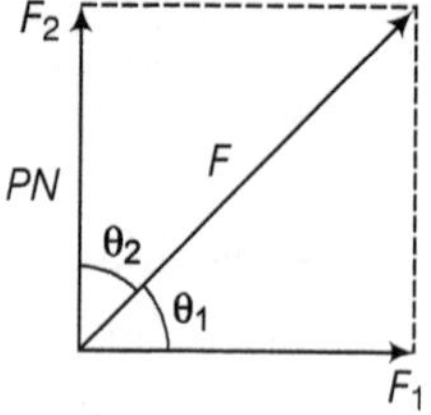

Given, mass $= m = 10\text{ kg.}$

$$F_1 = 6\text{N}, F_2 = 8\text{N}$$

$$\text{Resultant force} = F = \sqrt{F_1^2 + F_2^2} = \sqrt{36+64}$$

$$= 10\text{ N}$$

$$a = \frac{F}{m} = \frac{10}{10} = 1\text{ m/s}^2;\text{along } R.$$

Let θ_1 be angle between R and F_1

$$\tan\theta_1 = \frac{8}{6} = \frac{4}{3}$$

$$\theta_1 = \tan^{-1}(4/3)\text{ w.r.t. } F_1 = 6\text{N}$$

Let θ_2 be angle between F and F_2

$$\tan\theta_2 = \frac{6}{8} = \frac{3}{4}$$

$$\theta_2 = \tan^{-1}\left(\frac{3}{4}\right)\text{w.r.t. } F_2 = 8\text{ N}$$

Very Short Answer Type Questions

Q. 16 A girl riding a bicycle along a straight road with a speed of 5 ms^{-1} throws a stone of mass 0.5 kg which has a speed of 15 ms^{-1} with respect to the ground along her direction of motion. The mass of the girl and bicycle is 50 kg. Does the speed of the bicycle change after the stone is thrown? What is the change in speed, if so?

Thinking Process

In this problem, we have to apply conservation of linear momentum.

Ans. Given, total mass of girl, bicycle and stone = $m_1 = (50 + 0.5)$ kg = 50.5kg.

Velocity of bicycle $u_1 = 5$ m/s, Mass of stone $m_2 = 0.5$ kg

Velocity of stone $u_2 = 15$ m/s, Mass of girl and bicycle $m = 50$ kg

Yes, the speed of the bicycle changes after the stone is thrown.

Let after throwing the stone the speed of bicycle be v m/s.

According to law of conservation of linear momentum,

$$m_1 u_1 = m_2 u_2 + mv$$

$$50.5 \times 5 = 0.5 \times 15 + 50 \times v$$

$$252.5 - 7.5 = 50v$$

or $$v = \frac{245.0}{50}$$

$$v = 4.9 \text{ m/s}$$

Change in speed = 5 – 4.9 = 0.1 m/s.

Q. 17 A person of mass 50 kg stands on a weighing scale on a lift. If the lift is descending with a downward acceleration of 9 ms^{-2}, what would be the reading of the weighing scale? ($g = 10$ ms^{-2})

Ans. When a lift descends with a downward acceleration a the apparent weight of a body of mass m is given by

$$w' = R = m(g - a)$$

Mass of the person $m = 50$ kg

Descending acceleration $a = 9$ m/s^2

Acceleration due to gravity $g = 10$ m/s^2

Apparent weight of the person,

$$R = m(g - a)$$

$$= 50(10 - 9)$$

$$= 50 \text{ N}$$

$\therefore$ Reading of the weighing scale $= \frac{R}{g} = \frac{50}{10} = 5$ kg.

Q. 18 **The position-time graph of a body of mass 2 kg is as given in figure. What is the impulse on the body at $t = 0$ s and $t = 4$ s.**

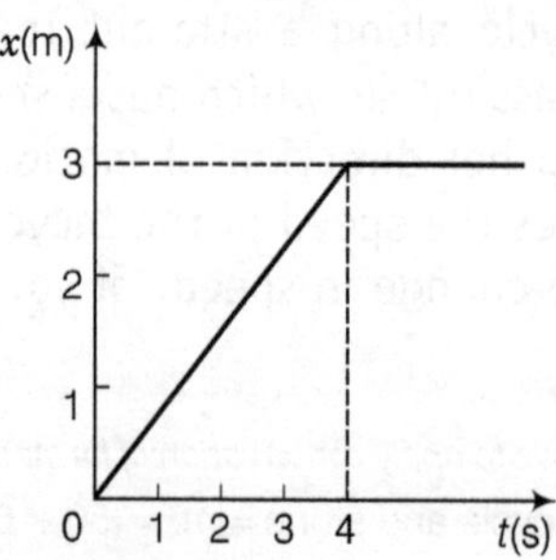

Ans. Given, mass of the body $(m) = 2$ kg

From the position-time graph, the body is at $x = 0$ when $t = 0$, *i.e.*, body is at rest.

$\therefore$ Impulse at $t = 0$, $s = 0$, is zero

From $t = 0$ s to $t = 4$ s, the position-time graph is a straight line, which shows that body moves with uniform velocity.

Beyond $t = 4$s, the graph is a straight line parallel to time axis, *i.e.*, body is at rest $(v = 0)$.

Velocity of the body = slope of position-time graph

$$= \tan\theta = \frac{3}{4} \text{ m/s}$$

Impulse (at $t = 4$ s) = change in momentum

$$= mv - mu$$
$$= m(v - u)$$
$$= 2\left(0 - \frac{3}{4}\right)$$
$$= -\frac{3}{2} \text{ kg-m/s} = -1.5 \text{ kg-m/s}$$

Q. 19 **A person driving a car suddenly applies the brakes on seeing a child on the road ahead. If he is not wearing seat belt, he falls forward and hits his head against the steering wheel. Why?**

Ans. When a person driving a car suddenly applies the brakes, the lower part of the body slower down with the car while upper part of the body continues to move forward due to inertia of motion.

If driver is not wearing seat belt, then he falls forward and his head hit against the steering wheel.

Q. 20 **The velocity of a body of mass 2 kg as a function of t is given by $\mathbf{v}(t) = 2t\,\hat{\mathbf{i}} + t^2\,\hat{\mathbf{j}}$. Find the momentum and the force acting on it, at time $t = 2$s.**

Ans. Given, mass of the body $m = 2$ kg.

Velocity of the body $\mathbf{v}(t) = 2t\,\hat{\mathbf{i}} + t^2\,\hat{\mathbf{j}}$

$\therefore$ Velocity of the body at $t = 2$s

$$\mathbf{v} = 2 \times 2\hat{\mathbf{i}} + (2)^2\,\hat{\mathbf{j}} = (4\hat{\mathbf{i}} + 4\hat{\mathbf{j}})$$

Momentum of the body $(p) = m\mathbf{v}$

$$= 2\,(4\hat{\mathbf{i}} + 4\hat{\mathbf{j}}) = (8\hat{\mathbf{i}} + 8\hat{\mathbf{j}}) \text{ kg-m/s}$$

Acceleration of the body $(a) = \frac{d\mathbf{v}}{dt}$

$$= \frac{d}{dt}(2t\,\hat{\mathbf{i}} + t^2\,\hat{\mathbf{j}})$$

$$= (2\hat{\mathbf{i}} + 2t\,\hat{\mathbf{j}})$$

At $t = 2$ s

$$\mathbf{a} = (2\hat{\mathbf{i}} + 2 \times 2\hat{\mathbf{j}})$$

$$= (2\hat{\mathbf{i}} + 4\hat{\mathbf{j}})$$

Force acting on the body $(\mathbf{F}) = m\mathbf{a}$

$$= 2\,(2\hat{\mathbf{i}} + 4\hat{\mathbf{j}})$$

$$= (4\hat{\mathbf{i}} + 8\hat{\mathbf{j}})\,\text{N}$$

Q. 21 **A block placed on a rough horizontal surface is pulled by a horizontal force F. Let f be the force applied by the rough surface on the block. Plot a graph of f *versus* F.**

Ans. *The approximate graph is shown in the diagram*

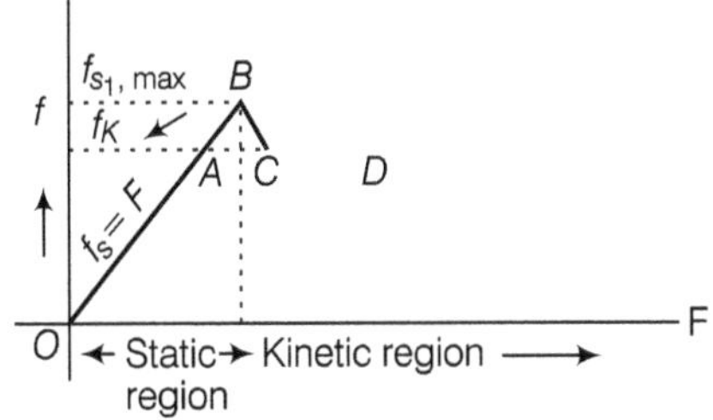

The frictional force f is shown on vertical axis and the applied force F is shown on the horizontal axis. The portion OA of graph represents static friction which is self adjusting. In this portion, $f = F$.

The point B corresponds to force of limiting friction which is the maximum value of static friction. $CD \| OX$ represents kinetic friction, when the body actually starts moving. The force of kinetic friction does not increase with applied force, and is slightly less than limiting friction.

Q. 22 **Why are porcelain objects wrapped in paper or straw before packing for transportation?**

Ans. Porcelain object are wrapped in paper or straw before packing to reduce the chances of damage during transportation. During transportation sudden jerks or even fall takes place, the force takes longer time to reach the porcelain objects through paper or straw for same change in momentum as $F = \frac{\Delta p}{\Delta t}$ and therefore, a lesser force acts on object.

Q. 23 **Why does a child feel more pain when she falls down on a hard cement floor, than when she falls on the soft muddy ground in the garden?**

Ans. When a child falls on a cement floor, her body comes to rest instantly. But $F \times \Delta t$ = change in momentum = constant. As time of stopping Δt decreases, therefore F increases and hence, child feel more pain.

When she falls on a soft muddy ground in the garden the time of stopping increases and hence, F decreases and she feels lesser pain.

Q. 24 A woman throws an object of mass 500 g with a speed of 25 ms^{-1}.

(a) What is the impulse imparted to the object?

(b) If the object hits a wall and rebounds with half the original speed, what is the change in momentum of the object?

Ans. Mass of the object $(m) = 500\text{ g} = 0.5\text{ kg}$

Speed of the object $(v) = 25\text{ m/s}$

(a) Impulse imparted to the object = change in momentum

$$= mv - mu$$
$$= m(v - u)$$
$$= 0.5\,(25 - 0) = 12.5\text{ N-s}$$

(b) Velocity of the object after rebounding

$$= -\frac{25}{2}\text{ m/s}$$
$$v' = -12.5\text{ m/s}$$

$\therefore$ Change in momentum $= m(v' - v)$

$$= 0.5\,(-12.5 - 25) = -18.75\text{ N-s}$$

Q. 25 Why are mountain roads generally made winding upwards rather than going straight up?

Ans. While going up a mountain, the force of friction acting on a vehicle of mass m is $f = \mu R = \mu mg\cos\theta$, where θ is the angle of slope of the road with the horizontal. To avoid skidding force of friction (f) should be large and therefore, $\cos\theta$ should be large and hence, θ should be small.

That's why mountain roads are generally made winding upwards rather than going straight upto avoid skidding.

Q. 26 A mass of 2 kg is suspended with thread *AB* (figure). Thread *CD* of the same type is attached to the other end of 2 kg mass. Lower thread is pulled gradually, harder and harder in the downward direction, so as to apply force on *AB*. Which of the threads will break and why?

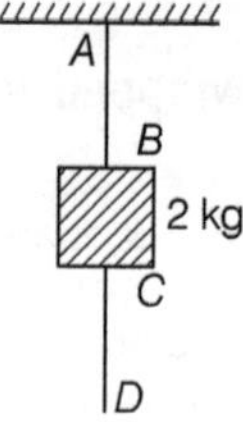

Ans. The thread *AB* will break earlier than the thread *CD*. This is because force acting on thread *CD* = applied force and force acting on thread *AB* = (applied force + weight of 2 kg mass). Hence, force acting on thread *AB* is larger than the force acting on thread *CD*.

Q. 27 In the above given problem if the lower thread is pulled with a jerk, what happens?

Ans. When the lower thread *CD* is pulled with a jerk, the thread *CD* itself break. Because pull on thread *CD* is not transmitted to the thread *AB* instantly.

Short Answer Type Questions

Q. 28 Two masses of 5 kg and 3 kg are suspended with help of massless inextensible strings as shown in figure. Calculate T_1 and T_2 when whole system is going upwards with acceleration = $2 m/s^2$ (use $g = 9.8 ms^{-2}$).

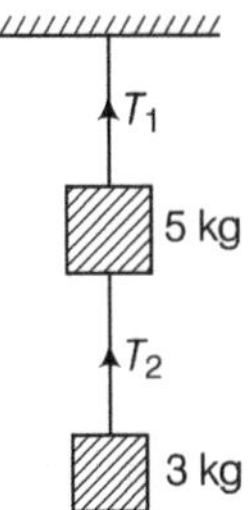

Thinking Process

As the whole system is going upward with an acceleration we have to apply Newton's laws.

Ans. Given, $m_1 = 5$ kg, $m_2 = 3$ kg

$g = 9.8 m/s^2$ and $a = 2 m/s^2$

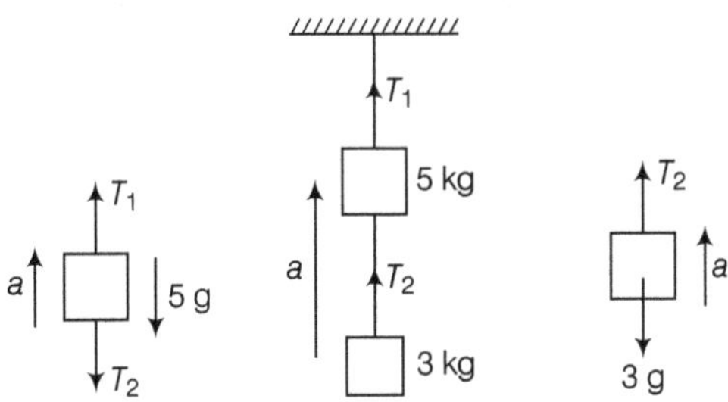

For the upper block

$$T_1 - T_2 - 5g = 5a$$

$\Rightarrow$ $$T_1 - T_2 = 5(g + a) \quad \text{...(i)}$$

For the lower block $$T_2 - 3g = 3a$$

$\Rightarrow$ $$T_2 = 3(g + a) = 3(9.8 + 2) = 35.4 \text{ N}$$

From Eq. (i) $$T_1 = T_2 + 5(g + a)$$
$$= 35.4 + 5(9.8 + 2) = 94.4 \text{ N}$$

Q. 29 Block A of weight 100 N rests on a frictionless inclined plane of slope angle 30°. A flexible cord attached to A passes over a frictionless pulley and is connected to block B of weight w. Find the weight w for which the system is in equilibrium.

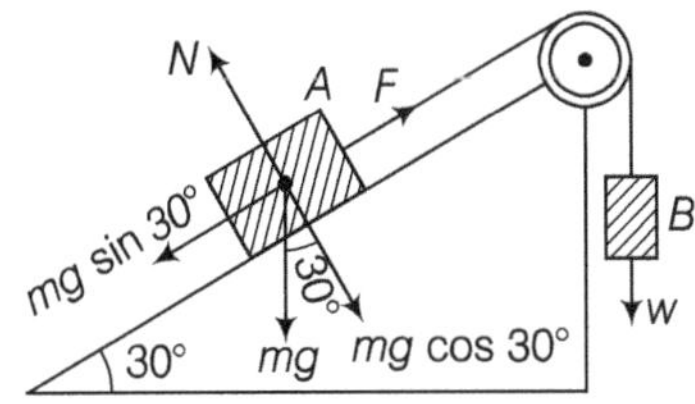

Ans. In equilibrium, the force $mg\sin\theta$ acting on block A parallel to the plane should be balanced by the tension in the string, *i.e.*,

$$mg\sin\theta = T = F \quad [\because T = F \text{given}] \quad ...(i)$$

and for block B, $$w = T = F \quad ...(ii)$$

where, w is the weight of block B.

From Eqs. (i) and (ii), we get,

$$\therefore \quad w = mg\sin\theta$$
$$= 100 \times \sin 30° \quad (\because mg = 100\text{ N})$$
$$= 100 \times \frac{1}{2}\text{ N} = 50\text{ N}$$

Note *While finding normal reaction in such cases, we should be careful it will be $N = mg\cos\theta$, where θ is angle of inclination.*

Q. 30 A block of mass M is held against a rough vertical wall by pressing it with a finger. If the coefficient of friction between the block and the wall is μ and the acceleration due to gravity is g, calculate the minimum force required to be applied by the finger to hold the block against the wall.

Ans. Given, mass of the block $= M$

Coefficient of friction between the block and the wall $= \mu$

Let a force F be applied on the block to hold the block against the wall. The normal reaction of mass be N and force of friction acting upward be f. In equilibrium, vertical and horizontal forces should be balanced separately.

$$\therefore \quad f = Mg \quad ...(i)$$

and $$F = N \quad ...(ii)$$

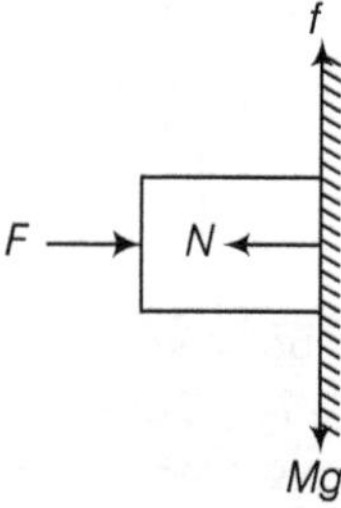

But force of friction $(f) = \mu N$

$$= \mu F \quad [\text{using Eq. (ii)}] \quad ...(iii)$$

From Eqs. (i) and (iii), we get $$\mu F = Mg$$

or $$F = \frac{Mg}{\mu}$$

Q. 31 **A 100 kg gun fires a ball of 1 kg horizontally from a cliff of height 500 m. It falls on the ground at a distance of 400 m from the bottom of the cliff. Find the recoil velocity of the gun.**
(acceleration due to gravity = 10 ms^{-2})

Ans. Given, mass of the gun $(m_1) = 100$ kg

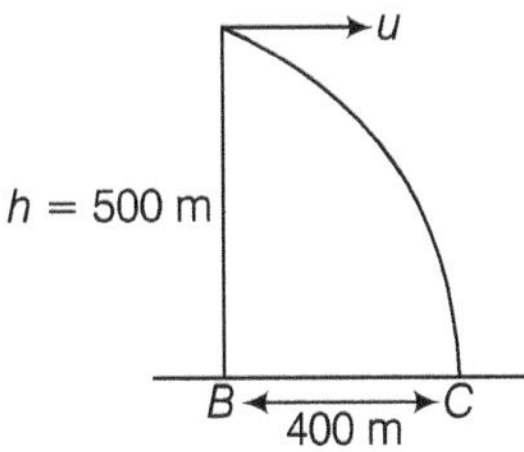

Mass of the ball $(m_2) = 1$ kg
Height of the cliff $(h) = 500$ m
Horizontal distance travelled by the ball $(x) = 400$ m

From $$h = \frac{1}{2} gt^2 \quad (\because \text{Initial velocity in downward direction is zero})$$

$$500 = \frac{1}{2} \times 10t^2$$

$$t = \sqrt{100} = 10\text{s}$$

From $$x = ut, u = \frac{x}{t} = \frac{400}{10} = 40 \text{ m/s}$$

If v is recoil velocity of gun, then according to principle of conservation of linear momentum,

$$m_1 v = m_2 u$$

$$v = \frac{m_2 u}{m_1} = \frac{1}{100} \times 40 = 0.4 \text{ m/s}$$

Q. 32 **Figure shows (x, t), (y, t) diagram of a particle moving in 2-dimensions.**

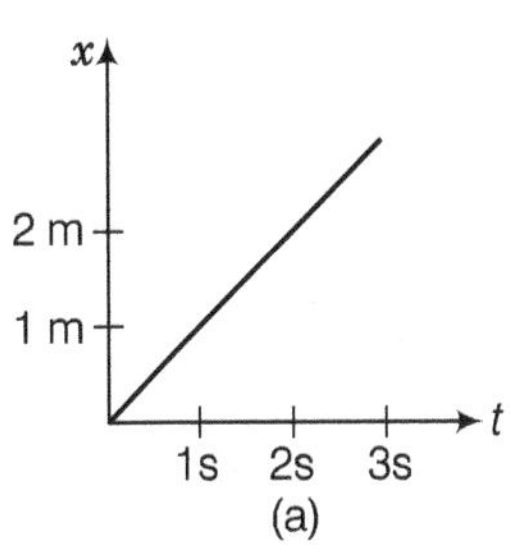

(a)

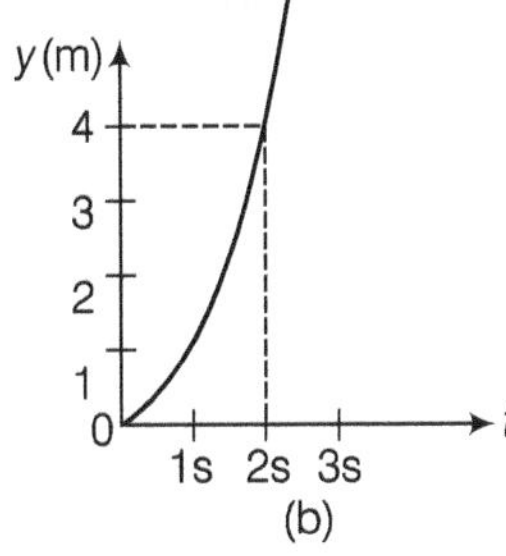

(b)

If the particle has a mass of 500 g, find the force (direction and magnitude) acting on the particle.

Thinking Process

To solve this question, we have to find the relation for x and time (t), y and time (t) from the given diagram.

Ans. Clearly from diagram (a), the variation can be related as

$$x = t \Rightarrow \frac{dx}{dt} = 1 \text{m/s}$$

$$a_x = 0$$

From diagram (b) $y = t^2$

$\Rightarrow \quad \frac{dy}{dt} = 2t$ or $a_y = \frac{d^2y}{dt^2} = 2 \text{ m/s}^2$

Hence, $I_y = ma_y = 500 \times 10^{-3} \times 2 = 1\text{N}$ $(\because m = 500 \text{ g})$

$F_x = ma_x = 0$

Hence, net force, $F = \sqrt{F_x^2 + F_y^2} = F_y = 1\text{N}$ (along y-axis)

Q. 33 **A person in an elevator accelerating upwards with an acceleration of 2 ms^{-2}, tosses a coin vertically upwards with a speed of 20 ms^{-1}. After how much time will the coin fall back into his hand? (g = 10 ms^{-2})**

Ans. Here, initial speed of the coin (u) = 20 m/s

Acceleration of the elevator (a) = 2 m/s^2 (upwards)

Acceleration due to gravity (g) = 10 m/s^2

$\therefore$ Effective acceleration $a' = g + a = 10 + 2 = 12 \text{ m/s}^2$ (here, acceleration is w.r.t. the lift)

If the time of ascent of the coin is t, then

$$v = u + at$$

$$0 = 20 + (-12) \times t$$

or $$t = \frac{20}{12} = \frac{5}{3}\text{s}$$

Time of ascent = Time of desent

$\therefore$ Total time after which the coin fall back into hand $= \left(\frac{5}{3} + \frac{5}{3}\right)\text{s} = \frac{10}{3}\text{s} = 3.33 \text{ s}$

Note *While calculating net acceleration we should be aware that if lift is going upward net acceleration is $(g + a)$ and for downward net acceleration is $(g - a)$.*

Long Answer Type Questions

Q. 34 **There are three forces $\mathbf{F_1}$, $\mathbf{F_2}$ and $\mathbf{F_3}$ acting on a body, all acting on a point P on the body. The body is found to move with uniform speed.**

(a) Show that the forces are coplanar.

(b) Show that the torque acting on the body about any point due to these three forces is zero.

Thinking Process

As the body is found to move with uniform velocity hence, we can say that total force acting will be zero.

Ans. As the body is moving with uniform speed (velocity) its acceleration $a = 0$.

$\therefore$ The sum of the forces is zero, $\mathbf{F_1 + F_2 + F_3 = 0}$

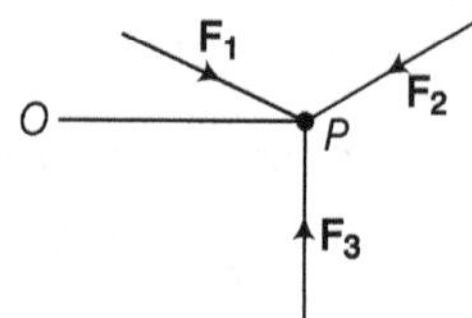

(a) Let $\mathbf{F}_1$, $\mathbf{F}_2$, $\mathbf{F}_3$ be the three forces passing through a point. Let $\mathbf{F}_1$ and $\mathbf{F}_2$ be in the plane A (one can always draw a plane having two intersecting lines such that the two lines lie on the plane). Then $\mathbf{F}_1 + \mathbf{F}_2$ must be in the plane A.

Since, $\mathbf{F}_3 = -(\mathbf{F}_1 + \mathbf{F}_2)$, $\mathbf{F}_3$ is also in the plane A.

(b) Consider the torque of the forces about P. Since, all the forces pass through P, the torque is zero. Now, consider torque about another point O. Then torque about O is

Torque $= \mathbf{OP} \times (\mathbf{F}_1 + \mathbf{F}_2 + \mathbf{F}_3)$

Since, $\mathbf{F}_1 + \mathbf{F}_2 + \mathbf{F}_3 = 0$, torque $= 0$

Q. 35 When a body slides down from rest along a smooth inclined plane making an angle of 45° with the horizontal, it takes time T. When the same body slides down from rest along a rough inclined plane making the same angle and through the same distance, it is seen to take time pT, where p is some number greater than 1. Calculate the coefficient of friction between the body and the rough plane.

Ans. Consider the diagram where a body slides down from along an inclined plane of inclination $\theta (= 45°)$.

On smooth inclined plane Acceleration of a body sliding down a smooth inclined plane

$$a = g \sin\theta$$

Here, $\theta = 45°$

$\therefore$ $$a = g \sin 45° = \frac{g}{\sqrt{2}}$$

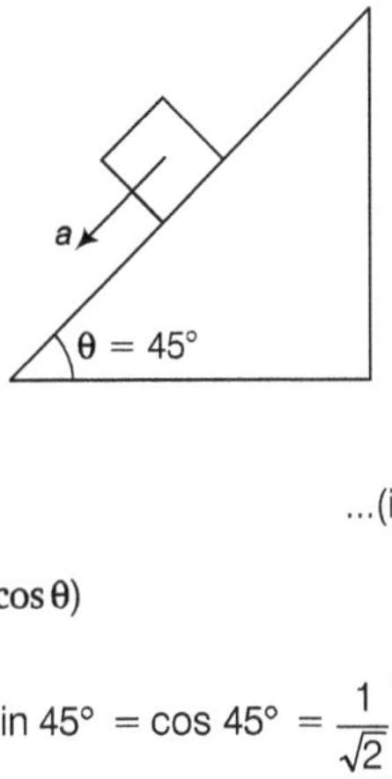

a

θ = 45°

Let the travelled distance be s.

Using equation of motion, $s = ut + \frac{1}{2}at^2$, we get

$$s = 0.t + \frac{1}{2}\frac{g}{\sqrt{2}}T^2$$

or $$s = \frac{gT^2}{2\sqrt{2}} \quad \text{...(i)}$$

On rough inclined plane Acceleration of the body $a = g(\sin\theta - \mu\cos\theta)$

$$= g(\sin 45° - \mu \cos 45°)$$

$$= \frac{g(1-\mu)}{\sqrt{2}} \quad \left(\text{As, } \sin 45° = \cos 45° = \frac{1}{\sqrt{2}}\right)$$

Again using equation of motion, $s = ut + \frac{1}{2}at^2$, we get

$$s = 0(pT) + \frac{1}{2}\frac{g(1-\mu)}{\sqrt{2}}(pT)^2$$

or $$s = \frac{g(1-\mu)p^2T^2}{2\sqrt{2}} \quad \text{...(ii)}$$

From Eqs. (i) and (ii), we get

$$\frac{gT^2}{2\sqrt{2}} = \frac{g(1-\mu)p^2T^2}{2\sqrt{2}}$$

or $$(1-\mu)p^2 = 1$$

or $$1-\mu = \frac{1}{p^2}$$

or $$\mu = \left(1 - \frac{1}{p^2}\right)$$

Q. 36 Figure shows (v_x, t), and (v_y, t) diagrams for a body of unit mass. Find the force as a function of time.

Ans. Consider figure (a)
$$v_x = 2t \text{ for } 0 < t < 1\text{s}$$
$$= 2(2 - t) \text{ for } 1 < t < 2\text{s}$$
$$= 0 \text{ for } t > 2\text{s}.$$

From figure (b)
$$v_y = t \text{ for } 0 < t < 1\text{s}$$
$$= 1 \text{ for } t > 1\text{s}$$

$\therefore$
$$F_x = ma_x = m\frac{dv_x}{dt}$$
$$= 1 \times 2 \quad \text{for } 0 < t < 1\text{s}$$
$$= 1(-2) \quad \text{for } 1 < t < 2\text{s}$$
$$\text{for } 2 < t$$

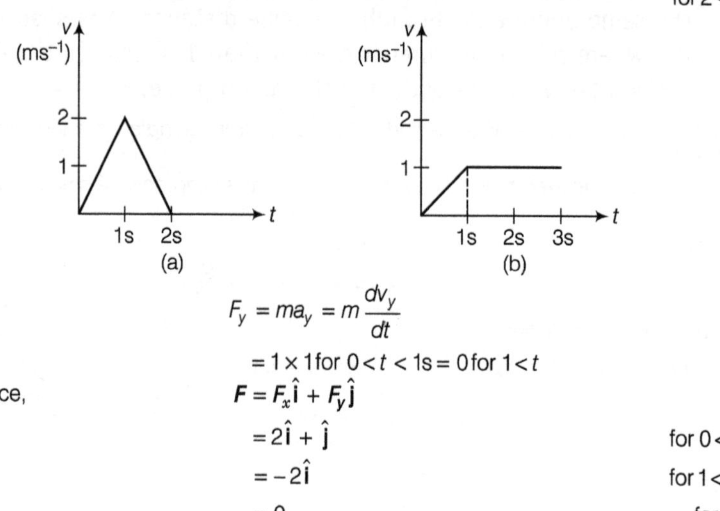

$$F_y = ma_y = m\frac{dv_y}{dt}$$
$$= 1 \times 1 \text{ for } 0 < t < 1\text{s} = 0 \text{ for } 1 < t$$

Hence,
$$\mathbf{F} = F_x\hat{i} + F_y\hat{j}$$
$$= 2\hat{i} + \hat{j} \quad \text{for } 0 < t < 1\text{s}$$
$$= -2\hat{i} \quad \text{for } 1 < t < 2\text{s}$$
$$= 0 \quad \text{for } t > 2\text{s}.$$

Q. 37 A racing car travels on a track (without banking) *ABCDEFA*. *ABC* is a circular arc of radius 2 *R*. *CD* and *FA* are straight paths of length *R* and *DEF* is a circular arc of radius $R = 100$ m. The coefficient of friction on the road is $\mu = 0.1$. The maximum speed of the car is 50 ms^{-1}. Find the minimum time for completing one round.

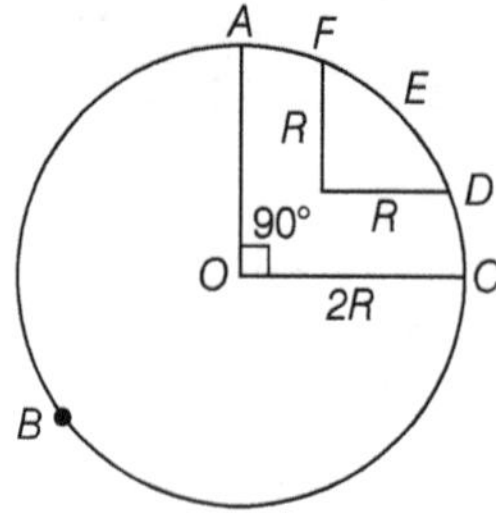

Thinking Process

The necessary centripetal force required for the circular motion will be provided by the frictional force.

Ans. Balancing frictional force for centripetal force $\frac{mv^2}{r} = f = \mu N = \mu mg$

where, N is normal reaction.

$$\therefore \quad v = \sqrt{\mu rg} \quad \text{(where, } r \text{ is radius of the circular track)}$$

For path ABC

$$\text{Path length} = \frac{3}{4}(2\pi\, 2R) = 3\pi R = 3\pi \times 100$$
$$= 300\pi \text{m}$$
$$v_1 = \sqrt{\mu 2Rg} = \sqrt{0.1 \times 2 \times 100 \times 10}$$
$$= 14.14 \text{ m/s}$$
$$\therefore \quad t_1 = \frac{300\pi}{14.14} = 66.6 \text{ s}$$

For path DEF

$$\text{Path length} = \frac{1}{4}(2\pi R) = \frac{\pi \times 100}{2} = 50\pi$$
$$v_2 = \sqrt{\mu Rg} = \sqrt{0.1 \times 100 \times 10} = 10 \text{ m/s}$$
$$t_2 = \frac{50\pi}{10} = 5\pi \text{ s} = 15.7 \text{s}$$

For paths, CD and FA

$$\text{Path length} = R + R = 2R = 200 \text{ m}$$
$$t_3 = \frac{200}{50} = 4.0 \text{ s.}$$

$\therefore$ Total time for completing one round

$$t = t_1 + t_2 + t_3 = 66.6 + 15.7 + 4.0 = 86.3 \text{ s}$$

Q. 38 The displacement vector of a particle of mass m is given by $\mathbf{r}(t) = \hat{\mathbf{i}}\, A \cos \omega t + \hat{\mathbf{j}}\, B \sin \omega t$.

(a) Show that the trajectory is an ellipse.

(b) Show that $F = -m\omega^2 \mathbf{r}$.

Thinking Process

To find trajectory, we will relate x and y in terms of constants A and B.

Ans. (a) Displacement vector of the particle of mass m is given by

$$\mathbf{r}(t) = \hat{\mathbf{i}} A \cos \omega t + \hat{\mathbf{j}} B \sin \omega t$$

$\therefore$ Displacement along x-axis is,

$$x = A \cos \omega t$$

or

$$\frac{x}{A} = \cos \omega t \quad \text{...(i)}$$

Displacement along y-axis *is*,

and

$$y = B \sin \omega t$$

or

$$\frac{y}{B} = \sin \omega t$$

Squaring and then adding Eqs. (i) and (ii), we get

$$\frac{x^2}{A^2} + \frac{y^2}{B^2} = \cos^2 \omega t + \sin^2 \omega t = 1$$

This is an equation of ellipse.

Therefore, trajectory of the particle is an ellipse.

(b) Velocity of the particle

$$\mathbf{v} = \frac{d\mathbf{r}}{dt} = \hat{\mathbf{i}}\frac{d}{dt}(A\cos\omega t) + \hat{\mathbf{j}}\frac{d}{dt}(B\sin\omega t)$$
$$= \hat{\mathbf{i}}[A(-\sin\omega t).\omega] + \hat{\mathbf{j}}[B(\cos\omega t).\omega]$$
$$= -\hat{i}\,A\omega\sin\omega t + \hat{j}\;B\omega\cos\omega t$$

Acceleration of the particle $(\mathbf{a}) = \dfrac{d\mathbf{v}}{dt}$

or
$$\mathbf{a} = -\hat{\mathbf{i}}\,A\omega\frac{d}{d}(\sin\omega t) + \hat{\mathbf{j}}\,B\omega\frac{d}{dt}(\cos\omega t)$$
$$= -\hat{\mathbf{i}}\,A\omega[\cos\omega t].\omega + \hat{\mathbf{j}}\,B\omega[-\sin\omega t].\omega$$
$$= -\hat{\mathbf{i}}\,A\omega^2\cos\omega t - \hat{\mathbf{j}}\,B\omega^2\sin\omega t$$
$$= -\omega^2[\hat{\mathbf{i}}\,A\cos\omega t + \hat{\mathbf{j}}\,B\sin\omega t]$$
$$= -\omega^2\,\mathbf{r}$$

$\therefore$ Force acting on the particle,

$$F = m\mathbf{a} = -\mathbf{m}\,\omega^2\mathbf{r},$$ **Hence proved.**

Q. 39 A cricket bowler releases the ball in two different ways

(a) giving it only horizontal velocity, and

(b) giving it horizontal velocity and a small downward velocity.

The speed v_s at the time of release is the same. Both are released at a height H from the ground. Which one will have greater speed when the ball hits the ground ? Neglect air resistance.

Thinking Process

The horizontal component of velocity will remain unaffected by gravity.

Ans. (a) **When ball is given only horizontal velocity** Horizontal velocity at the time of release $(u_x) = v_s$

During projectile motion, horizontal velocity remains unchanged,

Therefore, $v_x = u_x = v_s$

In vertical direction, $v_y^2 = u_y^2 + 2gH$

$$v_y = \sqrt{2gH} \qquad (\because u_y = 0)$$

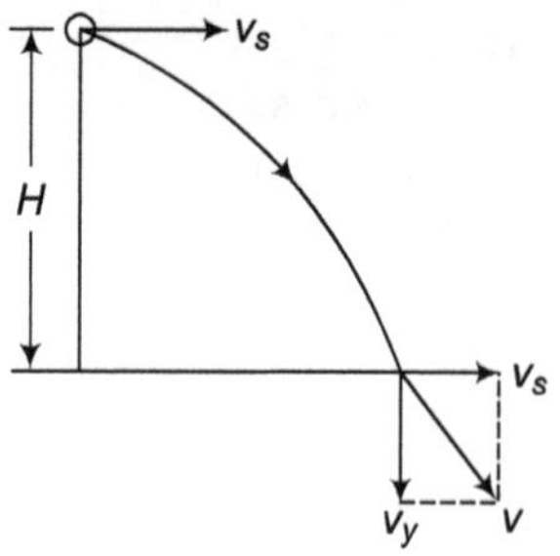

$\therefore$ Resultant speed of the ball at bottom,

$$v = \sqrt{v_x^2 + v_y^2}$$
$$= \sqrt{v_s^2 + 2gH} \qquad \text{...(i)}$$

(b) **When ball is given horizontal velocity and a small downward velocity**

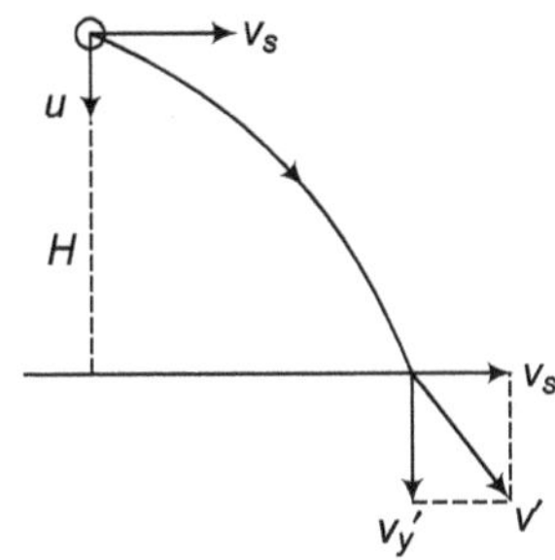

Let the ball be given a small downward velocity u.

In horizontal direction $\quad v'_x = u_x = v_s$

In vertical direction $\quad v'^2_y = u^2 + 2gH$

or $\quad v'_y = \sqrt{u^2 + 2gH}$

$\therefore$ Resultant speed of the ball at the bottom

$$v' = \sqrt{v'^2_x + v'^2_y} = \sqrt{v_s^2 + u^2 + 2gH} \quad \text{...(ii)}$$

From Eqs. (i) and (ii), we get $\quad v' > v$

Q. 40 There are four forces acting at a point P produced by strings as shown in figure. Which is at rest? Find the forces $\mathbf{F}_1$ and $\mathbf{F}_2$.

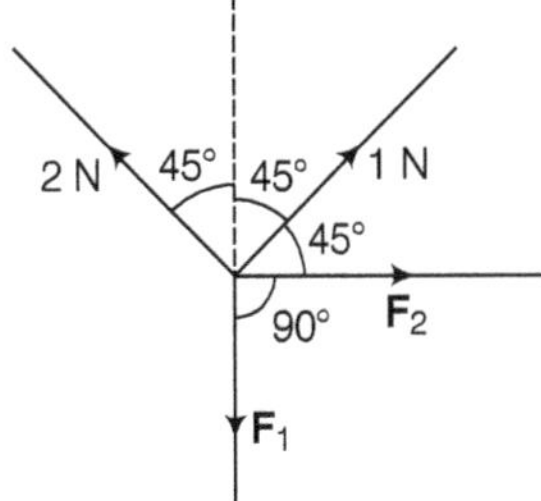

Thinking Process

To balance the forces, we have to resolve them along two mutually perpendicular directions.

Ans. Consider the adjacent diagram, in which forces are resolved.

On resolving forces into rectangular components, in equilibrium forces $\left(F_1 + \frac{1}{\sqrt{2}}\right)$ N are equal to $\sqrt{2}$ N and F_2 is equal to $\left(\sqrt{2} + \frac{1}{\sqrt{2}}\right)$ N.

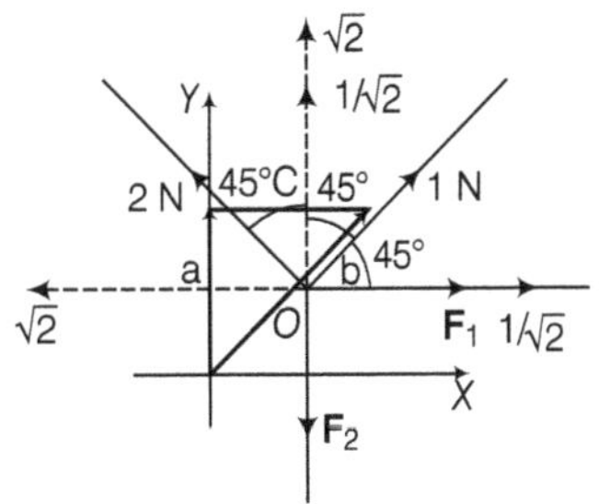

$$\therefore \quad F_1 + \frac{1}{\sqrt{2}} = \sqrt{2}$$

$$F_1 = \sqrt{2} - \frac{1}{\sqrt{2}} = \frac{2-1}{\sqrt{2}} = \frac{1}{\sqrt{2}} = 0.707 \text{ N}$$

and
$$F_2 = \sqrt{2} + \frac{1}{\sqrt{2}} = \frac{2+1}{\sqrt{2}} \text{ N} = \frac{3}{\sqrt{2}} \text{ N} = 2.121 \text{ N}$$

Q. 41 A rectangular box lies on a rough inclined surface. The coefficient of friction between the surface and the box is μ. Let the mass of the box be m.

(a) At what angle of inclination θ of the plane to the horizontal will the box just start to slide down the plane?

(b) What is the force acting on the box down the plane, if the angle of inclination of the plane is increased to $\alpha > \theta$?

(c) What is the force needed to be applied upwards along the plane to make the box either remain stationary or just move up with uniform speed?

(d) What is the force needed to be applied upwards along the plane to make the box move up the plane with acceleration a?

Ans. (a) Consider the adjacent diagram, force of friction on the box will act up the plane.

For the box to just starts sliding down mg

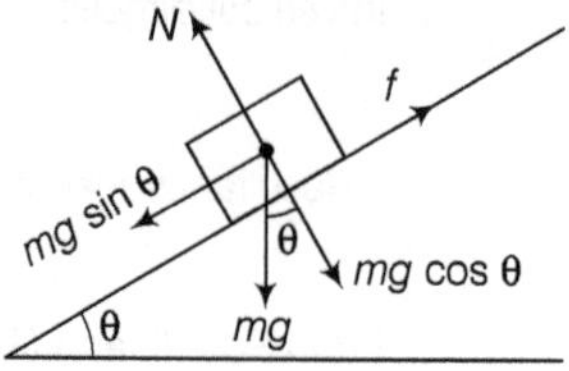

$$\sin\theta = f = \mu N = \mu\, mg\cos\theta$$

or

$$\tan\theta = \mu \Rightarrow \theta = \tan^{-1}(\mu)$$

N
f
mg sin θ
θ
mg cos θ
θ
mg

(b) When angle of inclination is increased to $\alpha > \theta$, then net force acting on the box, down the plane is

$$F_1 = mg\sin\alpha - f = mg\sin\alpha - \mu N$$
$$= mg(\sin\alpha - \mu\cos\alpha).$$

(c) To keep the box either stationary or just move it up with uniform speed, upward force needed, $F_2 = mg\sin\alpha + f = mg(\sin\alpha + \mu\cos\alpha)$ (In this case, friction would act down the plane).

(d) If the box is to be moved with an upward acceleration a, then upward force needed, $F_3 = mg(\sin\alpha + \mu\cos\alpha) + ma$.

Q. 42 A helicopter of mass 2000 kg rises with a vertical acceleration of 15 ms^{-2}. The total mass of the crew and passengers is 500 kg. Give the magnitude and direction of the ($g = 10\ ms^{-2}$)

(a) force on the floor of the helicopter by the crew and passengers.

(b) action of the rotor of the helicopter on the surrounding air.

(c) force on the helicopter due to the surrounding air.

Ans. Given, mass of helicopter $(m_1) = 2000$ kg

Mass of the crew and passengeres $m_2 = 500$ kg

Acceleration in vertical direction $a = 15\ m/s^2\ (\uparrow)$ and $g = 10\ m/s^2\ (\downarrow)$

(a) Force on the floor of the helicopter by the crew and passengers

$$m_2(g + a) = 500(10 + 15)\text{N}$$
$$500 \times 25\ \text{N} = 12500\ \text{N}$$

(b) Action of the rotor of the helicopter on the surrounding air $= (m_1 + m_2)(g + a)$

$$= (2000 + 500) \times (10 + 15) = 2500 \times 25$$
$$= 62500\ \text{N (downward)}$$

(c) Force on the helicopter due to the surrounding air

= reaction of force applied by helicopter.

= 62500 N (upward)

Note *We should be very clear when we are balancing action and reaction forces. We must know that which part is action and which part is reaction due to the action.*

5

Work, Energy and Power

Multiple Choice Questions (MCQs)

Q. 1 An electron and a proton are moving under the influence of mutual forces. In calculating the change in the kinetic energy of the system during motion, one ignores the magnetic force of one on another. This is, because

(a) the two magnetic forces are equal and opposite, so they produce no net effect

(b) the magnetic forces do not work on each particle

(c) the magnetic forces do equal and opposite (but non-zero) work on each particle

(d) the magnetic forces are necessarily negligible

Thinking Process

In this problem as the electron and proton are moving under the influence of mutual forces, they will perform circular motion about their centre (i.e., about middle point of the line joining them).

Ans. *(b)* When electron and proton are moving under influence of their mutual forces, the magnetic forces will be perpendicular to their motion hence no work is done by these forces.

Q. 2 A proton is kept at rest. A positively charged particle is released from rest at a distance d in its field. Consider two experiments; one in which the charged particle is also a proton and in another, a positron. In the same time t, the work done on the two moving charged particles is

(a) same as the same force law is involved in the two experiments

(b) less for the case of a positron, as the positron moves away more rapidly and the force on it weakens

(c) more for the case of a positron, as the positron moves away a larger distance

(d) same as the work done by charged particle on the stationary proton

Ans. *(c)* Force between two protons is same as that of between proton and a positron.

As positron is much lighter than proton, it moves away through much larger distance compared to proton.

We know that work done = force × distance. As forces are same in case of proton and positron but distance moved by positron is larger, hence, work done will be more.

Q. 3 **A man squatting on the ground gets straight up and stand. The force of reaction of ground on the man during the process is**

(a) constant and equal to mg in magnitude
(b) constant and greater than mg in magnitude
(c) variable but always greater than mg
(d) at first greater than mg and later becomes equal to mg

Ans. *(d)* When the man is squatting on the ground he is tilted somewhat, hence he also has to balance frictional force besides his weight in this case.

$$R = \text{reactional force} = \text{friction} + mg$$

$$\Rightarrow \quad R > mg$$

When the man gets straight up in that case friction ≈ 0

$$\Rightarrow \quad \text{Reactional force} \approx mg$$

Q. 4 **A bicyclist comes to a skidding stop in 10 m. During this process, the force on the bicycle due to the road is 200N and is directly opposed to the motion. The work done by the cycle on the road is**

(a) + 2000J (b) – 200J (c) zero (d) – 20,000J

Thinking Process

In this problem energy will be lost due to dissipation by friction.

Ans. *(c)* Here, work is done by the frictional force on the cycle and is equal to $-200 \times 10 = -2000$ J.

As the road is not moving, hence, work done by the cycle on the road = zero.

Note *We should be aware that here the energy of bicyclist is lost during the motion, but it is lost due to friction in the form of heat.*

Q. 5 **A body is falling freely under the action of gravity alone in vaccum. Which of the following quantities remain constant during the fall?**

(a) Kinetic energy (b) Potential energy
(c) Total mechanical energy (d) Total linear momentum

Ans. *(c)* As the body is falling freely under gravity, the potential energy decreases and kinetic energy increases but total mechanical energy (PE + KE) of the body and earth system will be constant as external force on the system is zero.

Q. 6 **During inelastic collision between two bodies, which of the following quantities always remain conserved?**

(a) Total kinetic energy (b) Total mechanical energy
(c) Total linear momentum (d) Speed of each body

Thinking Process

In an inelastic collision between two bodies due to some deformation, energy may be lost in the form of heat and sound etc.

Ans. *(c)* When we are considering the two bodies as system the total external force on the system will be zero.

Hence, total linear momentum of the system remain conserved.

Q. 7 Two inclined frictionless tracks, one gradual and the other steep meet at A from where two stones are allowed to slide down from rest, one on each track as shown in figure.

Which of the following statement is correct?

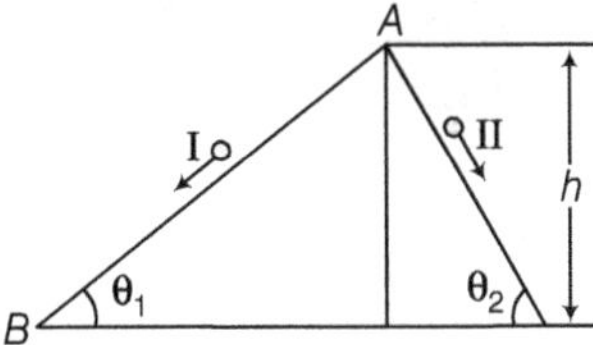

(a) Both the stones reach the bottom at the same time but not with the same speed

(b) Both the stones reach the bottom with the same speed and stone I reaches the bottom earlier than stone II

(c) Both the stones reach the bottom with the same speed and stone II reaches the bottom earlier than stone I

(d) Both the stones reach the bottom at different times and with different speeds

Ans. *(c)* As the given tracks are frictionless, hence, mechanical energy will be conserved. As both the tracks having common height, h.

From conservation of mechanical energy,

$$\frac{1}{2}mv^2 = mgh \quad \text{(for both tracks I and II)}$$

$$v = \sqrt{2gh}$$

Hence, speed is same for both stones. For stone I, a_1 = acceleration along inclined plane $= g\sin\theta_1$

Similarly, for stone II $a_2 = g\sin\theta_2$ as $\theta_2 > \theta_1$ hence, $a_2 > a_1$.

And both length for track II is also less hence, stone II reaches earlier than stone I.

Q. 8 The potential energy function for a particle executing linear SHM is given by $V(x) = \frac{1}{2}kx^2$ where k is the force constant of the oscillator (Fig). For $k = 0.5$ N/m, the graph of $V(x)$ *versus* x is shown in the figure. A particle of total energy E turns back when it reaches $x = \pm x_m$. If V and K indicate the PE and KE, respectively of the particle at $x = +x_m$, then which of the following is correct?

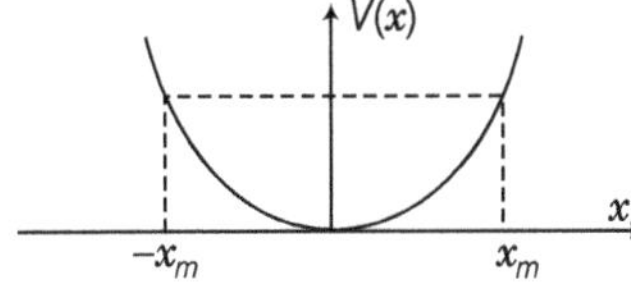

(a) $V = O$, $K = E$

(b) $V = E$, $K = O$

(c) $V < E$, $K = O$

(d) $V = O$, $K < E$

Ans. *(b)* Total energy is E = PE + KE ...(i)

When particle is at $x = x_m$ *i.e.*, at extreme position, returns back. Hence, at $x = x_m$; $x = 0$; K E = 0

From Eq. (i) $E = \text{PE} + 0 = \text{PE} = V(x_m) = \frac{1}{2}kx_m^2$

Q. 9 Two identical ball bearings in contact with each other and resting on a frictionless table are hit head-on by another ball bearing of the same mass moving initially with a speed v as shown in figure.

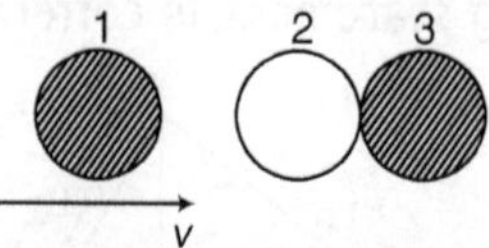

If the collision is elastic, which of the following (figure) is a possible result after collision?

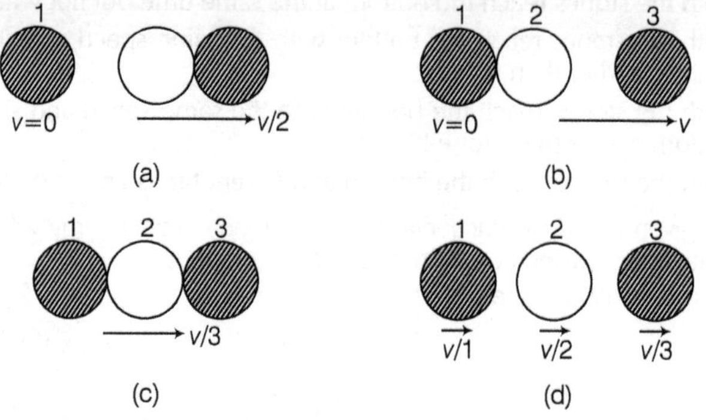

Ans. *(b)* When two bodies of equal masses collides elastically, their velocities are interchanged.

When ball 1 collides with ball-2, then velocity of ball-1, $v_1$becomes zero and velocity of ball-2, v_2 becomes v, *i.e.*, similarly.

$$v_1 = 0 \Rightarrow v_2 = v$$

when ball 2 collides will ball 3 $\quad v_2 = 0, v_3 = v$

Q. 10 A body of mass 0.5 kg travels in a straight line with velocity $v = a\,x^{3/2}$ where $a = 5\text{ m}^{-1/2}\text{s}^{-1}$. The work done by the net force during its displacement from $x = 0$ to $x = 2\text{ m}$ is

(a) 1.5 J (b) 50 J (c) 10 J (d) 100 J

Ans. Given, $v = ax^{3/2}$

$$m = 0.5\,\text{kg},\ a = 5\,\text{m}^{-1/2}\text{s}^{-1},\ \text{work done } (W) = ?$$

We know that

Acceleration $\quad a_0 = \dfrac{dv}{dt} = v\dfrac{dv}{dx} = ax^{3/2}\dfrac{d}{dx}(ax^{3/2})$

$$= ax^{3/2} \times a \times \frac{3}{2} \times x^{1/2} = \frac{3}{2}a^2x^2$$

Now, $\quad \text{Force} = ma_0 = m\dfrac{3}{2}a^2x^2$

$$\text{Work done} = \int_{x=0}^{x=2} F dx = \int_0^2 \frac{3}{2} ma^2x^2 dx$$

$$= \frac{3}{2} ma^2 \times (x^3/3)_0^2$$

$$= \frac{1}{2} ma^2 \times 8 = \frac{1}{2} \times (0.5) \times (25) \times 8 = 50\text{J}$$

Q. 11 A body is moving unidirectionally under the influence of a source of constant power supplying energy. Which of the diagrams shown in figure correctly shown the displacement-time curve for its motion?

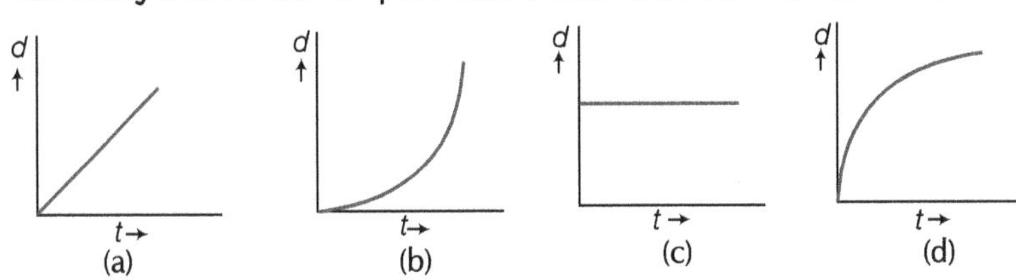

Ans. *(b)* Given, power = constant

We know that power (P)

$$P = \frac{dW}{dt} = \frac{\mathbf{F.ds}}{dt} = \frac{F\,ds}{dt} \qquad (\because \text{body is moving unidirectionally})$$

Hence, $$F.ds = Fds\cos 0°$$

$$P = \frac{Fds}{dt} = \text{constant} \qquad (\because P = \text{constant by question})$$

Now, writing dimensions

$$[F]\,[v] = \text{constant}$$

$$\Rightarrow \quad [MLT^{-2}]\,[LT^{-1}] = \text{constant}$$

$$\Rightarrow \quad L^2\,T^{-3} = \text{constant} \qquad (\because \text{mass is constant})$$

$$\Rightarrow \quad L \propto T^{3/2} \Rightarrow \text{Displacement } (d) \propto t^{3/2}$$

Q. 12 Which of the diagrams shown in figure most closely shows the variation in kinetic energy of the earth as it moves once around the sun in its elliptical orbit?

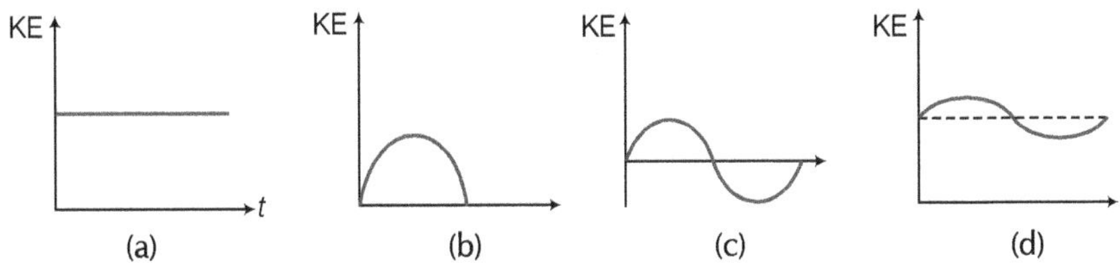

Ans. *(d)* When the earth is closest to the sun, speed of the earth is maximum, hence, KE is maximum. When the earth is farthest from the sun speed is minimum hence, KE is minimum but never zero and negative.

This variation is correctly represented by option(d).

Q. 13 Which of the diagrams shown in figure represents variation of total mechanical energy of a pendulum oscillating in air as function of time?

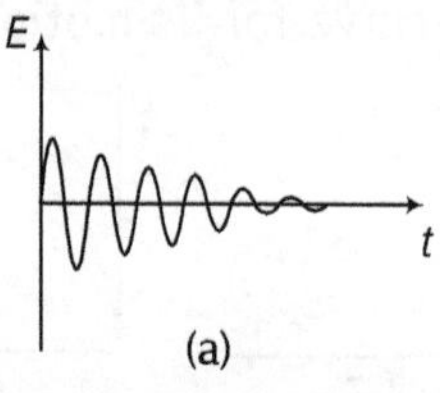

(a)

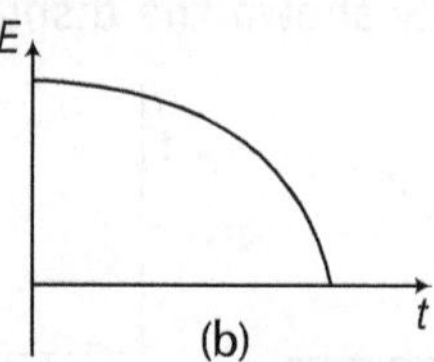

(b)

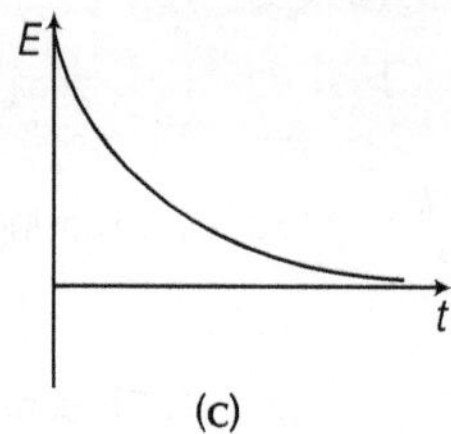

(c)

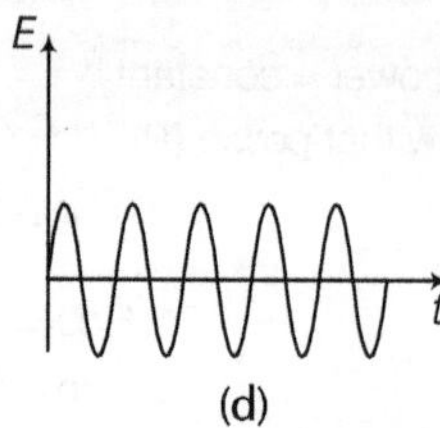

(d)

Ans. *(c)* When a pendulum oscillates in air, it will lose energy continuously in overcoming resistance due to air. Therefore, total mechanical energy of the pendulum decreases continuously with time.

The variation is correctly represented by curve (c).

Q. 14 A mass of 5 kg is moving along a circular path of radius 1 m. If the mass moves with 300 rev/min, its kinetic energy would be

(a) $250\pi^2$ (b) $100\pi^2$

(c) $5\pi^2$ (d) 0

Ans. *(a)* Given, mass $= m = 5$ kg

$$\text{Radius} = 1 \text{ m} = R$$

Revolution per minute

$$\omega = 300 \text{ rev/min}$$
$$= (300 \times 2\pi) \text{ rad/min}$$
$$= (300 \times 2 \times 3.14) \text{ rad/60 s}$$
$$= \frac{300 \times 2 \times 3.14}{60} \text{ rad/s} = 10\pi \text{ rad/s}$$

$\Rightarrow$

$$\text{linear speed} = v = \omega R$$
$$= \left(\frac{300 \times 2\pi}{60}\right)(1)$$
$$= 10\pi \text{ m/s}$$
$$\text{KE} = \frac{1}{2} mv^2$$
$$= \frac{1}{2} \times 5 \times (10\pi)^2$$
$$= 100\pi^2 \times 5 \times \frac{1}{2}$$
$$= 250\pi^2 \text{ J}$$

Q. 15 A raindrop falling from a height h above ground, attains a near terminal velocity when it has fallen through a height $(3/4)h$. Which of the diagrams shown in figure correctly shows the change in kinetic and potential energy of the drop during its fall up to the ground?

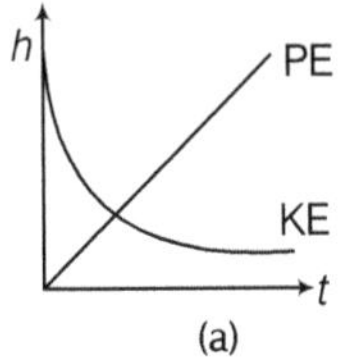

(a)

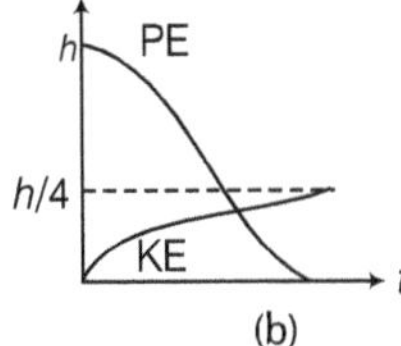

(b)

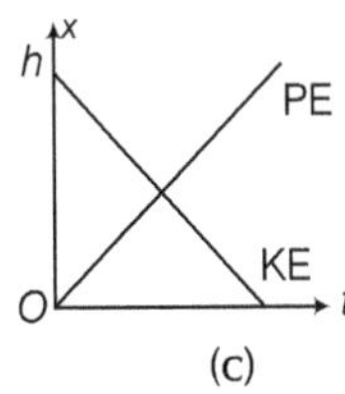

(c)

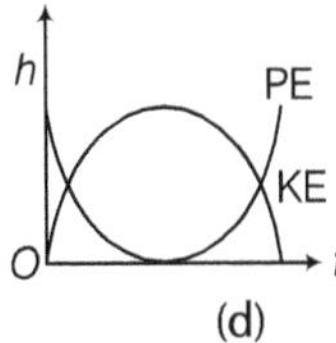

(d)

Thinking Process

During fall of a raindrop first velocity of the drop increases and then become constant after sometime.

Ans. *(b)* When drop falls first velocity increases, hence, first KE also increases. After sometime speed (velocity) is constant this is called terminal velocity, hence, KE also become constant. PE decreases continuously as the drop is falling continuously.

The variation in PE and KE is best represented by (b).

Q. 16 In a shotput event an athlete throws the shotput of mass 10 kg with an initial speed of 1 m s^{-1} at 45° from a height 1.5 m above ground. Assuming air resistance to be negligible and acceleration due to gravity to be 10 m s^{-2}, the kinetic energy of the shotput when it just reaches the ground will be

(a) 2.5 J (b) 5.0 J (c) 52.5 J (d) 155.0 J

Thinking Process

As air resistance is negligible, total mechanical energy of the system will remain constant.

Ans. *(d)* Given, $h = 1.5\,\text{m}$, $v = 1\,\text{m/s}$, $m = 10\,\text{kg}$, $g = 10\,\text{ms}^{-2}$

From conservation of mechanical energy.

$$(\text{PE})\,i + (\text{KE})\,i = (\text{PE})\,f + (\text{KE})\,f$$

$$\Rightarrow \quad mgh + \frac{1}{2}mv^2 = 0 + (\text{KE})\,f$$

$$\Rightarrow \quad (\text{KE})\,f = mgh + \frac{1}{2}mv^2$$

$$\Rightarrow \quad (\text{KE})\,f = 10 \times 10 \times 1.5 + \frac{1}{2} \times 10 \times (1)^2$$

$$= 150 + 5 = 155\,\text{J}$$

Note *We should be careful about the reference taken for PE, it may or may not be the ground.*

Q. 17 **Which of the diagrams in figure correctly shows the change in kinetic energy of an iron sphere falling freely in a lake having sufficient depth to impart it a terminal velocity?**

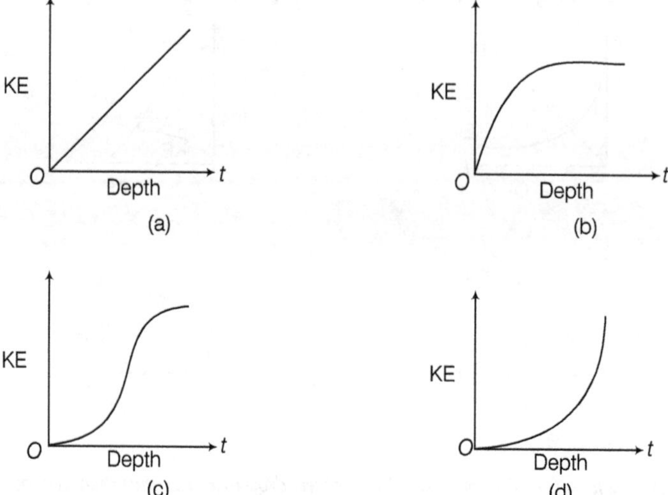

Ans. *(b)* First velocity of the iron sphere increases and after sometime becomes constant, called terminal velocity. Hence, accordingly first KE increases and then becomes constant which is best represented by (b).

Q. 18 **A cricket ball of mass 150 g moving with a speed of 126 km/h hits at the middle of the bat, held firmly at its position by the batsman. The ball moves straight back to the bowler after hitting the bat. Assuming that collision between ball and bat is completely elastic and the two remain in contact for 0.001s, the force that the batsman had to apply to hold the bat firmly at its place would be**

(a) 10.5 N (b) 21 N (c) 1.05×10^4 N (d) 2.1×10^4 N

Ans. *(c)* Given, $m = 150\text{g} = \frac{150}{1000}\text{kg} = \frac{3}{20}\text{kg}$

$$\Delta t = \text{time of contact} = 0.001\text{s}$$

$$u = 126\text{ km/h} = \frac{126 \times 1000}{60 \times 60}\text{ m/s} = 35\text{ m/s}$$

$$v = -126\text{ km/h} = -35\text{ m/s}$$

Change in momentum of the ball

$$\Delta p = m(v - u) = \frac{3}{20}(-35 - 35)\text{ kg-m/s}$$

$$= \frac{3}{20}(-70) = -\frac{21}{2}$$

We know that force $F = \frac{\Delta p}{\Delta t}$

$$= \frac{-21/2}{0.001}\text{N} = -1.05 \times 10^4\text{ N}$$

Here, – ve sign shown that force will be opposite to the direction of movement of the ball before hitting.

Multiple Choice Questions (More Than One Options)

Q. 19 A man of mass m, standing at the bottom of the staircase, of height L climbs it and stands at its top.

(a) Work done by all forces on man is equal to the rise in potential energy mgL

(b) Work done by all forces on man is zero

(c) Work done by the gravitational force on man is mgL

(d) The reaction force from a step does not do work because the point of application of the force does not move while the force exists

Ans. *(b, d)*

When a man of mass m climbs up the staircase of height L, work done by the gravitational force on the man is-mgl work done by internal muscular forces will be mgL as the change in kinetic energy is almost zero.

Hence, total work done $= -mgL + mgL = 0$

As the point of application of the contact forces does not move hence work done by reaction forces will be zero.

Note *Here work done by friction will also be zero as there is no dissipation or rubbing is involved.*

Q. 20 A bullet of mass m fired at 30° to the horizontal leaves the barrel of the gun with a velocity v. The bullet hits a soft target at a height h above the ground while it is moving downward and emerge out with half the kinetic energy it had before hitting the target.

Which of the following statements are correct in respect of bullet after it emerges out of the target?

(a) The velocity of the bullet will be reduced to half its initial value

(b) The velocity of the bullet will be more than half of its earlier velocity

(c) The bullet will continue to move along the same parabolic path

(d) The bullet will move in a different parabolic path

(e) The bullet will fall vertically downward after hitting the target

(f) The internal energy of the particles of the target will increase

Ans. *(b, d, f)*

Consider the adjacent diagram for the given situation in the question.

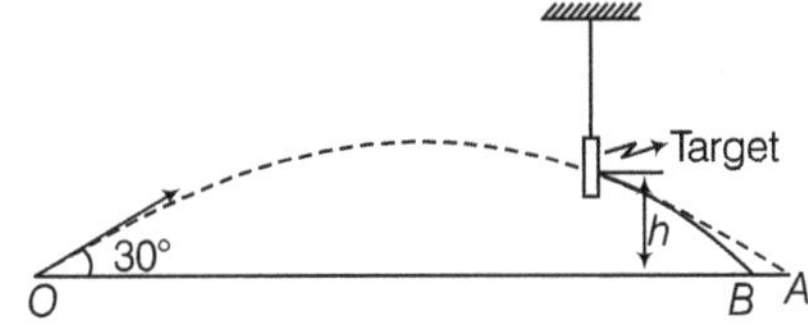

(b) Conserving energy between "O" and "A"

$$U_i + K_i = U_f + K_f$$

$$\Rightarrow \quad 0 + \frac{1}{2}mv^2 = mgh + \frac{1}{2}mv'$$

$$\Rightarrow \quad \frac{(v')^2}{2} = \frac{v^2}{2} = -gh$$

$$\Rightarrow \quad (v')^2 = v^2 - 2gh \Rightarrow v' = \sqrt{v^2 - 2gh} \quad ...(i)$$

where v' is speed of the bullet just before hitting the target. Let speed after emerging from the target is v'' then,

By question, $$= \frac{1}{2}(mv'')^2 = \frac{1}{2}\left[\frac{1}{2}m(v')^2\right]$$

$$\frac{1}{2}m(v'')^2 = \frac{1}{4}m(v')^2 = \frac{1}{4}m[v^2 - 2gh]$$

$$\Rightarrow \quad (v'')^2 = \frac{v^2 - 2gh}{2} = \frac{v^2}{2} - gh$$

$$\Rightarrow \quad v'' = \sqrt{\frac{v^2}{2} - gh} \quad \text{...(ii)}$$

From Eqs. (i) and (ii)

$$\frac{v'}{v''} = \frac{\sqrt{v^2 - 2gh}}{\frac{\sqrt{v^2 - 2gh}}{\sqrt{2}}} = \sqrt{2}$$

$$\Rightarrow \quad v'' = \frac{v'}{\sqrt{2}} = v^2\left(\frac{v'}{2}\right)$$

$$\Rightarrow \quad \frac{v''}{\frac{v'}{2}} = \sqrt{2} = 1.414 > 1$$

$$\Rightarrow \quad v'' > \frac{v'}{2}$$

Hence, after emerging from the target velocity of the bullet (v'') is more than half of its earlier velocity v' (velocity before emerging into the target).

(d) As the velocity of the bullet changes to v' which is less than v^1 hence, path, followed will change and the bullet reaches at point B instead of A', as shown in the figure.

(f) As the bullet is passing through the target the loss in energy of the bullet is transferred to particles of the target. Therefore, their internal energy increases.

Q. 21 Two blocks M_1 and M_2 having equal mass are free to move on a horizontal frictionless surface. M_2 is attached to a massless spring as shown in figure. Initially M_2 is at rest and M_1 is moving toward M_2 with speed v and collides head-on with M_2.

(a) While spring is fully compressed all the KE of M_1 is stored as PE of spring

(b) While spring is fully compressed the system momentum is not conserved, though final momentum is equal to initial momentum

(c) If spring is massless, the final state of the M_1 is state of rest

(d) If the surface on which blocks are moving has friction, then collision cannot be elastic

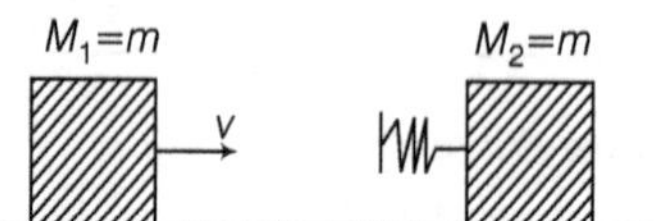

Ans. ***(c)*** Consider the adjacent diagram when M_1 comes in contact with the spring, M_1 is retarded by the spring force and M_2 is accelerated by the spring force.

(a) The spring will continue to compress until the two blocks acquire common velocity.

(b) As surfaces are frictionalless momentum of the system will be conserved.

(c) If spring is massless whole energy of M_1 will be imparted to M_2 and M_1 will be at rest, then

(d) Collision is inelastic, even if friction is not involved.

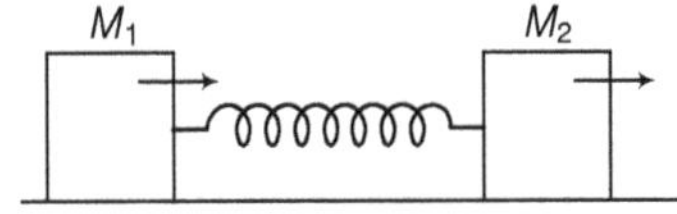

Very Short Answer Type Questions

Q. 22 A rough inclined plane is placed on a cart moving with a constant velocity u on horizontal ground. A block of mass M rests on the incline. Is any work done by force of friction between the block and incline? Is there then a dissipation of energy?

Ans. Consider the adjacent diagram. As the block M is at rest.

Hence, f = frictional force = $Mg \sin \theta$

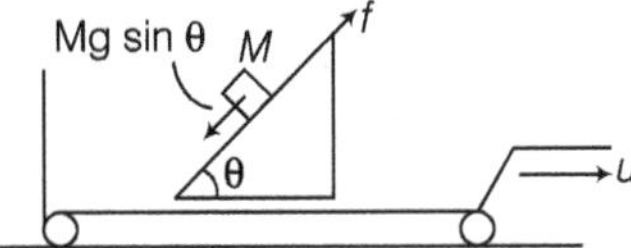

The force of friction acting between the block and incline opposes the tendency of sliding of the block. Since, block is not in motion, therefore, no work is done by the force of friction. Hence, no dissipation of energy takes place.

Q. 23 Why is electrical power required at all when the elevator is descending? Why should there be a limit on the number of passengers in this case?

Ans. When the elevator is descending, then electric power is required to prevent it from falling freely under gravity.

Also, as the weight inside the elevator increases, its speed of descending increases, therefore, there should be a limit on the number of passengers in the elevator to prevent the elevator from descending with large velocity.

Q. 24 A body is being raised to a height h from the surface of earth. What is the sign of work done by

(a) applied force and

(b) gravitational force?

Ans. (a) Force is applied on the body to lift it in upward direction and displacement of the body is also in upward direction, therefore, angle between the applied force and displacement is $\theta = 0°$

$\therefore$ Work done by the applied force

$$W = Fs\cos\theta = Fs\cos 0° = Fs \quad (\because \cos 0° = 1)$$

i.e., W = Positive

(b) The gravitational force acts in downward direction and displacement in upward direction, therefore, angle between them is $\theta = 180°$.

$\therefore$ Work done by the gravitational force

$$W = Fs\cos 180° = -Fs \qquad (\because \cos 180° = 1)$$

Q. 25 Calculate the work done by a car against gravity in moving along a straight horizontal road. The mass of the car is 400 kg and the distance moved is 2 m.

Ans. Force of gravity acts on the car vertically downward while car is moving along horizontal road, *i.e.*, angle between them is 90°.

Work done by the car against gravity

$$W = Fs\cos 90° = 0 \qquad (\because \cos 90° = 0)$$

Q. 26 A body falls towards earth in air. Will its total mechanical energy be conserved during the fall? Justify.

Ans. *No*, total mechanical energy of the body falling freely under gravity is not conserved, because a small part of its energy is utilised against resistive force of air, which is non-conservative force. In this condition, gain in KE < loss in PE.

Q. 27 A body is moved along a closed loop. Is the work done in moving the body necessarily zero? If not, state the condition under which work done over a closed path is always zero.

Ans. *No*, work done in moving along a closed loop is not necessarily zero. It is zero only when all the forces are conservative forces.

Q. 28 In an elastic collision of two billiard balls, which of the following quantities remain conserved during the short time of collision of the balls (*i.e.,* when they are in contact)?

(a) Kinetic energy.

(b) Total linear momentum.

Give reason for your answer in each case.

Ans. Total linear momentum of the system of two balls is always conserved. While balls are in contact, there may be deformation which means elastic PE which came from part of KE Therefore, KE may not be conserved.

Q. 29 Calculate the power of a crane in watts, which lifts a mass of 100 kg to a height of 10 m in 20s.

Ans. Given,

$$\text{mass} = m = 100\text{ kg}$$

$$\text{height} = h = 10\text{ m}, \quad \text{time duration } t = 20\text{s}$$

$$\text{power} = \text{Rate of work done}$$

$$= \frac{\text{change of PE}}{\text{time}} = \frac{mgh}{t}$$

$$= \frac{100 \times 9.8 \times 10}{20}$$

$$= 5 \times 98 = 490\text{ W}$$

Q. 30 The average work done by a human heart while it beats once is 0.5 J. Calculate the power used by heart if it beats 72 times in a minute.

Ans. Given, average work done by a human heart per beat = 0.5 J

Total work done during 72 beats

$$= 72 \times 0.5\,\text{J} = 36\,\text{J}$$

$$\text{Power} = \frac{\text{Work done}}{\text{Time}} = \frac{36\,\text{J}}{60\,\text{s}} = 0.6\,\text{W}$$

Q. 31 Give example of a situation in which an applied force does not result in a change in kinetic energy.

Ans. When a charged particle moves in a uniform normal magnetic field, the path of the particle is circular, as given field is uniform hence, radius of the circular path is also constant.

As the force is central and movement is tangential work done by the force is zero. As speed is also constant we can say that $\Delta K = 0$.

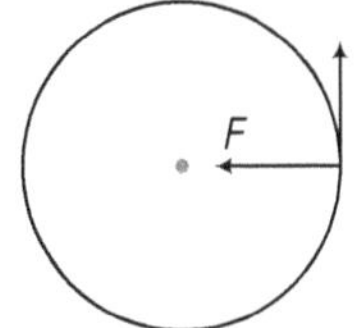

Q. 32 Two bodies of unequal mass are moving in the same direction with equal kinetic energy. The two bodies are brought to rest by applying retarding force of same magnitude. How would the distance moved by them before coming to rest compare?

Ans. According to work-energy theorem,

Change in KE = Work done by the retarding force

KE of the body = Retarding force × Displacement

As KE of the bodies and retarding forces applied on them are same, therefore, both bodies will travel equal distances before coming to rest.

Q. 33 A bob of mass *m* suspended by a light string of length *L* is whirled into a vertical circle as shown in figure. What will be the trajectory of the particle, if the string is cut at

(a) point *B*?

(b) point *C*?

(c) point *X*?

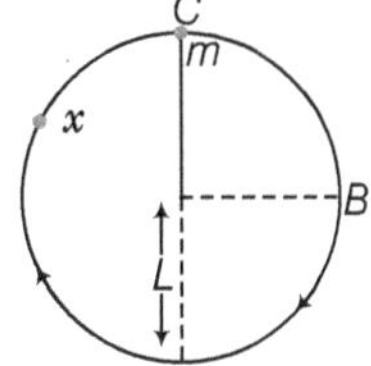

Thinking Process

In a uniform circular motion, velocity is always tangential in the direction of motion at any point.

Ans. When bob is whirled into a vertical circle, the required centripetal force is obtained from the tension in the string. When string is cut, tension in string becomes zero and centripetal force is not provided, hence, bob start to move in a straight line path along the direction of its velocity.

(a) At point *B*, the velocity of *B* is vertically downward, therefore, when string is cut at *B*, bob moves vertically downward.

(b) At point *C*, the velocity is along the horizontal towards right, therefore, when string is cut at *C*, bob moves horizontally towards right.

Also, the bob moves under gravity simultaneously with horizontal uniform speed. So, it traversed on a parabolic path with vertex at C.

(c) At point X, the velocity of the bob is along the tangent drawn at point X, therefore when string is cut at point C, bob moves along the tangent at that point X.

Also, the bob move under gravity simultaneously with horizontal uniform speed . So, it traversed on a parabolic path with vertex higher than C.

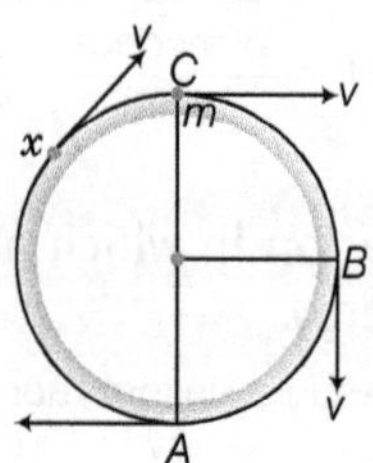

Short Answer Type Questions

Q. 34 **A graph of potential energy $V(x)$ *versus* x is shown in figure. A particle of energy E_0 is executing motion in it. Draw graph of velocity and kinetic energy *versus* x for one complete cycle *AFA*.**

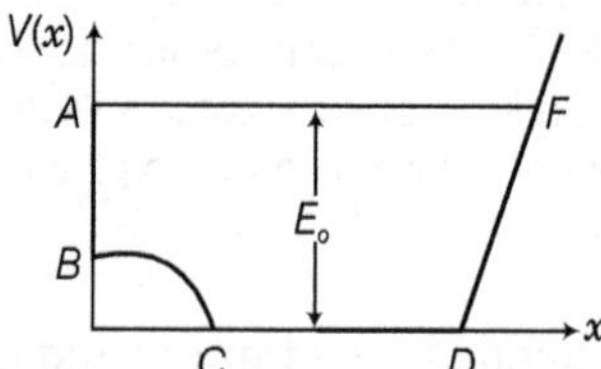

Thinking Process

We will assume total mechanical energy of the system to be constant.

Ans. **KE *versus* x graph**

We know that Total ME = KE + PE

$\Rightarrow$ $E_0 = \text{KE} + V(x)$

$\Rightarrow$ $\text{KE} = E_0 - V(x)$

at A_1 $x = 0$, $V(x) = E_0$

$\Rightarrow$ $\text{KE} = E_0 - E_0 = 0$

at B_1 $V(x) < E_0$

$\Rightarrow$ $\text{KE} > 0$ (positive)

at C and D_1 $V(x) = 0$

$\Rightarrow$ KE is maximum at F_1 $V(x) = E_0$

Hence, KE = 0

The variation is shown in adjacent diagram.

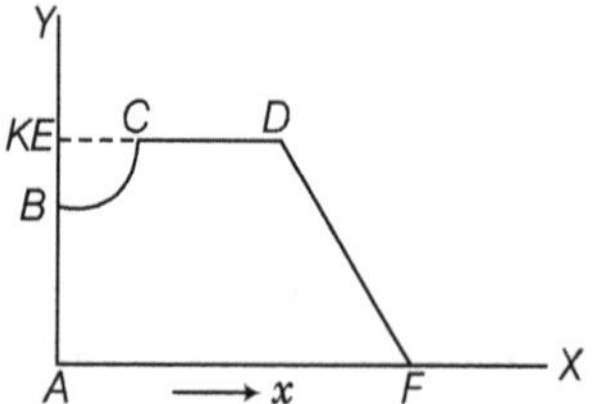

Velocity *versus* x graph

As $\text{KE} = \frac{1}{2} mv^2$

$\therefore$ At A and F, where KE = 0, $v = 0$.

At C and D, KE is maximum. Therefore, v is $\pm$ max.

At B, KE is positive but not maximum.

Therefore, v is $\pm$ some value (< max.)

The variation is shown in the diagram.

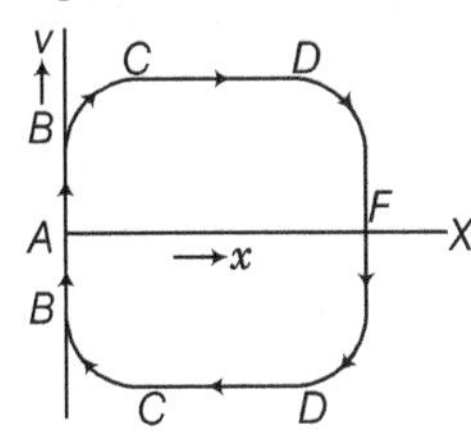

Q. 35 A ball of mass m, moving with a speed $2v_0$, collides inelastically ($e > 0$) with an identical ball at rest. Show that

(a) For head-on collision, both the balls move forward.

(b) For a general collision, the angle between the two velocities of scattered balls is less than 90°.

Ans. (a) Let v_1 and v_2 are velocities of the two balls after collision.

Now, by the principle of conservation of linear momentum,

$$2mv_0 = mv_1 + mv_2$$

or $$2v_0 = v_1 + v_2$$

and $$e = \frac{v_2 - v_1}{2v_0}$$

$\Rightarrow$ $$v_2 = v_1 + 2v_0 e$$

$\therefore$ $$2v_1 = 2v_0 - 2ev_0$$

$\therefore$ $$v_1 = v_0 (1 - e)$$

Since, $e < 1 \Rightarrow v_1$ has the same sign as v_0, therefore, the ball moves on after collision.

(b) Consider the diagram below for a general collision.

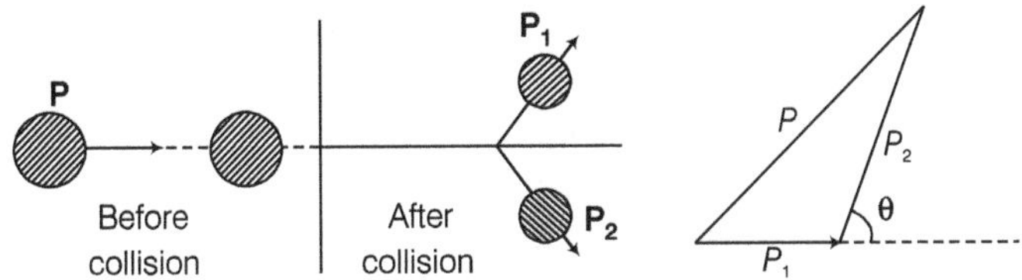

By principle of conservation of linear momentum,

$$\mathbf{P} = \mathbf{P}_1 + \mathbf{P}_2$$

For inelastic collision some KE is lost, hence $\frac{p^2}{2m} > \frac{p_1^2}{2m} + \frac{p_2^2}{2m}$

$\therefore$ $$p^2 > p_1^2 + p_2^2$$

Thus, $\mathbf{p}$, $\mathbf{p}_1$ and $\mathbf{p}_2$ are related as shown in the figure.

θ is acute (less than 90°) ($p^2 = p_1^2 + p_2^2$ would given $\theta = 90°$)

Q. 36 Consider a one-dimensional motion of a particle with total energy **E**. There are four regions *A*, *B*, *C* and *D* in which the relation between potential energy *V*, kinetic energy (*K*) and total energy *E* is as given below

Region A : $V > E$ **Region B :** $V < E$

Region C : $K < E$ **Region D :** $V > E$

State with reason in each case whether a particle can be found in the given region or not.

Thinking Process

A particle cannot be found in the given region when KE < O.

Ans. We know that

$$\text{Total energy } E = \text{PE} + \text{KE}$$

$$\Rightarrow \quad E = V + K \quad \text{...(i)}$$

For region A Given, $V > E$, From Eq. (i)

$$K = E - V$$

as $$V > E \Rightarrow E - V < 0$$

Hence, $K < 0$, this is not possible.

For region B Given, $V < E \Rightarrow E - V > 0$

This is possible because total energy can be greater than PE (V).

For region C Given, $K > E \Rightarrow K - E > 0$

from Eq. (i) **PE** $= V = E - K < 0$

Which is possible, because PE can be negative.

For region D Given, $V > K$

This is possible because for a system PE (V) may be greater than KE (K).

Q. 37 The bob *A* of a pendulum released from horizontal to the vertical hits another bob *B* of the same mass at rest on a table as shown in figure.

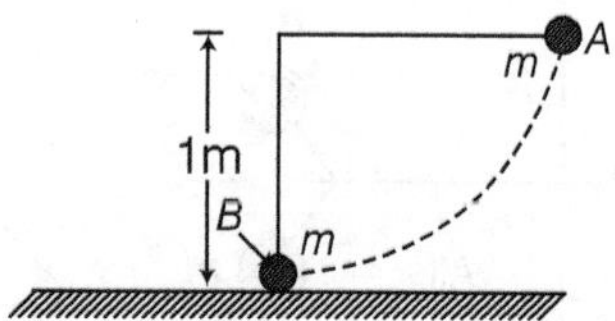

If the length of the pendulum is 1m, calculate

(a) the height to which bob A will rise after collision.

(b) the speed with which bob B starts moving.

Neglect the size of the bobs and assume the collision to be elastic.

Thinking Process

When two bodies of equal masses collides elastically momentum is interchanged. At the bottom point bob A is having almost horizontal velocity.

Ans. When ball *A* reaches bottom point its velocity is horizontal, hence, we can apply conservation of linear momentum in the horizontal direction.

(a) Two balls have same mass and the collision between them is elastic, therefore, ball A transfers its entire linear momentum to ball B. Hence, ball A will come to at rest after collision and does not rise at all.

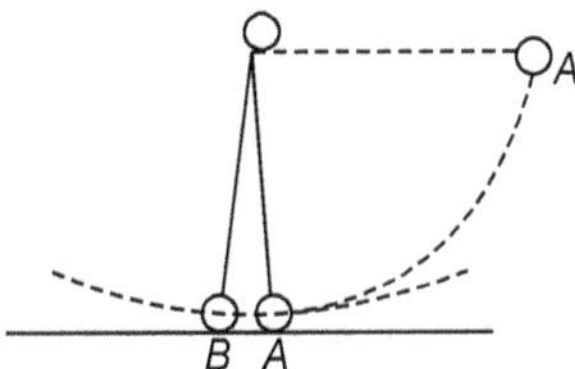

(b) Speed with which bob B starts moving

$$= \text{Speed with which bob } A \text{ hits bob } B$$
$$= \sqrt{2gh}$$
$$= \sqrt{2 \times 9.8 \times 1}$$
$$= \sqrt{19.6}$$
$$= 4.42 \text{m/s}$$

Note *When the bob A is at the bottommost point, its velocity is horizontal and tension is the external force on the bob but still momentum can be considered to be conserved in horizontal direction, because the tension has no effect in horizontal direction at the bottommost point.*

Q. 38 A raindrop of mass 1.00 g falling from a height of 1 km hits the ground with a speed of 50 m s^{-1}. Calculate

(a) the loss of PE of the drop.

(b) the gain in KE of the drop.

(c) Is the gain in KE equal to loss of PE? If not why?

Take, $g = 10 \text{ ms}^{-2}$.

Ans. Given, mass of the rain drop $(m) = 1.00 \text{ g}$

$$= 1 \times 10^{-3} \text{ kg}$$

Height of falling $(h) = 1 \text{ km} = 10^3 \text{ m}$

$$g = 10 \text{ m/s}^2$$

Speed of the rain drop $(v) = 50 \text{ m/s}$

(a) Loss of PE of the drop $= mgh$

$$= 1 \times 10^{-3} \times 10 \times 10^3 = 10 \text{J}$$

(b) Gain in KE of the drop $= \frac{1}{2} mv^2$

$$= \frac{1}{2} \times 1 \times 10^{-3} \times (50)^2$$
$$= \frac{1}{2} \times 10^{-3} \times 2500$$
$$= 1.250 \text{ J}$$

(c) *No*, gain in KE is not equal to the loss in its PE, because a part of PE is utilised in doing work against the viscous drag of air.

Q. 39 Two pendulums with identical bobs and lengths are suspended from a common support such that in rest position the two bobs are in contact (figure). One of the bobs is released after being displaced by 10° so that it collides elastically head-on with the other bob.

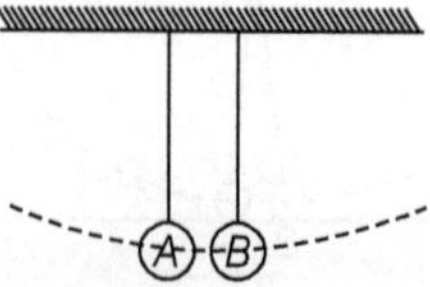

(a) Describe the motion of two bobs.

(b) Draw a graph showing variation in energy of either pendulum with time, for $0 \leq t \leq 2T$. where T is the period of each pendulum.

Thinking Process

As collision is elastic, mechanical energy of the system is conserved. We have to apply energy conservation principle to describe the motion of the two bobs.

Ans. (a) Consider the adjacent diagram in which the bob B is displaced through an angle θ and released.

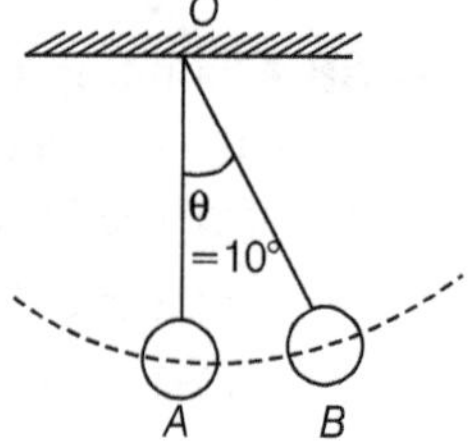

At $t = 0$, suppose bob B is displaced by $\theta = 10°$ to the right. It is given potential energy $E_1 = E$. Energy of A, $E_2 = 0$.

When B is released, it strikes A at $t = T/4$. In the head-on elastic collision between B and A comes to rest and A gets velocity of B. Therefore, $E_1 = 0$ and $E_2 = E$. At $t = 2T/4$, B reaches its extreme right position when KE of A is converted into PE $= E_2 = E$. Energy of B, $E_1 = 0$.

At $t = 3T/4$, A reaches its mean position, when its PE is converted into KE $= E_2 = E$. It collides elastically with B and transfers whole of its energy to B. Thus, $E_2 = 0$ and $E_1 = E$. The entire process is repeated.

(b) The values of energies of B and A at different time intervals are tabulated here. The plot of energy with time $0 \leq t \leq 2T$ is shown separately for B and A in the figure below.

Time (t)	**Energy of *A*** (E_1)	**Energy of *B*** (E_2)
0	E	0
$T/4$	0	E
$2T/4$	0	E
$3T/4$	E	0
$4T/4$	E	0
$5T/4$	0	E
$6T/4$	0	E
$7T/4$	E	0
$8T/4$	E	0

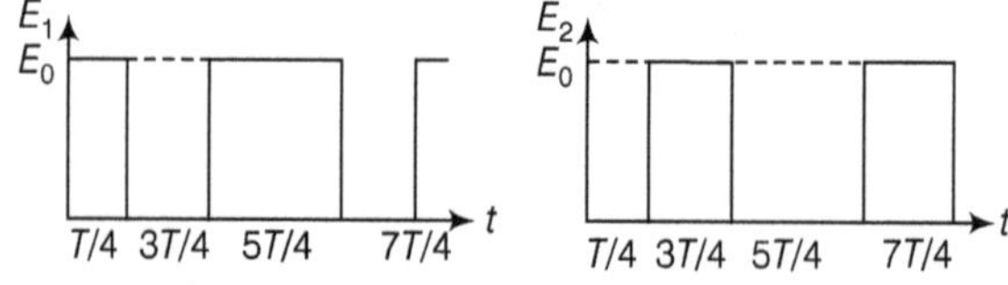

Q. 40 Suppose the average mass of raindrops is 3.0×10^{-5} kg and their average terminal velocity 9 m s^{-1}. Calculate the energy transferred by rain to each square metre of the surface at a place which receives 100cm of rain in a year.

Ans. Given, average mass of rain drop

$$(m) = 3.0 \times 10^{-5} \text{ kg}$$

Average terminal velocity $= (V) = 9$ m/s.

$$\text{Height } (h) = 100\,\text{cm} = 1\,\text{m}$$

$$\text{Density of water } (\rho) = 10^3 \text{ kg/m}^3$$

$$\text{Area of the surface } (A) = 1\,\text{m}^2$$

$$\text{Volume of the water due to rain (V)} = \text{Area} \times \text{height} = A \times h = 1 \times 1 = 1\,\text{m}^3$$

$$\text{Mass of the water due to rain } (M) = \text{Volume} \times \text{density} = V \times \rho = 1 \times 10^3 = 10^3 \text{ kg}$$

$$\therefore \text{ Energy transferred to the surface} = \frac{1}{2} mv^2 = \frac{1}{2} \times 10^3 \times (9)^2 = 40.5 \times 10^3 \text{ J} = 4.05 \times 10^4 \text{ J}$$

Q. 41 An engine is attached to a wagon through a shock absorber of length 1.5 m. The system with a total mass of 50,000 kg is moving with a speed of 36 kmh^{-1} when the brakes are applied to bring it to rest. In the process of the system being brought to rest, the spring of the shock absorber gets compressed by 1.0 m. If 90% of energy of the wagon is lost due to friction, calculate the spring constant.

Ans. Given, mass of the system $(m) = 50{,}000$ kg

$$\text{Speed of the system } (v) = 36\,\text{km/h} = \frac{36 \times 1000}{60 \times 60} = 10\,\text{m/s}$$

Compression of the spring $(x) = 1.0$ m

$$\text{KE of the system} = \frac{1}{2} mv^2 = \frac{1}{2} \times 50000 \times (10)^2 = 25000 \times 100 \text{ J} = 2.5 \times 10^6 \text{ J}$$

Since, 90% of KE of the system is lost due to friction, therefore, energy transferred to shock absorber, is given by

$$\Delta E = \frac{1}{2} kx^2 = 10\% \text{ of total KE of the system}$$

$$= \frac{10}{100} \times 2.5 \times 10^6 \text{ J} \quad \text{or} \quad k = \frac{2 \times 2.5 \times 10^6}{10 \times (1)^2}$$

$$= 5.0 \times 10^5 \text{ N/m}$$

Q. 42 **An adult weighting 600 N raises the centre of gravity of his body by 0.25m while taking each step of 1 m length in jogging. If he jogs for 6 km, calculate the energy utilised by him in jogging assuming that there is no energy loss due to friction of ground and air. Assuming that the body of the adult is capable of converting 10% of energy intake in the form of food, calculate the energy equivalents of food that would be required to compensate energy utilised for jogging.**

Thinking Process

Here, shift in centre of gravity of his body is equal to the height of each step.

Ans. Given, weight of the adult $(w) = mg = 600$ N

Height of each step $= h = 0.25$ m

Length of each step = 1 m

Total distance travelled = 6 km = 6000 m

$\therefore$ Total number of steps $= \frac{6000}{1} = 6000$

Total energy utilised in jogging $= n \times mgh$

$= 6000 \times 600 \times 0.25 \text{ J} = 9 \times 10^5 \text{ J}$

Since, 10% of intake energy is utilised in jogging.

$\therefore$ Total intake energy $= 10 \times 9 \times 10^5 \text{ J} = 9 \times 10^6$ J.

Q. 43 **On complete combustion a litre of petrol gives off heat equivalent to 3×10^7 J. In a test drive, a car weighing 1200 kg including the mass of driver, runs 15 km per litre while moving with a uniform speed on a straight track. Assuming that friction offered by the road surface and air to be uniform, calculate the force of friction acting on the car during the test drive, if the efficiency of the car engine were 0.5.**

Ans. Energy is given by the petrol in the form of heat of combustion.

Thus, by question,

Energy given by 1 litre of petrol $= 3 \times 10^7$ J

Efficiency of the car engine = 0.5

$\therefore$ Energy used by the car $= 0.5 \times 3 \times 10^7$ J

$E = 1.5 \times 10^7$ J

Total distance travelled $(s) = 15 \text{ km} = 15 \times 10^3$ m

If f is the force of friction then,

$E = f \times s$ ($\because$ Energy is utilised in working against friction)

$1.5 \times 10^7 = f \times 15 \times 10^3$

$\Rightarrow f = \frac{1.5 \times 10^7}{15 \times 10^3} = 10^3$ N

$f = 1000$ N

Long Answer Type Questions

Q. 44 A block of mass 1 kg is pushed up a surface inclined to horizontal at an angle of 30° by a force of 10 N parallel to the inclined surface (figure). The coefficient of friction between block and the incline is 0.1. If the block is pushed up by 10 m along the incline, calculate

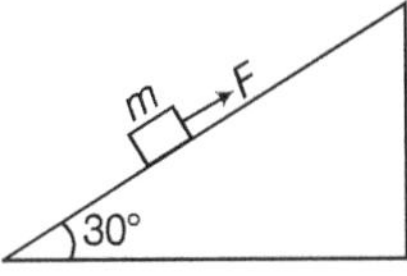

(a) work done against gravity

(b) work done against force of friction

(c) increases in potential energy

(d) increase in kinetic energy

(e) work done by applied force

Ans. Consider the adjacent diagram the block is pushed up by applying a force F.

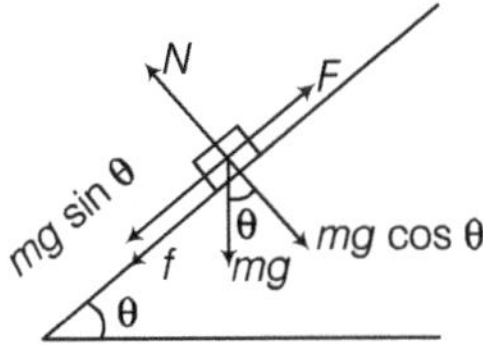

Normal reaction (N) and frictional force (f) is shown.

Given, mass $= m = 1$ kg, $\theta = 30°$

$F = 10$ N, $\mu = 0.1$ and s = distance moved by the block along the inclined plane = 10 m

(a) Work done against gravity = Increase in PE of the block

$$= mg \times \text{Vertical distance travelled}$$
$$= mg \times s\,(\sin\theta) = (mgs)\sin\theta$$
$$= 1 \times 10 \times 10 \times \sin 30° = 50 \text{ J} \qquad (\because g \leq 10 \text{ m/s}^2)$$

(b) Work done against friction

$$wf = f \times s = \mu N \times s = \mu\, mg\cos\theta \times s$$
$$= 0.1 \times 1 \times 10 \times \cos 30° \times 10$$
$$= 10 \times 0.866 = 8.66 \text{ J}$$

(c) Increase in PE $= mgh = mg\,(s\sin\theta)$

$$= 1 \times 10 \times 10 \times \sin 30°$$
$$= 100 \times \frac{1}{2} = 50 \text{ J}$$

(d) By work-energy theorem, we know that work done by all the forces = change in KE

$$(W) = \Delta K$$
$$\Delta k = W_g + W_f + W_f$$
$$\Rightarrow \quad = -mgh - fs + FS$$
$$= -50 - 8.66 + 10 \times 10$$
$$= 50 - 8.66 = 41.34 \text{ J}$$

(e) Work done by applied force, $F = FS$

$$= (10)(10) = 100 \text{ J}$$

Q. 45 A curved surface is shown in figure. The portion *BCD* is free of friction. There are three spherical balls of identical radii and masses. Balls are released from rest one by one from *A* which is at a slightly greater height than *C*.

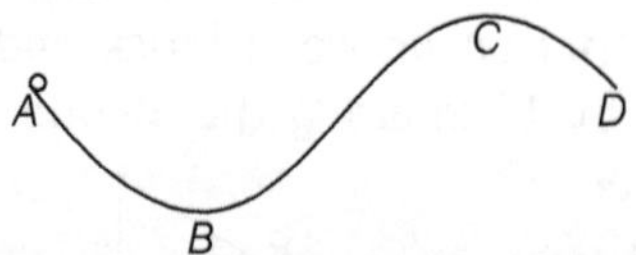

With the surface *AB*, ball 1 has large enough friction to cause rolling down without slipping; ball 2 has a small friction and ball 3 has a negligible friction.

(a) For which balls is total mechanical energy conserved?

(b) Which ball (s) can reach *D*?

(c) For balls which do not reach *D*, which of the balls can reach back *A*?

Ans. (a) As ball 1 is rolling down without slipping there is no dissipation of energy hence, total mechanical energy is conserved.

Ball 3 is having negligible friction hence, there is no loss of energy.

(b) Ball 1 acquires rotational energy, ball 2 loses energy by friction. They cannot cross at *C*. Ball 3 can cross over.

(c) Ball 1, 2 turn back before reaching *C*. Because of loss of energy, ball 2 cannot reach back to *A*. Ball 1 has a rotational motion in "wrong" sense when it reaches *B*. It cannot roll back to *A*, because of kinetic friction.

Q. 46 *A* rocket accelerates straight up by ejecting gas downwards. In a small time interval Δt, it ejects a gas of mass Δm at a relative speed u. Calculate KE of the entire system at $t + \Delta t$ and t and show that the device that ejects gas does work $= (1/2)\,\Delta m u^2$ in this time interval (negative gravity).

Thinking Process

As the gas is ejected, the rocket gets propelled in forward direction due to upward thrust.

Ans. Let M be the mass of rocket at any time t and v_1 the velocity of rocket at the same time t.

Let Δm = mass of gas ejected in time interval Δt.

Relative speed of gas ejected $= u$.

Consider at time $t + \Delta t$

$$(\text{KE})_t + \Delta t = \text{KE of rocket} + \text{KE of gas}$$

$$= \frac{1}{2}(M - \Delta m)(v + \Delta v)^2 + \frac{1}{2}\Delta m (v - u)^2$$

$$= \frac{1}{2}Mv^2 + Mv\Delta v - \Delta m v u + \frac{1}{2}\Delta m u^2$$

$$(\text{KE})_t = \text{KE of the rocket at time } t = \frac{1}{2}Mv^2$$

$$\Delta K = (\text{KE})_t + \Delta t - (\text{KE})_t$$

$$= (M\Delta v - \Delta m u)\,v + \frac{1}{2}\Delta m u^2$$

Since, action-reaction forces are equal.

Hence, $$M\frac{dv}{dt} = \frac{dm}{dt}|u|$$

$\Rightarrow$ $$M\Delta v = \Delta m u$$

$$\Delta K = \frac{1}{2}\Delta m u^2$$

Now, by work-energy theorem,

$$\Delta K = \Delta W$$

$\Rightarrow$ $$\Delta W = \frac{1}{2}\Delta m u^2$$

Q. 47 Two identical steel cubes (masses 50g, side 1 cm) collide head-on face to face with a space of 10 cm/s each. Find the maximum compression of each. Young's modulus for steel = $Y = 2 \times 10^{11}$ N/m^2.

Ans. Let $$m = 50g = 50 \times 10^{-3} \text{ kg}$$

$$\text{Side} = L = 1 \text{ cm} = 0.01 \text{ m}$$

$$\text{Speed} = v = 10 \text{ cm/s} = 0.1 \text{ m/s}$$

$$\text{Young's modulus} = Y = 2 \times 10^{11} \text{ N/m}^2$$

$$\text{Maximum compression } \Delta L = ?$$

In this case, all KE will be converted to PE

By Hooke's law , $$\frac{F}{A} = Y\frac{\Delta L}{L}$$

where A is the surface area and L is length of the side of the cube. If k is spring or compression constant, then

$$\text{force } F = k\,\Delta L$$

$\therefore$ $$k = Y\frac{A}{L} = YL$$

$$\text{Initial KE} = 2 \times \frac{1}{2}mv^2 = 5 \times 10^{-4} \text{ J}$$

$$\text{Final PE} = 2 \times \frac{1}{2}k(\Delta L)^2$$

$\therefore$ $$\Delta L = \sqrt{\frac{KE}{k}} = \sqrt{\frac{KE}{YL}} = \sqrt{\frac{5 \times 10^{-4}}{2 \times 10^{11} \times 0.1}} = 1.58 \times 10^{-7} \text{ m} \qquad [\because PE = KE]$$

Q. 48 A balloon filled with helium rises against gravity increasing its potential energy. The speed of the baloon also increases as it rises. How do you reconcile this with the law of conservation of mechanical energy? You can neglect viscous drag of air and assume that density of air is constant.

Thinking Process

In this problem, as viscous drag of air is neglected, hence there is no dissipation of energy.

Ans. Let m = Mass of balloon

$$V = \text{Volume of balloon}$$

$$\rho_{He} = \text{Density of helium}$$

$$\rho_{air} = \text{Density of air}$$

Volume V of balloon displaces volume V of air.

So, $$V(\rho_{air} - \rho_{He})g = ma = m\frac{dv}{dt} = \text{up thrust} \qquad \text{...(i)}$$

Integrating with respect to t,

$$V(\rho_{air} - \rho_{He})gt = mv \quad \text{...(ii)}$$

$$\Rightarrow \quad \frac{1}{2}mv^2 = \frac{1}{2}m\frac{V^2}{m^2}(\rho_{air} - \rho_{He})^2 g^2 t^2$$

$$= \frac{1}{2m}V^2(\rho_{air} - \rho_{He})^2 g^2 t^2$$

If the balloon rises to a height h, from $s = ut + \frac{1}{2}at^2$,

$$\text{We get } h = \frac{1}{2}at^2 = \frac{1}{2}\frac{V(\rho_{air} - \rho_{He})}{m}gt^2 \quad \text{...(iii)}$$

From Eqs. (iii) and (ii),

$$\frac{1}{2}mv^2 = [V(\rho_a - \rho_{He})g]\left[\frac{1}{2m}V(\rho_{air} - \rho_{He})gt^2\right]$$

$$= V(\rho_a - \rho_{He})gh$$

Rearranging the terms,

$$\Rightarrow \quad \frac{1}{2}mv^2 + V\rho_{He}gh = V_{\rho_{air}}hg$$

$$\Rightarrow \quad \text{KE}_{balloon} + \text{PE}_{balloon} = \text{Change in PE of air.}$$

So, as the balloon goes up, an equal volume of air comes down, increase in **PE** and **KE** of the balloon is at the cost of **PE** of air [which comes down].

6

System *of* Particles and Rotational Motion

Multiple Choice Questions (MCQs)

Q. 1 For which of the following does the centre of mass lie outside the body?

(a) A pencil (b) A shotput (c) A dice (d) A bangle

Ans. *(d)* A bangle is in the form of a ring as shown in the adjacent diagram. The centre of mass lies at the centre, which is outside the body (boundary).

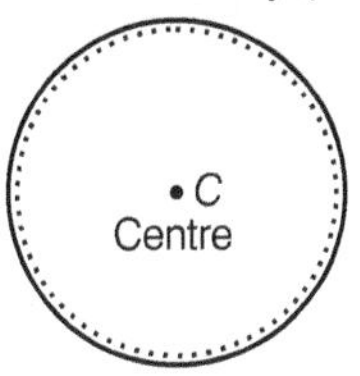

Q. 2 Which of the following points is the likely position of the centre of mass of the system shown in figure?

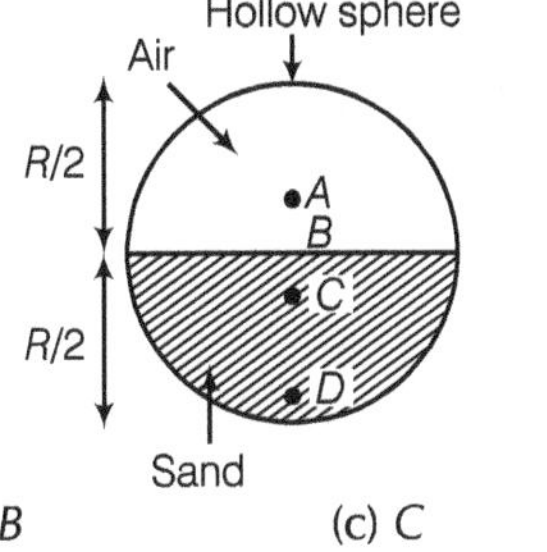

(a) A (b) B (c) C (d) D

Thinking Process

In a system of particles, the centre of mass of a body lies closer to heavier mass or masses.

Ans. *(c)* Centre of mass of a system lies towards the part of the system, having bigger mass. In the above diagram, lower part is heavier, hence CM of the system lies below the horizontal diameter.

Q. 3 **A particle of mass m is moving in yz-plane with a uniform velocity v with its trajectory running parallel to +ve y-axis and intersecting z-axis at $z = a$ in figure. The change in its angular momentum about the origin as it bounces elastically from a wall at y = constant is**

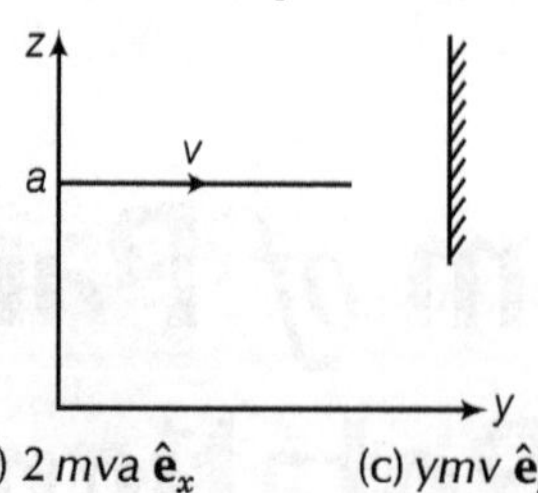

(a) $mva\,\hat{\mathbf{e}}_x$ (b) $2\,mva\,\hat{\mathbf{e}}_x$ (c) $ymv\,\hat{\mathbf{e}}_x$ (d) $2\,ymv\,\hat{\mathbf{e}}_x$

Thinking Process

In elastic collision, KE of the system remains conserved. Therefore, the ball will bounce back with the same speed v but in opposite direction i.e., along -ve y -axis.

Ans. *(b)* The initial velocity is $\mathbf{v}_i = \mathbf{v}\,\hat{\mathbf{e}}_y$ and after reflection from the wall, the final velocity is $\mathbf{v}_f = -\,v\hat{\mathbf{e}}_y$. The trajectory is described as position vector $\mathbf{r} = y\hat{\mathbf{e}}_y + a\hat{\mathbf{e}}_z$.

Hence, the change in angular momentum is $\mathbf{r} \times m(\mathbf{v}_f - \mathbf{v}_i) = 2mva\hat{\mathbf{e}}_x$.

Q. 4 **When a disc rotates with uniform angular velocity, which of the following is not true?**

(a) The sense of rotation remains same
(b) The orientation of the axis of rotation remains same
(c) The speed of rotation is non-zero and remains same
(d) The angular acceleration is non-zero and remains same

Ans. *(d)* We know that angular acceleration

$$\alpha = \frac{d\omega}{dt}, \text{ given } \omega = \text{constant}$$

where ω is angular velocity of the disc

$$\Rightarrow \qquad \alpha = \frac{d\omega}{dt} = \frac{0}{dt} = 0$$

Hence, angular acceleration is zero.

Q. 5 **A uniform square plate has a small piece Q of an irregular shape removed and glued to the centre of the plate leaving a hole behind in figure. The moment of inertia about the z-axis is then,**

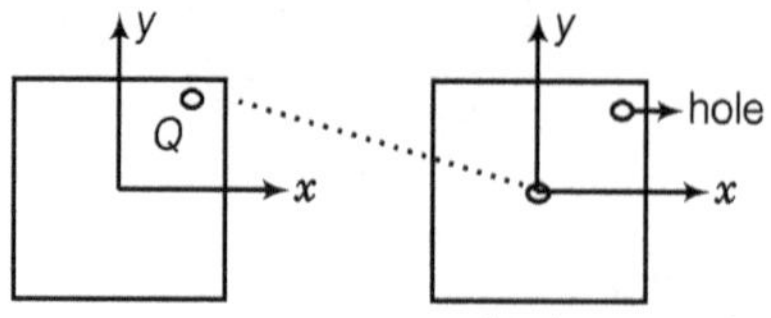

(a) increased (b) decreased
(c) the same (d) changed in unpredicted manner

Thinking Process

For two bodies having same mass, the body having mass distributed at greater distance from an axis, will have more moment of inertia.

Ans. *(b)* In the given diagrams, when the small piece *Q* removed and glued to the centre of the plate, the mass comes closer to the *z*-axis, hence, moment of inertia decreases.

Q. 6 **In problem 5, the CM of the plate is now in the following quadrant of *x*-*y* plane.**

(a) I (b) II (c) III (d) IV

Ans. *(c)* Consider the adjacent diagram, there is a line shown in the figure drawn along the diagonal. First, centre of mass of the system was on the dotted line and was shifted towards *Q* from the centre (Ist quadrant).

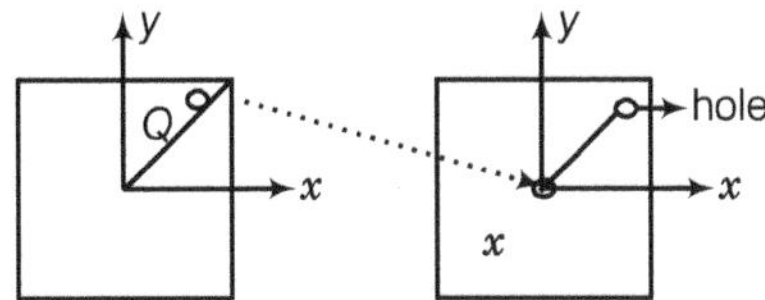

When mass is removed, it will be on the same line but shifted away from the centre and below (IIIrd quadrant). Position of CM is shown by *X* in the diagram.

Q. 7 **The density of a non-uniform rod of length 1m is given by $\rho(x) = a(1 + bx^2)$ where, *a* and *b* are constants and $0 \le x \le 1$. The centre of mass of the rod will be at**

(a) $\frac{3(2+b)}{4(3+b)}$ (b) $\frac{4(2+b)}{3(3+b)}$ (c) $\frac{3(3+b)}{4(2+b)}$ (d) $\frac{4(3+b)}{3(2+b)}$

Ans. *(a)* Density is given as $\rho(x) = a(1 + bx^2)$

where *a* and *b* are constants and $0 \le x \le 1$.

Let $b \to 0$, in this case

$$\rho(x) = a = \text{constant}$$

Hence, centre of mass will be at $x = 0.5$ m. (middle of the rod)

Putting, $b = 0$ in all the options, only (a) gives 0.5.

Note *We should not check options by putting $a = 0$, because $\rho = 0$ for $a = 0$.*

Q. 8 **A merry-go-round, made of a ring-like platform of radius *R* and mass *M*, is revolving with angular speed ω. A person of mass *M* is standing on it. At one instant, the person jumps off the round, radially away from the centre of the round (as seen from the round). The speed of the round of afterwards is**

(a) 2 ω (b) ω (c) $\frac{\omega}{2}$ (d) 0

Ans. *(a)* As no external torque acts on the system, angular momentum should be conserved.

Hence $I\omega = \text{constant}$ ...(i)

where, *I* is moment of inertia of the system and ω is angular velocity of the system.

From Eq. (i) $I_1\omega_1 = I_2\omega_2$

(where ω_1 and ω_2 are angular velocities before and after jumping)

$$\Rightarrow \quad I\omega = \frac{I}{2} \times \omega_2$$

(as mass reduced to half, hence, moment of inertia also reduced to half)

$$\Rightarrow \quad \omega_2 = 2\omega$$

Multiple Choice Questions (More Than One Options)

Q. 9 Choose the correct alternatives

(a) For a general rotational motion, angular momentum **L** and angular velocity ω need not be parallel.

(b) For a rotational motion about a fixed axis, angular momentum **L** and angular velocity ω are always parallel.

(c) For a general translational motion, momentum **p** and velocity **v** are always parallel.

(d) For a general translational motion, acceleration **a** and velocity **v** are always parallel.

Ans. *(a, c)*

For a general rotational motion ,where axis of rotation is not symmetric. Angular momentum **L** and angular velocity ω need not be parallel. For a general translational motion momentum $\mathbf{p} = m\mathbf{v}$, hence, **p** and **v** are always parallel.

Q. 10 Figure shows two identical particles 1 and 2, each of mass m, moving in opposite directions with same speed **v** along parallel lines. At a particular instant $\mathbf{r}_1$ and $\mathbf{r}_2$ are their respective position vectors drawn from point A which is in the plane of the parallel lines. Choose the correct options.

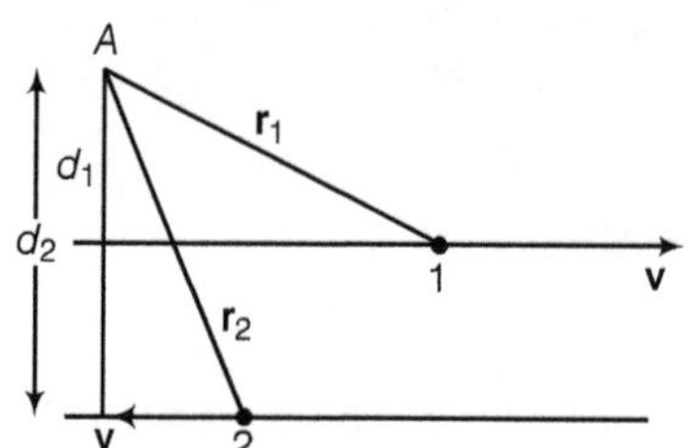

(a) Angular momentum I_1 of particle 1 about A is $I = mv(d_1) \odot$

(b) Angular momentum I_2 of particle 2 about A is $I_2 = mv\mathbf{r}_2 \odot$

(c) Total angular momentum of the system about A is $I = mv(\mathbf{r}_1 + \mathbf{r}_2) \odot$

(d) Total angular momentum of the system about A is $I = mv(d_2 - d_1) \otimes$

$\odot$ represents a unit vector coming out of the page.
$\otimes$ represents a unit vector going into the page.

Ans. *(a, b)*

The angular momentum **L** of a particle with respect to origin is defined to be $\mathbf{L} = \mathbf{r} \times \mathbf{p}$ where, **r** is the position vector of the particle and **p** is the linear momentum. The direction of **L** is perpendicular to both d **r** and **p** by right hand rule.

For particle 1, $I_1 = \mathbf{r}_1 \times m\mathbf{v}$, is out of plane of the paper and perpendicular to $\mathbf{r}_1$ and $\mathbf{p}(m\,\mathbf{v})$ Similarly $I_2 = \mathbf{r}_2 \times m(-\mathbf{v})$ is into the plane of the paper and perpendicular to $\mathbf{r}_2$ and $-\mathbf{p}$.

Hence, total angular momentum

$$l = l_1 + l_2 = \mathbf{r}_1 \times m\,\mathbf{v} + (-\mathbf{r}_2 \times m\,\mathbf{v})$$

$|l| = mv\,d_1 - mvd_2$ as $d_2 > d_1$, total angular momentum will be inward

Hence, $$I = m\,\mathbf{v}\,(d_2 - d_1) \otimes$$

Note *In the expression of angular momentum $I = \mathbf{r} \times \mathbf{p}$ the direction of l is taken by right hand rule.*

Q. 11 **The net external torque on a system of particles about an axis is zero. Which of the following are compatible with it?**

(a) The forces may be acting radially from a point on the axis

(b) The forces may be acting on the axis of rotation

(c) The forces may be acting parallel to the axis of rotation

(d) The torque caused by some forces may be equal and opposite to that caused by other forces

Ans. *(a, b, c, d)*

We know that torque on a system of particles $\tau = \mathbf{r} \times \mathbf{F} = F \sin\theta \hat{\mathbf{n}}$ ...(i)

where, θ is angle between **r** and **F**, and $\hat{\mathbf{n}}$ is a unit vector perpendicular to both **r** and **F**.

(a) When forces act radially, $\theta = 0$ hence $|\tau| = 0$ [from Eq. (i)]

(b) When forces are acting on the axis of rotation, $\mathbf{r} = 0, |\tau| = 0$ [from Eq. (i)]

(c) When forces acting parallel to the axis of rotation $\theta = 0°, |\tau| = 0$ [from Eq. (i)]

(d) When torque by forces are equal and opposite, $\tau_{net} = \tau_1 - \tau_2 = 0$

Q. 12 **Figure shows a lamina in *xy*-plane. Two axes *z* and *z′* pass perpendicular to its plane. A force F acts in the plane of lamina at point *P* as shown. Which of the following are true? (The point *P* is closer to *z′*-axis than the *z*-axis.)**

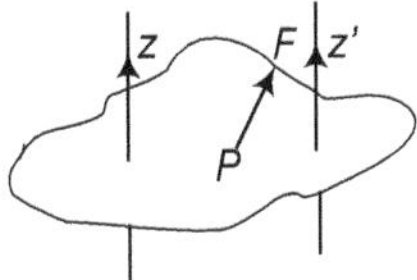

(a) Torque τ caused by **F** about z -axis is along $-\hat{\mathbf{k}}$

(b) Torque τ' caused by **F** about z′-axis is along $-\hat{\mathbf{k}}$

(c) Torque τ caused by **F** about z-axis is greater in magnitude than that about z-axis

(d) Total torque is given be $\tau = \tau + \tau'$

Thinking Process

Torque of a force **F** *about an axis is* $\mathbf{r} \times \mathbf{F}$ *which is perpendicular to the plane containing* **r** *and* **F**.

Ans. *(b, c)*

(a) Consider the adjacent diagram, where $r > r'$

Torque τ about z-axis $\tau = \mathbf{r} \times \mathbf{F}$ which is along $\hat{\mathbf{k}}$

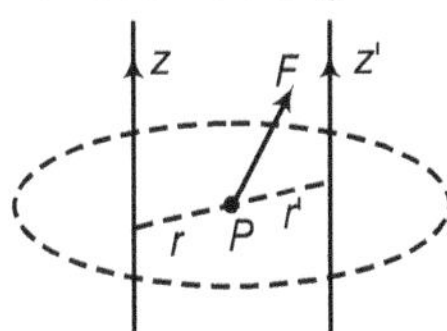

(b) $\tau' = \mathbf{r}' \times \mathbf{F}$ which is along $-\hat{\mathbf{k}}$

(c) $|\tau|_z = Fr_\perp$ = magnitude of torque about z-axis where $r_\perp$ is perpendicular distance between F and z-axis.

Similarly, $|\tau|_{z'} = F r_\perp'$

Clearly $r_\perp > r_\perp' \Rightarrow |\tau|_z > |\tau|_{z'}$

(d) We are always calculating resultant torque about a common axis.

Hence, total torque $\tau \neq \tau + \tau'$, because τ and τ' are not about common axis.

Q. 13 **With reference to figure of a cube of edge *a* and mass *m*, state whether the following are true or false. (O is the centre of the cube.)**

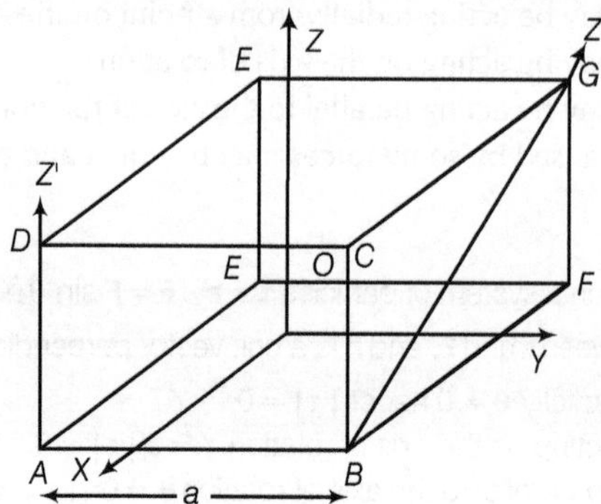

(a) The moment of inertia of cube about z-axis is $I_z = I_x + I_y$

(b) The moment of inertia of cube about z′-axis is $I_z = I_z + \frac{ma^2}{2}$

(c) The moment of inertia of cube about z″-axis is $= I_z + \frac{ma^2}{2}$

(d) $I_x = I_y$

Thinking Process

Moment of inertia about two symmetrical axes are same. To calculate net moment of inertia we can apply the concept of symmetry.

Ans. *(a, b, d)*

(a) Theorem of perpendicular axes is applicable only for laminar (plane) objects. Thus, option (a) is false.

(b) As z′ || z and distance between them $= a\frac{\sqrt{2}}{2} = \frac{a}{\sqrt{2}}$

Now, by theorem of parallel axes

$$I_{z'} = I_z + m\left(\frac{a}{\sqrt{2}}\right)^2 = I_z + \frac{ma^2}{2}$$

Hence, choice (b) is true.

(c) z″ is not parallel to z hence, theorem of parallel axis cannot be applied. Thus, option (c) is false.

(d) As x and y-axes are symmetrical.

Hence, $I_x = I_y$

Thus, option (d) is true.

Very Short Answer Type Questions

Q. 14 The centre of gravity of a body on the earth coincides with its centre of mass for a small object whereas for an extended object it may not. What is the qualitative meaning of small and extended in this regard?
For which of the following two coincides? A building, a pond, a lake, a mountain?

Thinking Process

Centre of gravity is centre of a given structure but centre of mass is a point where whole mass of the body can be assumed to be concentrated.

Ans. When the vertical height of the object is very small as compared to the earth's radius, we call the object small, otherwise it is extended.

(i) Building and pond are small objects.

(ii) A deep lake and a mountain are examples of extended objects.

Q. 15 Why does a solid sphere have smaller moment of inertia than a hollow cylinder of same mass and radius, about an axis passing through their axes of symmetry?

Ans. The moment of inertia of a body is given by $I = \Sigma m_i r_i^2$ [sum of moment of inertia of each constituent particles]

All the mass in a cylinder lies at distance R from the axis of symmetry but most of the mass of a solid sphere lies at a smaller distance than R.

Q. 16 The variation of angular position θ, of a point on a rotating rigid body, with time t is shown in figure. Is the body rotating clockwise or anti-clockwise?

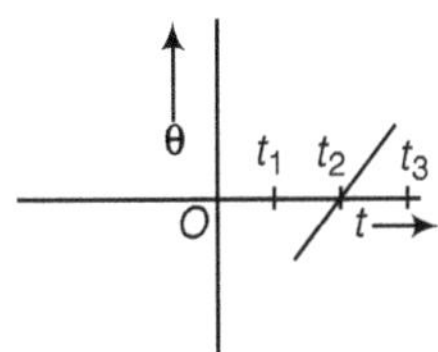

Ans. As the slope of θ-t graph is positive and positive slope indicates anti-clockwise rotation which is traditionally taken as positive.

Q. 17 A uniform cube of mass m and side a is placed on a frictionless horizontal surface. A vertical force F is applied to the edge as shown in figure. Match the following (most appropriate choice)

(a)	$mg/4 < F < mg/2$	(i)	Cube will move up.
(b)	$F > mg/2$	(ii)	Cube will not exhibit motion.
(c)	$F > mg$	(iii)	Cube will begin to rotate and slip at A.
(d)	$F = mg/4$	(iv)	Normal reaction effectively at $a/3$ from A, no motion.

Ans. Consider the below diagram

Moment of the force F about point A, $\tau_1 = F \times a$ (anti-clockwise)

Moment of weight mg of the cube about point A,

$$\tau_2 = mg \times \frac{a}{2} \text{ (clockwise)}$$

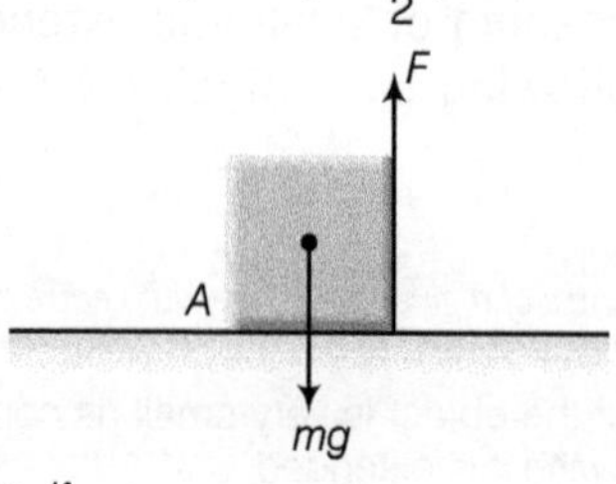

Cube will not exhibit motion, if $\tau_1 = \tau_2$

($\because$ In this case, both the torque will cancel the effect of each other)

$\therefore$ $$F \times a = mg \times \frac{a}{2} \Rightarrow F = \frac{mg}{2}$$

Cube will rotate only when, $\tau_1 > \tau_2$

$\Rightarrow$ $$F \times a > mg \times \frac{a}{2} \Rightarrow F > \frac{mg}{2}$$

Let normal reaction is acting at $\frac{a}{3}$ from point A, then

$$mg \times \frac{a}{3} = F \times a \text{ or } F = \frac{mg}{3}$$ (For no motion)

When $F = \frac{mg}{4}$ which is less than $\frac{mg}{3}$,. $\left(F < \frac{mg}{3}\right)$

there will be no motion.

$\therefore$ (a) → (ii) (b) → (iii) (c) → (i) (d) → (iv)

Q. 18 A uniform sphere of mass m and radius R is placed on a rough horizontal surface (figure). The sphere is struck horizontally at a height h from the floor. Match the following

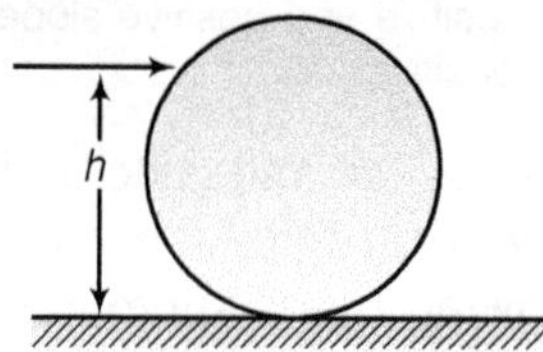

(a)	$h = R/2$	(i)	Sphere rolls without slipping with a constant velocity and no loss of energy.
(b)	$h = R$	(ii)	Sphere spins clockwise, loses energy by friction.
(c)	$h = 3R/2$	(iii)	Sphere spins anti-clockwise, loses energy by friction.
(d)	$h = 7R/5$	(iv)	Sphere has only a translational motion, looses energy by friction.

Ans. Consider the diagram where a sphere of m and radius R, struck horizontally at height h above the floor

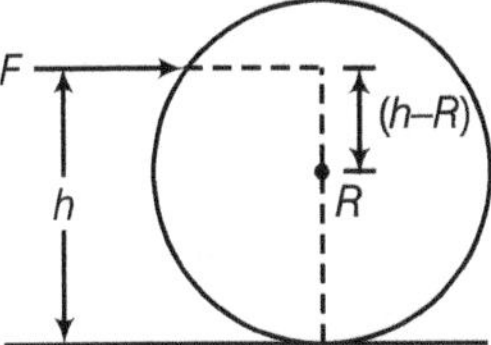

The sphere will roll without slipping when $\omega = \frac{v}{r}$, where, v is linear velocity and ω is angular velocity of the sphere.

Now, angular momentum of sphere, about centre of mass

[We are applying conservation of angular momentum just before and after struck]

$$mv(h-R) = I\omega = \left(\frac{2}{5}mR^2\right)\left(\frac{v}{R}\right)$$

$$\Rightarrow \quad mv(h-R) = \frac{2}{5}mvR$$

$$h - R = \frac{2}{5}R \Rightarrow h = \frac{7}{5}R$$

Therefore, the sphere will roll without slipping with a constant velocity and hence, no loss of energy, so (d) →(i)

Torque due to applied force, F about centre of mass

$$\tau = F(h-R) \quad \text{(clockwise)}$$

For $\tau = 0$, $h = R$, sphere will have only translational motion. It would lose energy by friction.

Hence, (b) → (iv)

The sphere will spin clockwise when $\tau > 0 \Rightarrow h > R$

Therefore, (c) → (ii)

The sphere will spin anti-clockwise when $\tau < 0 \Rightarrow h < R$, (a) → (iii)

Short Answer Type Questions

Q. 19 The vector sum of a system of non-collinear forces acting on a rigid body is given to be non-zero. If the vector sum of all the torques due to the system of forces about a certain point is found to be zero, does this mean that it is necessarily zero about any arbitrary point?

Ans. *No*, not necessarily.

Given, $\sum_i F_i \neq 0$

The sum of torques about a certain point O, $\sum_i \mathbf{r}_i \times \mathbf{F}_i = 0$

The sum of torques about any other point O'

$$\sum_i (\mathbf{r}_i - \mathbf{a}) \times \mathbf{F}_i = \sum_i \mathbf{r}_i \times \mathbf{F}_i - \mathbf{a} \times \sum_i \mathbf{F}_i$$

Here, the second term need not vanish.

Therefore, sum of all the torques about any arbitrary point need not be zero necessarily.

Q. 20 **A wheel in uniform motion about an axis passing through its centre and perpendicular to its plane is considered to be in mechanical (translational plus rotational) equilibrium because no net external force or torque is required to sustain its motion. However, the particles that constitute the wheel do experience a centripetal the acceleration directed towards the centre. How do you reconcile this fact with the wheel being in equilibrium?**

How would you set a half wheel into uniform motion about an axis passing through the centre of mass of the wheel and perpendicular to its plane? Will you require external forces to sustain the motion?

Ans. Wheel is a rigid body. The particles that constitute the wheel do experience a centripetal acceleration directed towards the centre. This acceleration arises due to internal elastic forces, which cancel out in pairs.

In a half wheel, the distribution of mass about its centre of mass (through which axis of rotation passes) is not symmetrical. Therefore, the direction of angular momentum of the wheel does not coincide with the direction of its angular velocity. Hence, an external torque is required to maintain the motion of the half wheel.

Q. 21 **A door is hinged at one end and is free to rotate about a vertical axis (figure). Does its weight cause any torque about this axis? Give reason for your answer.**

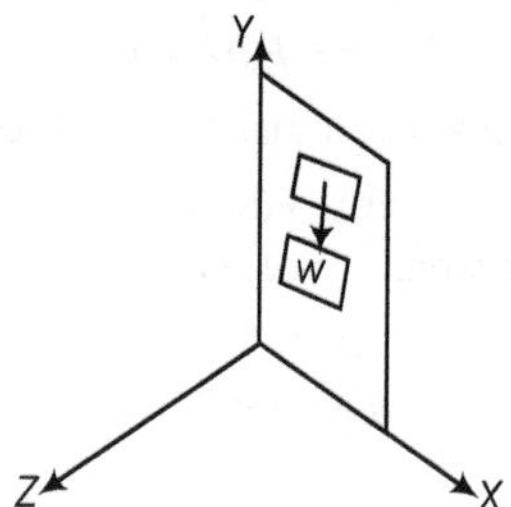

Ans. Consider the diagram, where weight of the door acts along negative y-axis.

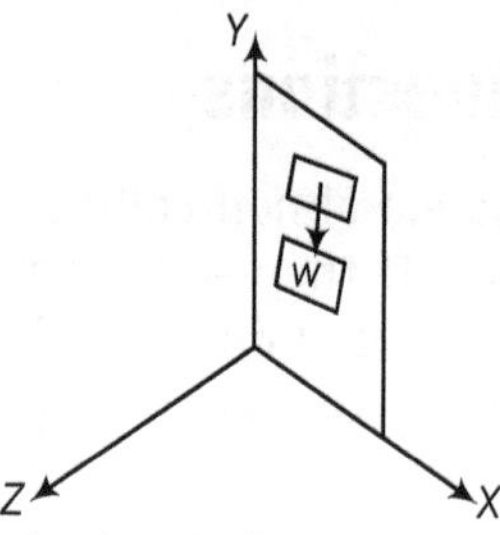

A force can produce torque only along a direction normal to itself as $\tau = \mathbf{r} \times \mathbf{F}$. So, when the door is in the xy-plane, the torque produced by gravity can only be along $\pm z$ direction, never about an axis passing through y-direction.

Hence, the weight will not produce any torque about y-axis.

Q. 22 $(n-1)$ equal point masses each of mass m are placed at the vertices of a regular n-polygon. The vacant vertex has a position vector **a** with respect to the centre of the polygon. Find the position vector of centre of mass.

Thinking Process

The centre of mass of a regular n-polygon lies at its geometrical centre.

Ans. Let **b** be the position vector of the centre of mass of a regular n-polygon.

$(n-1)$ equal point masses are placed at $(n-1)$ vertices of the regular n-polygon, therefore, for its centre of mass

$$r_{CM} = \frac{(n-1)\,mb + ma}{(n-1)\,m + m} = 0 \quad (\because \text{Centre of mass lies at centre})$$

$$\Rightarrow \quad (n-1)\,mb + ma = 0$$

$$\Rightarrow \quad b = -\frac{a}{(n-1)}$$

Long Answer Type Questions

Q. 23 Find the centre of mass of a uniform (a) half-disc, (b) quarter-disc.

Ans. Let M and R be the mass and radius of the half-disc, mass per unit area of the half-disc

$$m = \frac{M}{\frac{1}{2}\pi R^2} = \frac{2M}{\pi R^2}$$

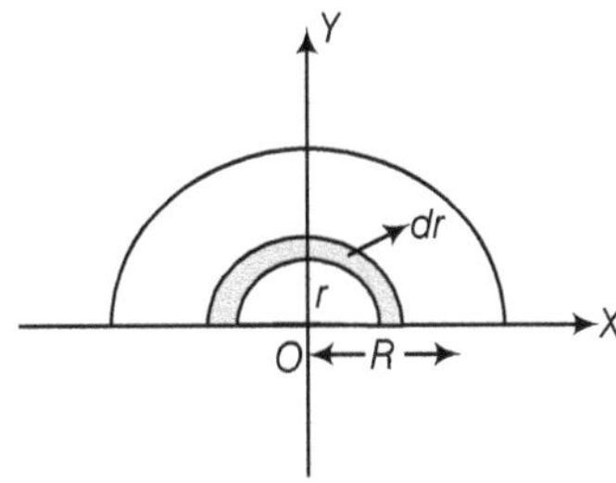

(a) The half-disc can be supposed to be consists of a large number of semicircular rings of mass dm and thickness dr and radii ranging from $r = 0$ to $r = R$.

Surface area of semicircular ring of radius r and of thickness $dr = \frac{1}{2} 2\pi r \times dr = \pi r dr$

$\therefore$ Mass of this elementary ring, $dm = \pi r dr \times \frac{2M}{\pi R^2}$

$$dm = \frac{2M}{R^2} r dr$$

If (x, y) are coordinates of centre of mass of this element,

then, $$(x, y) = \left(0, \frac{2r}{\pi}\right)$$

Therefore, $$x = 0 \text{ and } y = \frac{2r}{\pi}$$

Let x_{CM} and y_{CM} be the coordinates of the centre of mass of the semicircular disc.

Then
$$x_{CM} = \frac{1}{M}\int_0^R x\,dm = \frac{1}{M}\int_0^R 0\,dm = 0$$
$$y_{CM} = \frac{1}{M}\int_0^R y\,dm = \frac{1}{M}\int_0^R \frac{2r}{\pi} \times \left(\frac{2M}{R^2}\,rdr\right)$$
$$= \frac{4}{\pi R^2}\int_0^R r^2 dr = \frac{4}{\pi R^2}\left[\frac{r^3}{3}\right]_0^R$$
$$= \frac{4}{\pi R^2} \times \left(\frac{R^3}{3} - 0\right) = \frac{4R}{3\pi}$$

$\therefore$ Centre of mass of the semicircular disc $= \left(0, \frac{4R}{3\pi}\right)$

(b) Centre of mass of a uniform quarter disc.

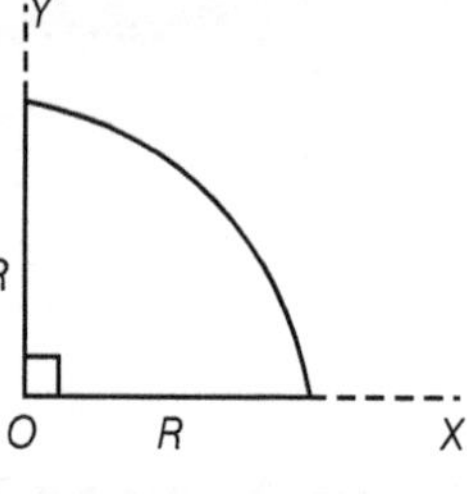

Mass per unit area of the quarter disc $= \dfrac{M}{\dfrac{\pi R^2}{4}} = \dfrac{4M}{\pi R^2}$

Using symmetry

For a half-disc along y-axis centre of mass will be at $x = \dfrac{4R}{3\pi}$

For a half-disc along x-axis centre of mass will be at $x = \dfrac{4R}{3\pi}$

Hence, for the quarter disc centre of mass $= \left(\dfrac{4R}{3\pi}, \dfrac{4R}{3\pi}\right)$

Q. 24 **Two discs of moments of inertia I_1 and I_2 about their respective axes (normal to the disc and passing through the centre), and rotating with angular speed ω_1 and ω_2 are brought into contact face to face with their axes of rotation coincident.**

(a) Does the law of conservation of angular momentum apply to the situation? Why?

(b) Find the angular speed of the two discs system.

(c) Calculate the loss in kinetic energy of the system in the process.

(d) Account for this loss.

Thinking Process

Due to friction between the two discs, the system will acquire common angular speed after sometime.

Ans. Consider the diagram below

Let the common angular velocity of the system is ω.

(a) *Yes*, the law of conservation of angular momentum can be applied. Because, there is no net external torque on the system of the two discs.

External forces, gravitation and normal reaction, act through the axis of rotation, hence, produce no torque.

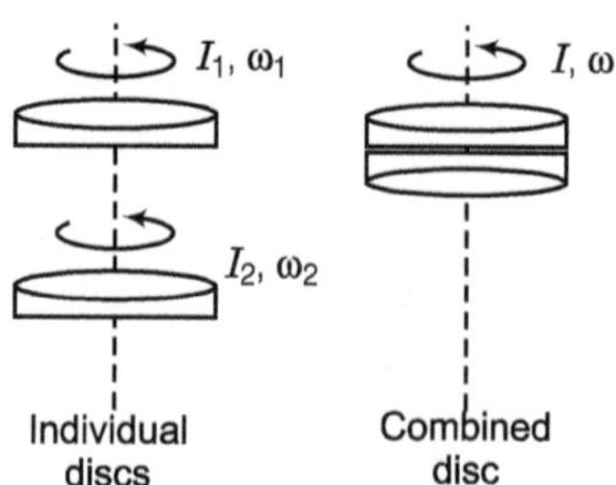

(b) By conservation of angular momentum

$$L_f = L_i$$

$$\Rightarrow \quad I\omega = I_1\omega_1 + I_2\omega_2$$

$$\Rightarrow \quad \omega = \frac{I_1\omega_1 + I_2\omega_2}{I} = \frac{I_1\omega_1 + I_2\omega_2}{I_1 + I_2} \qquad (\because I = I_1 + I_2)$$

(c) $K_f = \frac{1}{2}(I_1 + I_2)\frac{(I_1\omega_1 + I_2\omega_2)^2}{(I_1 + I_2)^2} = \frac{1}{2}\frac{(I_1\omega_1 + I_2\omega_2)^2}{(I_1 + I_2)}$

$K_i = \frac{1}{2}(I_1\omega_1^2 + I_2\omega_2^2)$

$\Delta K = K_f - K_i = -\frac{I_1 I_2}{2(I_1 + I_2)}(\omega_1 - \omega_2)^2 < 0$

(d) Hence, there is loss in KE of the system. The loss in kinetic energy is mainly due to the work against the friction between the two discs.

Q. 25 A disc of radius R is rotating with an angular ω_0 about a horizontal axis. It is placed on a horizontal table. The coefficient of kinetic friction is μ_K.

(a) What was the velocity of its centre of mass before being brought in contact with the table?

(b) What happens to the linear velocity of a point on its rim when placed in contact with the table?

(c) What happens to the linear speed of the centre of mass when disc is placed in contact with the table?

(d) Which force is responsible for the effects in (b) and (c)?

(e) What condition should be satisfied for rolling to begin?

(f) Calculate the time taken for the rolling to begin.

Ans. (a) Before being brought in contact with the table the disc was in pure rotational motion hence, $v_{CM} = 0$.

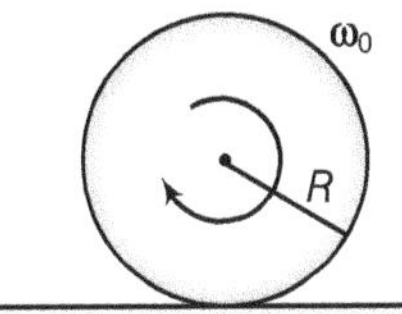

(b) When the disc is placed in contact with the table due to friction velocity of a point on the rim decreases.

(c) When the rotating disc is placed in contact with the table due to friction centre of mass acquires some linear velocity.

(d) Friction is responsible for the effects in (b) and (c) .

(e) When rolling starts $v_{CM} = \omega R$.

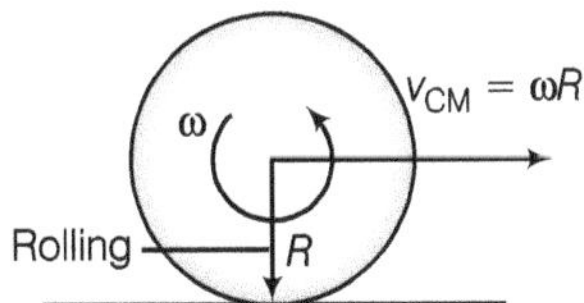

where ω is angular speed of the disc when rolling just starts.

(f) Acceleration produced in centre of mass due to friction

$$a_{CM} = \frac{F}{m} = \frac{\mu_k mg}{m} = \mu_k g.$$

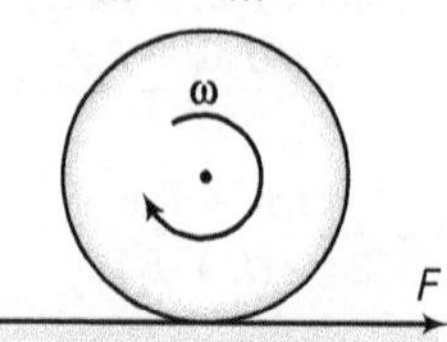

Angular retardation produced by the torque due to friction.

$$\alpha = \frac{\tau}{I} = \frac{\mu_K mgR}{I} \qquad [\because \tau = (\mu_k N)R = \mu_k mgR]$$

$\therefore$ $$v_{CM} = u_{CM} + a_{CM}t$$

$\Rightarrow$ $$v_{CM} = \mu_k gt \qquad (\because u_{CM} = 0)$$

and $$\omega = \omega_0 + \alpha t$$

$\Rightarrow$ $$\omega = \omega_0 - \frac{\mu_k mgR}{I}t$$

For rolling without slipping, $\frac{v_{CM}}{R} = \omega$

$\Rightarrow$ $$\frac{v_{CM}}{R} = \omega_0 - \frac{\mu_k mgR}{I}t$$

$$\frac{\mu_k gt}{R} = \omega_0 - \frac{\mu_k mgR}{I}t$$

$$t = \frac{R\omega_0}{\mu_k g\left(1 + \frac{mR^2}{I}\right)}$$

Note *In this problem, frictional force helps in setting pure rolling motion.*

Q. 26 Two cylindrical hollow drums of radii R and $2R$, and of a common height h, are rotating with angular velocities ω (anti-clockwise) and ω (clockwise), respectively. Their axes, fixed are parallel and in a horizontal plane separated by $3R + \delta$. They are now brought in contact $(\delta \to 0)$

(a) Show the frictional forces just after contact.

(b) Identify forces and torques external to the system just after contact.

(c) What would be the ratio of final angular velocities when friction ceases?

Ans. (a) Consider the situation shown below, we have shown the frictional forces.

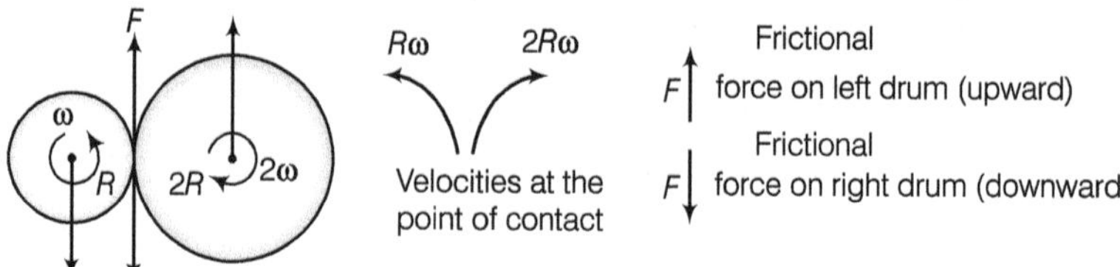

(b) $F' = F = F''$ where F' and F'' are external forces through support.

$\Rightarrow$ $F_{net} = 0$ (one each cylinder)

External torque $= F \times 3R$, (anti-clockwise)

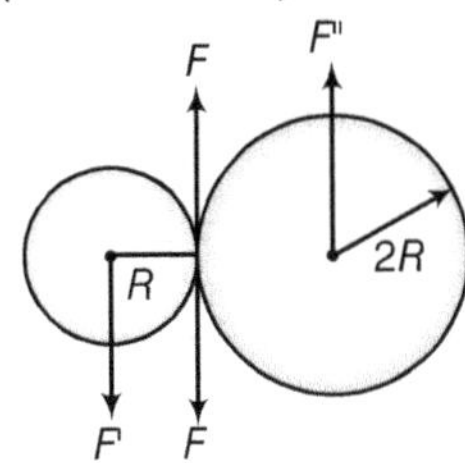

(c) Let ω_1 and ω_2 be final angular velocities of smaller and bigger drum respectively (anti-clockwise and clockwise respectively)

Finally, there will be no friction.

Hence, $R\omega_1 = 2R\omega_2 \Rightarrow \dfrac{\omega_1}{\omega_2} = 2$

Note *We should be very careful while indicating direction of frictional forces.*

Q. 27 **A uniform square plate S (side c) and a uniform rectangular plate R (sides b, a) have identical areas and masses.**

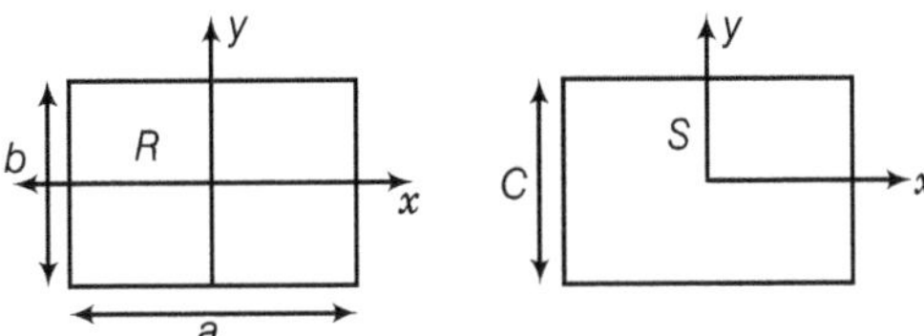

Show that

(a) $I_{xR} / I_{xS} < 1$ (b) $I_{yR} / I_{yS} > 1$ (c) $I_{zR} / I_{zS} > 1$

Ans. By given question

Area of square = Area of rectangular plate

$\Rightarrow$ $c^2 = a \times b \Rightarrow c^2 = ab$

Now by definition

(a) $$\frac{I_{xR}}{I_{xS}} = \frac{b^2}{c^2} \qquad [\because I \propto (\text{area})^2]$$

From the diagram $b < c$

$\Rightarrow$ $$\frac{I_{xR}}{I_{xS}} = \left(\frac{b}{c}\right)^2 < 1 \Rightarrow I_{xR} < I_{xS}$$

(b) $$\frac{I_{yR}}{I_{yS}} = \frac{a^2}{c^2}$$

as $a > c$

$$\frac{I_{yR}}{I_{yS}} = \left(\frac{a}{c}\right)^2 > 1$$

(c) $I_{zR} - I_{zS} \propto (a^2 + b^2 - 2c^2) = a^2 + b^2 - 2ab = (a-b)^2 \quad [\because c^2 = ab]$

$\Rightarrow$ $$(I_{zR} - I_{zS}) > 0 \Rightarrow \frac{I_{zR}}{I_{zS}} > 1$$

Q. 28 A uniform disc of radius R, is resting on a table on its rim. The coefficient of friction between disc and table is μ (figure). Now, the disc is pulled with a force F as shown in the figure. What is the maximum value of F for which the disc rolls without slipping?

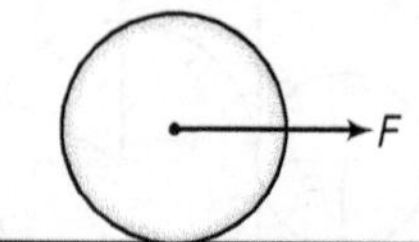

Thinking Process

Frictional force on the disc will be in opposite direction of F and supports the rotation of the disc in clockwise direction.

Ans. Consider the diagram below

Frictional force (f) is acting in the opposite direction of F.

Let the acceleration of centre of mass of disc be a then

$$F - f = Ma \quad \text{...(i)}$$

where M is mass of the disc

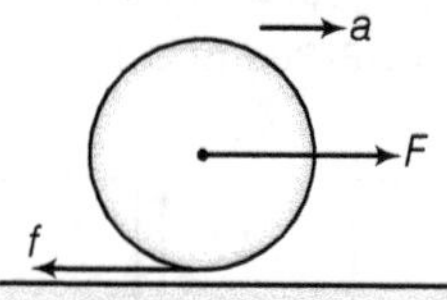

The angular acceleration of the disc is

$$\alpha = a/R \quad \text{(for pure rolling)}$$

from $$\tau = I\alpha$$

$\Rightarrow$ $$fR = \left(\frac{1}{2}MR^2\right)\alpha \Rightarrow fR = \left(\frac{1}{2}MR^2\right)\left(\frac{a}{R}\right)$$

$\Rightarrow$ $$Ma = 2f \quad \text{...(ii)}$$

From Eqs. (i) and (ii), we get

$$f = F/3 \quad [\because N = Mg]$$

$\because$ $$f \leq \mu N = \mu Mg$$

$\Rightarrow$ $$\frac{F}{3} \leq \mu Mg \Rightarrow F \leq 3\mu Mg$$

$\Rightarrow$ $$F_{max} = 3\mu Mg$$

7

Gravitation

Multiple Choice Questions (MCQs)

Q. 1 The earth is an approximate sphere. If the interior contained matter which is not of the same density everywhere, then on the surface of the earth, the acceleration due to gravity

(a) will be directed towards the centre but not the same everywhere

(b) will have the same value everywhere but not directed towards the centre

(c) will be same everywhere in magnitude directed towards the centre

(d) cannot be zero at any point

Ans. *(d)* If we assume the earth as a sphere of uniform density, then it can be treated as point mass placed at its centre. In this case acceleration due to gravity $g = 0$, at the centre.

It is not so, if the earth is considered as a sphere of non-uniform density, in that case value of g will be different at different points and cannot be zero at any point.

Q. 2 As observed from the earth, the sun appears to move in an approximate circular orbit. For the motion of another planet like mercury as observed from the earth, this would

(a) be similarly true

(b) not be true because the force between the earth and mercury is not inverse square law

(c) not be true because the major gravitational force on mercury is due to the sun

(d) not be true because mercury is influenced by forces other than gravitational forces

Ans. *(c)* As observed from the earth, the sun appears to move in an approximate circular orbit. The gravitational force of attraction between the earth and the sun always follows inverse square law.

Due to relative motion between the earth and mercury, the orbit of mercury, as observed from the earth will not be approximately circular, since the major gravitational force on mercury is due to the sun.

Q. 3 Different points in the earth are at slightly different distances from the sun and hence experience different forces due to gravitation. For a rigid body, we know that if various forces act at various points in it, the resultant motion is as if a net force acts on the CM (centre of mass) causing translation and a net torque at the CM causing rotation around an axis through the CM. For the earth-sun system (approximating the earth as a uniform density sphere).

(a) the torque is zero

(b) the torque causes the earth to spin

(c) the rigid body result is not applicable since the earth is not even approximately a rigid body

(d) the torque causes the earth to move around the sun

Ans. *(a)* As the earth is revolving around the sun in a circular motion due to gravitational attraction. The force of attraction will be of radial nature *i.e.*, angle between position vector **r** and force **F** is zero. So, torque $= |\tau| = |\mathbf{r} \times \mathbf{F}| = rF\sin 0° = 0$

Q. 4 Satellites orbitting the earth have finite life and sometimes debris of satellites fall to the earth. This is because

(a) the solar cells and batteries in satellites run out

(b) the laws of gravitation predict a trajectory spiralling inwards

(c) of viscous forces causing the speed of satellite and hence height to gradually decrease

(d) of collisions with other satellites

Ans. *(c)* As the total energy of the earth satellite bounded system is negative $\left(\frac{-GM}{2a}\right)$.
where, a is radius of the satellite and M is mass of the earth.

Due to the viscous force acting on satellite, energy decreases continuously and radius of the orbit or height decreases gradually.

Q. 5 Both the earth and the moon are subject to the gravitational force of the sun. As observed from the sun, the orbit of the moon

(a) will be elliptical

(b) will not be strictly elliptical because the total gravitational force on it is not central

(c) is not elliptical but will necessarily be a closed curve

(d) deviates considerably from being elliptical due to influence of planets other than the earth

Ans. *(b)* As observed from the sun, two types of forces are acting on the moon one is due to gravitational attraction between the sun and the moon and the other is due to gravitational attraction between the earth and the moon. Hence, total force on the moon is not central.

Q. 6 In our solar system, the inter-planetary region has chunks of matter (much smaller in size compared to planets) called asteroids. They

(a) will not move around the sun, since they have very small masses compared to the sun

(b) will move in an irregular way because of their small masses and will drift away into outer space

(c) will move around the sun in closed orbits but not obey Kepler's laws

(d) will move in orbits like planets and obey Kepler's laws

Ans. *(d)* Asteroids are also being acted upon by central gravitational forces, hence they are moving in circular orbits like planets and obey Kepler's laws.

Q. 7 Choose the wrong option.

(a) Inertial mass is a measure of difficulty of accelerating a body by an external force whereas the gravitational mass is relevant in determining the gravitational force on it by an external mass

(b) That the gravitational mass and inertial mass are equal is an experimental result

(c) That the acceleration due to gravity on the earth is the same for all bodies is due to the equality of gravitational mass and inertial mass

(d) Gravitational mass of a particle like proton can depend on the presence of neighbouring heavy objects but the inertial mass cannot

Ans. *(d)* Gravitational mass of proton is equivalent to its inertial mass and is independent of presence neighbouring heavy objects.

Q. 8 Particles of masses $2M$, m and M are respectively at points A, B and C with $AB = \frac{1}{2}(BC)$. m is much-much smaller than M and at time $t = 0$, they are all at rest as given in figure.

At subsequent times before any collision takes place.

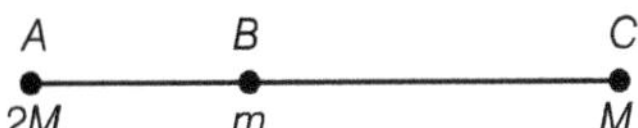

(a) m will remain at rest

(b) m will move towards M

(c) m will move towards $2M$

(d) m will have oscillatory motion

Thinking Process

The particle B will move towards the greater force, between forces by A and B.

Ans. *(c)* Force on B due to $A = F_{BA} = \frac{G(2Mm)}{(AB)^2}$ towards BA

Force on B due to $C = F_{BC} = \frac{GMm}{(BC)^2}$ towards BC

As, $(BC) = 2AB$

$$\Rightarrow \quad F_{BC} = \frac{GMm}{(2AB)^2} = \frac{GMm}{4(AB)^2} < F_{BA}$$

Hence, m will move towards BA (*i.e.*, $2M$)

Multiple Choice Questions (More Than One Options)

Q. 9 Which of the following options are correct?

(a) Acceleration due to gravity decreases with increasing altitude

(b) Acceleration due to gravity increases with increasing depth (assume the earth to be a sphere of uniform density)

(c) Acceleration due to gravity increases with increasing latitude

(d) Acceleration due to gravity is independent of the mass of the earth

Thinking Process

Acceleration due to gravity is maximum on the surface of the earth, it decreases in both cases while going upward or at a depth.

Ans. *(a, c, d)*

Acceleration due to gravity at altitude h, $g_h = \dfrac{g}{(1+h/R)^2} \approx g\left(1-\dfrac{2h}{R}\right)$

At depth d, $$g_d = g\left(1-\frac{d}{R}\right)$$

In both cases with increase in h and d, g decreases.

At latitude ϕ, $$g_\phi = g - \omega^2 R\cos^2\phi$$

As ϕ increases g_ϕ increases.

Also, we can conclude from the formulae, that it is independent of mass.

Q. 10 If the law of gravitation, instead of being inverse square law, becomes an inverse cube law

(a) planets will not have elliptic orbits

(b) circular orbits of planets is not possible

(c) projectile motion of a stone thrown by hand on the surface of the earth will be approximately parabolic

(d) there will be no gravitational force inside a spherical shell of uniform density

Ans. *(a, c)*

If the law of gravitation becomes an inverse cube law, then we can write, for a planet of mass m revolving around the sun of mass M,

$$F = \frac{GMm}{a^3} = \frac{mv^2}{a} \quad \text{(where } a \text{ is radius of orbiting planet)}$$

$$\Rightarrow \quad v = \text{orbital speed} = \frac{\sqrt{GM}}{a} \Rightarrow v \propto \frac{1}{a}$$

Time period of revolution of a planet $T = \dfrac{2\pi a}{v} = \dfrac{2\pi a}{\frac{\sqrt{GM}}{a}} = \dfrac{2\pi a^2}{\sqrt{GM}}$

$$\Rightarrow \quad T^2 \propto a^4$$

Hence, orbit will not be elliptical. [for elliptical orbit $T^2 \propto a^3$]

As force $$F = \left(\frac{GM}{a^3}\right)m = g'm$$

where, $$g' = \frac{GM}{a^3}$$

As g', acceleration due to gravity is constant, hence path followed by a projectile will be approximately parabolic. (as $T \propto a^2$)

Q. 11 If the mass of the sun were ten times smaller and gravitational constant G were ten times larger in magnitude. Then,

(a) walking on ground would become more difficult

(b) the acceleration due to gravity on the earth will not change

(c) raindrops will fall much faster

(d) airplanes will have to travel much faster

Ans. *(a, c, d)*

Given, $G' = 10G$

Consider the adjacent diagram.

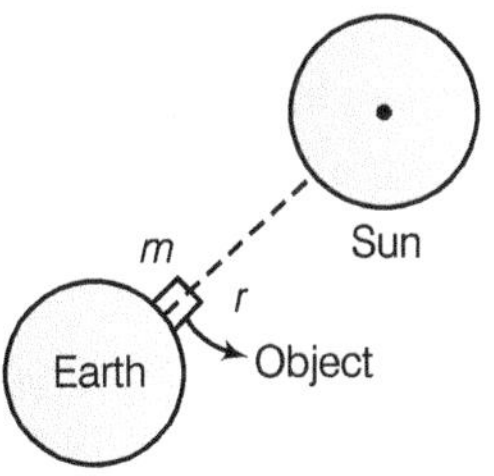

Force on the object due to the earth $= \frac{G'M_e m}{R^2} = \frac{10GM_e m}{R^2}$ $[\because G' = 10G \text{ given}]$

$$= 10\left(\frac{GM_e m}{R^2}\right)$$

$$= (10g)\,m = 10\,mg \qquad \left[\because g = \frac{GM_e}{R^2}\right] \quad ...(i)$$

Force on the object due to the sun $F = \frac{GM_s' m}{r^2}$

$$= \frac{G(M_s)m}{10r^2} \qquad \left[\because M_s' = \frac{M_s}{10} \text{ (given)}\right]$$

As $r >> R$ (radius of the earth) $\Rightarrow F$ will be very small.

So, the effect of the sun will be neglected.

Now, as $g' = 10\,g$

Hence, weight of person $= mg' = 10\,mg$ [from Eq. (i)]

i.e., gravity pull on the person will increase. Due to it, walking on ground would become more difficult.

Critical velocity, v_c is proportional to g *i.e.*,

$$v_c \propto g$$

As, $g' > g$

$\Rightarrow$ $v_c' > v_c$

Hence, rain drops will fall much faster.

To overcome the increased gravitational force of the earth, the aeroplanes will have to travel much faster.

Q. 12 If the sun and the planets carried huge amounts of opposite charges,

(a) all three of Kepler's laws would still be valid

(b) only the third law will be valid

(c) the second law will not change

(d) the first law will still be valid

Thinking Process

Electrostatic force of attraction acts between two opposite charges.

Ans. *(a, c, d)*

Due to huge amounts of opposite charges on the sun and the earth electrostatic force of attraction will be large. Gravitational force is also attractive in nature have both forces will be added.

Both the forces obey inverse square law and are central forces. As both the forces are of same nature, hence all the three **Kepler's laws** will be valid.

Q. 13 **There have been suggestions that the value of the gravitational constant G becomes smaller when considered over very large time period (in billions of years) in the future. If that happens, for our earth,**

(a) nothing will change

(b) we will become hotter after billions of years

(c) we will be going around but not strictly in closed orbits

(d) after sufficiently long time we will leave the solar system

Ans. *(c, d)*

We know that gravitational force between the earth and the sun.

$F_G = \frac{GMm}{r^2}$, where M is mass of the sun and m is mass of the earth.

When G decreases with time, the gravitational force F_G will become weaker with time. As F_G is changing with time. Due to it, the earth will be going around the sun not strictly in closed orbit and radius also increases, since the attraction force is getting weaker.

Hence, after long time the earth will leave the solar system.

Q. 14 **Supposing Newton's law of gravitation for gravitation forces $\mathbf{F}_1$ and $\mathbf{F}_2$ between two masses m_1 and m_2 at positions $\mathbf{r}_1$ and $\mathbf{r}_2$ read**

$$\mathbf{F}_1 = -\mathbf{F}_2 = -\frac{\mathbf{r}_{12}}{r_{12}^3} GM_0^2 \left(\frac{m_1 m_2}{M_0^2}\right)^n$$

where M_0 is a constant of dimension of mass, $\mathbf{r}_{12} = \mathbf{r}_1 - \mathbf{r}_2$ and n is a number. In such a case,

(a) the acceleration due to gravity on the earth will be different for different objects

(b) none of the three laws of Kepler will be valid

(c) only the third law will become invalid

(d) for n negative, an object lighter than water will sink in water

Ans. *(a,c, d)*

Given, $$\mathbf{F}_1 = -\mathbf{F}_2 = \frac{-\mathbf{r}_{12}}{r_{12}^3} GM_0^2 \left(\frac{m_1 m_2}{M_0^2}\right)^n$$

$$\mathbf{r}_{12} = \mathbf{r}_1 - \mathbf{r}_2$$

Acceleration due to gravity, $g = \frac{|F|}{\text{mass}}$

$$= \frac{GM_0^2 (m_1 m_2)^n}{r_{12}^2 (M_0)^{2n}} \times \frac{1}{(\text{mass})}$$

Since, g depends upon position vector, hence it will be different for different objects. As g is not constant, hence constant of proportionality will not be constant in Kepler's third law. Hence, Kepler's third law will not be valid.

As the force is of central nature. $\left[\because \text{force} \propto \frac{1}{r^2}\right]$

Hence, first two Kepler's laws will be valid.

For negative n,
$$g = \frac{GM_0^2 (m_1 m_2)^{-n}}{r_{12}^2 (M_0)^{-2n}} \times \frac{1}{(\text{mass})}$$
$$= \frac{GM_0^{2(1+n)}}{r_{12}^2} \frac{(m_1 m_2)^{-n}}{(\text{mass})}$$
$$g = \frac{GM_0^2}{r_{12}^2} \left(\frac{M_0^2}{m_1 m_2}\right)^n \times \frac{1}{\text{mass}}$$

As $M_0 > m_1$ or m_2

$g > 0$, hence in this case situation will reverse *i.e.*, object lighter than water will sink in water.

Q. 15 Which of the following are true?

(a) A polar satellite goes around the earth's pole in north-south direction

(b) A geostationary satellite goes around the earth in east-west direction

(c) A geostationary satellite goes around the earth in west-east direction

(d) A polar satellite goes around the earth in east-west direction

Ans. *(a, c)*

A geostationary satellite is having same sense of rotation as that of earth *i.e.*, west-east direction.

A polar satellite goes around the earth's pole in north-south direction.

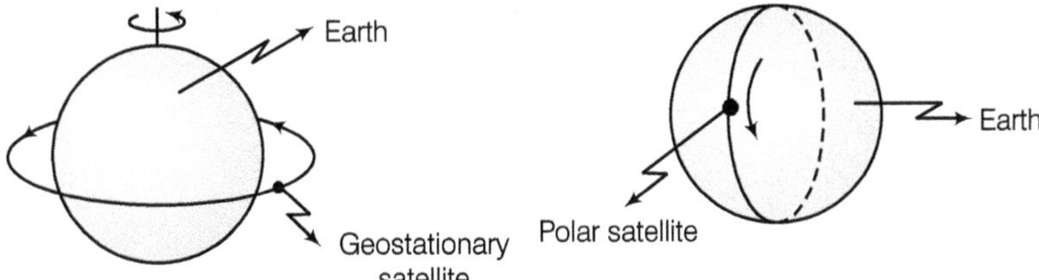

Q. 16 The centre of mass of an extended body on the surface of the earth and its centre of gravity

(a) are always at the same point for any size of the body

(b) are always at the same point only for spherical bodies

(c) can never be at the same point

(d) is close to each other for objects, say of sizes less than 100 m

(e) both can change if the object is taken deep inside the earth

Ans. *(d)*

For small objects, say of sizes less than 100 m centre of mass is very close with the centre of gravity of the body. But when the size of object increases, its weight changes and its CM and CG become far from each other.

Very Short Answer Type Questions

Q. 17 Molecules in air in the atmosphere are attracted by gravitational force of the earth. Explain why all of them do not fall into the earth just like an apple falling from a tree.

Ans. Air molecules in the atmosphere are attracted vertically downward by gravitational force of the earth just like an apple falling from a tree. Air molecules move randomly due to their thermal velocity and hence the resultant motion of air molecules is not exactly in the vertical downward direction.

But in case of apple, only vertical motion dominates because of being heavier than air molecules. But due to gravity, the density of atmosphere increases near to the earth's surface.

Q. 18 Give one example each of central force and non-central force.

Ans. **Example of central force** Gravitational force, electrostatic force etc.

Example of non-central force Nuclear force, magnetic force acting between two current carrying loops etc.

Q. 19 Draw areal velocity *versus* time graph for mars.

Ans. Areal velocity of a planet revolving around the sun is constant with time. Therefore, graph between areal velocity and time is a straight line (*AB*) parallel to time axis.(Kepler's second law).

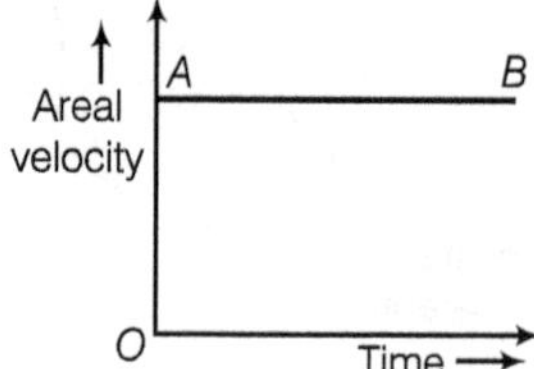

Q. 20 What is the direction of areal velocity of the earth around the sun?

Ans. Areal velocity of the earth around the sun is given by

$$\frac{dA}{dt} = \frac{\mathbf{L}}{2m}$$

where, **L** is the angular momentum and m is the mass of the earth.

But angular momentum $\mathbf{L} = \mathbf{r} \times \mathbf{p} = \mathbf{r} \times m\mathbf{v}$

$\therefore$ Areal velocity $\left(\frac{dA}{dt}\right) = \frac{1}{2m}(\mathbf{r} \times m\mathbf{v}) = \frac{1}{2}(\mathbf{r} \times \mathbf{v})$

Therefore, the direction of areal velocity $\left(\frac{dA}{dt}\right)$ is in the direction of $(\mathbf{r} \times \mathbf{v})$, *i.e.*, perpendicular to the plane containing **r** and **v** and directed as given by right hand rule.

Q. 21 How is the gravitational force between two point masses affected when they are dipped in water keeping the separation between them the same?

Ans. Gravitational force acting between two point masses m_1 and m_2, $F = \frac{Gm_1m_2}{r^2}$, is independent of the nature of medium between them. Therefore, gravitational force acting between two point masses will remain unaffected when they are dipped in water.

Q. 22 Is it possible for a body to have inertia but no weight?

Ans. Yes, a body can have inertia (*i.e.*, mass) but no weight. Everybody always have inertia (*i.e.*, mass) but its weight (mg) can be zero, when it is taken at the centre of the earth or during free fall under gravity.

e.g., In the tunnel through the centre of the earth, the object moves only due to inertia at the centre while its weight becomes zero.

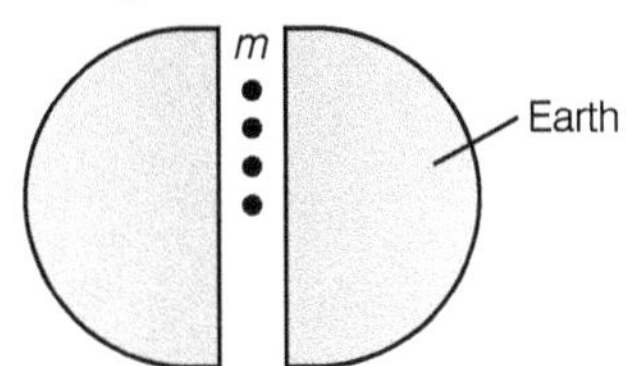

Q. 23 We can shield a charge from electric fields by putting it inside a hollow conductor. Can we shield a body from the gravitational influence of nearby matter by putting it inside a hollow sphere or by some other means?

Ans. A body cannot be shielded from the gravitational influence of nearby matter, because gravitational force between two point mass bodies is independent of the intervening medium between them.

It is due to the above reason, we cannot shield a body from the gravitational influence of nearby matter by putting it either inside a hollow sphere or by some other means.

Q. 24 An astronaut inside a small spaceship orbitting around the earth cannot detect gravity. If the space station orbitting around the earth has a large size, can he hope to detect gravity?

Ans. Inside a small spaceship orbitting around the earth, the value of acceleration due to gravity g, can be considered as constant and hence astronaut feels weightlessness.

If the space station orbitting around the earth has a large size, such that variation in g matters in that case astronaut inside the spaceship will experience gravitational force and hence can detect gravity. *e.g.*, On the moon, due to larger size gravity can be detected.

Q. 25 The gravitational force between a hollow spherical shell (of radius R and uniform density) and a point mass is F. Show the nature of F *versus* r graph where r is the distance of the point from the centre of the hollow spherical shell of uniform density.

Ans. Consider the diagram, density of the shell is constant. Let it is ρ.

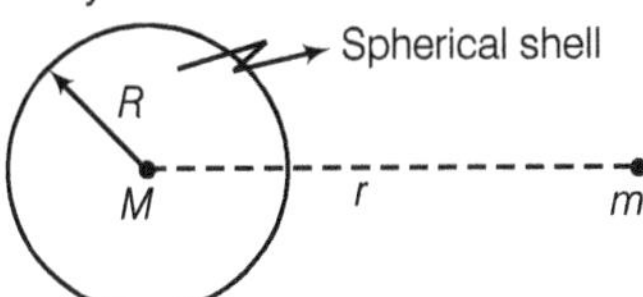

Mass of the shell = (density) × (volume)

$$= (\rho) \times \frac{4}{3}\pi R^3 = M$$

As the density of the shell is uniform, it can be treated as a point mass placed at its centre.

Therefore, F = gravitational force between M and $m = \frac{GMm}{r^2}$

$$F = 0 \text{ for } r < R \quad (\textit{i.e.}, \text{ force inside the shell is zero})$$

$$= \frac{GM}{r^2} \text{ for } r \geq R$$

The variation of F *versus* r is shown in the diagram.

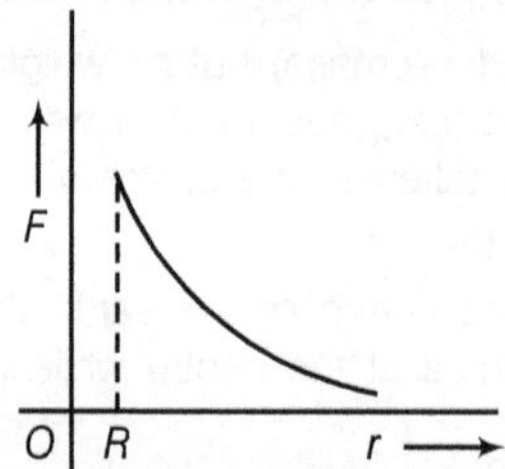

Note *When r tends to infinity, force tends to zero, also force is maximum on the surface of the hollow spherical shell.*

Q. 26 Out of aphelion and perihelion, where is the speed of the earth more and why?

Ans. Aphelion is the location of the earth where it is at the greatest distance from the sun and perihelion is the location of the earth where it is at the nearest distance from the sun.

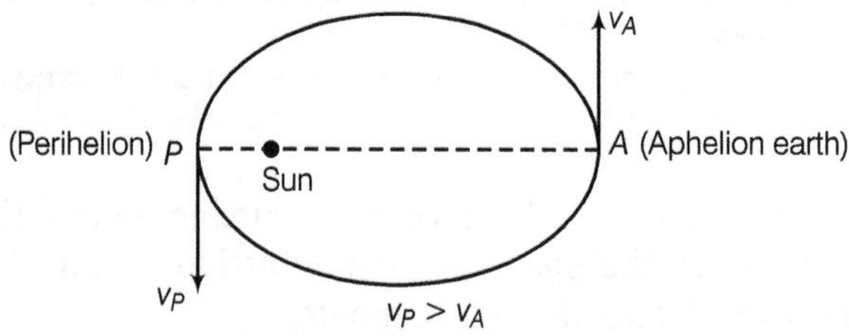

The areal velocity $\left(\frac{1}{2}\mathbf{r} \times \mathbf{v}\right)$ of the earth around the sun is constant (Kepler's IInd law).

Therefore, the speed of the earth is more at the perihelion than at the aphelion.

Q. 27 What is the angle between the equatorial plane and the orbital plane of
(a) polar satellite?
(b) geostationary satellite?

Ans. Consider the diagram where plane of geostationary and polar satellite are shown.

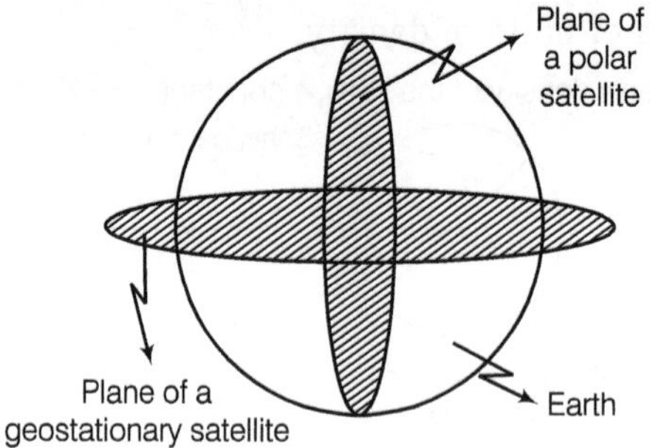

Clearly

(a) Angle between the equatorial plane and orbital plane of a polar satellite is 90°.

(b) Angle between equatorial plane and orbital plane of a geostationary satellite is 0°.

Short Answer Type Questions

Q. 28 **Mean solar day is the time interval between two successive noon when sun passes through zenith point (meridian).**

Sidereal day is the time interval between two successive transit of a distant star through the zenith point (meridian).

By drawing appropriate diagram showing the earth's spin and orbital motion, show that mean solar day is 4 min longer than the sidereal day. In other words, distant stars would rise 4 min early every successive day.

Ans. Consider the diagram below, the earth moves from the point P to Q in one solar day.

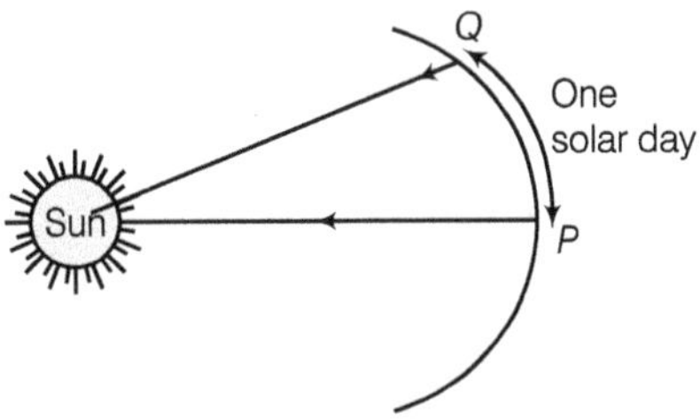

Every day the earth advances in the orbit by approximately 1°. Then, it will have to rotate by 361° (which we define as 1 day) to have the sun at zenith point again.

$\because$ 361° corresponds to 24 h.

$\therefore$ 1° corresponds to $\frac{24}{361} \times 1 = 0.066\text{ h} = 3.99\text{ min} \approx 4\text{ min}$

Hence, distant stars would rise 4 min early every successive day.

Q. 29 **Two identical heavy spheres are separated by a distance 10 times their radius. Will an object placed at the mid-point of the line joining their centres be in stable equilibrium or unstable equilibrium? Give reason for your answer.**

Thinking Process

To determine the nature of equilibrium, we have to displace the object through a small distance, from the middle point and then force will be calculated in displaced position.

Ans. Let the mass and radius of each identical heavy sphere be M and R respectively. An object of mass m be placed at the mid-point P of the line joining their centres.

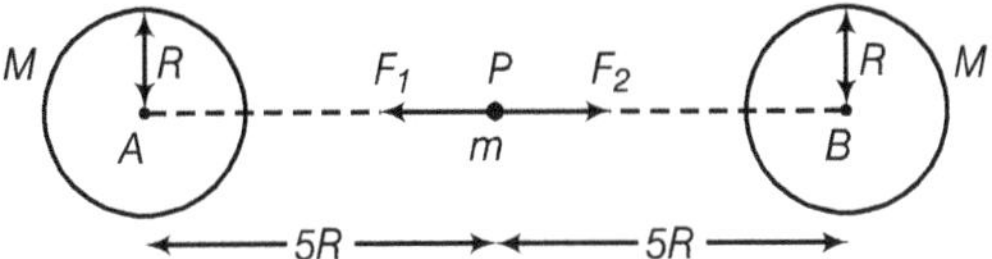

Force acting on the object placed at the mid-point,

$$F_1 = F_2 = \frac{GMm}{(5R)^2}$$

The direction of forces are opposite, therefore net force acting on the object is zero.

To check the stability of the equilibrium, we displace the object through a small distance x towards sphere A.

Now, force acting towards sphere *A*, $F_1' = \dfrac{GMm}{(5R - x)^2}$

Force acting towards sphere *B*, $F_2' = \dfrac{GMm}{(5R + x)^2}$

As $F_1' > F_2'$, therefore a resultant force $(F_1' - F_2')$ acts on the object towards sphere *A*, therefore object start to move towards sphere *A* and hence equilibrium is unstable.

Q. 30 Show the nature of the following graph for a satellite orbitting the earth.

(a) KE *versus* orbital radius *R*

(b) PE *versus* orbital radius *R*

(c) TE *versus* orbital radius *R*

Ans. Consider the diagram, where a satellite of mass *m*, moving around the earth in a circular orbit of radius *R*.

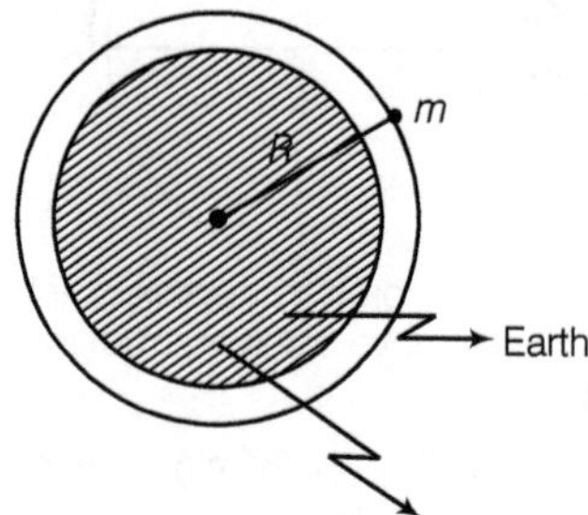

Orbital speed of the satellite orbitting the earth is given by $v_o = \sqrt{\dfrac{GM}{R}}$

where, *M* and *R* are the mass and radius of the earth.

(a) $\therefore$ KE of a satellite of mass *m*, $E_K = \dfrac{1}{2}mv_o^2 = \dfrac{1}{2}m \times \dfrac{GM}{R}$

$\therefore \qquad E_K \propto \dfrac{1}{R}$

It means the KE decreases exponentially with radius.

The graph for KE *versus* orbital radius *R* is shown in figure.

(b) Potential energy of a satellite $E_P = -\dfrac{GMm}{R}$

$$E_P \propto -\frac{1}{R}$$

The graph for PE *versus* orbital radius *R* is shown in figure.

(c) Total energy of the satellite $E = E_K + E_P = \dfrac{GMm}{2R} - \dfrac{GMm}{R}$

$$= -\frac{GMm}{2R}$$

The graph for total energy *versus* orbital radius *R* is shown in the figure.

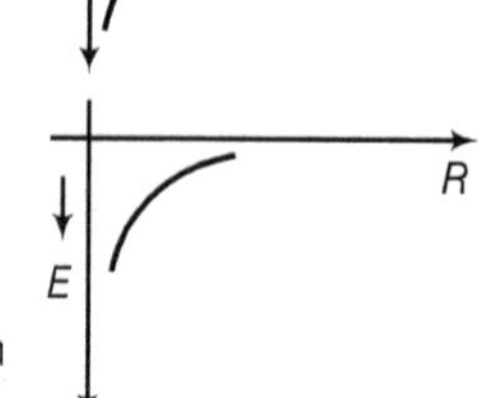

Note *We should keep in mind that Potential Energy (PE) and Kinetic Energy (KE) of the satellite-earth system is always negative.*

Q. 31 **Shown are several curves [fig. (a), (b), (c), (d), (e), (f)]. Explain with reason, which ones amongst them can be possible trajectories traced by a projectile (neglect air friction).**

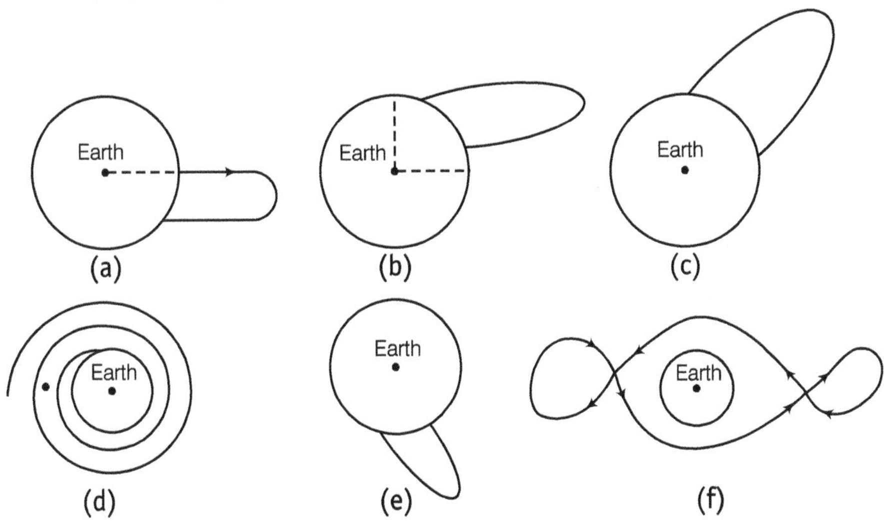

Ans. The trajectory of a particle under gravitational force of the earth will be a conic section (for motion outside the earth) with the centre of the earth as a focus. Only (c) meets this requirement.

Note *The trajectory of the particle depends upon the velocity of projection. Depending upon the magnitude and direction of velocity it may be parabolic or elliptical.*

Q. 32 **An object of mass *m* is raised from the surface of the earth to a height equal to the radius of the earth, that is, taken from a distance *R* to 2*R* from the centre of the earth. What is the gain in its potential energy?**

Ans. Consider the diagram where an object of mass *m* is raised from the surface of the earth to a distance (height) equal to the radius of the earth (*R*).

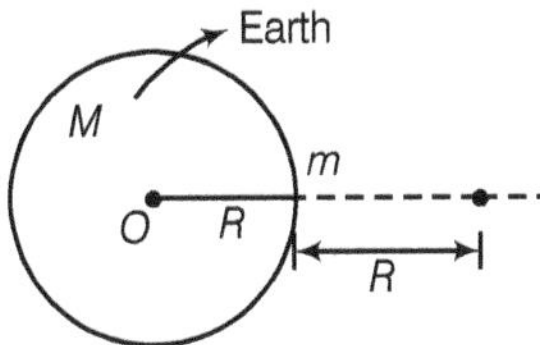

Potential energy of the object at the surface of the earth $= -\dfrac{GMm}{R}$

PE of the object at a height equal to the radius of the earth $= -\dfrac{GMm}{2R}$

$$\therefore \quad \text{Gain in PE of the object} = \frac{-GMm}{2R} - \left(-\frac{GMm}{R}\right)$$

$$= \frac{-GMm + 2GMm}{2R} = +\frac{GMm}{2R}$$

$$= \frac{gR^2 \times m}{2R} = \frac{1}{2}mgR \qquad (\because GM = gR^2)$$

Q. 33 **A mass m is placed at P a distance h along the normal through the centre O of a thin circular ring of mass M and radius r (figure).**

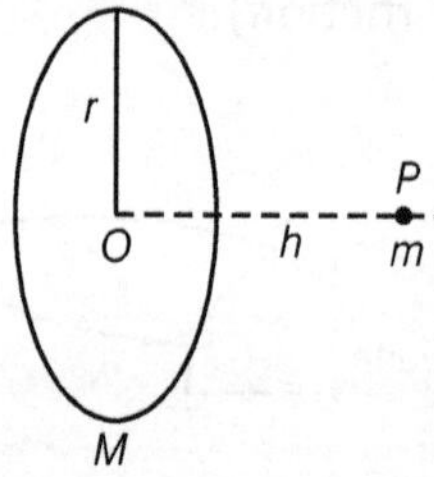

If the mass is moved further away such that OP becomes $2h$, by what factor the force of gravitation will decrease, if $h = r$?

Ans. Consider the diagram, in which a system consisting of a ring and a point mass is shown.

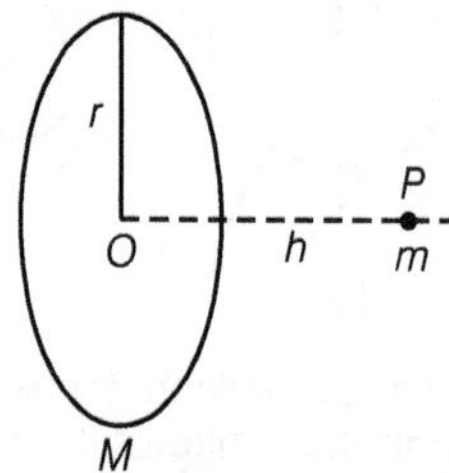

Gravitational force acting on an object of mass m, placed at point P at a distance h along the normal through the centre of a circular ring of mass M and radius r is given by

$$F = \frac{GMmh}{(r^2 + h^2)^{3/2}} \quad \text{(along } PO) \ldots \text{(i)}$$

When mass is displaced upto distance $2h$, then

$$F' = \frac{GMm \times 2h}{[r^2 + (2h)^2]^{3/2}} \quad [\because h = 2r]$$

$$= \frac{2GMmh}{(r^2 + 4h^2)^{3/2}} \quad \ldots \text{(ii)}$$

When $h = r$, then from Eq.(i)

$$F = \frac{GMm \times r}{(r^2 + r^2)^{3/2}} \Rightarrow F = \frac{GMm}{2\sqrt{2}r^2}$$

and

$$F' = \frac{2GMmr}{(r^2 + 4r^2)^{3/2}} = \frac{2GMm}{5\sqrt{5}r^2} \quad \text{[From Eq. (ii) substituting } h = r]$$

$\therefore$

$$\frac{F'}{F} = \frac{4\sqrt{2}}{5\sqrt{5}}$$

$\Rightarrow$

$$F' = \frac{4\sqrt{2}}{5\sqrt{5}} F$$

Long Answer Type Questions

Q. 34 A star like the sun has several bodies moving around it at different distances. Consider that all of them are moving in circular orbits. Let r be the distance of the body from the centre of the star and let its linear velocity be v, angular velocity ω, kinetic energy K, gravitational potential energy U, total energy E and angular momentum l. As the radius r of the orbit increases, determine which of the above quantities increase and which ones decrease.

Ans. The situation is shown in the diagram, where a body of mass m is revolving around a star of mass M.

N, O, r, m, Star

Linear velocity of the body $v = \sqrt{\frac{GM}{r}}$

$\Rightarrow$ $v \propto \frac{1}{\sqrt{r}}$

Therefore, when r increases, v decreases.

Angular velocity of the body $\omega = \frac{2\pi}{T}$

According to Kepler's law of period,

$$T^2 \propto r^3 \Rightarrow T = kr^{3/2}$$

where k is a constant

$\therefore$ $$\omega = \frac{2\pi}{kr^{3/2}} \Rightarrow \omega \propto \frac{1}{r^{3/2}} \qquad \left(\because \omega = \frac{2\pi}{T}\right)$$

Therefore, when r increases, ω decreases.

Kinetic energy of the body $K = \frac{1}{2}mv^2 = \frac{1}{2}m \times \frac{GM}{r} = \frac{GMm}{2r}$

$\therefore$ $K \propto \frac{1}{r}$

Therefore, when r increases, KE decreases.

Gravitational potential energy of the body,

$$U = -\frac{GMm}{r} \Rightarrow U \propto -\frac{1}{r}$$

Therefore, when r increases, PE becomes less negative *i.e.,* increases.

Total energy of the body $E = \text{KE} + \text{PE} = \frac{GMm}{2r} + \left(-\frac{GMm}{r}\right) = -\frac{GMm}{2r}$

Therefore, when r increases, total energy becomes less negative, *i.e.*, increases.

Angular momentum of the body $L = mvr = mr\sqrt{\frac{GM}{r}} = m\sqrt{GMr}$

$\therefore$ $L \propto \sqrt{r}$

Therefore, when r increases, angular momentum L increases.

Note *In this case, we have not considered the sun-object system as isolated and the force on the system is not zero. So, angular momentum is not conserved.*

Q. 35 **Six point masses of mass *m* each are at the vertices of a regular hexagon of side *l*. Calculate the force on any of the masses.**

Thinking Process

To calculate resultant force, we will apply principle of superposition i.e., net force will be equal to sum of individual forces by each point mass (m).

Ans. Consider the diagram below, in which six point masses are placed at six vertices *A,B,C,D,E* and *F*.

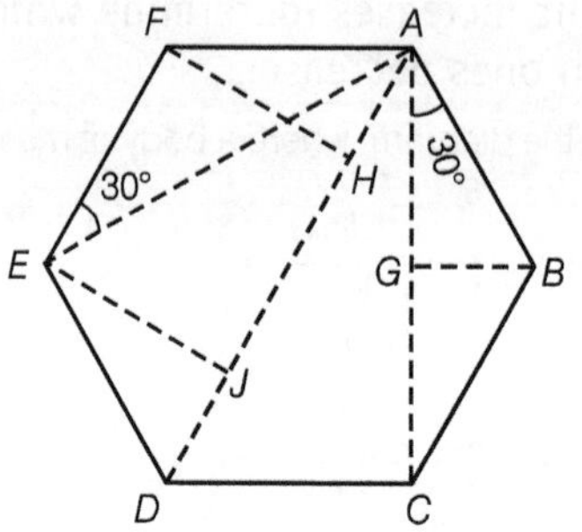

F A 30° H 30° E G B J D C

$$AC = AG + GC = 2AG$$
$$= 2l\cos 30° = 2l\sqrt{3}/2$$
$$= \sqrt{3}l = AE$$
$$AD = AH + HJ + JD$$
$$= l\sin 30° + l + l\sin 30° = 2l$$

Force on mass *m* at *A* due to mass *m* at *B* is, $f_1 = \frac{Gmm}{l^2}$ along *AB*.

Force on mass *m* at *A* due to mass *m* at C is, $f_2 = \frac{Gm \times m}{(\sqrt{3}l)^2} = \frac{Gm^2}{3l^2}$ along *AC*.

$[\because AC = \sqrt{3}l]$

Force on mass *m* at *A* due to mass *m* at *D* is, $f_3 = \frac{Gm \times m}{(2l)^2} = \frac{Gm^2}{4l^2}$ along *AD*. $[\because AD = 2l]$

Force on mass *m* at *A* due to mass *m* at *E* is, $f_4 = \frac{Gm \times m}{(\sqrt{3}l)^2} = \frac{Gm^2}{3l^2}$ along *AE*.

Force on mass *m* at *A* due to mass *m* at *F* is, $f_5 = \frac{Gm \times m}{l^2} = \frac{Gm^2}{l^2}$ along *AF*.

Resultant force due to f_1 and f_5 is, $F_1 = \sqrt{f_1^2 + f_5^2 + 2f_1f_5\cos 120°} = \frac{Gm^2}{l^2}$ along *AD*.

$[\because$ Angle between f_1 and $f_5 = 120°]$

Resultant force due to f_2 and f_4 is, $F_2 = \sqrt{f_2^2 + f_4^2 + 2f_2f_4\cos 60°}$

$$= \frac{\sqrt{3}Gm^2}{3l^2} = \frac{Gm^2}{\sqrt{3}l^2} \text{ along } AD.$$

So, net force along $AD = F_1 + F_2 + F_3 = \frac{Gm^2}{l^2} + \frac{Gm^2}{\sqrt{3}l^2} + \frac{Gm^2}{4l^2} = \frac{Gm^2}{l^2}\left(1 + \frac{1}{\sqrt{3}} + \frac{1}{4}\right)$.

Q. 36 A satellite is to be placed in equatorial geostationary orbit around the earth for communication.

(a) Calculate height of such a satellite.

(b) Find out the minimum number of satellites that are needed to cover entire earth, so that atleast one satellite is visible from any point on the equator.

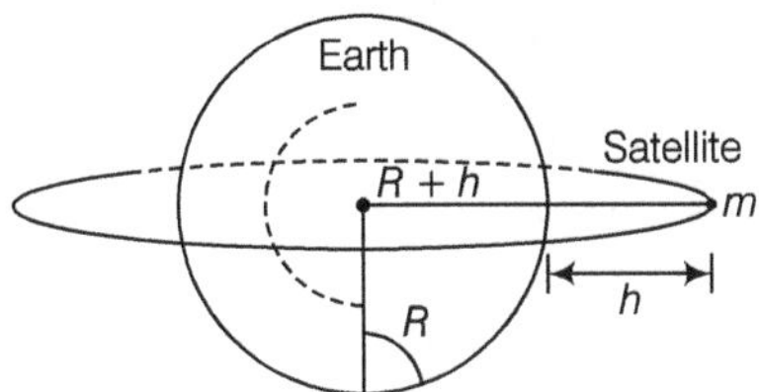

$[M = 6 \times 10^{24}$ kg, $R = 6400$ km, $T = 24$h, $G = 6.67 \times 10^{-11}$ SI unit]

Ans. Consider the adjacent diagram

Given, mass of the earth $M = 6 \times 10^{24}$ kg

Radius of the earth, $R = 6400\text{ km} = 6.4 \times 10^6$ m

Time period $T = 24$ h

$= 24 \times 60 \times 60 = 86400$ s

$G = 6.67 \times 10^{-11}\ \text{N-m}^2/\text{kg}^2$

(a) Time period
$$T = 2\pi\sqrt{\frac{(R+h)^3}{GM}} \qquad \left[\because v_o = \sqrt{\frac{GM}{R+h}} \text{ and } T = \frac{2\pi(R+h)}{v_o}\right]$$

$$\Rightarrow \quad T^2 = 4\pi^2 \frac{(R+h)^3}{GM} \Rightarrow (R+h)^3 = \frac{T^2 GM}{4\pi^2}$$

$$\Rightarrow \quad R + h = \left(\frac{T^2 GM}{4\pi^2}\right)^{1/3} \Rightarrow h = \left(\frac{T^2 GM}{4\pi^2}\right)^{1/3} - R$$

$$\Rightarrow \quad h = \left[\frac{(24 \times 60 \times 60)^2 \times 6.67 \times 10^{-11} \times 6 \times 10^{24}}{4 \times (3.14)^2}\right]^{1/3} - 6.4 \times 10^6$$

$$= 4.23 \times 10^7 - 6.4 \times 10^6$$

$$= (42.3 - 6.4) \times 10^6$$

$$= 35.9 \times 10^6 \text{ m}$$

$$= 3.59 \times 10^7 \text{ m}$$

(b) If satellite is at height h from the earth's surface, then according to the diagram.

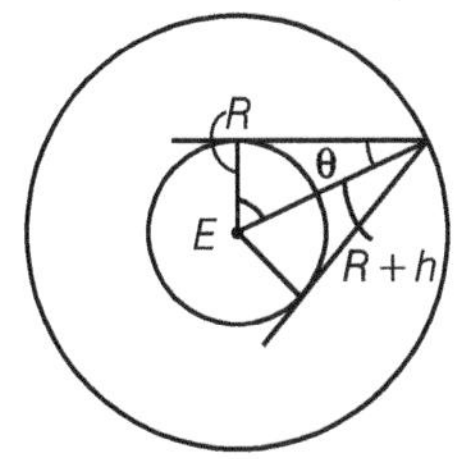

$$\cos\theta = \frac{R}{R+h} = \frac{1}{\left(1+\frac{h}{R}\right)} = \frac{1}{\left(1+\frac{3.59\times10^7}{6.4\times10^6}\right)}$$

$$= \frac{1}{1+5.61} = \frac{1}{6.61} = 0.1513 = \cos 81°18'$$

$$\theta = 81°18'$$

$\therefore$ $$2\theta = 2\times(81°18') = 162°36'$$

If n is the number of satellites needed to cover entire the earth, then

$$n = \frac{360°}{2\theta} = \frac{360°}{162°36'} = 2.31$$

$\therefore$ Minimum 3 satellites are required to cover entire the earth.

Q. 37 Earth's orbit is an ellipse with eccentricity 0.0167. Thus, the earth's distance from the sun and speed as it moves around the sun varies from day-to-day. This means that the length of the solar day is not constant through the year. Assume that the earth's spin axis is normal to its orbital plane and find out the length of the shortest and the longest day. A day should be taken from noon to noon. Does this explain variation of length of the day during the year?

Thinking Process

As the earth orbits the sun, the angular momentum is conserved and areal velocity is constant.

Ans. Consider the diagram. Let m be the mass of the earth, v_p, v_a be the velocity of the earth at perigee and apogee respectively. Similarly, ω_p and ω_a are corresponding angular velocities.

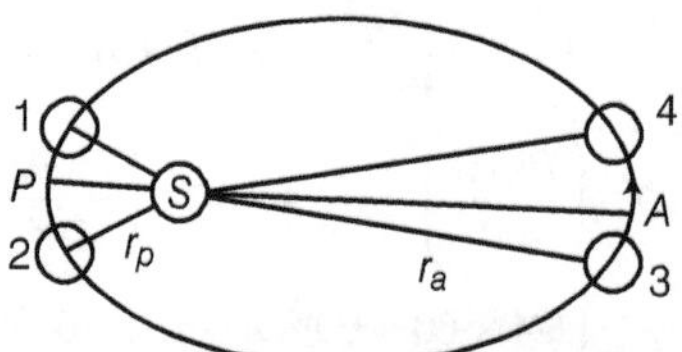

Angular momentum and areal velocity are constant as the earth orbits the sun.

At perigee, $r_p^2\omega_p = r_a^2\omega_a$ at apogee ...(i)

If a is the semi-major axis of the earth's orbit, then $r_p = a(1-e)$ and $r_a = a(1+e)$ ...(ii)

$\therefore$ $$\frac{\omega_p}{\omega_a} = \left(\frac{1+e}{1-e}\right)^2, e = 0.0167$$ [from Eqs. (i) and (ii)]

$\therefore$ $$\frac{\omega_p}{\omega_a} = 1.0691$$

Let ω be angular speed which is geometric mean of ω_p and ω_a and corresponds to mean solar day,

$\therefore$ $$\left(\frac{\omega_p}{\omega}\right)\left(\frac{\omega}{\omega_a}\right) = 1.0691$$

$\therefore$ $$\frac{\omega_p}{\omega} = \frac{\omega}{\omega_a} = 1.034$$

If ω corresponds to 1° per day (mean angular speed), then $\omega_p = 1.034°$ per day and $\omega_a = 0.967°$ per day. Since, $361° = 24$, mean solar day, we get 361.034° which corresponds to 24 h, 8.14" (8.1" longer) and 360.967° corresponds to 23 h 59 min 52" (7.9" smaller).

This does not explain the actual variation of the length of the day during the year.

Q. 38 A satellite is in an elliptic orbit around the earth with aphelion of $6R$ and perihelion of $2R$ where $R = 6400$ km is the radius of the earth. Find eccentricity of the orbit. Find the velocity of the satellite at apogee and perigee. What should be done if this satellite has to be transferred to a circular orbit of radius $6R$?

[$G = 6.67 \times 10^{-11}$ SI unit and $M = 6 \times 10^{24}$ kg]

Ans. Given, r_p = radius of perihelion $= 2R$

r_a = radius of apnelion $= 6R$

Hence, we can write

$$r_a = a(1+e) = 6R \quad \text{...(i)}$$

$$r_p = a(1-e) = 2R \quad \text{...(ii)}$$

Solving Eqs. (i) and (ii), we get

$$\text{eccentricity, } e = \frac{1}{2}$$

By conservation of angular momentum, angular momentum at perigee = angular momentum at apogee

$$\therefore \quad mv_p r_p = mv_a r_a$$

$$\therefore \quad \frac{v_a}{v_p} = \frac{1}{3}$$

where m is mass of the satellite.

Applying conservation of energy, energy at perigee = energy at apogee

$$\frac{1}{2}mv_p^2 - \frac{GMm}{r_p} = \frac{1}{2}mv_a^2 - \frac{GMm}{r_a}$$

where M is the mass of the earth.

$$\therefore \quad v_p^2\left(1-\frac{1}{9}\right) = -2GM\left(\frac{1}{r_a}-\frac{1}{r_p}\right) = 2GM\left(\frac{1}{r_p}-\frac{1}{r_a}\right) \quad \left(\text{By putting } v_a = \frac{v_p}{3}\right)$$

$$v_p = \frac{\left[2GM\left(\frac{1}{r_p}-\frac{1}{r_a}\right)\right]^{1/2}}{\left[1-(V_a/V_p)^2\right]^{1/2}} = \left[\frac{\frac{2GM}{R}\left(\frac{1}{2}-\frac{1}{6}\right)}{\left(1-\frac{1}{9}\right)}\right]^{1/2}$$

$$= \left(\frac{2/3}{8/9}\frac{GM}{R}\right)^{1/2} = \sqrt{\frac{3}{4}\frac{GM}{R}} = 6.85 \text{ km/s}$$

$$v_p = 6.85 \text{ km/s}, \; v_a = 2.28 \text{ km/s}$$

For circular orbit of radius r,

$$v_c = \text{orbital velocity} = \sqrt{\frac{GM}{r}}$$

For $$r = 6R, \; v_c = \sqrt{\frac{GM}{6R}} = 3.23 \text{ km/s.}$$

Hence, to transfer to a circular orbit at apogee, we have to boost the velocity by $\Delta = (3.23 - 2.28) = 0.95$ km/s. This can be done by suitably firing rockets from the satellite.

8

Mechanical Properties *of* Solids

Multiple Choice Questions (MCQs)

Q. 1 Modulus of rigidity of ideal liquids is

(a) infinity
(b) zero
(c) unity
(d) some finite small non-zero constant value

Ans. *(b)* No frictional (viscous) force exists in case of ideal fluid, hence, tangential forces are zero so there is no stress developed.

Q. 2 The maximum load a wire can withstand without breaking, when its length is reduced to half of its original length, will

(a) be double
(b) be half
(c) be four times
(d) remain same

Ans. *(d)* We know that, Breaking stress $= \dfrac{\text{Breaking force}}{\text{Area of cross-section}}$ ... (i)

When length of the wire changes, area of cross-section remains same.
Hence, breaking force will be same when length changes.

Q. 3 The temperature of a wire is doubled. The Young's modulus of elasticity

(a) will also double
(b) will become four times
(c) will remain same
(d) will decrease

Ans. *(d)* We know that with increase in temperature length of a wire changes as

$$L_t = L_o\,(1+\alpha\,\Delta T)$$

where ΔT is change in the temperature, L_0 is original length, α is coefficient of linear expansion and L_t is Length at temperature T.

Now we can write $\Delta L = L_t - L_o = L_o\,\alpha\,\Delta T$

where α is coefficient of linear expansion.

$$\text{Young's modulus } (Y) = \frac{\text{Stress}}{\text{Strain}} = \frac{F\,L_o}{A \times \Delta L} = \frac{FL_o}{AL_o\,\alpha\,\Delta T} \propto \frac{1}{\Delta T}$$

As, $Y \propto \dfrac{1}{\Delta T}$

When temperature increases ΔT increases, hence, Y decreases.

Q. 4 A spring is stretched by applying a load to its free end. The strain produced in the spring is

(a) volumetric (b) shear
(c) longitudinal and shear (d) longitudinal

Ans. *(c)* Consider the diagram where a spring is stretched by applying a load to its free end. Clearly the length and shape of the spring changes.

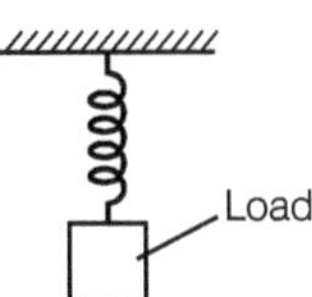

The change in length corresponds to longitudinal strain and change in shape corresponds to shearing strain.

Q. 5 A rigid bar of mass M is supported symmetrically by three wires each of length l. Those at each end are of copper and the middle one is of iron. The ratio of their diameters, if each is to have the same tension, is equal to

(a) Y_{copper}/Y_{iron} (b) $\sqrt{\frac{Y_{iron}}{Y_{copper}}}$

(c) $\frac{Y^2{}_{iron}}{Y^2{}_{copper}}$ (d) $\frac{Y_{iron}}{Y_{copper}}$

Ans. *(b)* We know that Young's modulus

$$Y = \frac{\text{Stress}}{\text{Strain}} = \frac{F/A}{\Delta L/L} = F/A \times \frac{L}{\Delta L}$$

$$= \frac{F}{\pi (D/2)^2} \times \frac{L}{\Delta L} = \frac{4FL}{\pi D^2 \Delta L}$$

$$\Rightarrow \qquad D^2 = \frac{4FL}{\pi \Delta LY} \Rightarrow D = \sqrt{\frac{4FL}{\pi \Delta LY}}$$

As F and $\frac{L}{\Delta L}$ are constants.

Hence, $$D \propto \sqrt{\frac{1}{Y}}$$

Now, we can find ratio as $\frac{D_{copper}}{D_{iron}} = \sqrt{\frac{Y_{iron}}{Y_{copper}}}$

Q. 6 A mild steel wire of length $2L$ and cross-sectional area A is stretched, well within elastic limit, horizontally between two pillars (figure). A mass m is suspended from the mid-point of the wire. Strain in the wire is

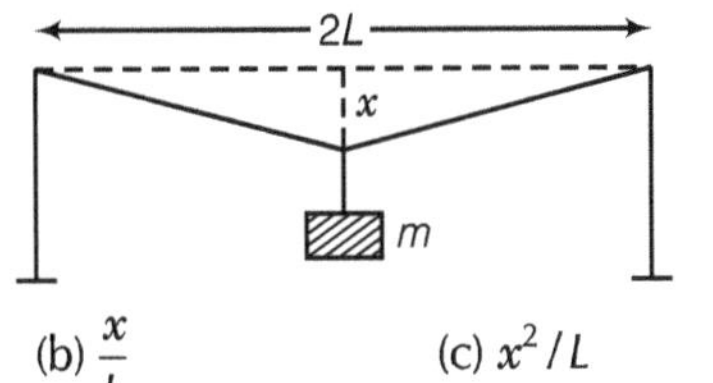

(a) $\frac{x^2}{2L^2}$ (b) $\frac{x}{L}$ (c) x^2/L (d) $x^2/2L$

Thinking Process

We will assume the vertical displacement x to be very small compared to L. Change in the length will be calculated by difference of final total length and initial length $2L$.

Ans. *(a)* Consider the diagram below

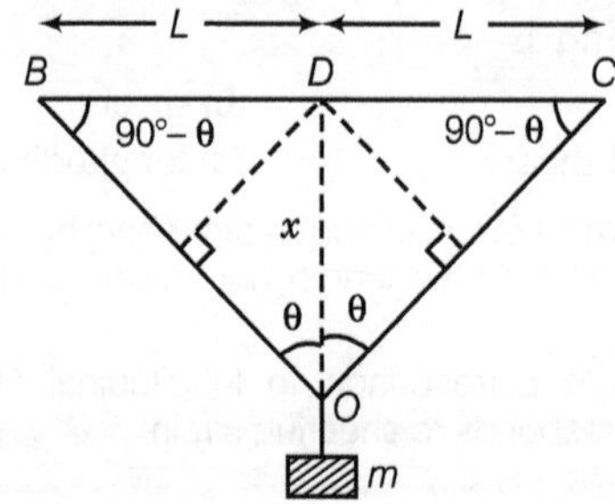

Hence, change in length

$$\Delta L = BO + OC - (BD + DC)$$
$$= 2BO - 2BD \qquad (\because BO = OC, BD = DC)$$
$$= 2[BO - BD]$$
$$= 2[(x^2 + L^2)^{1/2} - L]$$
$$= 2L\left[\left(1 + \frac{x^2}{L^2}\right)^{1/2} - 1\right]$$
$$\approx 2L\left[1 + \frac{1}{2}\frac{x^2}{L^2} - 1\right] = \frac{x^2}{L} \qquad [\because x << L]$$

$$\therefore \qquad \text{Strain} = \frac{\Delta L}{2L} = \frac{x^2/L}{2L} = \frac{x^2}{2L^2}$$

Q. 7 **A rectangular frame is to be suspended symmetrically by two strings of equal length on two supports (figure). It can be done in one of the following three ways;**

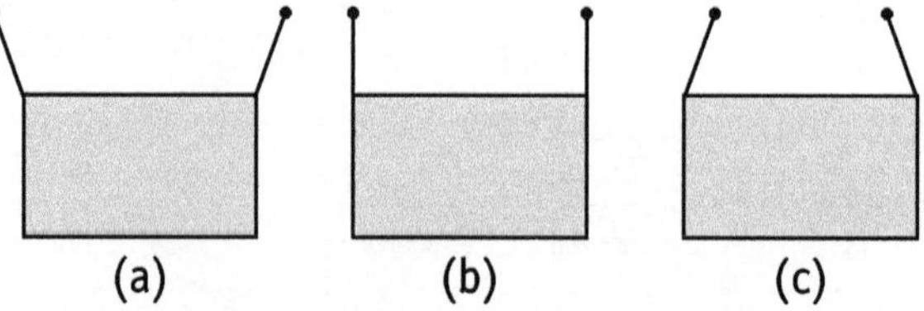

The tension in the strings will be

(a) the same in all cases
(b) least in (a)
(c) least in (b)
(d) least in (c)

Ans. *(c)* Consider the FBD diagram of the rectangular frame

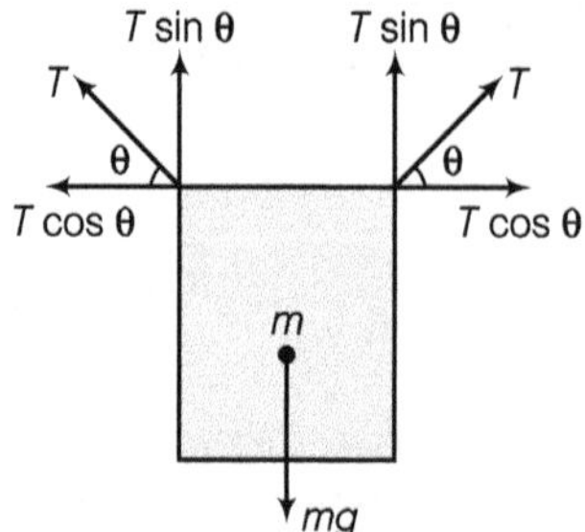

Balancing vertical forces $2T \sin\theta - mg = 0$ [T is tension in the string]

$\Rightarrow$ $2T \sin\theta = mg$ ...(i)

Total horizontal force $= T\cos\theta - T\cos\theta = 0$

Now from Eq. (i), $T = \dfrac{mg}{2\sin\theta}$

As mg is constant

$$\Rightarrow \quad T \propto \frac{1}{\sin\theta} \Rightarrow T_{max} = \frac{mg}{2\sin\theta_{min}}$$

$$\sin\theta_{min} = 0 \Rightarrow \theta_{min} = 0$$

No option matches with $\theta = 0°$

$$T_{min} = \frac{mg}{2\sin\theta_{max}} \quad (\text{since, } \sin\theta_{max} = 1)$$

$$\sin\theta_{max} = 1 \Rightarrow \theta = 90°$$

Matches with option (b)

Hence, tension is least for the case (b).

Note *We should be careful when measuring the angle, it must be in the direction as given in the diagram.*

Q. 8 Consider two cylindrical rods of identical dimensions, one of rubber and the other of steel. Both the rods are fixed rigidly at one end to the roof. A mass *M* is attached to each of the free ends at the centre of the rods.

(a) Both the rods will elongate but there shall be no perceptible change in shape

(b) The steel rod will elongate and change shape but the rubber rod will only elongate

(c) The steel rod will elongate without any perceptible change in shape, but the rubber rod will elongate and the shape of the bottom edge will change to an ellipse

(d) The steel rod will elongate, without any perceptible change in shape, but the rubber rod will elongate with the shape of the bottom edge tapered to a tip at the centre

Ans. *(d)* Consider the diagram.

A mass M is attached at the centre. As the mass is attached to both the rods, both rod will be elongated, but due to different elastic properties of material rubber changes shape also.

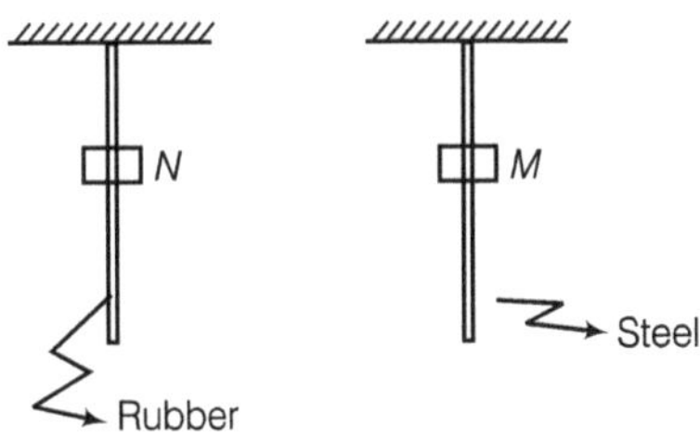

Multiple Choice Questions (More Than One Options)

Q. 9 The stress-strain graphs for two materials are shown in figure. (assume same scale)

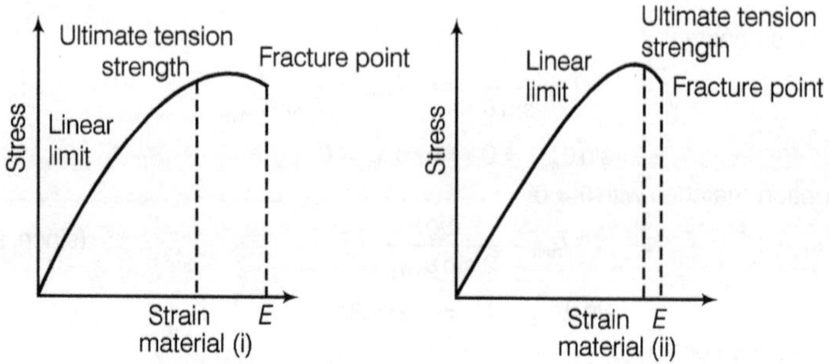

(a) Material (ii) is more elastic than material (i) and hence material (ii) is more brittle
(b) Material (i) and (ii) have the same elasticity and the same brittleness
(c) Material (ii) is elastic over a larger region of strain as compared to (i)
(d) Material (ii) is more brittle than material (i)

Thinking Process

We have to compare ultimate tensile strength for each material. Material having more ultimate tensile strength will be elastic over larger region.

Ans. *(c, d)*

It is clear from the two graphs, the ultimate tensile strength for material (ii) is greater, hence material (ii) is elastic over larger region as compared to material (i).
For material (ii) fracture point is nearer, hence it is more brittle.

Q. 10 A wire is suspended from the ceiling and stretched under the action of a weight F suspended from its other end. The force exerted by the ceiling on its is equal and opposite to the weight.

(a) Tensile stress at any cross-section A of the wire is F/A
(b) Tensile stress at any cross-section is zero
(c) Tensile stress at any cross-section A of the wire is $2F/A$
(d) Tension at any cross-section A of the wire is F

Ans. *(a, d)*

As shown in the diagram
Clearly, forces at each cross-section is F.

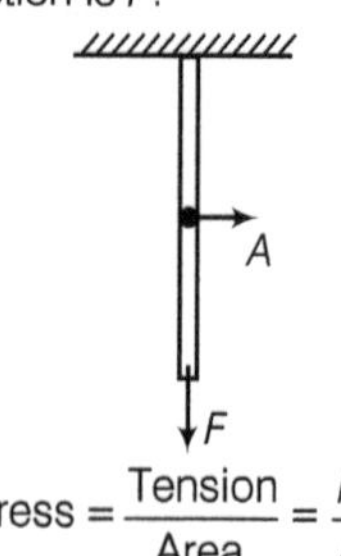

Now applying formula, $$\text{Stress} = \frac{\text{Tension}}{\text{Area}} = \frac{F}{A}$$

$$\text{Tension} = \text{Applied force} = F$$

Q. 11 A rod of length l and negligible mass is suspended at its two ends by two wires of steel (wire A) and aluminium (wire B) of equal lengths (figure). The cross-sectional areas of wires A and B are 1.0 mm^2 and 2.0 mm^2, respectively. $(Y_{Al} = 70 \times 10^9 \text{Nm}^{-2}$ and $Y_{steel} = 200 \times 10^9 \text{Nm}^{-2})$

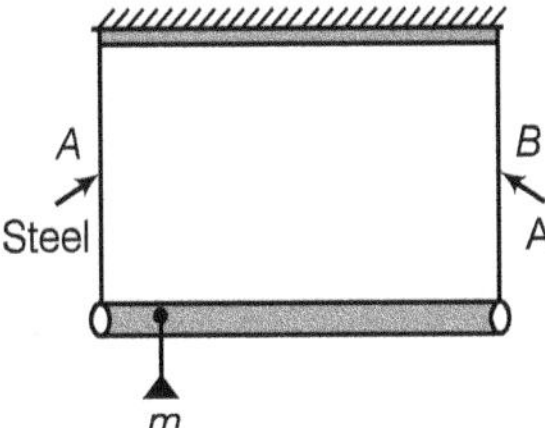

(a) Mass m should be suspended close to wire A to have equal stresses in both the wires

(b) Mass m should be suspended close to B to have equal stresses in both the wires

(c) Mass m should be suspended at the middle of the wires to have equal stresses in both the wires

(d) Mass m should be suspended close to wire A to have equal strain in both wires

Ans. *(b, d)*

Let the mass is placed at x from the end B.

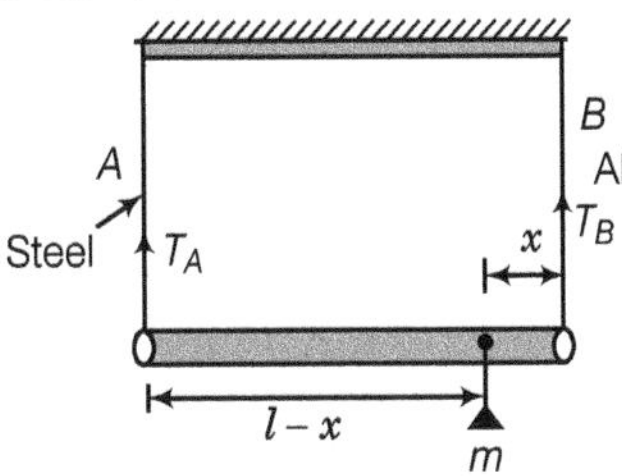

Let T_A and T_B be the tensions in wire A and wire B respectively.

For the rotational equilibrium of the system,

$$\Sigma\tau = 0 \qquad \text{(Total torque = 0)}$$

$$\Rightarrow \quad T_B x - T_A (l - x) = 0$$

$$\Rightarrow \quad \frac{T_B}{T_A} = \frac{l-x}{x} \qquad \text{...(i)}$$

$$\text{Stress in wire } A = S_A = \frac{T_A}{a_A}$$

$$\text{Stress in wire } B = S_B = \frac{T_B}{a_B}$$

where a_A and a_B are cross-sectional areas of wire A and B respectively.

By question $a_B = 2\,a_A$

Now, **for equal stress** $\quad S_A = S_B$

$$\Rightarrow \quad \frac{T_A}{a_A} = \frac{T_B}{a_B} \Rightarrow \frac{T_B}{T_A} = \frac{a_B}{a_A} = 2$$

$$\Rightarrow \quad \frac{l-x}{x} = 2 \Rightarrow \frac{l}{x} - 1 = 2$$

$$\Rightarrow \quad x = \frac{l}{3} \Rightarrow l - x = l - l/3 = \frac{2\,l}{3}$$

Hence, mass m should be placed closer to B.

For equal strain, $(\text{strain})_A = (\text{strain})_B$

$$\Rightarrow \quad \frac{(Y_A)}{S_A} = \frac{Y_B}{S_B} \quad \text{(where } Y_A \text{ and } Y_B \text{ are Young modulii)}$$

$$\Rightarrow \quad \frac{Y_{\text{steel}}}{T_A/a_A} = \frac{Y_{\text{Al}}}{T_B/a_B}$$

$$\Rightarrow \quad \frac{Y_{\text{steel}}}{Y_{\text{Al}}} = \frac{T_A}{T_B} \times \frac{a_B}{a_A} = \left(\frac{x}{l-x}\right)\left(\frac{2a_A}{a_A}\right)$$

$$\Rightarrow \quad \frac{200 \times 10^9}{70 \times 10^9} = \frac{2x}{l-x} \Rightarrow \frac{20}{7} = \frac{2x}{l-x}$$

$$\Rightarrow \quad \frac{10}{7} = \frac{x}{l-x} \Rightarrow 10l - 10x = 7x$$

$$\Rightarrow \quad 17x = 10l \Rightarrow x = \frac{10l}{17}$$

$$l - x = l - \frac{10l}{17} = \frac{7l}{17}$$

Hence, mass m should be placed closer to wire A.

Q. 12 For an ideal liquid,

(a) the bulk modulus is infinite
(b) the bulk modulus is zero
(c) the shear modulus is infinite
(d) the shear modulus is zero

Ans. *(a, d)*

As an ideal liquid is not compressible.

Hence, change in volume, $\Delta V = 0$

$$\text{Bulk modulus } B = \frac{\text{Stress}}{\text{Volume strain}} = \frac{F/A}{\Delta V/V} = \frac{F}{A} \times \frac{V}{\Delta V} = \infty$$

$$\text{Compressibility, } K = \frac{1}{B} = \frac{1}{\infty} = 0$$

As there is no tangential (viscous) force exists in case of an ideal fluid, hence, shear modulus = 0.

Q. 13 A copper and a steel wire of the same diameter are connected end to end. A deforming force F is applied to this composite wire which causes a total elongation of 1 cm. The two wires will have

(a) the same stress (b) different stress (c) the same strain (d) different strain

Ans. *(a, d)*

Consider the diagram where a deforming force F is applied to the combination.

$$\text{For steel wire, } Y_{\text{steel}} = \frac{\text{Stress}}{\text{Strain}} = \frac{F/A}{\text{Strain}}$$

where F is tension in each wire and A is cross-section area of each wires.

As F and A are same for both the wire, hence, stress will be same for both the wire.

$$(\text{Strain})_{\text{steel}} = \frac{\text{Stress}}{Y_{\text{steel}}}, \quad (\text{Strain})_{\text{copper}} = \frac{\text{Stress}}{Y_{\text{copper}}}$$

As, $Y_{\text{steel}} \neq Y_{\text{copper}}$

Hence, the two wires will have differents strain.

Very Short Answer Type Questions

Q. 14 The Young's modulus for steel is much more than that for rubber. For the same longitudinal strain, which one will have greater tensile stress?

Ans. Young's modulus $(Y) = \dfrac{\text{Stress}}{\text{Longitudinal strain}}$

For same longitudinal strain, $Y \propto \text{stress}$

$$\therefore \quad \frac{Y_{\text{steel}}}{Y_{\text{rubber}}} = \frac{(\text{stress})_{\text{steel}}}{(\text{stress})_{\text{rubber}}} \quad \ldots(\text{i})$$

But $Y_{\text{steel}} > Y_{\text{rubber}}$

$$\therefore \quad \frac{Y_{\text{steel}}}{Y_{\text{rubber}}} > 1$$

Therefore, from Eq. (i),

$$\frac{(\text{stress})_{\text{steel}}}{(\text{stress})_{\text{rubber}}} > 1$$

$$\Rightarrow \quad (\text{stress})_{\text{steel}} > (\text{stress})_{\text{rubber}}$$

Q. 15 Is stress a vector quantity?

Ans. Stress $= \dfrac{\text{Magnitude of internal reaction force}}{\text{Area of cross-section}}$

Therefore, stress is a scalar quantity not a vector quantity.

Q. 16 Identical springs of steel and copper are equally stretched. On which, more work will have to be done?

Ans. Work done in stretching a wire is given by $W = \frac{1}{2} F \times \Delta l$

[where F is applicd force and Δl is extension in the wire]

As springs of steel and copper are equally stretched. Therefore, for same force (F),

$$W \propto \Delta l \quad \ldots(\text{i})$$

$$\text{Young's modulus } (Y) = \frac{F}{A} \times \frac{l}{\Delta l} \Rightarrow \Delta l = \frac{F}{A} \times \frac{l}{Y}$$

As both springs are identical, $\Delta l \propto \dfrac{1}{Y}$ ...(ii)

From Eqs. (i) and (ii), we get $W \propto \dfrac{1}{Y}$

$$\therefore \quad \frac{W_{\text{steel}}}{W_{\text{copper}}} = \frac{Y_{\text{copper}}}{Y_{\text{steel}}} < 1 \quad (\text{As, } Y_{\text{steel}} > Y_{\text{copper}})$$

$$\Rightarrow \quad W_{\text{steel}} < W_{\text{copper}}$$

Therefore, more work will be done for stretching copper spring.

Q. 17 What is the Young's modulus for a perfect rigid body?

Ans. Young's modulus $(Y) = \dfrac{F}{A} \times \dfrac{l}{\Delta l}$

For a perfectly rigid body, change in length $\Delta l = 0$

$$\therefore \quad Y = \frac{F}{A} \times \frac{l}{0} = \infty$$

Therefore, Young's modulus for a perfectly rigid body is infinite(∞).

Q. 18 What is the Bulk modulus for a perfect rigid body?

Ans. Bulk modulus $(K) = \frac{p}{\Delta V / V} = \frac{pV}{\Delta V}$

For perfectly rigid body, change in volume $\Delta V = 0$

$$\therefore \quad K = \frac{pV}{0} = \infty$$

Therefore, bulk modulus for a perfectly rigid body is infinity (∞).

Q. 19 A wire of length L and radius r is clamped rigidly at one end. When the other end of the wire is pulled by a force f, its length increases by l. Another wire of the same material of length $2L$ and radius $2r$, is pulled by a force $2f$. Find the increase in length of this wire.

Thinking Process

In this problem, we have to apply Hooke's law and then elongation in each wire will be compared.

Ans. The situation is shown in the diagram.

Now, Young's modulus $(Y) = \frac{f}{A} \times \frac{L}{l}$

For first wire, $$Y = \frac{f}{\pi r^2} \times \frac{L}{l} \quad \ldots(i)$$

For second wire, $$Y = \frac{2f}{\pi (2r)^2} \times \frac{2L}{l'}$$

$$= \frac{f}{\pi r^2} \times \frac{L}{l'} \quad \ldots(ii)$$

From Eqs. (i) and (ii), $$\frac{f}{\pi r^2} \times \frac{L}{l} = \frac{f}{\pi r^2} \times \frac{L}{l'}$$

$$\therefore \quad l = l'$$

($\because$ Both wires are of same material, hence, Young's modulus will be same.)

Q. 20 A steel rod ($Y = 2.0 \times 10^{11}$ N/m^2 and $\alpha = 10^{-50}$ °C^{-1}) of length 1 m and area of cross-section 1 cm^2 is heated from 0°C to 200° C, without being allowed to extend or bend. What is the tension produced in the rod?

Thinking Process

Due to increase in temperature of the rod, length, increases. The equation of thermal expansion for linear expansion will be applied.

Ans. Given, Young's modulus of steel $Y = 2.0 \times 10^{11}$ N/m^2

Coefficient of thermal expansion $\alpha = 10^{-5}$ °C^{-1}

Length $l = 1$ m

Area of cross-section $A = 1 \text{ cm}^2 = 1 \times 10^{-4} \text{ m}^2$

Increase in temperature $\Delta t = 200°\text{C} - 0°\text{C} = 200°\text{C}$

Tension produced in steel rod $(F) = YA\alpha\Delta t$

$$= 2.0 \times 10^{11} \times 1 \times 10^{-4} \times 10^{-5} \times 200$$

$$= 4 \times 10^4 \text{N}$$

Q. 21 To what depth must a rubber ball be taken in deep sea so that its volume is decreased by 0.1%. (The bulk modulus of rubber is 9.8×10^8 N/m^2; and the density of sea water is 10^3 kg/m^3)

Ans. Given, Bulk modulus of rubber $(K) = 9.8 \times 10^8$ N/m^2

Density of sea water $(\rho) = 10^3$ kg/m^3

Percentage decrease in volume, $\left(\frac{\Delta V}{V} \times 100\right) = 0.1 \Rightarrow \frac{\Delta V}{V} = \frac{0.1}{100}$

$$\Rightarrow \frac{\Delta V}{V} = \frac{1}{1000}$$

Let the rubber ball be taken upto depth h.

$\therefore$ Change in pressure $(p) = h\rho g$

$$\therefore \text{Bulk modulus } (K) = \left|\frac{p}{\Delta V / V}\right| = \frac{h\rho g}{(\Delta V / V)}$$

$$\Rightarrow h = \frac{K \times (\Delta V / V)}{\rho g} = \frac{9.8 \times 10^8 \times \frac{1}{1000}}{10^3 \times 9.8} = 100 \text{ m}$$

Q. 22 A truck is pulling a car out of a ditch by means of a steel cable that is 9.1 m long and has a radius of 5 mm. When the car just begins to move, the tension in the cable is 800 N. How much has the cable stretched? (Young's modulus for steel is 2×10^{11} N/m^2)

Ans. Length of steel cable $l = 9.1$ m

Radius $r = 5 \text{ mm} = 5 \times 10^{-3}$ m

Tension in the cable $F = 800$ N

Young's modulus for steel $Y = 2 \times 10^{11}$ N/m^2

Change in length $\Delta l = ?$

$$\text{Young's modulus } (Y) = \frac{F}{A} \times \frac{l}{\Delta l} \Rightarrow \Delta l = \frac{F}{\pi r^2} \times \frac{l}{Y}$$

$$= \frac{800}{3.14 \times (5 \times 10^{-3})^2} \times \frac{9.1}{2 \times 10^{11}}$$

$$= 4.64 \times 10^{-4} \text{ m}$$

Q. 23 Two identical solid balls, one of ivory and the other of wet-clay, are dropped from the same height on the floor. Which one will rise to a greater height after striking the floor and why?

Ans. Since, ivory ball is more elastic than wet-clay ball, therefore, ivory ball tries to regain its original shape quickly. Hence, more energy and momentum is transferred to the ivory ball in comparison to the wet clay ball and therefore, ivory ball will rise higher after striking the floor.

Q. 24 **Consider a long steel bar under a tensile stress due to forces F acting at the edges along the length of the bar (figure). Consider a plane making an angle θ with the length. What are the tensile and shearing stresses on this plane?**

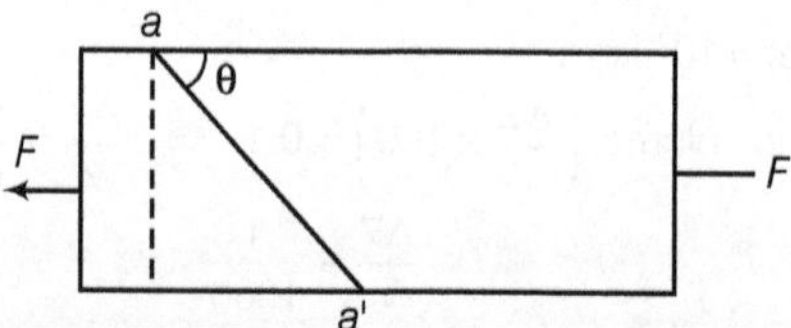

(a) For what angle is the tensile stress a maximum?
(b) For what angle is the shearing stress a maximum?

Thinking Process

To solve this question, we have to resolve the force along and perpendicular to the inclined plane. Now, we can easily calculate the tensile and shearing stress.

Ans. Consider the adjacent diagram.

Let the cross-sectional area of the bar be A. Consider the equilibrium of the plane aa'. A force F must be acting on this plane making an angle $\frac{\pi}{2} - \theta$ with the normal ON. Resolving F into components, along the plane (F_P)and normal to the plane.

$$F_P = F \cos \theta$$
$$F_N = F \sin \theta$$

Let the area of the face aa' be A', then

$$\frac{A}{A'} = \sin \theta$$

$$\therefore \quad A' = \frac{A}{\sin \theta}$$

$$\text{The tensile stress} = \frac{\text{Normal force}}{\text{Area}} = \frac{F \sin \theta}{A'}$$
$$= \frac{F \sin \theta}{A / \sin \theta} = \frac{F}{A} \sin^2 \theta$$

$$\text{Shearing stress} = \frac{\text{Parallel force}}{\text{Area}}$$
$$= \frac{F \cos \theta}{A / \sin \theta} = \frac{F}{A} \sin \theta . \cos \theta$$
$$= \frac{F}{2A} (2 \sin \theta . \cos \theta) = \frac{F}{2A} \sin 2\theta$$

(a) For tensile stress to be maximum, $\sin^2 \theta = 1$

$$\Rightarrow \quad \sin \theta = 1$$
$$\Rightarrow \quad \theta = \frac{\pi}{2}$$

(b) For shearing stress to be maximum,

$$\sin 2\theta = 1$$
$$\Rightarrow \quad 2\theta = \frac{\pi}{2}$$
$$\Rightarrow \quad \theta = \frac{\pi}{4}$$

Note *We must not apply the formula for stress directly, forces must be resolved.*

Q. 25 (a) A steel wire of mass μ per unit length with a circular cross-section has a radius of 0.1 cm. The wire is of length 10 m when measured lying horizontal, and hangs from a hook on the wall. A mass of 25 kg is hung from the free end of the wire. Assuming, the wire to be uniform and lateral strains << longitudinal strains, find the extension in the length of the wire. The density of steel is 7860 kg m^{-3}.
(Young's modulus $Y = 2 \times 10^{11}$ Nm^{-2}.

(b) If the yield strength of steel is 2.5×10^8 Nm^{-2}, what is the maximum weight that can be hung at the lower end of the wire?

Thinking Process

When the wire is hanging different part of the wire will be acted upon by different forces. To find the tension due to whole wire, consider a small element and find the tension there and then integrate for the whole wire.

Ans. Consider the diagram when a small element of length dx is considered at x from the load ($x = 0$).

(a) Let $T(x)$ and $T(x + dx)$ are tensions on the two cross-sections a distance dx apart, then --

$-T(x + dx) + T(x) = dmg = \mu dxg$ (where μ is the mass/length). $(\because dm = \mu dx)$

$$dT = \mu g dx \qquad [\because dT = T(x + dx) - T(x)]$$

$$\Rightarrow \quad T(x) = \mu g x + C \qquad \text{(on integrating)}$$

At $x = 0$, $T(0) = Mg \Rightarrow C = Mg$

$$\therefore \quad T(x) = \mu g x + Mg$$

Let the length dx at x increase by dr, then

$$\text{Young's modulus } Y = \frac{\text{Stress}}{\text{Strain}}$$

$$\frac{T(x)/A}{dr/dx} = Y$$

$$\Rightarrow \quad \frac{dr}{dx} = \frac{1}{YA} T(x)$$

$$\Rightarrow \quad r = \frac{1}{YA}\int_0^L (\mu g x + Mg)dx$$

$$= \frac{1}{YA}\left[\frac{\mu g x^2}{2} + Mgx\right]_0^L$$

$$= \frac{1}{YA}\left[\frac{mgL^2}{2} + MgL\right]$$

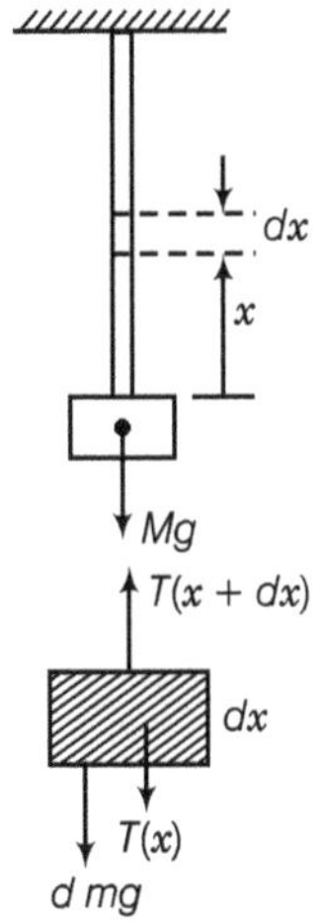

Mg
T(x + dx)
dx
T(x)
d mg
x

(m is the mass of the wire)

$$A = \pi \times (10^{-3})^2 \text{ m}^2$$

$$Y = 200 \times 10^9 \text{ Nm}^{-2}$$

$$m = \pi \times (10^{-3})^2 \times 10 \times 7860 \text{ kg}$$

$$\therefore \quad r = \frac{1}{2 \times 10^{11} \times \pi \times 10^{-6}}\left[\frac{\pi \times 786 \times 10^{-3} \times 10 \times 10}{2} + 25 \times 10 \times 10\right]$$

$$= [196.5 \times 10^{-6} + 3.98 \times 10^{-3}] \approx 4 \times 10^{-3} \text{m}$$

(b) Clearly tension will be maximum at $x = L$

$\therefore$ $$T = \mu gL + Mg = (m + M)g \quad [\because m = \mu L]$$

The yield force = (Yield strength Y) area $= 250 \times 10^6 \times \pi \times (10^{-3})^2 = 250 \times \pi$N

At yield point T = Yield force

$\Rightarrow$ $$(m + M)g = 250 \times \pi$$

$$m = \pi \times (10^{-3})^2 \times 10 \times 7860 << M$$

$\therefore$ $$Mg \approx 250 \times \pi$$

Hence, $$M = \frac{250 \times \pi}{10} = 25 \times \pi \approx 75 \text{ kg.}$$

Q. 26 A steel rod of length $2l$, cross-sectional area A and mass M is set rotating in a horizontal plane about an axis passing through the centre. If Y is the Young's modulus for steel, find the extension in the length of the rod. (assume the rod is uniform)

Thinking Process

To solve this question, we have to consider a small element, find tension in the rod at this element and then calculate for the whole rod.

Ans. Consider an element of width dr at r as shown in the diagram.

Let $T(r)$ and $T(r + dr)$ be the tensions at r and $r + dr$ respectively.

Net centrifugal force on the element $= \omega^2 r dm$ (where ω is angular velocity of the rod)

$$= \omega^2 r \mu dr \quad (\because \mu = \text{mass/length})$$

$\Rightarrow$ $$T(r) - T(r + dr) = \mu \omega^2 r dr$$

$\Rightarrow$ $$-dT = \mu \omega^2 r dr$$

[$\because$ Tension and centrifugal forces are opposite]

$\therefore$ $$-\int_{T=0}^{T} dT = \int_{r=l}^{r=r} \mu\omega^2 r dr \quad [\because T = 0 \text{ at } r = l]$$

$\Rightarrow$ $$T(r) = \frac{\mu\omega^2}{2}(l^2 - r^2)$$

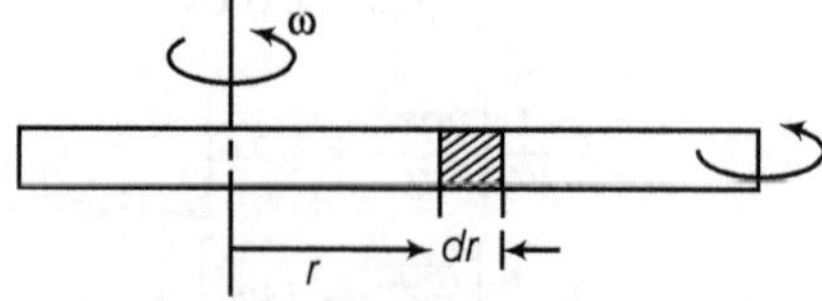

Let the increase in length of the element dr be Δr

So, $$\text{Young's modulus } Y = \frac{\text{Stress}}{\text{Strain}} = \frac{T(r)/A}{\frac{\Delta r}{dr}}$$

ω²r dm ω² (r + dr)

$\therefore$ $$\frac{\Delta r}{dr} = \frac{T(r)}{A} = \frac{\mu\omega^2}{2YA}(l^2 - r^2)$$

$\therefore$ $$\Delta r = \frac{1}{YA}\frac{\mu\omega^2}{2}(l^2 - r^2)dr$$

$\therefore$ Δ = change in length in right part $= \frac{1}{YA}\frac{\mu\omega^2}{2}\int_0^l (l^2 - r^2)dr$

$$= \left(\frac{1}{YA}\right)\frac{\mu\omega^2}{2}\left[l^3 - \frac{l^3}{3}\right] = \frac{1}{3YA}\mu\omega^2 L^2$$

$\therefore$ $$\text{Total change in length} = 2\Delta = \frac{2}{3YA}\mu\omega^2 l^2$$

Q. 27 An equilateral triangle ABC is formed by two Cu rods AB and BC and one Al rod. It is heated in such a way that temperature of each rod increases by ΔT. Find change in the angle ABC. [Coeffecient of linear expansion for Cu is α_1, coefficient of linear expansion for Al is α_2]

Thinking Process

Due to increase in temperature length of each side will change, hence, the angle corresponding to any vertex also changes.

Ans. Consider the diagram shown

Let $l_1 = AB, l_2 = AC, l_3 = BC$

$$\therefore \quad \cos\theta = \frac{l_3^2 + l_1^2 - l_2^2}{2l_3 l_1} \qquad \text{(assume } \angle ABC = \theta\text{)}$$

$$\Rightarrow \quad 2l_3 l_1 \cos\theta = l_3^2 + l_1^2 - l_2^2$$

Differentiating $2(l_3 dl_1 + l_1 dl_3)\cos\theta - 2l_1 l_3 \sin\theta d\theta$

$$= 2l_3 dl_1 + 2l_1 dl_1 - 2l_2 dl_2$$

Now, $dl_1 = l_1\alpha_1 \Delta t$ (where, Δt = change in temperature)

$$dl_2 = l_2\alpha_1 \Delta t \quad \Rightarrow \quad dl_3 = l_3\alpha_2\Delta t$$

and $l_1 = l_2 = l_3 = l$

$$(l^2 \alpha_1\Delta t + l^2 \alpha_1 \Delta t)\cos\theta + l^2 \sin\theta d\theta = l^2 \alpha_1\Delta t + l^2\alpha_1\Delta t - l^2\alpha_2 \Delta t$$

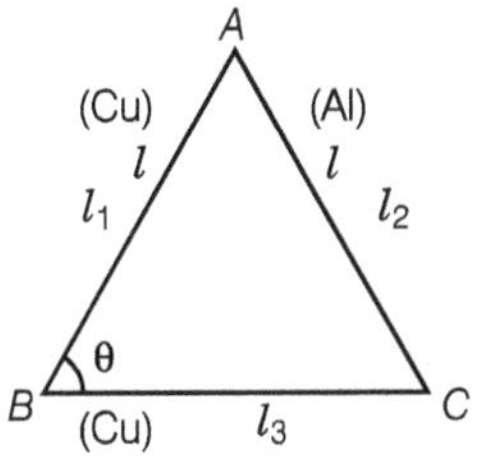

$$\sin\theta d\theta = 2\alpha_1 \Delta t (1 - \cos\theta) - \alpha_2\Delta t$$

Putting $\theta = 60°$ (for equilateral triangle)

$$d\theta \times \sin 60° = 2\alpha_1 \Delta t (1 - \cos 60°) - \alpha_2\Delta t$$

$$= 2\alpha_1\Delta t \times \frac{1}{2} - \alpha_2\Delta t = (\alpha_1 - \alpha_2)\Delta t$$

$\Rightarrow$ $d\theta$ = change in the angle $\angle ABC$

$$= \frac{(\alpha_1 - \alpha_2)\Delta T}{\sin 60°} = \frac{2(\alpha_1 - \alpha_2)\Delta T}{\sqrt{3}} \qquad (\because \Delta t = \Delta T \text{ given})$$

Q. 28 In nature, the failure of structural members usually result from large torque because of twisting or bending rather than due to tensile or compressive strains. This process of structural breakdown is called buckling and in cases of tall cylindrical structures like trees, the torque is caused by its own weight bending the structure. Thus, the vertical through the centre of gravity does not fall within the base. The elastic torque caused because of this bending about the central axis of the tree is given by $\frac{Y\pi r^4}{4R}$. Y is the Young's modulus, r is the radius of the trunk and R is the radius of curvature of the bent surface along the height of the tree containing the centre of gravity (the neutral surface). Estimate the critical height of a tree for a given radius of the trunk.

Thinking Process

In this question, the elastic torque is given we have to find the torque caused by the weight due to bending and equate with the given value.

Ans. Consider the diagram according to the question, the bending torque on the trunk of radius r of the tree $= \frac{Y\pi r^4}{4R}$

where R is the radius of curvature of the bent surface.

When the tree is about to buckle $Wd = \frac{Y\pi r^4}{4R}$

If $R \gg h$, then the centre of gravity is at a height $l \approx \frac{1}{2}h$ from the ground.

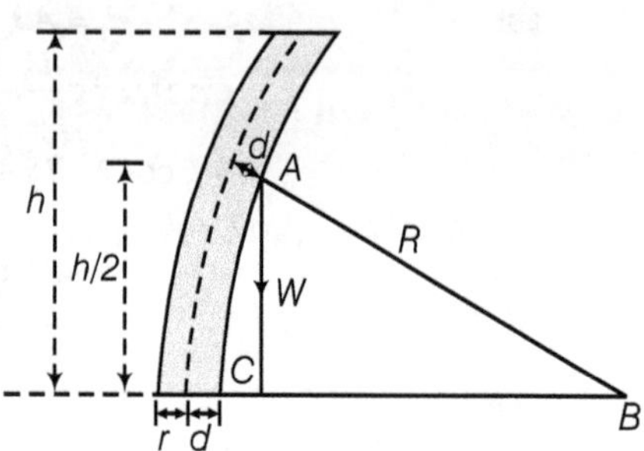

From $\Delta ABC \; R^2 \simeq (R-d)^2 + \left(\frac{1}{2}h\right)^2$

if $d \ll R$, $\quad R^2 \simeq R^2 - 2Rd + \frac{1}{4}h^2$

$\therefore \quad d = \frac{h^2}{8R}$

If ω_0 is the weight/volume

$$\frac{Y\pi r^4}{4R} = \omega_0 \,(\pi r^2 h)\, \frac{h^2}{8R} \qquad [\because \text{Torque is caused by the weight}]$$

$$\Rightarrow \quad h \simeq \left(\frac{2Y}{\omega_0}\right)^{1/3} r^{2/3}$$

Hence, critical height $= h = \left(\frac{2Y}{\omega_0}\right)^{1/3} r^{2/3}$.

Q. 29 **A stone of mass m is tied to an elastic string of negligible mass and spring constant k. The unstretched length of the string is L and has negligible mass. The other end of the string is fixed to a nail at a point P. Initially the stone is at the same level as the point P. The stone is dropped vertically from point P.**

(a) Find the distance y from the top when the mass comes to rest for an instant, for the first time.

(b) What is the maximum velocity attained by the stone in this drop?

(c) What shall be the nature of the motion after the stone has reached its lowest point?

Thinking Process

In this problem ,the given string is elastic and there is no dissipation of energy we can apply conservation of mechanical energy.

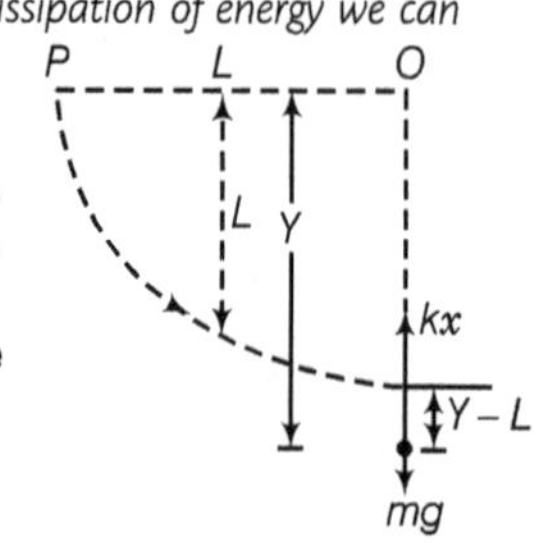

Ans. Consider the diagram the stone is dropped from point p.

(a) Till the stone drops through a length L it will be in free fall. After that the elasticity of the string will force it to a SHM. Let the stone come to rest instantaneously at y.

The loss in PE of the stone is the PE stored in the stretched string.

$$mgy = \frac{1}{2}k(y-L)^2$$

$$\Rightarrow \qquad mgy = \frac{1}{2}ky^2 - kyL + \frac{1}{2}kL^2 \Rightarrow \frac{1}{2}ky^2 - (kL + mg)y + \frac{1}{2}kL^2 = 0$$

$$y = \frac{(kL + mg) \pm \sqrt{(kL + mg)^2 - k^2L^2}}{k} = \frac{(kL + mg) \pm \sqrt{2mgkL + m^2g^2}}{k}$$

Retain the positive sign.

$$\therefore \qquad y = \frac{(kL + mg) + \sqrt{2mgkL + m^2g^2}}{k}$$

(b) In SHM, the maximum velocity is attained when the body passes, through the "equilibrium, position" *i.e.,* when the instantaneous acceleration is zero. That is $mg - kx = 0$, where x is the extension from L.

$$\Rightarrow \qquad mg = kx$$

Let the velocity be v. Then,

$$\frac{1}{2}mv^2 + \frac{1}{2}kx^2 = mg\,(L + x) \qquad \text{(from conservation of energy)}$$

$$\frac{1}{2}mv^2 = mg\,(L + x) - \frac{1}{2}kx^2$$

Now, $$mg = kx \Rightarrow x = \frac{mg}{k}$$

$$\therefore \qquad \frac{1}{2}mv^2 = mg\left(L + \frac{mg}{k}\right) - \frac{1}{2}k\frac{m^2g^2}{k^2} = mgL + \frac{m^2g^2}{k} - \frac{1}{2}\frac{m^2g^2}{k}$$

$$\frac{1}{2}mv^2 = mgL + \frac{1}{2}\frac{m^2g^2}{k}$$

$$\therefore \qquad v^2 = 2gL + mg^2/k$$

$$v = (2gL + mg^2/k)^{1/2}$$

(c) When stone is at the lowest position *i.e.*, at instantaneous distance Y from P, then equation of motion of the stone is

$$\frac{md^2y}{dt^2} = mg - k\,(y - L) \Rightarrow \frac{d^2y}{dt^2} + \frac{k}{m}(y - L) - g = 0$$

Make a transformation of variables, $z = \frac{k}{m}(y - L) - g$

$$\therefore \qquad \frac{d^2z}{dt^2} + \frac{k}{m}z = 0$$

It is a differential equation of second order which represents SHM.

Comparing with equation $\frac{d^2z}{dt^2} + \omega^2 z = 0$

Angular frequency of harmonic motion $\omega = \sqrt{\frac{k}{m}}$

The solution of above equation will be of the type $z = A\cos(\omega t + \phi)$; where $\omega = \sqrt{\frac{k}{m}}$

$$y = \left(L + \frac{mg}{k}\right) + A'\cos(\omega t + \phi)$$

Thus, the stone will perform SHM with angular frequency $\omega = \sqrt{k/m}$ about a point $y_0 = L + \frac{mg}{k}$.

9

Mechanical Properties *of* Fluids

Multiple Choice Questions (MCQs)

Q. 1 A tall cylinder is filled with viscous oil. A round pebble is dropped from the top with zero initial velocity. From the plot shown in figure, indicate the one that represents the velocity (v) of the pebble as a function of time (t).

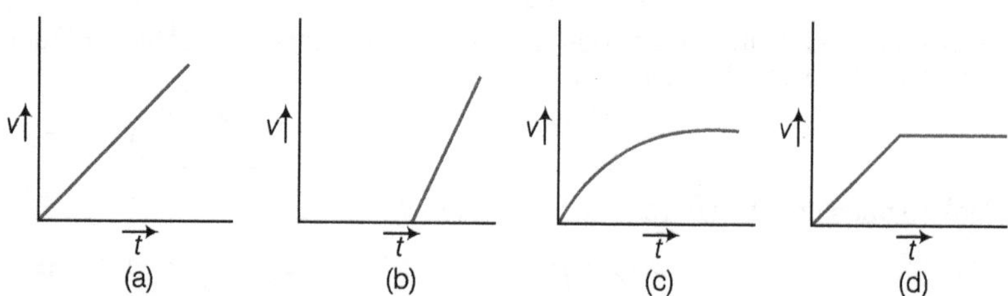

Thinking Process

When the pebble is dropped from the top, a variable force called viscous force will act which increases with increase in speed. And at equilibrium this velocity becomes constant.

Ans. *(c)* When the pebble is falling through the viscous oil the viscous force is

$$F = 6\pi\eta r v$$

where r is radius of the pebble, v is instantaneous speed, η is coefficient of viscosity.

As the force is variable, hence acceleration is also variable so v-t graph will not be straight line.First velocity increases and then becomes constant known as terminal velocity.

Q. 2 Which of the following diagrams does not represent a streamline flow?

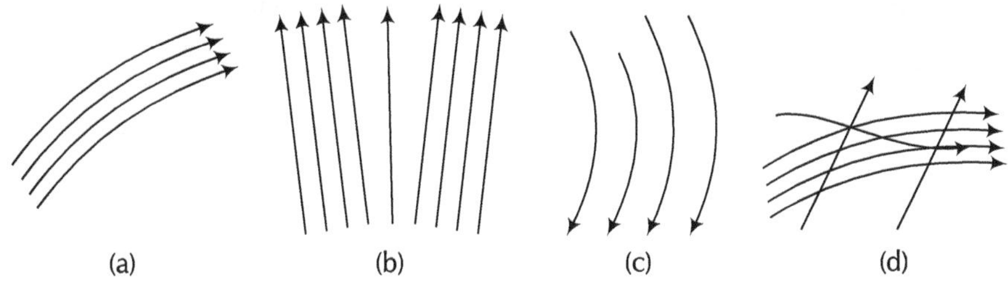

Ans. *(d)* In a streamline flow at any given point, the velocity of each passing fluid particles remaines constant. If we consider a cross-sectional area, then a point on the area cannot have different velocities at the same time, hence two streamlines of flow cannot cross each other.

Q. 3 Along a streamline,

(a) the velocity of a fluid particle remains constant
(b) the velocity of all fluid particles crossing a given position is constant
(c) the velocity of all fluid particles at a given instant is constant
(d) the speed of a fluid particle remains constant

Ans. *(b)* As we know for a streamline flow of a liquid velocity of each particle at a particular cross-section is constant, because Av = constant (law of continuity) between two cross-section of a tube of flow.

Q. 4 An ideal fluid flows through a pipe of circular cross-section made of two sections with diameters 2.5 cm and 3.75 cm. The ratio of the velocities in the two pipes is

(a) 9 : 4 (b) 3 : 2 (c) $\sqrt{3}:\sqrt{2}$ (d) $\sqrt{2}:\sqrt{3}$

Ans. *(a)* Consider the diagram where an ideal fluid is flowing through a pipe.

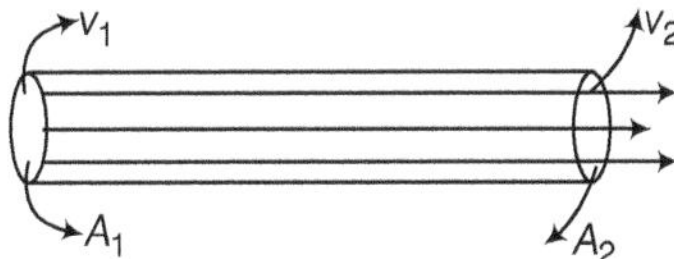

As given

d_1 = Diameter at 1st point is 2.5.

d_2 = Diameter at 2nd point is 3.75.

Applying equation of continuity for cross-sections A_1 and A_2.

$$\Rightarrow \qquad A_1v_1 = A_2v_2$$

$$\Rightarrow \qquad \frac{v_1}{v_2} = \frac{A_2}{A_1} = \frac{\pi(r_2^2)}{\pi(r_1^2)} = \left(\frac{r_2}{r_1}\right)^2$$

$$= \left(\frac{\frac{3.75}{2}}{\frac{2.5}{2}}\right)^2 = \left(\frac{3.75}{2.5}\right)^2 = \frac{9}{4} \qquad \left[\begin{array}{l} r_2 = \frac{d_2}{2} \\ r_1 = \frac{d_1}{2} \end{array}\right]$$

Q. 5 The angle of contact at the interface of water-glass is 0°, ethyl alcohol-glass is 0°, mercury-glass is 140° and methyliodide-glass is 30°. A glass capillary is put in a trough containing one of these four liquids. It is observed that the meniscus is convex. The liquid in the trough is

(a) water (b) ethylalcohol (c) mercury (d) methyliodide

Ans. *(c)* According to the question, the observed meniscus is of convex figure shape. Which is only possible when angle of contact is obtuse. Hence, the combination will be of mercury-glass (140°)

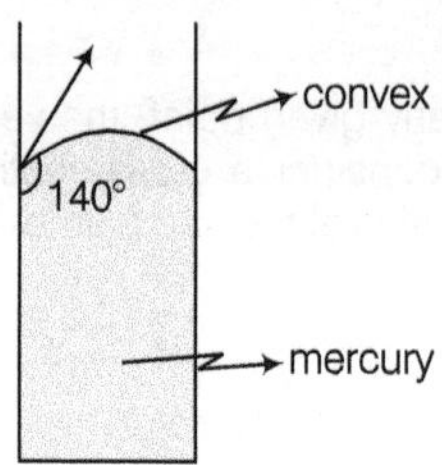

Multiple Choice Questioins (More Than One Options)

Q. 6 For a surface molecule,

(a) the net force on it is zero
(b) there is a net downward force
(c) the potential energy is less than that of a molecule inside
(d) the potential energy is more than that of a molecule inside

Ans. *(b, d)*

Consider the diagram where two molecules of a liquid are shown. One is well inside the liquid and other is on the surface. The molecule (*A*) which is well inside experiences equal forces from all directions, hence net force on it will be zero.

And molecules on the liquid surface have some extra energy as it surrounded surraind by only lower half side of liquid molecules.

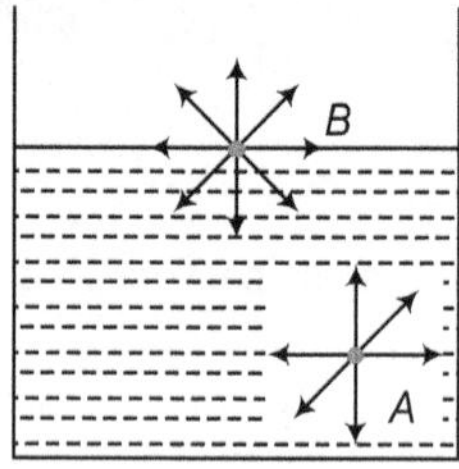

Q. 7 Pressure is a scalar quantity, because

(a) it is the ratio of force to area and both force and area are vectors
(b) it is the ratio of the magnitude of the force to area
(c) it is the ratio of the component of the force normal to the area
(d) it does not depend on the size of the area chosen

Ans. *(b, c)*

Pressure is defined as the ratio of magnitude of component of the force normal to the area and the area under consideration.

As magnitude of component is considered, hence, it will not have any direction. So, pressure is a scalar quantity.

Q. 8 A wooden block with a coin placed on its top, floats in water as shown in figure.

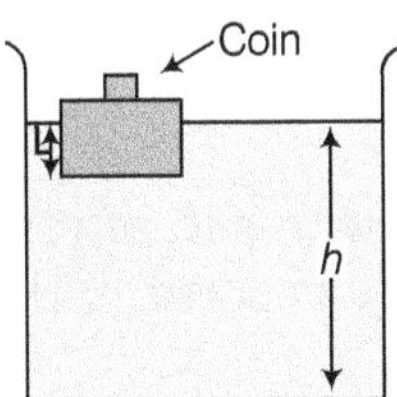

The distance l and h are shown in the figure. After sometime, the coin falls into the water. Then,

(a) l decreases (b) h decreases (c) l increases (d) h increases

Thinking Process

When any body floats in a liquid, the upthrust force acting on the body due to the displaced liquid is balanced by its weight.

Ans. *(a,b)*

When the coin falls into the water, weight of the (block + coin) system decreases, which was balanced by the upthrust force earlier. As weight of the system decreases, hence upthrust force will also decrease which is only possible when l decreases.

As l decreases volume of water displaced by the block decreases, hence h decreases.

Note *As the coin falls into water, it displaces some volume of water which is very less hence, we neglect volume of the coin.*

Q. 9 With increase in temperature, the viscosity of

(a) gases decreases
(b) liquids increases
(c) gases increases
(d) liquids decreases

Ans. *(c, d)*

For liquids coefficient of viscosity, $\eta \propto \frac{1}{\sqrt{T}}$

i.e., with increase in temperature η decreases.

For gases coefficient of viscosity, $\eta \propto \sqrt{T}$

i.e., with increase in temperature η increases.

Q. 10 Streamline flow is more likely for liquids with

(a) high density
(b) high viscosity
(c) low density
(d) low viscosity

Ans. *(b, c)*

Streamline flow is more likely for liquids having low density. We know that greater the coefficient of viscosity of a liquid more will be velocity gradient hence each line of flow can be easily differentiated. Also higher the coefficient of viscosity lower will be Reynolds number, hence flow more like to be streamline.

Very Short Answer Type Questions

Q. 11 Is viscosity a vector?

Ans. Viscosity is a property of liquid it does not have any direction, hence it is a scalar quantity.

Q. 12 Is surface tension a vector?

Ans. *No*, surface tension is a scalar quantity.

Surface tension $= \dfrac{\text{Work done}}{\text{Surface area}}$, where work done and surface area both are scalar quantities.

Q. 13 Iceberg floats in water with part of it submerged. What is the fraction of the volume of iceberg submerged, if the density of ice is $\rho_i = 0.917\text{ g cm}^{-3}$?

Ans. Given, density of ice $(\rho_{ice}) = 0.917\text{g /cm}^3$

Density of water $(\rho_w) = 1\text{ g/cm}^3$

Let V be the total volume of the iceberg and V' of its volume be submerged in water.
In floating condition.
Weight of the iceberg = Weight of the water displaced by the submerged part by ice

$$V\rho_{ice}g = V'\rho_w g$$

or $$\frac{V'}{V} = \frac{\rho_{ice}}{\rho_w} = \frac{0.917}{1} = 0.917 \qquad (\because \text{Weight}=mg=v\rho g)$$

Q. 14 A vessel filled with water is kept on a weighing pan and the scale adjusted to zero. A block of mass M and density ρ is suspended by a massless spring of spring constant k. This block is submerged inside into the water in the vessel. What is the reading of the scale?

Ans. Consider the diagram,

The scale is adjusted to zero, therefore, when the block suspended to a spring is immersed in water, then the reading of the scale will be equal to the thrust on the block due to water.

Thrust = weight of water displaced

$= V\rho_w g$ (where V is volume of the block and ρ_w is density of water)

$= \dfrac{m}{\rho}\rho_w g = \left(\dfrac{\rho_w}{\rho}\right)mg$

$$\left(\because \text{Density of the block } \rho = \frac{\text{mass}}{\text{volume}} = \frac{m}{V}\right)$$

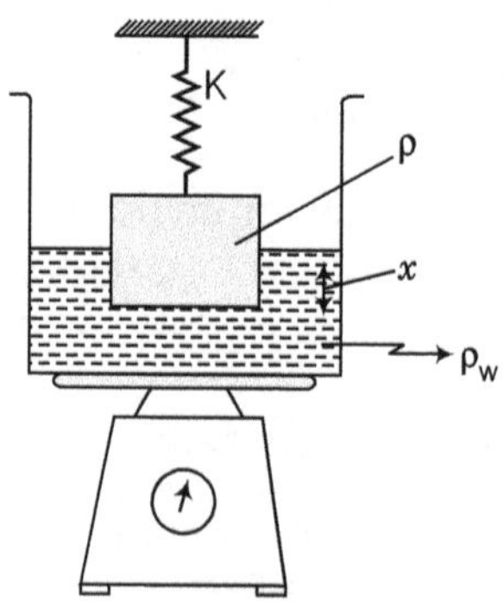

Q. 15 **A cubical block of density ρ is floating on the surface of water. Out of its height L, fraction x is submerged in water. The vessel is in an elevator accelerating upward with acceleration a. What is the fraction immersed?**

Thinking Process

As the elevator is accelerating upward the net acceleration of the block with respect to the elevator can be calculate by the concept of pseudo force.

Ans. Consider the diagram.

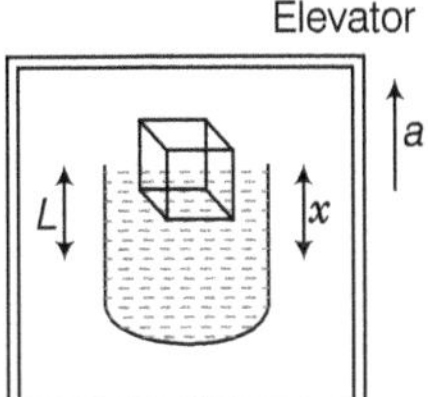

Let the density of water be ρ_w and a cubical block of ice of side L be floating in water with x of its height (L) submerged in water.

$$\text{Volume of the block } (V) = L^3$$

$$\text{Mass of the block } (m) = V\rho = L^3\rho$$

$$\text{Weight of the block} = mg = L^3\rho g$$

1st case

Volume of the water displaced by the submerged part of the block $= xL^2$

∴ Weight of the water displaced by the block

In floating condition, $xL^2\rho_w g$

Weight of the block = Weight of the water displaced by the block

$$L^3\rho g = xL^2\rho_w g$$

or
$$\frac{x}{L} = \frac{\rho}{\rho_w} = x$$

2nd case

When elevator is accelerating upward with an acceleration a, then effective acceleration

$$= (g + a) \qquad (\because \text{Pseudo force is downward})$$

Then, weight of the block
$$= m(g + a)$$
$$= L^3\rho(g + a)$$

Let x_1 fraction be submerged in water when elevator is accelerating upwards.

Now, in the floating condition, weight of the block = weight of the displaced water

$$L^3\rho(g + a) = (x_1L^2)\rho_w(g + a)$$

or
$$\frac{x_1}{L} = \frac{\rho}{\rho_w} = x$$

From 1st and 2nd case,

We see that,the fraction of the block submerged in water is independent of the acceleration of the elevator.

Note *We should not confuse with the concept of pseudo force, i.e., pseudo force is downward, hence fraction will change due to increased force.*

Short Answer Type Questions

Q. 16 The sap in trees, which consists mainly of water in summer, rises in a system of capillaries of radius $r = 2.5 \times 10^{-5}$ m. The surface tension of sap is $T = 7.28 \times 10^{-2}$ Nm^{-1} and the angle of contact is 0°. Does surface tension alone account for the supply of water to the top of all trees?

Ans. Given, radius $(r) = 2.5 \times 10^{-5}$ m

Surface tension $(S) = 7.28 \times 10^{-2}$ N/m

Angle of contact $(\theta) = 0°$

The maximum height to which sap can rise in trees through capillarity action is given by

$$h = \frac{2S\cos\theta}{r\rho g} \text{ where } S = \text{Surface tension}, \rho = \text{Density}, r = \text{Radius}$$

$$= \frac{2 \times 7.28 \times 10^{-2} \times \cos 0°}{2.5 \times 10^{-5} \times 1 \times 10^{-3} \times 9.8} = 0.6 \text{ m}$$

This is the maximum height to which the sap can rise due to surface tension. Since, many trees have heights much more than this, capillary action alone cannot account for the rise of water in all trees.

Q. 17 The free surface of oil in a tanker, at rest, is horizontal. If the tanker starts accelerating the free surface will be titled by an angle θ. If the acceleration is a ms^{-2}, what will be the slope of the free surface?

Thinking Process

As the tanker starts accelerating, free surface of the tanker will not be horizontal because pseudo force acts.

Ans. Consider the diagram where a tanker is accelerating with acceleration a.

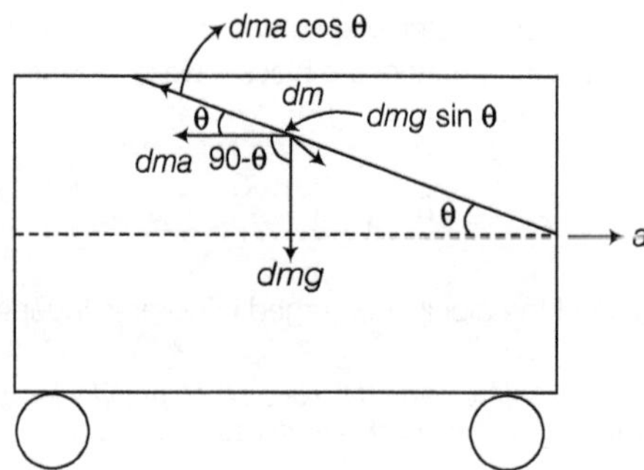

Consider an elementary particle of the fluid of mass dm.

The acting forces on the particle with respect to the tanker are shown above .

Now, balancing forces (as the particle is in equilibrium) along the inclined direction component of weight = component of pseudo force $dmg \sin\theta = dma \cos\theta$ (we have assumed that the surface is inclined at an angle θ) where, dma is pseudo force

$\Rightarrow$ $$g\sin\theta = a\cos\theta$$

$\Rightarrow$ $$a = g\tan\theta$$

$\Rightarrow$ $$\tan\theta = \frac{a}{g} = \text{slope}$$

Q. 18 Two mercury droplets of radii 0.1 cm and 0.2 cm collapse into one single drop. What amount of energy is released? The surface tension of mercury $T = 435.5 \times 10^{-3}\ \text{Nm}^{-1}$.

Thinking Process

In this process, conservation of mass will be applied. Before and after collapse, mass and hence, volume of the system remains conserved.

Ans. Consider the diagram.

Radii of mercury droplets $r_1 = 0.1\,\text{cm} = 1 \times 10^{-3}\ \text{m}$

$$r_2 = 0.2\ \text{cm} = 2 \times 10^{-3}\ \text{m}$$

Surface tension $(T) = 435.5 \times 10^{-3}$ N/m

Let the radius of the big drop formed by collapsing be R.

$\therefore$ Volume of big drop = Volume of small droplets

$$\frac{4}{3}\pi R^3 = \frac{4}{3}\pi r_1^3 + \frac{4}{3}\pi r_2^2$$

or
$$R^3 = r_1^3 + r_2^3$$
$$= (0.1)^3 + (0.2)^3$$
$$= 0.001 + 0.008$$
$$= 0.009$$

or
$$R = 0.21\,\text{cm} = 2.1 \times 10^{-3}\ \text{m}$$

$\therefore$ Change in surface area
$$\Delta A = 4\pi R^2 - (4\pi r_1^2 + 4\pi r_2^2)$$
$$= 4\pi[R^2 - (r_1^2 + r_2^2)]$$

$\therefore$ Energy released $= T \cdot \Delta A$ (where T is surface tension of mercury)
$$= T \times 4\pi[R^2 - (r_1^2 + r_2^2)]$$
$$= 435.5 \times 10^{-3} \times 4 \times 3.14[(2.1 \times 10^{-3})^2 - (1 \times 10^{-6} + 4 \times 10^{-6})]$$
$$= 435.5 \times 4 \times 3.14[4.41 - 5] \times 10^{-6} \times 10^{-3}$$
$$= -\,32.23 \times 10^{-7}$$ (Negative sign shows absorption)

Therefore, 3.22×10^{-6} J energy will be absorbed.

Note *In this process, energy is not conserved. Energy is lst due to the collapsing, in the form of radiations.*

Q. 19 If a drop of liquid breaks into smaller droplets, it results in lowering of temperature of the droplets. Let a drop of radius R, break into N small droplets each of radius r. Estimate the drop in temperature.

Ans. When a big drop of radius R, breaks into N droplets each of radius r, the volume remains constant.

$\therefore$ Volume of big drop = $N \times$ Volume of each small drop

$$\frac{4}{3}\pi R^3 = N \times \frac{4}{3}\pi r^3$$

or
$$R^3 = Nr^3$$

or
$$N = \frac{R^3}{r^3}$$

Now, change in surface area $= 4\pi R^2 - N4\pi r^2$
$$= 4\pi(R^2 - Nr^2)$$

Energy released $= T \times \Delta A$ $= S \times 4\pi(R^2 - Nr^2)$ [T = Surface tension]

Due to releasing of this energy, the temperature is lowered.

If ρ is the density and s is specific heat of liquid and its temperature is lowered by $\Delta\theta$, then energy released $= ms\Delta\theta$ [s = specific heat $\Delta\theta$ = change in temperature]

$$T \times 4\pi(R^2 - Nr^2) = \left(\frac{4}{3} \times R^3 \times \rho\right)s\Delta\theta \qquad [\because m = v\rho = \frac{4}{3}\pi R^3\rho]$$

$$\Rightarrow \quad \Delta\theta = \frac{T \times 4\pi(R^2 - Nr^2)}{\frac{4}{3}\pi R^3 \rho \times s}$$

$$= \frac{3T}{\rho s}\left[\frac{R^2}{R^3} - \frac{Nr^2}{R^3}\right]$$

$$= \frac{3T}{\rho s}\left[\frac{1}{R} - \frac{(R^3/r^3) \times r^2}{R^3}\right]$$

$$= \frac{3T}{\rho s}\left[\frac{1}{R} - \frac{1}{r}\right]$$

Q. 20 **The surface tension and vapour pressure of water at 20°C is 7.28×10^{-2} Nm^{-1} and 2.33×10^3 Pa, respectively. What is the radius of the smallest spherical water droplet which can form without evaporating at 20°C?**

Ans. Given, surface tension of water

$$(S) = 7.28 \times 10^{-2} \text{ N/m}$$

Vapour pressure $(p) = 2.33 \times 10^3$ Pa

The drop will evaporate, if the water pressure is greater than the vapour pressure.

Let a water droplet or radius R can be formed without evaporating.

Vapour pressure = Excess pressure in drop.

$$\therefore \quad p = \frac{2S}{R}$$

$$\text{or} \quad R = \frac{2S}{p} = \frac{2 \times 7.28 \times 10^{-2}}{2.33 \times 10^3}$$

$$= 6.25 \times 10^{-5} \text{ m}$$

Long Answer Type Questions

Q. 21 **(a) Pressure decreases as one ascends the atmosphere. If the density of air is ρ, what is the change in pressure dp over a differential height dh?**

(b) Considering the pressure p to be proportional to the density, find the pressure p at a height h if the pressure on the surface of the earth is p_0.

(c) If $p_0 = 1.03 \times 10^5$ Nm^{-2}, $\rho_0 = 1.29$ kg m^{-3} and $g = 9.8$ ms^{-2}, at what height will be pressure drop to (1/10) the value at the surface of the earth?

(d) This model of the atmosphere works for relatively small distances. Identify the underlying assumption that limits the model.

Thinking Process

As we are going up in the atmosphere, thickness of the gases above us decreases hence, pressure also decreases.

Ans. (a) Consider a horizontal parcel of air with cross-section A and height dh.

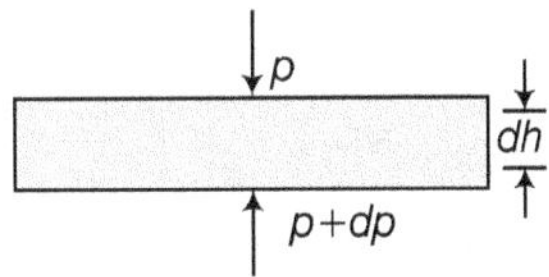

Let the pressure on the top surface and bottom surface be p and $p + dp$. If the parcel is in equilibrium, then the net upward force must be balanced by the weight.

i.e., $$(p + dp)A - pA = -\rho gAdh \quad (\because \text{Weight} = \text{Density} \times \text{Volume} \times g)$$

$$= -\rho \times Adh \times g$$

$\Rightarrow$ $$dp = -\rho gdh. \quad (\rho = \text{density of air})$$

Negative sign shows that pressure decreases with height.

(b) Let p_0 be the density of air on the surface of the earth.

As per question, pressure $\propto$ density

$\Rightarrow$ $$\frac{p}{p_0} = \frac{\rho}{\rho_0}$$

$\Rightarrow$ $$\rho = \frac{\rho_0}{p_0} p$$

$\therefore$ $$dp = -\frac{\rho_0 g}{p_0} pdh \quad [\because dp = -\rho gdh]$$

$\Rightarrow$ $$\frac{dp}{p} = -\frac{\rho_0 g}{p_0} dh$$

$\Rightarrow$ $$\int_{p_0}^{p} \frac{dp}{p} = -\frac{\rho_0 g}{p_0} \int_0^h dh \quad \left[\begin{matrix}\because \text{at } h = o, r = p_0 \\ \text{and} \quad \text{at } h = h, p = p\end{matrix}\right]$$

$\Rightarrow$ $$\ln \frac{p}{p_0} = -\frac{\rho_0 g}{p_0} h$$

By removing log, $$p = p_0 e \left(-\frac{\rho_0 gh}{p_0}\right)$$

(c) As $p = p_0 e^{-\frac{\rho_0 gh}{p_0}}$,

$\Rightarrow$ $$\ln \frac{p}{p_0} = -\frac{\rho_0 gh}{P_0}$$

By question, $$p = \frac{1}{10} p_0$$

$\Rightarrow$ $$\ln \left(\frac{\frac{1}{10} p_0}{p_0}\right) = -\frac{\rho_0 g}{p_0} h$$

$\Rightarrow$ $$\ln \frac{1}{10} = -\frac{\rho_0 g}{p_0} h\rho_0$$

$$\therefore \quad h = -\frac{p_0}{\rho_0 g}\ln\frac{1}{10} = -\frac{p_0}{\rho_0 g}\ln(10)^{-1} = \frac{p_0}{\rho_0 g}\ln 10$$

$$= \frac{p_0}{\rho_0 g} \times 2.303 \qquad [\because \ln(x) = 2.303 \log_{10}(x)]$$

$$= \frac{1.013 \times 10^5}{1.22 \times 9.8} \times 2.303 = 0.16 \times 10^5 \text{m}$$

$$= 16 \times 10^3 \text{ m}$$

(d) We know that $p \propto \rho$ (when T = constant *i.e.*, isothermal pressure)

Temperature (T) remains constant only near the surface of the earth, not at greater heights.

Q. 22 Surface tension is exhibited by liquids due to force of attraction between molecules of the liquid. The surface tension decreases with increase in temperature and vanishes at boiling point. Given that the latent heat of vaporisation for water $L_v = 540$ k cal kg^{-1}, the mechanical equivalent of heat $J = 4.2$ J cal^{-1}, density of water $\rho_w = 10^3$ kg l^{-1}, Avagardro's number $N_A = 6.0 \times 10^{26}$ k mole^{-1} and the molecular weight of water $M_A = 10$ kg for 1 k mole.

(a) Estimate the energy required for one molecule of water to evaporate.

(b) Show that the inter-molecular distance for water is $d = \left[\frac{M_A}{N_A} \times \frac{1}{\rho_w}\right]^{1/3}$ and find its value.

(c) 1 g of water in the vapour state at 1 atm occupies 1601cm^3. Estimate the inter-molecular distance at boiling point, in the vapour state.

(d) During vaporisation a molecule overcomes a force F, assumed constant, to go from an inter-molecular distance d to d'. Estimate the value of F.

(e) Calculate F / d, which is a measure of the surface tension.

Ans. (a) Given , $L_v = 540 \text{ kcal kg}^{-1}$

$$= 540 \times 10^3 \text{ cal kg}^{-1} = 540 \times 10^3 \times 4.2 \text{ J kg}^{-1}$$

$\because$ Energy required to evaporate 1 kg of water = L_v kcal

$\therefore$ M_A kg of water requires $M_A L_v$ kcal $[\because Q = mL]$

Since, there are N_A molecules in M_A kg of water the energy required for 1 molecule to evaporate is

$$U = \frac{M_A L_v}{N_A} \text{J} \qquad [\text{where } N_A = 6 \times 10^{26} = \text{Avogadro number}]$$

$$= \frac{18 \times 540 \times 4.2 \times 10^3}{6 \times 10^{26}} \text{ J}$$

$$= 90 \times 18 \times 4.2 \times 10^{-23} \text{ J}$$

$$= 6.8 \times 10^{-20} \text{J}$$

(b) Let the water molecules to be points and are separated at distance d from each other.

Volume of N_A molecule of water $= \frac{M_A}{\rho_w}$ $\left[\because V = \frac{M}{\rho}\right]$

Thus, the volume around one molecule is $= \frac{M_A}{N_A \rho_w}$

The volume around one molecule is

$$d^3 = (M_A / N_A \rho_w)$$

$$\therefore \quad d = \left(\frac{M_A}{N_A \rho_w}\right)^{1/3} = \left(\frac{18}{6 \times 10^{26} \times 10^3}\right)^{1/3}$$

$$(30 \times 10^{-30})^{1/3} \text{ m} \approx 3.1 \times 10^{-10} \text{ m}$$

(c) $\because$ 1 kg of vapour occupies volume $= 1601 \times 10^{-3} \text{m}^3$

$\therefore$ 18 kg of vapour occupies $18 \times 1601 \times 10^{-3} \text{m}^3$

6×10^{26} molecules occupies $18 \times 1601 \times 10^{-3} \text{m}^3$

$\therefore$ 1 molecule occupies $\frac{18 \times 1601 \times 10^{-3}}{6 \times 10^{26}} \text{m}^3$

If d is the inter- molecular distance, then

$$d_1^3 = (3 \times 1601 \times 10^{-29}) \text{ m}^3$$

$$\therefore \quad d_1 = (30 \times 1601)^{1/3} \times 10^{-10} \text{m}$$

$$= 36.3 \times 10^{-10} \text{m}$$

(d) Work done to change the distance from d to d_1 is $= F(d_1 - d)$

This work done is equal to energy required to evaporate 1 molecule.

$$\therefore \quad F(d_1 - d) = 6.8 \times 10^{-20}$$

or

$$F = \frac{6.8 \times 10^{-20}}{d_1 - d}$$

$$= \frac{6.8 \times 10^{-20}}{(36.3 \times 10^{-10} - 3.1 \times 10^{-10})}$$

$$= 2.05 \times 10^{-11} \text{N}$$

(e) Surface tension $= \frac{F}{d} = \frac{2.05 \times 10^{-11}}{3.1 \times 10^{-10}} = 6.6 \times 10^{-2}$ N/m.

Q. 23 A hot air balloon is a sphere of radius 8 m. The air inside is at a temperature of 60°C. How large a mass can the balloon lift when the outside temperature is 20°C? Assume air in an ideal gas, $R = 8.314$ J mole^{-1}K^{-1}, 1 atm $= 1.013 \times 10^5$ Pa, the membrane tension is 5 Nm^{-1}.

Thinking Process

Pressure inside the curved surface will be greater than of outside pressure.

Ans. Let the pressure inside the balloon be p_i and the outside pressure be p_o, then excess pressure is $p_i - p_o = \frac{2S}{r}$.

where, S = Surface tension
r = radius of balloon

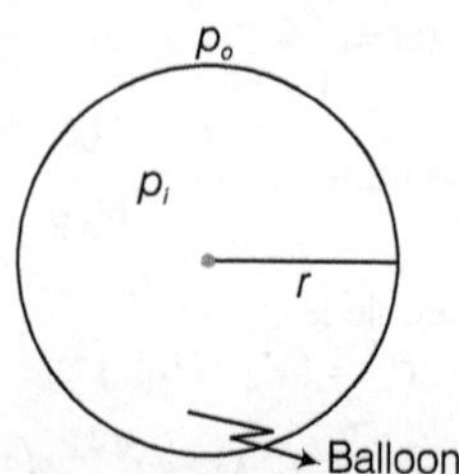

Considering the air to be an ideal gas $p_i V = n_i RT_i$ where, V is the volume of the air inside the balloon, n_i is the number of moles inside and T_i is the temperature inside, and $p_o\ V = n_o RT_o$ where V is the volume of the air displaced and n_o is the number of moles displaced and T_o is the temperature outside.

So. $$n_i = \frac{p_i V}{RT_i} = \frac{M_i}{M_A}$$

where, M_i is the mass of air inside and M_A is the molar mass of air

and $$n_o = \frac{p_o V}{RT_o} = \frac{M_o}{M_A}$$

where, M_o is the mass of air outside that has been displaced. If w is the load it can raise, then $w + M_i g = M_o g$

$$\Rightarrow \quad w = M_o g - M_i g$$

As in atmosphere 21% O_2 and 79% N_2-is present

$\therefore$ Molar mass of air

$$M_i = 0.21 \times 32 + 0.79 \times 28 = 28.84\,\text{g}.$$

$\therefore$ Weight raised by the balloon

$$w = (M_o - M_i)g$$

$$\Rightarrow \quad w = \frac{M_A V}{R}\left(\frac{p_o}{T_o} - \frac{p_i}{T_i}\right)g$$

$$= \frac{0.02884 \times \frac{4}{3}\pi \times 8^3 \times 9.8}{8.314} \left(\frac{1.013 \times 10^5}{293} - \frac{1.013 \times 10^5}{333} - \frac{2 \times 5}{8 \times 313}\right)$$

$$= \frac{0.02884\ \frac{4}{3}\pi \times 8^3}{8.314} \times 1.013 \times 10^5 \left(\frac{1}{293} - \frac{1}{333}\right) \times 9.8$$

$$= 3044.2\ \text{N}$$

$$\therefore \quad \text{Mass lifted by the balloon} = \frac{w}{g} = \frac{3044.2}{10} \approx 304.42\ \text{kg}.$$

$$\approx 305\ \text{kg}.$$

10

Thermal Properties *of* Matter

Multiple Choice Questions (MCQs)

Q. 1 A bimetallic strip is made of aluminium and steel ($\alpha_{Al} > \alpha_{steel}$). On heating, the strip will

(a) remain straight
(b) get twisted
(c) will bend with aluminium on concave side
(d) will bend with steel on concave side

Thinking Process

The metallic strip with higher coefficient of linear expansion (α_{Al}) will expand more.

Ans. *(d)* As $\alpha_{Al} > \alpha$steel, aluminium will expand more. So, it should have larger radius of curvature. Hence, aluminium will be on convex side.

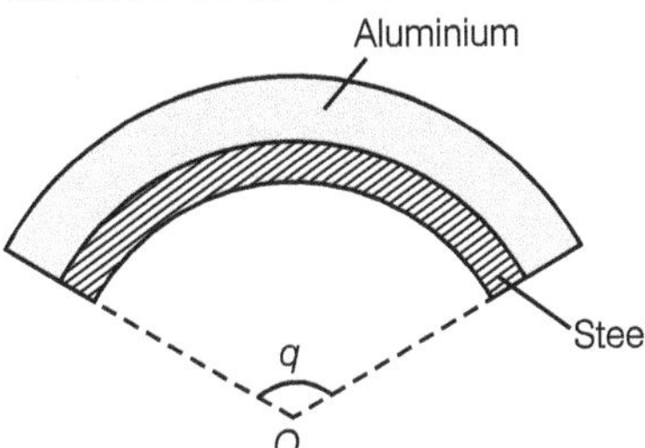

Q. 2 A uniform metallic rod rotates about its perpendicular bisector with constant angular speed. If it is heated uniformly to raise its temperature slightly

(a) its speed of rotation increases
(b) its speed of rotation decreases
(c) its speed of rotation remains same
(d) its speed increases because its moment of inertia increases

Ans. *(b)* As the rod is heated, it expands. No external torque is acting on the system so angular momentum should be conserved.

$$L = \text{Angular momentum} = I\omega = \text{constant}$$

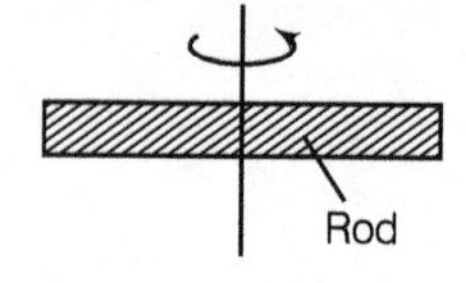

$$\Rightarrow \quad I_1\omega_1 = I_2\omega_2$$

Due to expansion of the rod $I_2 > I_1$

$$\Rightarrow \quad \frac{\omega_2}{\omega_1} = \frac{I_1}{I_2} < 1$$

$$\Rightarrow \quad \omega_2 < \omega_1$$

So, angular velocity (speed of rotation) decreases.

Q. 3 **The graph between two temperature scales *A* and *B* is shown in figure between upper fixed point and lower fixed point there are 150 equal division on scale *A* and 100 on scale *B*. The relationship for conversion between the two scales is given by**

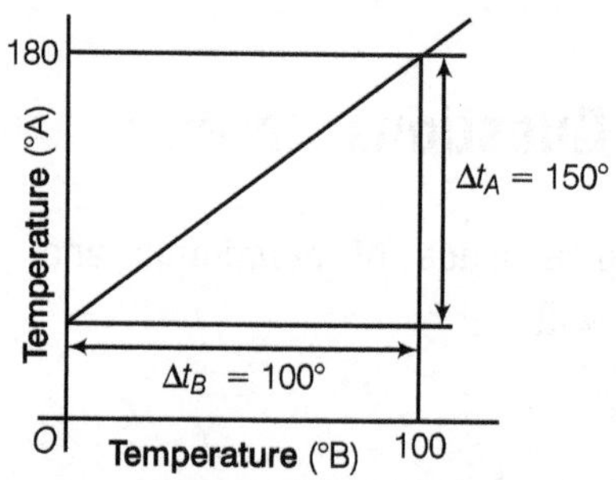

(a) $\frac{t_A - 180}{100} = \frac{t_B}{150}$ (b) $\frac{t_A - 30}{150} = \frac{t_B}{100}$ (c) $\frac{t_B - 180}{150} = \frac{t_A}{100}$ (d) $\frac{t_B - 40}{100} = \frac{t_A}{180}$

Ans. *(b)* It is clear from the graph that lowest point for scale *A* is 30° and lowest point for scale *B* is 0°. Highest point for the scale *A* is 180° and for scale B is 100°. Hence, correct relation is

$$\frac{t_A - (\text{LFP})_A}{(\text{UFP})_A - (\text{LFP})_A} = \frac{t_B - (\text{LFP})_B}{(\text{UFP})_B - (\text{LFP})_B}$$

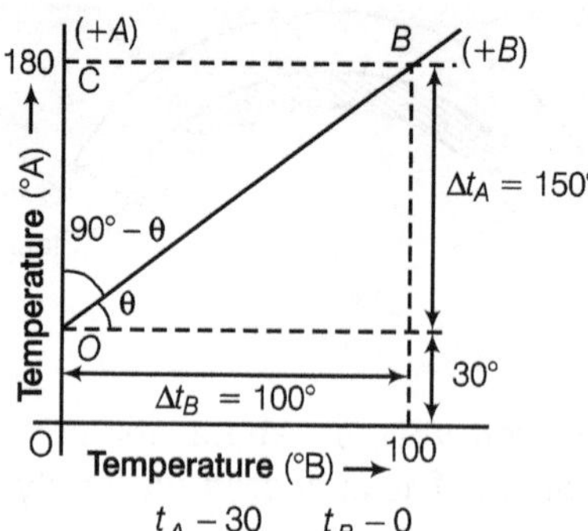

$$\Rightarrow \quad \frac{t_A - 30}{180 - 30} = \frac{t_B - 0}{100 - 0}$$

$$\Rightarrow \quad \frac{t_A - 30}{150} = \frac{t_B}{100}$$

where, LFP → Lower fixed point

UFP → Upper fixed point

Q. 4 **An aluminium sphere is dipped into water. Which of the following is true?**

(a) Buoyancy will be less in water at 0°C than that in water at 4°C
(b) Buoyancy will be more in water at 0°C than that in water at 4°C
(c) Buoyancy in water at 0°C will be same as that in water at 4°C
(d) Buoyancy may be more or less in water at 4°C depending on the radius of the sphere

Thinking Process

Density of water is maximum at 4°C, this is because of anomalous expansion of water.

Ans. *(a)* Let volume of the sphere is V and ρ is its density, then we can write buoyant force

$$F = V\rho G \quad (g = \text{acceleration due to gravity})$$

$$\Rightarrow \quad F \propto \rho \quad (\because V \text{ and } g \text{ are almost constant})$$

$$\Rightarrow \quad \frac{F_{4°C}}{F_{0°C}} = \frac{\rho_{4°C}}{\rho_{0°C}} > 1 \quad (\because \rho_{4°C} > \rho_{0°C})$$

$$\Rightarrow \quad F_{4°C} > F_{0°C}$$

Hence, buoyancy will be less in water at 0°C than that in water at 4°C.

Q. 5 **As the temperature is increased, the period of a pendulum**

(a) increases as its effective length increases even though its centre of mass still remains at the centre of the bob
(b) decreases as its effective length increases even though its centre of mass still remains at the centre of the bob
(c) increases as its effective length increases due to shifting to centre of mass below the centre of the bob
(d) decreases as its effective length remains same but the centre of mass shifts above the centre of the bob

Ans. *(a)* As the temperature is increased length of the pendulum increases. We know that time period of pendulum $T = 2\pi\sqrt{\frac{L}{g}}$

$$\Rightarrow \quad T \propto \sqrt{L}, \text{ as } L, \text{ increases.}$$

So, time period (T) also increases.

L

Pendulum

Q. 6 **Heat is associated with**

(a) kinetic energy of random motion of molecules
(b) kinetic energy of orderly motion of molecules
(c) total kinetic energy of random and orderly motion of molecules
(d) kinetic energy of random motion in some cases and kinetic energy of orderly motion in other

Ans. *(a)* We know that as temperature increases vibration of molecules about their mean position increases hence, kinetic energy associated with random motion of molecules increases.

Q. 7 **The radius of a metal sphere at room temperature T is R and the coefficient of linear expansion of the metal is α. The sphere heated a little by a temperature ΔT so that its new temperature is $T + \Delta T$. The increase in the volume of the sphere is approximately.**

(a) $2\pi R\alpha \Delta T$
(b) $\pi R^2\alpha \Delta T$
(c) $4\pi R^3\alpha \Delta T/3$
(d) $4\pi R^3\alpha \Delta T$

Ans. *(d)* Let the radius of the sphere is R. As the temperature increases radius of the sphere increases as shown.

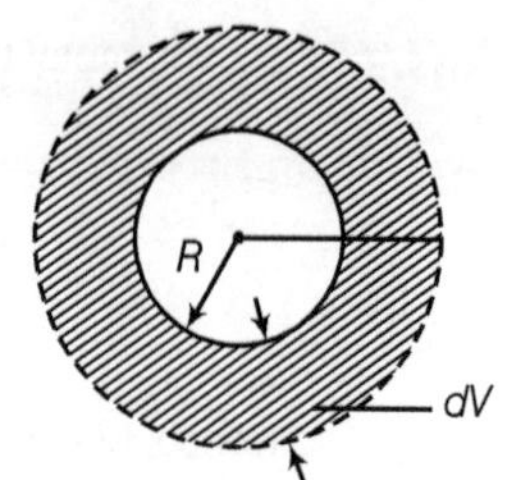

$$\text{Original volume } V_0 = \frac{4}{3}\pi R^3$$

Coefficient of linear expansion $= \alpha$

$\therefore$ Coefficient of volume expansion $= 3\alpha$

$$\therefore \quad \frac{1}{V}\frac{dV}{dT} = 3\alpha \Rightarrow dV = 3V\alpha dt \simeq 4\pi R^3\alpha\Delta T$$

$=$ Increase in the volume

Q. 8 **A sphere, a cube and a thin circular plate, all of same material and same mass are initially heated to same high temperature.**

(a) Plate will cool fastest and cube the slowest
(b) Sphere will cool fastest and cube the slowest
(c) Plate will cool fastest and sphere the slowest
(d) Cube will cool fastest and plate the slowest

Thinking Process

In this problem the cooling will be in the form of radiations that is according to Stefan's law. Since, emissive power directly proportional to surface. Here, for given volume, sphere have least surface area and circular plate of greatest surface area.

Ans. *(c)* Consider the diagram where all the three objects are heated to same temperature T. We know that density, $\rho = \frac{\text{mass}}{\text{volume}}$ as ρ is same for all the three objects hence, volume will also be same.

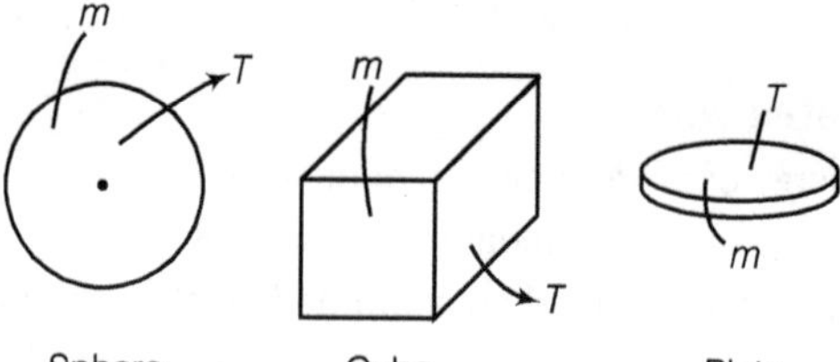

As thickness of the plate is least hence, surface area of the plate is maximum.
We know that, according to Stefan's law of heat loss $H \alpha AT^4$
where, A is surface area of for object and T is temperature.

Hence,
$$H_{\text{sphere}} : H_{\text{cube}} : H_{\text{plate}}$$
$$= A_{\text{sphere}} : A_{\text{cube}} : A_{\text{plate}}$$

As A_{plate} is maximum.
Hence, the plate will cool fastest.
As, the sphere is having minimum surface area hence, the sphere cools slowest.

Multiple Choice Questions (More Than One Options)

Q. 9 Mark the correct options

(a) A system X is in thermal equilibrium with Y but not with Z. The systems Y and Z may be in thermal equilibrium with each other.

(b) A system X is in thermal equilibrium with Y but not with Z.The systems Y and Z are not in thermal equilibrium with each other.

(c) A system X is neither in thermal equilibrium with Y nor with Z. The systems Y and Z must be in thermal equilibrium with each other.

(d) A system X is neither in thermal equilibrium with Y nor with Z. The systems Y and Z may be in thermal equilibrium with each other.

Ans. *(b, d)*

According to question

$$T_x = T_y \quad (\because x \text{ and } y \text{ are in thermal equilibrium})$$

$$T_x \neq T_z \quad (\because x \text{ is not in thermal equilibrium with } z)$$

Clearly, $T_y \neq T_z$

Hence, y and z are not in thermal equilibrium.

(d) Given, $T_x \neq T_y$

and $T_x \neq T_z$

We cannot say about equilibrium of Y and Z, they may or may not be in equilibrium.

Q. 10 Gulab namuns (assumed to be spherical) are to be heated in an oven. They are available in two sizes, one twice bigger (in radius) than the other. Pizzas (assumed to be discs) are also to be heated in oven. They are also in two sizes, one twice bigger (in radius) than the other. All four are put together to be heated to oven temperature. Choose the correct option from the following.

(a) Both size gulab jamuns will get heated in the same time

(b) Smaller gulab jamuns are heated before bigger ones

(c) Smaller pizzas are heated before bigger ones

(d) Bigger pizzas are heated before smaller

Ans. *(b, c)*

Smaller gulab jamuns are having least surface area hence, they will be heated first.

As in case of smaller gulab jamun heat radiates will be less

Similarly, smaller pizzas are heated before bigger ones because they are of small surface areas.

Q. 11 Refer to the plot of temperature *versus* time (figure) showing the changes in the state if ice on heating (not to scale). Which of the following is correct?

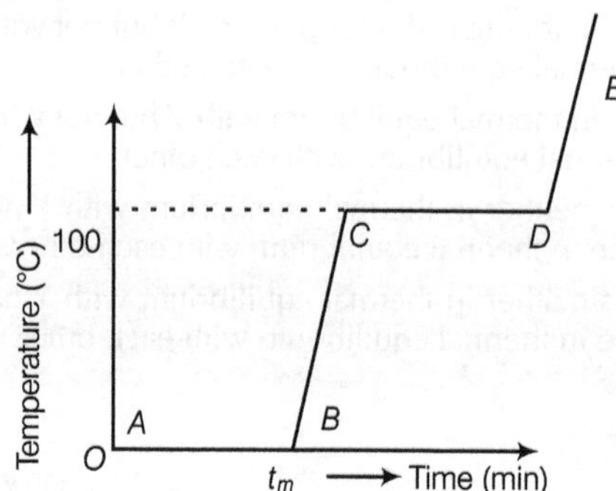

(a) The region *AB* represent ice and water in thermal equilibrium

(b) At *B* water starts boiling

(c) At *C* all the water gets converted into steam

(d) *C* to *D* represents water and steam in equilibrium at boiling point

Thinking Process

During phase change process, temperature of the system remains constant.

Ans. *(a, d)*

During the process *AB* temperature of the system is 0°C Hence, it represents phase change that is transformation of ice into water while temperature remains 0°C.

BC represents rise in temperature of water from 0°C to 100°C (at *C*).

Now, water starts converting into steam which is represent by *CD*.

Q. 12 A glass full of hot milk is poured on the table. It begins to cool gradually. Which of the following is correct?

(a) The rate of cooling is constant till milk attains the temperature of the surrounding

(b) The temperature of milk falls off exponentially with time

(c) While cooling, there is a flow of heat from milk to the surrounding as well as from surrounding to the milk but the net flow of heat is from milk to the surrounding and that is why it cools

(d) All three phenomenon, conduction, convection and radiation are responsible for the loss of heat from milk to the surroundings

Ans. *(b, c, d)*

When hot milk spread on the table heat is transferred to the surroundings by conduction, convection and radiation.

According to Newton's law of cooling temperature of the milk falls off exponentially. Heat also will be transferred from surroundings to the milk but will be lesser than that of transferred from milk to the surroundings.

Very Short Answer Type Questions

Q. 13 Is the bulb of a thermometer made of diathermic or adiabatic wall?

Ans. As diathermic walls alow exchange of heat energy between two systems and adiabatic walls do not, hence, diathermic walls are used to make the bulb of a thermometer.

Q. 14 A student records the initial length l, change in temperature ΔT and change in length Δl of a rod as follows

S. No.	l(m)	ΔT (°C)	Δl(m)
1.	2	10	4×10^{-4}
2.	1	10	4×10^{-4}
3.	2	20	2×10^{-4}
4.	3	10	6×10^{-4}

If the first observation is correct, what can you say about observation 2, 3 and 4.

Ans. From the 1st observation $\alpha = \dfrac{\Delta l}{l\Delta T} \Rightarrow \alpha = \dfrac{4\times10^{-4}}{2\times10} = 2\times10^{-5}\,°C^{-1}$

For 2nd observation $\Delta l = \alpha l \Delta T$

$= 2\times10^{-5}\times1\times10 = 2\times10^{-4}\text{m} \neq 4\times10^{-4}\text{m}$ (Wrong)

For 3rd observation $\Delta l = \alpha l \Delta T$

$= 2\times10^{-5}\times2\times20 = 8\times10^{-4}\text{m} \neq 2\times10^{-4}\text{m}$ (Wrong)

For 4th observation $\Delta l = \alpha l \Delta T$

$= 2\times10^{-5}\times3\times10 = 6\times10^{-4}\text{m} = 6\times10^{-4}\text{m}$

[*i.e.*, observed value (Correct)]

Q. 15 Why does a metal bar appear hotter than a wooden bar at the same temperature? Equivalently it also appears cooler than wooden bar if they are both colder than room temperature.

Thinking Process

According to Kirchhoff's law, good radiator are good absorbers.

Ans. Due to difference in conductivity, metals having high conductivity compared to wood. On touch with a finger, heat from the surrounding flows faster to the finger from metals and so one feels the heat.

Similarly, when one touches a cold metal the heat from the finger flows away to the surroundings faster.

Q. 16 Calculate the temperature which has numeral value on Celsius and Fahrenheit scale.

Ans. Let Q be the value of temperature having same value an Celsius and Fahrenheit scale.

Now, we can write

$$\frac{°F-32}{180} = \frac{°C}{100}$$

$\Rightarrow$ Let $F = C = Q$

$$\Rightarrow \frac{Q-32}{180} = \frac{Q}{100} = Q = -40°C \text{ or } -40°F$$

Q. 17 These days people use steel utensiles with copper bottom. This is supposed to be good for uniform heating of food. Explain this effect using the fact that copper is the better conductor.

Ans. As copper is a good conductor of heat as compared to steel. The steel utensils with copper bottom absorbs heat more quickly than steel and give it to the food in utensil. As a result, of it, the food in utensil is heated uniformly and quickly.

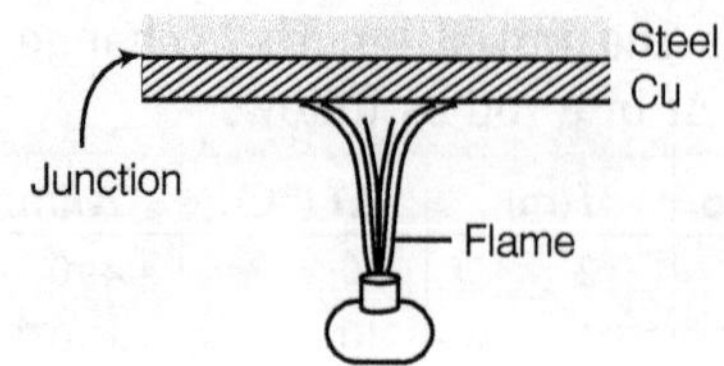

Short Answer Type Questions

Q. 18 Find out the increase in moment of inertia I of a uniform rod (coefficient of linear expansion α) about its perpendicular bisector when its temperature is slightly increased by ΔT.

Thinking Process

As temperature increases length of the rod also increases hence, moment of inertia of the rod also increases.

Ans. Let the mass and length of a uniform rod be M and l respectively.

Moment of inertia of the rod about its perpendicular bisector. $(I) = \dfrac{Ml^2}{12}$

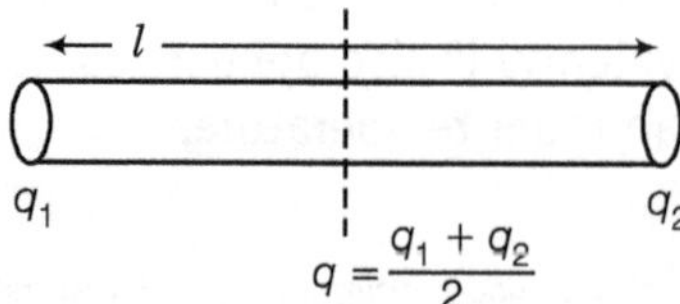

Increase in length of the rod when temperature is increased by ΔT, is given by

$$\Delta l = l\alpha\Delta T \quad \text{...(i)}$$

$\therefore$ New moment of inertia of the rod $(I') = \dfrac{M}{12}(l + \Delta l)^2 = \dfrac{M}{12}(l^2 + \Delta l^2 + 2I\Delta l)$

As change in length Δl is very small, therefore, neglecting $(\Delta l)^2$, we get

$$I' = \frac{M}{12}(l^2 + 2l\Delta l)$$

$$= \frac{Ml^2}{12} + \frac{MI\Delta l}{6} = l + \frac{MI\Delta l}{6}$$

$\therefore$ Increase in moment of inertia

$$\Delta I = I' - I = \frac{Ml\Delta l}{6} = 2 \times \left(\frac{Ml^2}{12}\right)\frac{\Delta l}{l}$$

$$\Delta I = 2 \cdot I\alpha\Delta T \quad \text{[Using Eq. (i)]}$$

Q. 19 **During summers in India, one of the common practice to keep cool is to make ice balls of crushed ice, dip it in flavoured sugar syrup and sip it. For this a stick is inserted into crushed ice and is squeezed in the palm to make it into the ball. Equivalently in winter in those areas where it snows, people make snow balls and throw around. Explain the formation of ball out of crushed ice or snow in the light of *p-T* diagram of water.**

Ans. Refer to the *p-T* diagram of water and double headed arrow. Increasing pressure at 0°C and 1 atm takes ice into liquid state and decreasing pressure in liquid state at 0°C and 1 atm takes water to ice state.

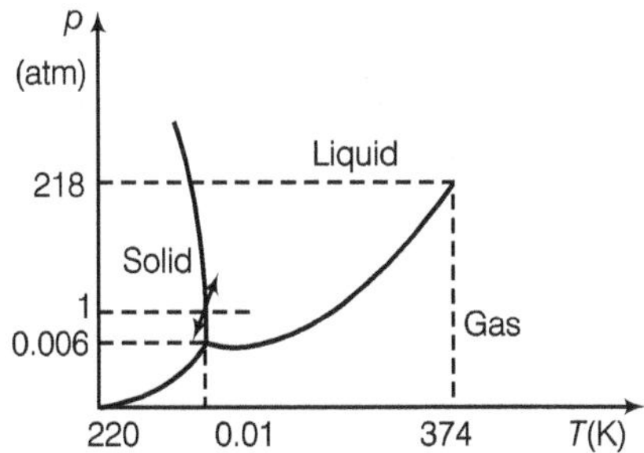

When crushed ice is squeezed, some of it melts, filling up gap between ice flakes upon releasing pressure. This water freezes, binding all ice flakes and making the ball more stable.

Q. 20 **100 g of water is supercooled to −10°C. At this point, due to some disturbance mechanised or otherwise some of it suddenly freezes to ice. What will be the temperature of the resultant mixture and how much mass would freeze? [$S_w = 1\text{cal} / \text{g}/°\text{C}$ and $L^{W}_{\text{Fusion}} = 80$ cal / g]**

Ans. Given, mass of water $(m) = 100$

Change in temperature $\Delta T = 0-(-10) = 10°\text{C}$

Specific heat of water $(S_w) = 1$ cal /g/°C

Latent heat of fusion of water $L^{w}_{\text{fusion}} = 80$ cal / g

Heat required to bring water in super cooling from −10°C to 0°C,

$$Q = ms_w\Delta T$$
$$= 100 \times 1 \times 10 = 1000 \text{ cal}$$

Let m gram of ice be melted.

$\therefore$ $$Q = mL$$

or $$m = \frac{Q}{L} = \frac{1000}{80} = 12.5 \text{ g}$$

As small mass of ice is melted, therefore the temperature of the mixture will remain 0°C.

Note *To find the temperature of the mixture we must go through the two steps* ($Q = ms$DT) *and* ($Q = mL$)*, we should not directly apply first one.*

Q. 21 One day in the morning. Ramesh filled up 1/3 bucket of hot water from geyser, to take bath. Remaining 2/3 was to be filled by cold water (at room temperature) to bring mixture to a comfortable temperature. Suddenly Ramesh had to attend to something which would take some times, say 5-10 min before he could take bath. Now, he had two options (i) fill the remaining bucket completely by cold water and then attend to the work, (ii) first attend to the work and fill the remaining bucket just before taking bath. Which option do you think would have kept water warmer? Explain

Thinking Process

We should apply logic in this problem in the context of Newton's law of cooling which gives a consequence about rate of fall of temperature of a body with respect to the difference of temperature of body and surroundings.

Ans. The first option would have kept water warmer because according to Newton's law of cooling, the rate of loss of heat is directly proportional to the difference of temperature of the body and the surrounding and in the first case the temperature difference is less, so, rate of loss of heat will be less.

Long Answers Type Questions

Q. 22 We would like to prepare a scale whose length does not change with temperature. It is proposed to prepare a unit scale of this type whose length remains, say 10 cm. We can use a bimetallic strip made of brass and iron each of different length whose length (both components) would change in such a way that difference between their length B remain constant. If $\alpha_{\text{iron}} = 1.2 \times 10^{-5}$ /K and $\alpha_{\text{brass}} = 1.8 \times 10^{-5}$ /K, what should we take as length of each strip?

Ans. According to question $l_{\text{iron}} - l_{\text{brass}} = 10\text{ cm} = \text{constant}$ at all temperatures

Let l_0 be length at temperature 0°C and l be the length after change in temperature of Δt.

Now, we can write $\quad l_{\text{iron}} - l_{\text{brass}} = 10$ cm at all temperatures

$$l_{\text{iron}}(1 + \alpha_{\text{iron}}\Delta t) - l_{\text{brass}}(1 + \alpha_{\text{brass}}\Delta t) = 10\text{ cm}$$

$$l_{\text{iron}}\, \alpha_{\text{iron}} = l_{\text{brass}}\, \alpha_{\text{brass}}$$

$$\therefore \quad \frac{l_{\text{iron}}}{l_{\text{brass}}} = \frac{1.8}{1.2} = \frac{3}{2}$$

$$\therefore \quad \frac{1}{2} l_{\text{brass}} = 10\text{ cm}$$

$$\Rightarrow \quad l_{\text{brass}} = 20\text{ cm and } l_{\text{iron}}\ 30\text{ cm}$$

Q 23 We would like to make a vessel whose volume does not change with temperature (take a hint from the problem above). We can use brass and iron ($\beta_{vbrass} = 6 \times 10^{-5}$ /K and $\beta_{viron} = 3.55 \times 10^{-5}$/K) to create a volume of 100 cc. How do you think you can achieve this?

Ans. In the previous problem the difference in the length was constant.
In this problem the difference in volume is constant.
The situation is shown in the diagram.

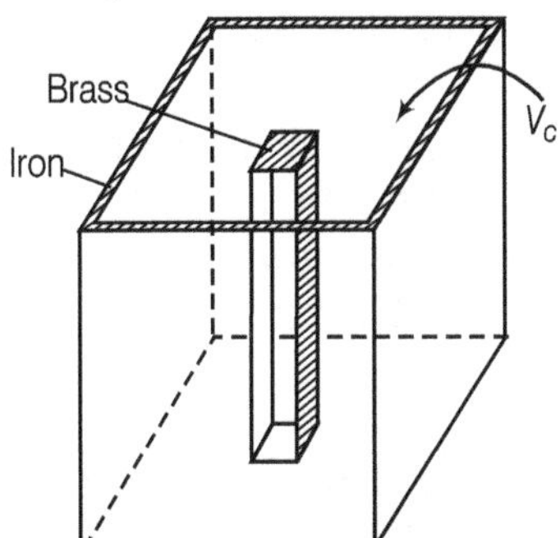

Let V_{io}, V_{bo} be the volume of iron and brass vessel at 0°C
V_i, V_b be the volume of iron and brass vessel at $\Delta\theta$°C,
γ_i, γ_b be the coefficicnt, of volume expansion of iron and brass.

As per question, $$V_{io} - V_{bo} = 100 \text{ cc} = V_i - V_b \quad \ldots(i)$$

Now,
$$V_i = V_{io}(1 + \gamma_i \Delta\theta)$$
$$V_b = V_{bo}(1 + \gamma_b \Delta\theta)$$
$$V_i - V_b = (V_{io} - V_{bo}) + \Delta\theta(V_{io}\gamma_i - V_{bo}\gamma_b)$$

Since, $V_i - V_b =$ constant.

So,
$$V_{io}\gamma_i = V_{bo}\gamma_b$$

$$\Rightarrow \quad \frac{V_{io}}{V_{bo}} = \frac{\gamma_b}{\gamma_i} = \frac{\frac{3}{2}\beta_b}{\frac{3}{2}\beta_i} = \frac{\beta_b}{\beta_i} = \frac{6 \times 10^{-5}}{3.55 \times 10^{-5}} = \frac{6}{3.55}$$

$$\frac{V_{io}}{V_{bo}} = \frac{6}{3.55} \quad \ldots(ii)$$

Solving Eqs. (i) and (ii), we get
$$V_{io} = 244.9 \text{ cc}$$
$$V_{bo} = 144.9 \text{ cc}$$

Q. 24 Calculate the stress developed inside a tooth cavity filled with copper when hot tea at temperature of 57°C is drunk. You can take body (tooth) temperature to be 37°C and $\alpha = 1.7 \times 10^{-5}$/°C bulk modulus for copper $= 140 \times 10^9$ N/m^2.

Ans. Given, decrease in temperature $(\Delta t) = 57 - 37 = 20$°C
Coefficient of linear expansion $(\alpha) = 1.7 \times 10^{-5}$/°C
Bulk modulus for copper $(B) = 140 \times 10^9$ N/m^2
Coefficient of cubical expansion $(\gamma) = 3\alpha = 5.1 \times 10^{-5}$/°C
Let initial volume of the cavity be V and its volume increases by ΔV due to increase in temperature.

$\therefore \qquad \Delta V = \gamma V \Delta t$

$\Rightarrow \qquad \dfrac{\Delta V}{V} = \gamma \Delta t \qquad \ldots(i)$

Thermal stress produced = $B \times$ Volumetric strain

$$= B \times \frac{\Delta V}{V} = B \times \gamma \Delta t$$

$$= 140 \times 10^9 \times (5.1 \times 10^{-5} \times 20)$$

$$= 1{,}428 \times 10^8 \text{ N/m}^2$$

This is about 10^3 times of atmospheric pressure.

Q. 25 A rail track made of steel having length 10 m is clamped on a railway line at its two ends (figure). On a summer day due to rise in temperature by 20° C. It is deformed as shown in figure. Find x (displacement of the centre) if $\alpha_{steel} = 1.2 \times 10^{-5}/°$ C.

Ans. Consider the diagram.

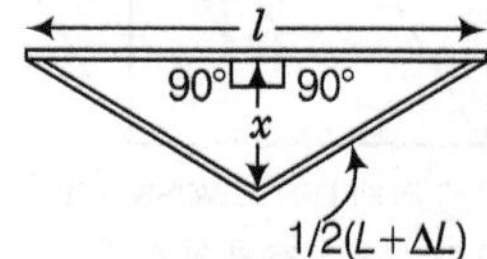

Applying Pythagorus theorem in right angled triangle in figure.

$$\left(\frac{L + \Delta L}{2}\right)^2 = \left(\frac{L}{2}\right)^2 + x^2$$

$$\Rightarrow \qquad x = \sqrt{\left(\frac{L + \Delta L}{2}\right)^2 - \left(\frac{L}{2}\right)^2}$$

$$= \frac{1}{2}\sqrt{(L + \Delta L)^2 - L^2}$$

$$= \frac{1}{2}\sqrt{(L^2 + \Delta L^2 + 2L\Delta L) - L^2}$$

$$= \frac{1}{2}\sqrt{(\Delta L^2 + 2L\Delta L)}$$

As increase in length ΔL is very small, therefore, neglecting $(\Delta L)^2$, we get

$$x = \frac{1}{2} \times \sqrt{2L\Delta L} \qquad \ldots(i)$$

But $\qquad \Delta L = L\alpha\Delta t \qquad \ldots(ii)$

Substituting value of ΔL in Eq. (i) from Eq. (ii)

$$x = \frac{1}{2}\sqrt{2L \times L\alpha\,\Delta t} = \frac{1}{2}L\sqrt{2\alpha\,\Delta t}$$

$$= \frac{10}{2} \times \sqrt{2 \times 1.2 \times 10^{-5} \times 20}$$

$$= 5 \times \sqrt{4 \times 1.2 \times 10^{-4}}$$

$$= 5 \times 2 \times 1.1 \times 10^{-2} = 0.11 \text{m} = 11 \text{cm}$$

Note *Here we have assumed ΔLto be very small so that it can be neglected compared to L.*

Q. 26 A thin rod having length L_0 at 0°C and coefficient of linear expansion α has its two ends maintained at temperatures θ_1 and θ_2, respectively. Find its new length.

Thinking Process

When temperature of a rod varies linearly, temperature of the middle point of the rod can be taken as mean of temperatures at the two ends.

Ans. Consider the diagram

θ_1 ⬭ θ_2

$$\theta = \frac{\theta_1 + \theta_2}{2}$$

Let temperature varies linearly in the rod from its one end to other end. Let θ be the temperature of the mid-point of the rod. At steady state,

Rate of flow of heat,

$$\left(\frac{dQ}{dt}\right) = \frac{KA\,(\theta_1 - \theta)}{(L_0/2)} = \frac{KA(\theta - \theta_2)}{(L_0/2)}$$

where, K is coefficient of thermal conductivity of the rod.

or ⇒ $$\theta_1 - \theta = \theta - \theta_2$$

or ⇒ $$\theta = \frac{\theta_1 + \theta_2}{2}$$

Using relation, $$L = L_0\,(1 + \alpha\,\theta)$$

or $$L = L_0\left[1 + \alpha\left(\frac{\theta_1 + \theta_2}{2}\right)\right]$$

Q. 27 According to Stefan's law of radiation, a black body radiates energy σT^4 from its unit surface area every second where T is the surface temperature of the black body and $\sigma = 5.67 \times 10^{-8}$ W/ m^{2}K^4 is known as Stefan's constant. A nuclear weapon may be thought of as a ball of radius 0.5 m. When detonated, it reaches temperature of 10^6K and can be treated as a black body.

(a) Estimate the power it radiates.

(b) If surrounding has water at 30°C, how much water can 10% of the energy produced evaporate in 1 s?

$[S_w = 4186.0$ J / kg K and $L_v = 22.6 \times 10^5$ J / kg]

(c) If all this energy U is in the form of radiation, corresponding momentum is $p = U/c$. How much momentum per unit time does it impart on unit area at a distance of 1 km?

Ans. Given, $\sigma = 5.67 \times 10^{-8}$ W/m^2 kg

Radius, $= R = 0.5$ m, $T = 10^6$ K

(a) Power radiated by Stefan's law

$$P = \sigma A T^4 = (4\pi R^2)T^4$$
$$= (5.67 \times 10^{-4} \times 4 \times (3.14) \times (0.5)^2 \times (10^6)\,4$$
$$= 1.78 \times 10^{17}\text{ J/s} = 1.8 \times 10^{17}\text{ J/s}$$

(b) Energy available per second, $U = 1.8 \times 10^{17}$ J/s $= 18 \times 10^{16}$ J/s

Actual energy required to evaporate water = 10% of 1.8×10^{17} J/s

$$= 1.8 \times 10^{16}\text{ J/s}$$

Energy used per second to raise the temperature of m kg of water from 30°C to 100°C and then into vapour at 100°C

$$= ms_w\,\Delta\theta + m\,L_v = m \times 4186 \times (100 - 30) + m \times 22.6 \times 10^5$$
$$= 2.93 \times 10^5\,m + 22.6 \times 10^5\,m = 25.53 \times 10^5\,m\text{ J/s}$$

As per question, $25.53 \times 10^5\,m = 1.8 \times 10^{16}$

or
$$m = \frac{1.8 \times 10^{16}}{25.33 \times 10^5} = 7.0 \times 10^9\text{ kg}$$

(c) Momentum per unit time,

$$p = \frac{U}{c} = \frac{U}{c} = \frac{1.8 \times 10^{17}}{3 \times 10^8} = 6 \times 10^8\text{ kg-m/s}^2 \qquad \begin{bmatrix} P = \text{momentum} \\ V = \text{energy} \\ C = \text{velocity of Light} \end{bmatrix}$$

Momentum per unit time per unit

$$\text{area } p = \frac{p}{4\pi R^2} = \frac{6 \times 10^8}{4 \times 3.14 \times (10^3)^2}$$

$$\Rightarrow \qquad d = 47.7\text{ N/m}^2 \qquad [4\pi R^2 = \text{Surface area}]$$

11

Thermodynamics

Multiple Choice Questions (MCQs)

Q. 1 An ideal gas undergoes four different processes from the same initial state (figure). Four processes are adiabatic, isothermal, isobaric and isochoric. Out of 1, 2, 3 and 4 which one is adiabatic?

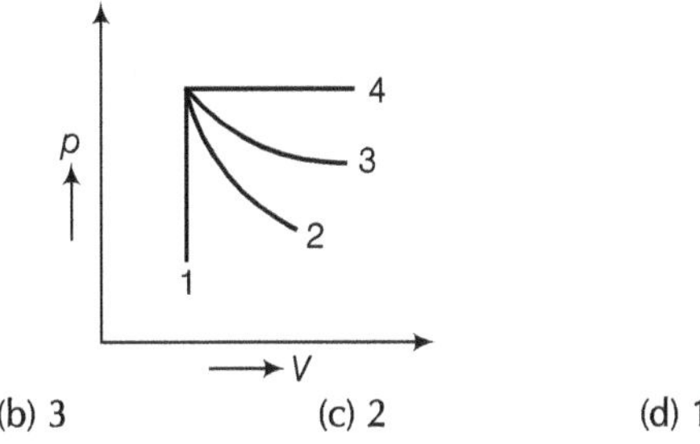

(a) 4 (b) 3 (c) 2 (d) 1

Thinking Process

The slope of the curve for the adiabatic process will be more that is the curve will be steeper. Slope of p-V curve in adiabatic process $= \gamma (p/V)$ where as slope of is otemal process $= -p/v$

Ans. *(c)* For the curve 4 pressure is constant, so this is an isobaric process.

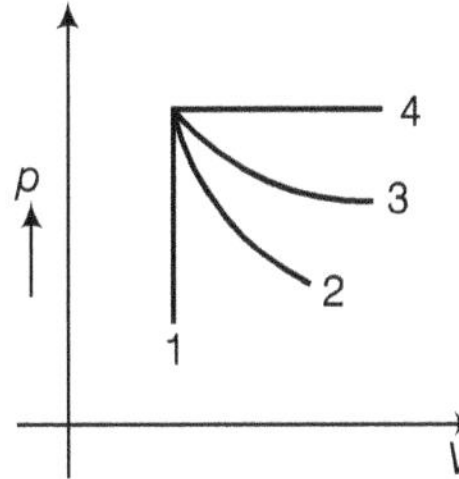

For the curve 1, volume is constant, so it is isochoric process. Between curves 3 and 2, curve 2 is steeper, so it is adiabatic and 3 is isothermal.

Note *We should be careful while deciding between isothermal and adiabatic curves because these curves look similar.*

Q. 2 If an average person jogs, he produces 14.5×10^3 cal/min. This is removed by the evaporation of sweat. The amount of sweat evaporated per minute (assuming 1 kg requires 580×10^3 cal for evaporation) is

(a) 0.25 kg (b) 2.25 kg (c) 0.05 kg (d) 0.20 kg

Ans. *(a)* Amount of sweat evaporated/minute

$$= \frac{\text{Sweat produced / minute}}{\text{Number of calories required for evaporation / kg}}$$

$$= \frac{\text{Amount of heat produced per minute in jogging}}{\text{Latent heat (in cal / kg)}}$$

$$= \frac{14.5 \times 10^3}{580 \times 10^3} = \frac{145}{580} = 0.25 \text{ kg}$$

Q. 3 Consider p-V diagram for an ideal gas shown in figure.

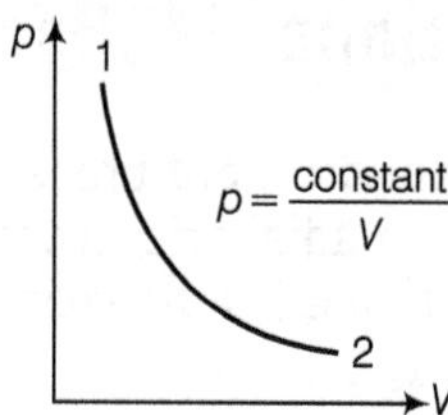

Out of the following diagrams, which figure represents the T-p diagram?

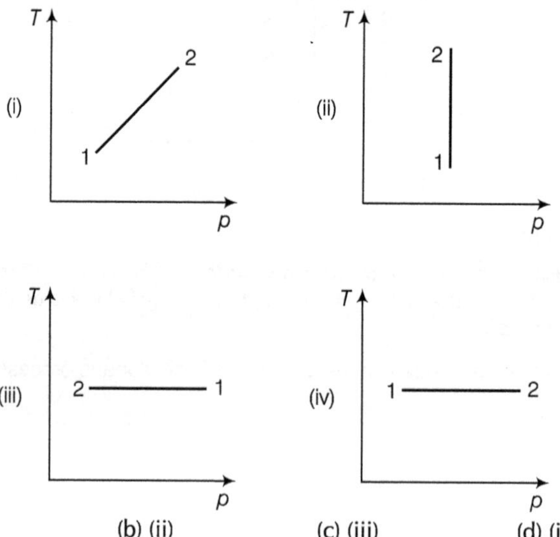

(a) (iv) (b) (ii) (c) (iii) (d) (i)

Ans. *(c)* According to the question given that $pV = \text{constant}$

Hence, we can say that the gas is going through an isothermal process.

Clearly, from the graph that between process 1 and 2 temperature is constant and the gas expands and pressure decreases *i.e.*, $p_2 < p_1$ which corresponds to diagram (iii).

Q. 4 An ideal gas undergoes cyclic process *ABCDA* as shown in given *p-V* diagram. The amount of work done by the gas is

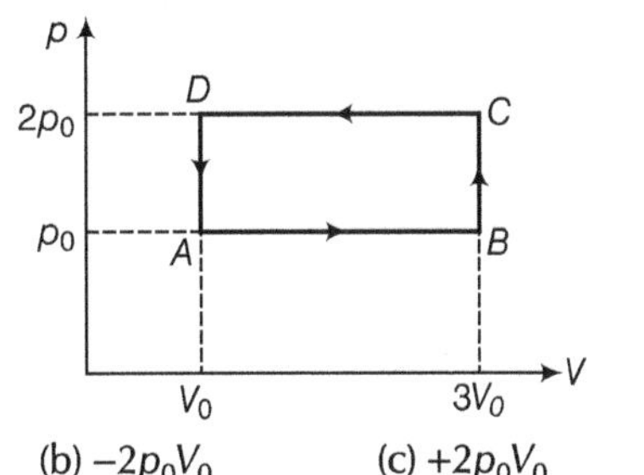

(a) $6p_0V_0$ (b) $-2p_0V_0$ (c) $+2p_0V_0$ (d) $+4p_0V_0$

Thinking Process

Work done in a process by which a gas is going through can be calculated by area of the p-V diagram.

Ans. *(b)* Consider the *p-V* diagram given in the question.

Work done in the process *ABCD* = area of rectangle *ABCDA*

$$= (AB) \times BC = (3V_0 - V_0) \times (2p_0 - p_0)$$
$$= 2V_0 \times p_0 = 2\, p_0\, V_0$$

As the process is going anti-clockwise, hence there is a net compression in the gas. So, work done by the gas $= -2\, p_0\, V_0$.

Q. 5 Consider two containers *A* and *B* containing identical gases at the same pressure, volume and temperature. The gas in container *A* is compressed to half of its original volume isothermally while the gas in container *B* is compressed to half of its original value adiabatically. The ratio of final pressure of gas in *B* to that of gas in *A* is

(a) $2^{\gamma-1}$ (b) $\left(\frac{1}{2}\right)^{\gamma-1}$ (c) $\left(\frac{1}{1-\gamma}\right)^2$ (d) $\left(\frac{1}{\gamma-1}\right)^2$

Ans. *(a)* Consider the *p-V* diagram shown for the container *A* (isothermal) and for container *B* (adiabatic).

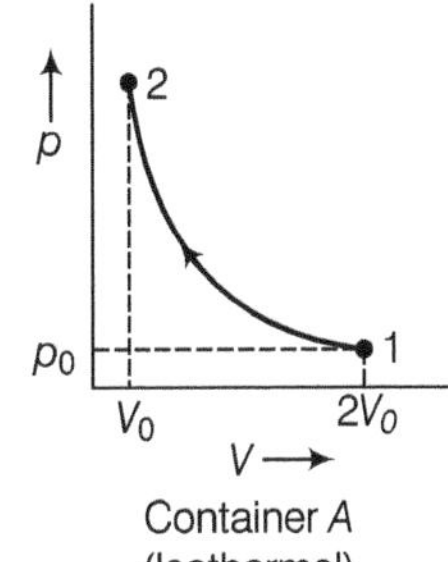

Container *A* (Isothermal)

Container *B* (Adiabatic)

Both the process involving compression of the gas.

For isothermal process (gas *A*) (during $1 \rightarrow 2$)

$$p_1V_1 = p_2V_2$$
$$\Rightarrow \quad p_0\,(2\,V_0) = p_2\,(V_0)$$
$$\Rightarrow \quad p_2 = 2p_0$$

For adiabatic process, (gas B) (during $1 \rightarrow 2$)

$$p_1 V_1^{\gamma} = p_2 V_2^{\gamma}$$

$$\Rightarrow \quad p_0 (2V_0)^{\gamma} = p_2 (V_0)^{\gamma}$$

$$\Rightarrow \quad p_2 = \left(\frac{2V_0}{V_0}\right)^{\gamma} p_0 = (2)^{\gamma} p_0$$

Hence, $\dfrac{(p_2)_B}{(p_2)_A}$ = Ratio of final pressure $= \dfrac{(2)^{\gamma} p_0}{2p_0} = 2^{\gamma - 1}$

where, γ is ratio of specific heat capacities for the gas.

Q. 6 **Three copper blocks of masses M_1, M_2 and M_3 kg respectively are brought into thermal contact till they reach equilibrium. Before contact, they were at T_1, T_2, T_3 $(T_1 > T_2 > T_3)$. Assuming there is no heat loss to the surroundings, the equilibrium temperature T is (s is specific heat of copper)**

(a) $T = \dfrac{T_1 + T_2 + T_3}{3}$

(b) $T = \dfrac{M_1T_1 + M_2T_2 + M_3T_3}{M_1 + M_2 + M_3}$

(c) $T = \dfrac{M_1T_1 + M_2T_2 + M_3T_3}{3(M_1 + M_2 + M_3)}$

(d) $T = \dfrac{M_1T_1s + M_2T_2s + M_3T_3s}{M_1 + M_2 + M_3}$

Ans. *(b)* Let the equilibrium temperature of the system is T.

Let us assume that $T_1, T_2 < T < T_3$.

According to question, there is no net loss to the surroundings.

Heat lost by M_3 = Heat gained by M_1 + Heat gained by M_2

$$\Rightarrow \quad M_3 s(T_3 - T) = M_1 s(T - T_1) + M_2 s(T - T_2)$$

(where, s is specific heat of the copper material)

$$\Rightarrow \quad T[M_1 + M_2 + M_3] = M_3T_3 + M_1T_1 + M_2T_2$$

$$\Rightarrow \quad T = \frac{M_1T_1 + M_2T_2 + M_3T_3}{M_1 + M_2 + M_3}$$

Multiple Choice Questions (More Than One Options)

Q. 7 **Which of the processes described below are irreversible?**

(a) The increase in temperature of an iron rod by hammering it

(b) A gas in a small container at a temperature T_1 is brought in contact with a big reservoir at a higher temperature T_2 which increases the temperature of the gas

(c) A quasi-static isothermal expansion of an ideal gas in cylinder fitted with a frictionless piston

(d) An ideal gas is enclosed in a piston cylinder arrangement with adiabatic walls. A weight w is added to the piston, resulting in compression of gas

Thinking Process

If any process can be returned back such that both, the system and the surroundings return to their original states, with no other change anywhere else in the universe, then this process is called reversible process.

Ans. *(a, b, d)*

(a) When the rod is hammered, the external work is done on the rod which increases its temperature. The process cannot be retraced itself.

(b) In this process energy in the form of heat is transferred to the gas in the small container by big reservoir at temperature T_2.

(d) As the weight is added to the cylinder arrangement in the form of external pressure hence, it cannot be reversed back itself.

Q. 8 An ideal gas undergoes isothermal process from some initial state *i* to final state *f*. Choose the correct alternatives.

(a) $dU = 0$ (b) $dQ = 0$ (c) $dQ = dU$ (d) $dQ = dW$

Ans. *(a, d)*

For an isothermal process change in temperature of the system $dT = 0 \Rightarrow T = \text{constant}$.

We know that for an ideal gas dU = change in internal energy $= nC_V\ dT = 0$

[where, n is number of moles and C_V is specific heat capacity at constant volume]

From first law of thermodynamics,

$$dQ = dU + dW$$
$$= 0 + dW \Rightarrow dQ = dW$$

Q. 9 Figure shows the *p-V* diagram of an ideal gas undergoing a change of state from *A* to *B*. Four different parts I, II, III and IV as shown in the figure may lead to the same change of state.

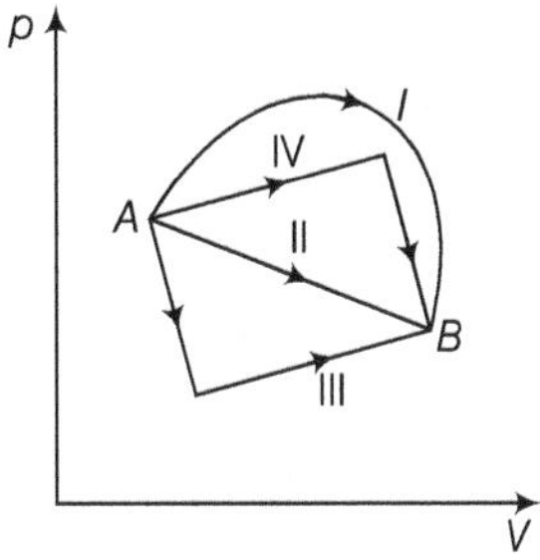

(a) Change in internal energy is same in IV and III cases, but not in I and II

(b) Change in internal energy is same in all the four cases

(c) Work done is maximum in case I

(d) Work done is minimum in case II

Thinking Process

Internal energy is a state function and work done by the gas is a path dependent function.The work done in a thermodynamical process is equal to the area bounded between p-V curve.

Ans. *(b, c)*

Change in internal energy for the process A to B

$$dU_{A \to B} = nC_V\, dT = nC_V(T_B - T_A)$$

which depends only on temperatures at A and B.

Work done for A to B, $dW_{A \to B}$ = Area under the p-V curve which is maximum for the path I.

Q. 10 Consider a cycle followed by an engine (figure.)

1 to 2 is isothermal

2 to 3 is adiabatic

3 to 1 is adiabatic

Such a process does not exist, because

(a) heat is completely converted to mechanical energy in such a process, which is not possible

(b) mechanical energy is completely converted to heat in this process, which is not possible

(c) curves representing two adiabatic processes don't intersect

(d) curves representing an adiabatic process and an isothermal process don't intersect

Ans. *(a, c)*

(a) The given process is a cyclic process *i.e.*, it returns to the original state 1.

Hence, change in internal energy $dU = 0$

$\Rightarrow \qquad dQ = dU + dW = 0 + dW = dW$

Hence, total heat supplied is converted to work done by the gas (mechanical energy) which is not possible by second law of thermodynamics.

(c) When the gas expands adiabatically from 2 to 3. It is not possible to return to the same state without being heat supplied, hence the process 3 to 1 cannot be adiabatic.

Q. 11 Consider a heat engine as shown in figure. Q_1 and Q_2 are heat added both to T_1 and heat taken from T_2 in one cycle of engine. W is the mechanical work done on the engine.

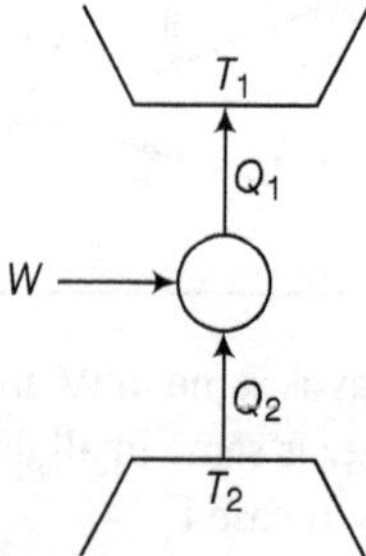

If $W > 0$, then possibilities are

(a) $Q_1 > Q_2 > 0$

(b) $Q_2 > Q_1 > 0$

(c) $Q_2 < Q_1 < 0$

(d) $Q_1 < 0, Q_2 > 0$

Ans. *(a, c)*

Consider the figure we can write $Q_1 = W + Q_2$

$\Rightarrow \qquad W = Q_1 - Q_2 > 0 \qquad$ (By question)

$\Rightarrow \qquad Q_1 > Q_2 > 0 \qquad$ (If both Q_1 and Q_2 are positive)

We can also, write $Q_2 < Q_1 < 0$ (If both Q_1 and Q_2 are negative).

Very Short Answer Type Questions

Q. 12 Can a system be heated and its temperature remains constant?

Ans. Yes, this is possible when the entire heat supplied to the system is utilised in expansion. *i.e.,* its working against the surroundings.

Q. 13 A system goes from P to Q by two different paths in the p-V diagram as shown in figure. Heat given to the system in path 1 is 1000 J. The work done by the system along path 1 is more than path 2 by 100 J. What is the heat exchanged by the system in path 2?

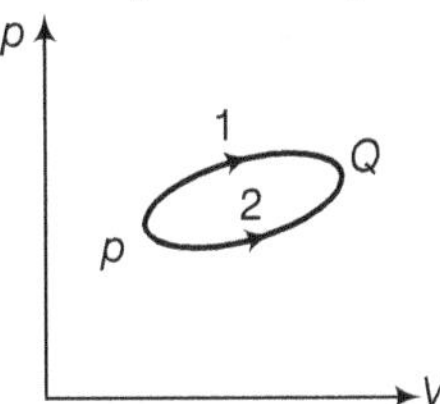

Thinking Process

We have to apply first law of thermodynamics for each path.

Ans. **For path 1,** Heat given $Q_1 = +1000$ J

Work done $= W_1$ (let)

For path 2,

Work done $(W_2) = (W_1 - 100)$ J

Heat given $Q_2 = ?$

As change in internal energy between two states for different path is same.

$$\therefore \quad \Delta U = Q_1 - W_1 = Q_2 - W_2$$

$$1000 - W_1 = Q_2 - (W_1 - 100)$$

$$\Rightarrow \quad Q_2 = 1000 - 100 = 900 \text{ J}$$

Q. 14 If a refrigerator's door is kept open, will the room become cool or hot? Explain.

Ans. If a refrigerator's door is kept open, then room will become hot, because amount of heat removed would be less than the amount of heat released in the room.

Q. 15 Is it possible to increase the temperature of a gas without adding heat to it? Explain.

Ans. Yes, during adiabatic compression the temperature of a gas increases while no heat is given to it.

In adiabatic compression, $dQ = 0$

$\therefore$ From first law of thermodynamics, $dU = dQ - dW$

$$dU = -dW$$

In compression work is done on the gas *i.e.,* work done is negative.

Therefore, $dU =$ Positive

Hence, internal energy of the gas increases due to which its temperature increases.

Q. 16 Air pressure in a car tyre increases during driving. Explain.

Ans. During, driving, temperature of the gas increases while its volume remains constant.

So, according to Charle's law, at constant volume (V),

$$\text{Pressure } (p) \propto \text{Temperature } (T)$$

Therefore, pressure of gas increases.

Short Answer Type Questions

Q. 17 Consider a Carnot's cycle operating between $T_1 = 500$ K and $T_2 = 300$ K producing 1 kJ of mechanical work per cycle. Find the heat transferred to the engine by the reservoirs.

Thinking Process

The efficiency of a Carnot's engine is $\eta = 1 - \frac{T_2}{T_1}$,

where, T_2 *is temperature of the sink and* T_1 *is temperature of the source.*

Ans. Given, temperature of the source $T_1 = 500$ K

Temperature of the sink $T_2 = 300$ K

Work done per cycle $W = 1\text{k J} = 1000$ J

Heat transferred to the engine per cycle $Q_1 = ?$

Efficiency of a Carnot engine $(\eta) = 1 - \frac{T_2}{T_1} = 1 - \frac{300}{500} = \frac{200}{500} = \frac{2}{5}$

and $$\eta = \frac{W}{Q_1}$$

$\Rightarrow$ $$Q_1 = \frac{W}{\eta} = \frac{1000}{(2/5)} = 2500 \text{ J}$$

Q. 18 A person of mass 60 kg wants to lose 5kg by going up and down a 10 m high stairs. Assume he burns twice as much fat while going up than coming down. If 1 kg of fat is burnt on expending 7000 k cal, how many times must he go up and down to reduce his weight by 5 kg?

Thinking Process

Potential energy(PE) of an object at height (h) is mgh. The energy in the form of fat will be utilised to increase PE of the person. Thus, the calorie consumed by the person in going up is mgh, then according to problem calorie consumed by the person in coming down is $\frac{1}{2}mgh$.

Ans. Given, height of the stairs $= h = 10$ m

Energy produced by burning 1 kg of fat = 7000 kcal

$\therefore$ Energy produced by burning 5 kg of fat $= 5 \times 7000 = 35000$ kcal

$= 35 \times 10^6$ cal

Energy utilised in going up and down one time

$$= mgh + \frac{1}{2}mgh = \frac{3}{2}mgh$$

$$= \frac{3}{2} \times 60 \times 10 \times 10$$

$$= 9000 \text{ J} = \frac{9000}{4.2} = \frac{3000}{1.4} \text{ cal}$$

$\therefore$ Number of times, the person has to go up and down the stairs

$$= \frac{35 \times 10^6}{(3000/1.4)} = \frac{35 \times 1.4 \times 10^6}{3000}$$

$$= 16.3 \times 10^3 \text{ times}$$

Q. 19 Consider a cycle tyre being filled with air by a pump. Let V be the volume of the tyre (fixed) and at each stroke of the pump $\Delta V(<<V)$ of air is transferred to the tube adiabatically. What is the work done when the pressure in the tube is increased from p_1 to p_2?

Thinking Process

There is no exchange of heat in the process, hence this can be considered as an adiabatic process.

Ans. Let, volume is increased by ΔV and pressure is increased by Δp by an stroke.

For just before and after an stroke, we can write

$$p_1 V_1^\gamma = p_2 V_2^\gamma$$

$$\Rightarrow \quad p(V+\Delta V)^\gamma = (p+\Delta p)V^\gamma \qquad (\because \text{ volume is fixed})$$

$$\Rightarrow \quad pV^\gamma\left(1+\frac{\Delta V}{V}\right)^\gamma = p\left(1+\frac{\Delta p}{p}\right)V^\gamma$$

$$\Rightarrow \quad pV^\gamma\left(1+\gamma\frac{\Delta V}{V}\right) \approx pV^\gamma\left(1+\frac{\Delta p}{p}\right) \qquad (\because \Delta v << v)$$

$$\Rightarrow \quad \gamma\frac{\Delta V}{V} = \frac{\Delta p}{p} \Rightarrow \Delta V = \frac{1}{\gamma}\frac{V}{p}\Delta p$$

$$\Rightarrow \quad dV = \frac{1}{\gamma}\frac{V}{p}dp$$

Hence, work done is increasing the pressure from p_1 to p_2

$$W = \int_{p_1}^{p_2} p\,dV = \int_{p_1}^{p_2} p \times \frac{1}{\gamma}\frac{V}{p}dp$$

$$= \frac{V}{\gamma}\int_{p_1}^{p_2} dp = \frac{V}{\gamma}(p_2 - p_1)$$

$$\Rightarrow \quad W = \frac{(p_2 - p_1)}{\gamma}V$$

Q. 20 In a refrigerator one removes heat from a lower temperature and deposits to the surroundings at a higher temperature. In this process, mechanical work has to be done, which is provided by an electric motor. If the motor is of 1kW power and heat transferred from −3°C to 27°C, find the heat taken out of the refrigerator per second assuming its efficiency is 50% of a perfect engine.

Thinking Process

The Carnot engine is the most efficient heat engine operating between two given temperature. This is why it is known as perfect engine. The efficiency of Carnot engine is

$$\eta = 1 - \frac{T_2}{T_1}.$$

Ans. Given, temperature of the source is 27°C

$$\Rightarrow \quad T_1 = (27+273)\text{K} = 300\text{K}$$

Temperature of sink $\quad T_2 = (-3+273)\text{K} = 270\text{K}$

Efficiency of a perfect heat engine is given by

$$\eta = 1 - \frac{T_2}{T_1} = 1 - \frac{270}{300} = \frac{1}{10}$$

Efficiency of refrigerator is 50% of a perfect engine

$$\therefore \quad \eta' = 0.5 \times \eta = \frac{1}{2}\eta = \frac{1}{20}$$

$\therefore$ Coefficient of performance of the refrigerator

$$\beta = \frac{Q_2}{W} = \frac{1-\eta'}{\eta'}$$

$$= \frac{1-(1/20)}{(1/20)} = \frac{19/20}{1/20} = 19$$

$\Rightarrow$ $$Q_2 = \beta W = 19W \qquad \left(\because \beta = \frac{Q_2}{W}\right)$$

$$= 19 \times (1\text{kW}) = 19\text{kW} = 19\text{kJ/s}.$$

Therefore, heat is taken out of the refrigerator at a rate of 19 kJ per second.

Q. 21 If the coefficient of performance of a refrigerator is 5 and operates at the room temperature (27°C), find the temperature inside the refrigerator.

Thinking Process

Coefficient of performance (β) of a refrigerator is ratio of quantity of heat removed per cycle (Q_2) to the amount of work done on the refrigerator.

Ans. Given, coefficient of performace (β) = 5

$$T_1 = (27+273)\,K = 300\text{ K}, \; T_2 = ?$$

Coefficient of performance $(\beta) = \dfrac{T_2}{T_1 - T_2}$

$$5 = \frac{T_2}{300 - T_2} \Rightarrow 1500 - 5T_2 = T_2$$

$\Rightarrow$ $$6T_2 = 1500 \Rightarrow T_2 = 250\text{K}$$

$\Rightarrow$ $$T_2 = (250 - 273)°\text{C} = -23°\text{C}$$

Q. 22 The initial state of a certain gas is (p_i, V_i, T_i). It undergoes expansion till its volume becomes V_f. Consider the following two cases

(a) the expansion takes place at constant temperature.

(b) the expansion takes place at constant pressure.

Plot the p-V diagram for each case. In which of the two cases, is the work done by the gas more?

Ans. Consider the diagram p-V, where variation is shown for each process.

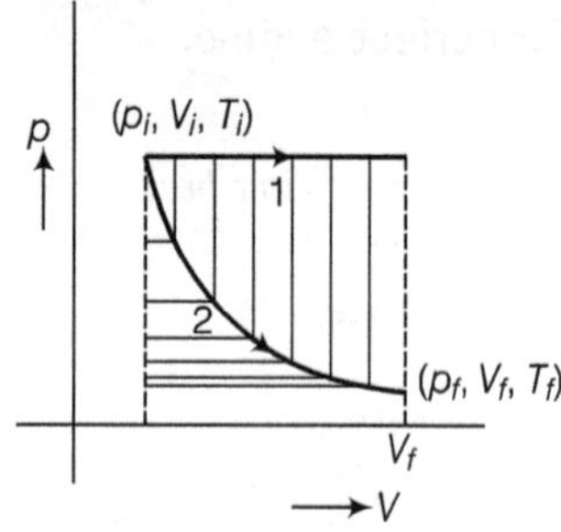

Process 1 is isobaric and process 2 is isothermal.

Since, work done = area under the p-V curve. Here, area under the p-V curve 1 is more . So, work done is more when the gas expands in isobaric process.

Long Answer Type Questions

Q. 23 Consider a p-V diagram in which the path followed by one mole of perfect gas in a cylindrical container is shown in figure.

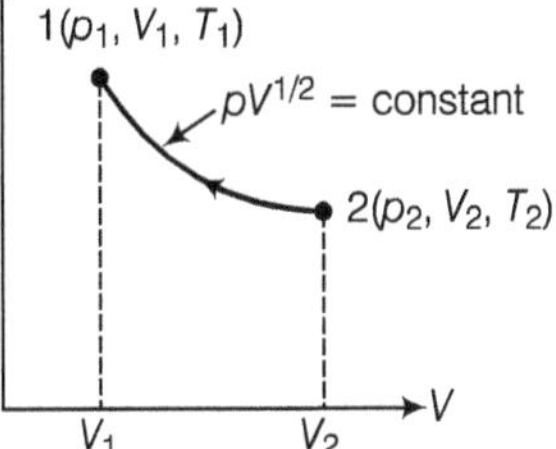

(a) Find the work done when the gas is taken from state 1 to state 2.

(b) What is the ratio of temperature T_1/T_2, if $V_2 = 2V_1$?

(c) Given the internal energy for one mole of gas at temperature T is $(3/2)RT$, find the heat supplied to the gas when it is taken from state 1 to 2, with $V_2 = 2V_1$.

Ans. Let $pV^{1/2} = \text{Constant} = K, \ p = \frac{K}{\sqrt{V}}$

(a) Work done for the process 1 to 2,

$$W = \int_{V_1}^{V_2} p dV = K\int_{V_1}^{V_2} \frac{dV}{\sqrt{V}} = K\left[\frac{\sqrt{V}}{1/2}\right]_{V_1}^{V_2} = 2K(\sqrt{V_2} - \sqrt{V_1})$$

$$= 2p_1V_1^{1/2}(\sqrt{V_2} - \sqrt{V_1}) = 2p_2V_2^{1/2}(\sqrt{V_2} - \sqrt{V_1})$$

(b) From ideal gas equation,

$$pV = nRT \quad \Rightarrow \quad T = \frac{pV}{nR} = \frac{p\sqrt{V}\sqrt{V}}{nR}$$

$$\Rightarrow \quad T = \frac{K\sqrt{V}}{nR} \qquad (\text{As, } p\sqrt{V} = K)$$

Hence,

$$T_1 = \frac{K\sqrt{V_1}}{nR} \Rightarrow T_2 = \frac{K\sqrt{V_2}}{nR}$$

$$\Rightarrow \quad \frac{T_1}{T_2} = \frac{\frac{K\sqrt{V_1}}{nR}}{\frac{K\sqrt{V_2}}{nR}} = \sqrt{\frac{V_1}{V_2}} = \sqrt{\frac{V_1}{2V_1}} = \frac{1}{\sqrt{2}} \qquad (\because V_2 = 2V_1)$$

(c) Given, internal energy of the gas $= U = \left(\frac{3}{2}\right)RT$

$$\Delta U = U_2 - U_1 = \frac{3}{2}R(T_2 - T_1)$$

$$= \frac{3}{2}RT_1(\sqrt{V} - 1) \qquad [\because T_2 = \sqrt{2}\,T_1 \text{ from (b)}]$$

$$\Delta W = 2p_1V_1^{1/2}(\sqrt{V_2} - \sqrt{V_1})$$

$$= 2p_1V_1^{1/2}(\sqrt{2} \times \sqrt{V_1} - \sqrt{V_1})$$

$$= 2p_1V_1(\sqrt{2} - 1) = 2RT_1(\sqrt{2} - 1)$$

$\because$

$$\Delta Q = \Delta U + \Delta W$$

$$= \frac{3}{2}RT_1(\sqrt{2} - 1) + 2RT_1(\sqrt{2} - 1)$$

$$= (\sqrt{2} - 1)RT_1(2 + 3/2)$$

$$= \left(\frac{7}{2}\right)RT_1(\sqrt{2} - 1)$$

This is the amount of heat supplied.

Q. 24 A cycle followed by an engine (made of one mole of perfect gas in a cylinder with a piston) is shown in figure.

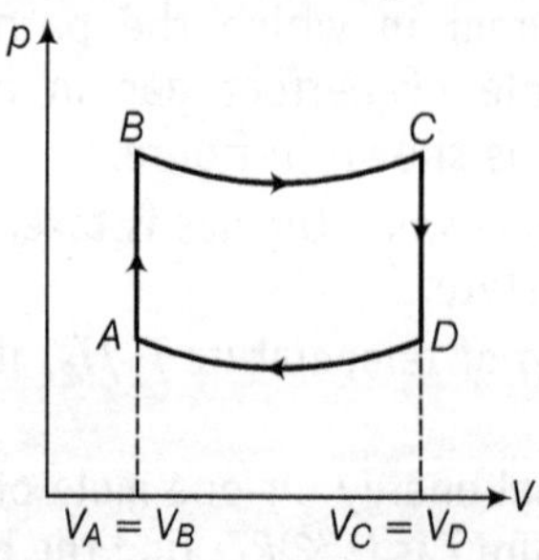

A to B volume constant, B to C adiabatic, C to D volume constant and D to A adiabatic

$$V_C = V_D = 2V_A = 2V_B$$

(a) In which part of the cycle heat is supplied to the engine from outside?

(b) In which part of the cycle heat is being given to the surrounding by the engine?

(c) What is the work done by the engine in one cycle? Write your answer in term of p_A, p_B, V_A?

(d) What is the efficiency of the engine?

$$\left(\gamma = \frac{5}{3} \text{ for the gas}\right), \left(C_V = \frac{3}{2}R \text{ for one mole}\right)$$

Ans. (a) For the process AB,

$$dV = 0 \Rightarrow dW = 0 \qquad (\because \text{volume is constant})$$

$$dQ = dU + dW = dU$$

$\Rightarrow$ $dQ = dU =$ Change in internal energy.

Hence, in this process heat supplied is utilised to increase, internal energy of the system.

Since, $p = \left(\frac{nR}{V}\right)T$, in isochoric process, $T \propto p$. So temperature increases with increases of pressure in process AB which inturn increases internal energy of the system *i.e.*, $dU > 0$. This imply that $dQ > 0$. So heat is supplied to the system in process AB.

(b) For the process CD, volume is constant but pressure decreases.
Hence, temperature also decreases so heat is given to surroundings.

(c) To calculate work done by the engine in one cycle, we calculate work done in each part separately.

$$W_{AB} = \int_A^B pdV = 0, \; W_{CD} = \int_{V_C}^{V_D} pdV = 0 \qquad (\because dV = 0)$$

$$W_{BC} = \int_{V_B}^{V_C} pdV = k\int_{V_B}^{V_C} \frac{dV}{V^\gamma} = \frac{k}{1-\gamma}[V^{1-\gamma}]_{V_B}^{V_C}$$

$$= \frac{1}{1-\gamma}[pV]_{V_B}^{V_C} = \frac{(p_C V_C - p_B V_B)}{1-\gamma}$$

Similarly, $$W_{DA} = \frac{p_A V_A - p_D V_D}{1-\gamma} \qquad [\because BC \text{ is adiabatic process}]$$

$\because$ B and C lies on adiabatic curve BC.

$\therefore \qquad p_B V_B^{\gamma} = p_C V_C^{\gamma}$

$$p_C = p_B \left(\frac{V_B}{V_C}\right)^{\gamma} = p_B \left(\frac{1}{2}\right)^{\gamma} = 2^{-\gamma} p_B$$

Similarly, $\qquad p_D = 2^{-\gamma} p_A$

Total work done by the engine in one cycle $ABCDA$.

$$W = W_{AB} + W_{BC} + W_{CD} + W_{DA} = W_{BC} + W_{DA}$$

$$= \frac{(p_C V_C - p_B V_B)}{1-\gamma} + \frac{(p_A V_A - p_D V_D)}{1-\gamma}$$

$$W = \frac{1}{1-\gamma}[2^{-\gamma} p_B (2V_B) - p_B V_B + p_A V_A - 2^{-\gamma} p_B (2V_B)]$$

$$= \frac{1}{1-\gamma}[p_B V_B (2^{-\gamma+1} - 1) - p_A V_A (2^{-\gamma+1} - 1)$$

$$= \frac{1}{1-\gamma}(2^{1-\gamma} - 1)(p_B - p_A)V_A$$

$$= \frac{3}{2}\left[1 - \left(\frac{1}{2}\right)^{2/3}\right](p_B - p_A)V_A$$

Q. 25 A cycle followed by an engine (made of one mole of an ideal gas in a cylinder with a piston) is shown in figure. Find heat exchanged by the engine, with the surroundings for each section of the cycle. $[C_V = (3/2)R]$

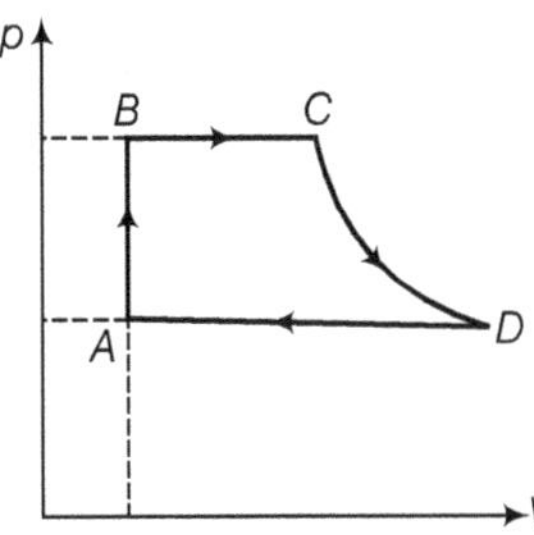

(a) AB : constant volume

(b) BC : constant pressure

(c) CD : adiabatic

(d) DA : constant pressure

Thinking Process

Find amount of heat associated with each process by using first law of thermodynamics.

Ans. (a) For process AB,

Volume is constant, hence work done $dW = 0$

Now, by first law of thermodynamics,

$$dQ = dU + dW = dU + 0 = dU$$

$$= nCv\, dT = nCv\,(T_B - T_A)$$

$$= \frac{3}{2}R\,(T_B - T_A) \qquad (\because n = 1)$$

$$= \frac{3}{2}(RT_B - RT_A) = \frac{3}{2}(p_B V_B - p_A V_A)$$

Heat exchanged $= \frac{3}{2}(p_B V_B - p_A V_A)$

(b) For process BC, p = constant

$$dQ = dU + dW = \frac{3}{2}R(T_C - T_B) + p_B(V_C - V_B)$$

$$= \frac{3}{2}(p_C V_C - p_B V_B) + p_B(V_C - V_B) = \frac{5}{2} p_B(V_C - V_B)$$

Heat exchanged $= \frac{5}{2} p_B(V_C - V_A)$ $(\because p_B = p_C \text{ and } p_B = V_A)$

(c) For process CD, Because CD is adiabatic, dQ = Heat exchanged = 0

(d) DA involves compression of gas from V_D to V_A at constant pressure p_A.

$\therefore$ Heat exchanged can be calculated by similar way as BC_1,

Hence, $dQ = \frac{5}{2} p_A(V_A - V_D)$.

Q. 26 Consider that an ideal gas (n moles) is expanding in a process given by $p = f(V)$, which passes through a point (V_0, p_0). Show that the gas is absorbing heat at (p_0, V_0) if the slope of the curve $p = f(V)$ is larger than the slope of the adiabatic passing through (p_0, V_0).

Ans. According to question, slope of the curve = $f(V)$, where V is volume.

$\therefore$ Slope of $p = f(V)$ curve at $(V_0, p_0) = f(V_0)$

Slope of adiabatic at $(V_0, p_0) = k(-\gamma) V_0^{-1-\gamma} = -\gamma p_0/V_0$

Now heat absorbed in the process $p = f(V)$

$$dQ = dU + dW = nC_V dT + p dV \quad \ldots\text{(i)}$$

$$\because \quad pV = nRT \Rightarrow T = \left(\frac{1}{nR}\right) pV$$

$$\Rightarrow \quad T = \left(\frac{1}{nR}\right) V f(V)$$

$$\Rightarrow \quad dT = \left(\frac{1}{nR}\right)[f(V) + Vf'(V)]dV \quad \ldots\text{(ii)}$$

Now from Eq. (i)

$$\frac{dQ}{dV} = nC_V\frac{dT}{dV} + p\frac{dV}{dV} = nC_V\frac{dT}{dV} + p$$

$$= \frac{nC_V}{nR} \times [f(V) + V f'(V)] + p \quad \text{[from Eq. (ii)]}$$

$$= \frac{C_V}{R}[f(V) + V f'(V)] + f(V) \quad [\because p = f(V)]$$

$$\Rightarrow \quad \left[\frac{dQ}{dV}\right]_{V=V_0} = \frac{C_V}{R}[f(V_0) + V_0 f'](V_0)] + f(V_0)$$

$$= f(V_0)\left[\frac{C_V}{R} + 1\right] + V_0 f'(V_0)\frac{C_V}{R}$$

$$\because \quad C_V = \frac{R}{\gamma - 1} \Rightarrow \frac{C_V}{R} = \frac{1}{\gamma - 1}$$

$$\Rightarrow \quad \left[\frac{dQ}{dv}\right]_{V=V_0} = \left[\frac{1}{\gamma - 1} + 1\right] f(V_0) + \frac{V_0 f'(V_0)}{\gamma - 1}$$

$$= \frac{\gamma}{\gamma - 1} p_0 + \frac{V_0}{\gamma - 1} f'(V_0)$$

Heat is absorbed where $\frac{dQ}{dV} > 0$, when gas expands

Hence, $\gamma p_0 + V_0 f'(V_0) > 0$ or $f'(V_0) > \left(-\gamma \frac{p_0}{V_0}\right)$

Q. 27 Consider one mole of perfect gas in a cylinder of unit cross-section with a piston attached (figure). A spring (spring constant k)is attached (unstretched length L) to the piston and to the bottom of the cylinder. Initially the spring is unstretched and the gas is in equilibrium. A certain amount of heat Q is supplied to the gas causing an increase of value from V_0 to V_1.

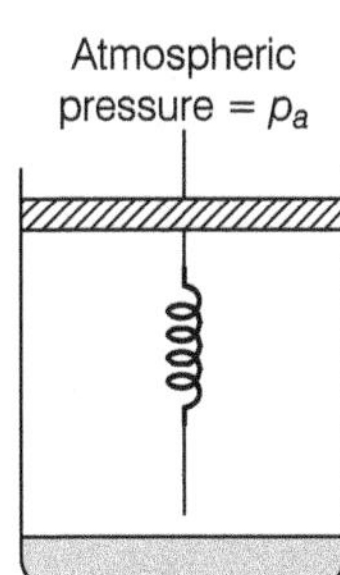

(a) What is the initial pressure of the system?

(b) What is the final pressure of the system?

(c) Using the first law of thermodynamics, write down a relation between Q, p_a, V, V_0 and k.

Thinking Process

We will assume the piston is massless, hence, at equilibrium atmospheric pressure and inside pressure will be same.

Ans. (a) Initially the piston is in equilibrium hence, $p_i = p_a$

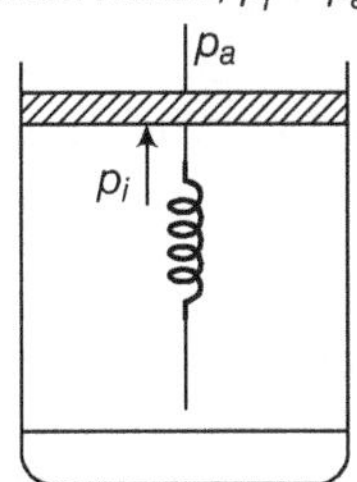

(b) On supplying heat, the gas expands from V_0 to V_1

$\therefore$ Increase in volume of the gas $= V_1 - V_0$

As the piston is of unit cross-sectional area hence, extension in the spring

$$x = \frac{V_1 - V_0}{\text{Area}} = V_1 - V_0 \quad \text{[Area=1]}$$

$\therefore$ Force exerted by the spring on the piston

$$= F = kx = k(V_1 - V_0)$$

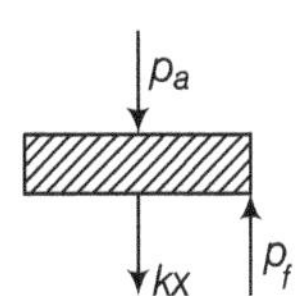

Hence, final pressure $= p_f = p_a + kx$

$$= p_a + k \times (V_1 - V_0)$$

(c) From first law of thermodynamics $dQ = dU + dW$

If T is final temperature of the gas, then increase in internal energy

$$dU = C_V(T_1 - T_0) = C_V(T_1 - T_0)$$

We can write, $$T = \frac{p_f V_1}{R} = \left[\frac{p_a + k(V_1 - V_0)}{R}\right]\frac{V_1}{R}$$

Work done by the gas $= pdV +$ increase in PE of the spring

$$= p_a(V_1 - V_0) + \frac{1}{2}kx^2$$

Now, we can write $dQ = dU + dW$

$$= C_V(T - T_0) + p_a(V - V_0) + \frac{1}{2}kx^2$$

$$= C_V(T - T_0) + p_a(V - V_0) + \frac{1}{2}(V_1 - V_0)^2$$

This is the required relation.

12

Kinetic Theory

Multiple Choice Questions (MCQs)

Q. 1 A cubic vessel (with face horizontal + vertical) contains an ideal gas at NTP. The vessel is being carried by a rocket which is moving at a speed of 500 m s^{-1} in vertical direction. The pressure of the gas inside the vessel as observed by us on the ground

(a) remains the same because 500 ms^{-1} is very much smaller than v_{rms} of the gas

(b) remains the same because motion of the vessel as a whole does not affect the relative motion of the gas molecules and the walls

(c) will increase by a factor equal to $(v_{rms}^2 + (500)^2) / v_{rms}^2$ where v_{rms} was the original mean square velocity of the gas

(d) will be different on the top wall and bottom wall of the vessel

Thinking Process

This phenomenon is based on the concept of relative motion that is when collision takes place, it is the relative velocity which changes.

Ans. *(b)* As the motion of the vessel as a whole does not effect the relative motion of the gas molecules with respect to the walls of the vessel, hence pressure of the gas inside the vessel, as observed by us, on the ground remains the same.

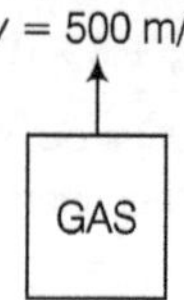

Q. 2 1 mole of an ideal gas is contained in a cubical volume *V*, *ABCDEFGH* at 300K (figure). One face of the cube (*EFGH*) is made up of a material which totally absorbs any gas molecule incident on it. At any given time,

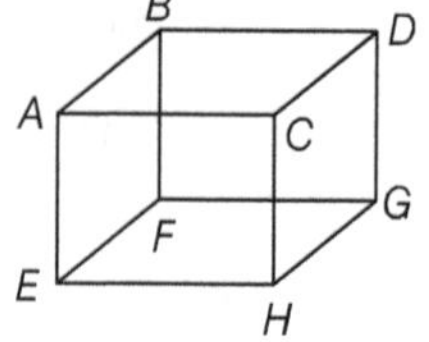

(a) the pressure on *EFGH* would be zero

(b) the pressure on all the faces will the equal

(c) the pressure of *EFGH* would be double the pressure on *ABCD*

(d) the pressure on *EFGH* would be half that on *ABCD*

Ans. *(d)* In an ideal gas, when a molecule collides elastically with a wall, the momentum transferred to each molecule will be twice the magnitude of its normal momentum.

For the face *EFGH*, it transfers only half of that.

Q. 3 Boyle's law is applicable for an

(a) adiabatic process
(b) isothermal process
(c) isobaric process
(d) isochoric process

Ans *(b)* Boyle's law is applicable when temperature is constant

i.e., $pV = nRT = \text{constant}$

$\Rightarrow$ $pV = \text{constant}$ (at constant temperature)

i.e., $p \propto \frac{1}{V}$ [where , p=pressure, V=volume]

So, this process can be called as isothermal process.

Q. 4 A cylinder containing an ideal gas is in vertical position and has a piston of mass *M* that is able to move up or down without friction (figure). If the temperature is increased

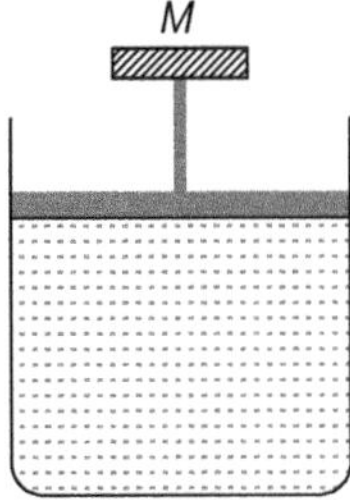

(a) both p and V of the gas will change
(b) only p will increase according to Charles' law
(c) V will change but not p
(d) p will change but not V

Ans. *(c)* Consider the diagram where an ideal gas is contained in a cylinder, having a piston of mass *M*. Friction is absent.

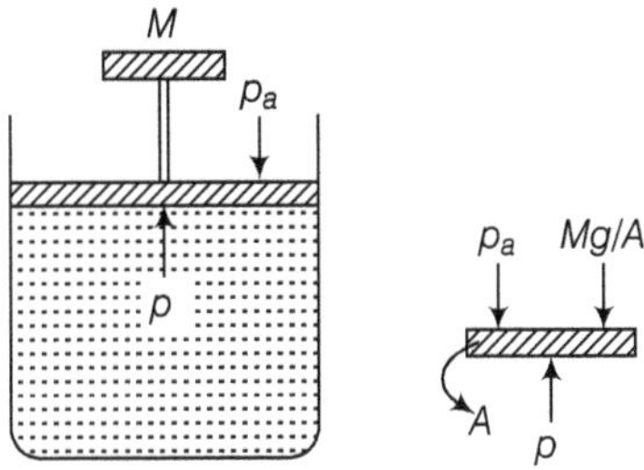

The pressure inside the gas will be

$$p = p_a + Mg/A$$

where, p_a = atmospheric pressure

A = area of cross-section of the piston.

Mg = weight of piston

Hence, p = constant.

When temperature increases

as $pV = nRT \Rightarrow$ volume (V) increases at constant pressure.

Q. 5 Volume *versus* temperature graphs for a given mass of an ideal gas are shown in figure. At two different values of constant pressure. What can be inferred about relation between p_1 and p_2?

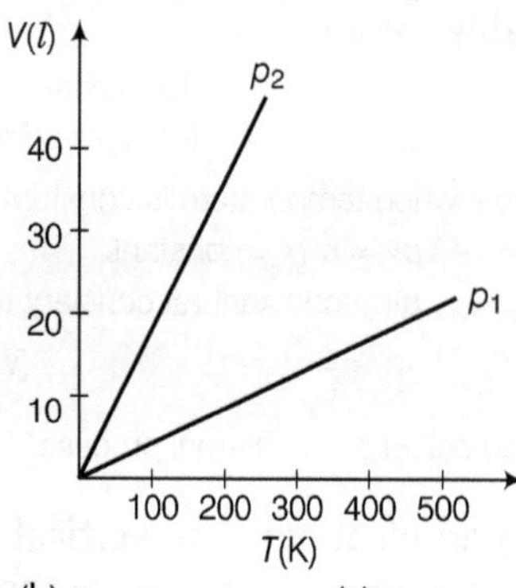

(a) $p_1 > p_2$ (b) $p_1 = p_2$ (c) $p_1 < p_2$ (d) Data is insufficient

Thinking Process

To find the required relation, we have to consider slope of the V – T graph. By ideal gas equation, the slope of V-T curve is V/T = nR/p. This imply that greater the slope, smaller the pressure and vice-versa.

Ans. *(a)* We know for an ideal gas,

$$pV = nRT \Rightarrow V = \left(\frac{nR}{p}\right)T$$

Slope of the $V-T$ graph, $m = \frac{dV}{dT} = \frac{nR}{p}$ [m = slope of $V-t$ graph]

$\Rightarrow$ $m \propto \frac{1}{p}$ [$\because nR$ = constant]

$\Rightarrow$ $p \propto \frac{1}{m}$

hence, $\frac{p_1}{p_2} = \frac{m_2}{m_1} < 1$

$\begin{bmatrix} P = \text{pressure} \\ V = \text{volume} \\ n = \text{number of moles of gases} \\ R = \text{gas constant} \\ T = \text{temperature} \end{bmatrix}$

where, m_1 is slope of the graph corresponding to p_1 and similarly m_2 is slope corresponding to p_2.

$\Rightarrow$ $p_2 < p_1$ or $p_1 > p_2$

Q. 6 1 mole of H_2 gas is contained in a box of volume $V = 1.00 \text{ m}^3$ at $T = 300$ K. The gas is heated to a temperature of $T = 3000$ K and the gas gets converted to a gas of hydrogen atoms. The final pressure would be (considering all gases to be ideal)

(a) same as the pressure initially (b) 2 times the pressure initially

(c) 10 times the pressure initially (d) 20 times the pressure initially

Ans. *(d)* Consider the diagram, when the molecules breaks into atoms, the number of moles would become twice.

Now, by ideal gas equation

P = Pressure of gas, n = Number of moles

R = Gas constant, T = Temperature

$pV = nRT$

As volume (V) of the container is constant.

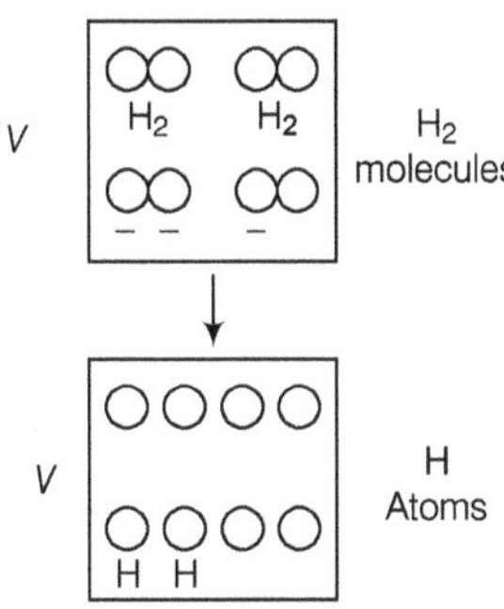

As gases breaks number of moles becomes twice of initial, so $n_2 = 2n_1$

So, $$p \propto nT$$

$\Rightarrow$ $$\frac{p_2}{p_1} = \frac{n_2 T_2}{n_1 T_1} = \frac{(2n_1)(3000)}{n_1 (300)} = 20$$

$\Rightarrow$ $$p_2 = 20p_1$$

Hence, final pressure of the gas would be 20 times the pressure initially.

Q. 7 **A vessel of volume V contains a mixture of 1 mole of hydrogen and 1 mole oxygen (both considered as ideal). Let $f_1(v)dv$, denote the fraction of molecules with speed between v and $(v + dv)$ with $f_2(v)dv$, similarly for oxygen. Then,**

(a) $f_1(v) + f_2(v) = f(v)$ obeys the Maxwell's distribution law

(b) $f_1(v)$, $f_2(v)$ will obey the Maxwell's distribution law separately

(c) neither $f_1(v)$, nor $f_2(v)$ will obey the Maxwell's distribution law

(d) $f_2(v)$ and $f_1(v)$ will be the same

Ans. *(b)* For a function $f(v)$, the number of molecules $n = f(v)$, which are having speeds between v and $v + dv$.

For each function $f_1(v)$ and $f_2(v)$, n will be different, hence each function $f_1(v)$ and $f_2(v)$ will obey the Maxwell's distribution law separately.

Q. 8 **An inflated rubber balloon contains one mole of an ideal gas, has a pressure p, volume V and temperature T. If the temperature rises to 1.1 T, and the volume is increased to 1.05 V, the final pressure will be**

(a) 1.1 p (b) p (c) less than p (d) between p and1.1

Ans. *(d)* We know for an ideal gas, $pV = nRT$ (Ideal gas equation)

$\Rightarrow$ n = Number of moles, p = Pressure, V = Volume

R = Gas constant, T = Temperature

$$= \frac{pV}{RT}$$

As number of moles of the gas remains fixed, hence, we can write

$$\frac{p_1 V_1}{RT_1} = \frac{p_2 V_2}{RT_2}$$

$$\Rightarrow \quad p_2 = (p_1 V_1)\left(\frac{T_2}{V_2 T_1}\right)$$

$$= \frac{(p)(V)(1.1T)}{(1.05)V(T)} \qquad \left[\begin{matrix} p_1 = p \\ V_2 = 1.05V \text{and } T_2 = 1.1T \end{matrix}\right]$$

$$= p \times \left(\frac{1.1}{1.05}\right)$$

$$= p(1.0476) \approx 1.05\,p$$

Hence, final pressure p_2 lies between p and $1.1p$.

Multiple Choice Questions (More Than One Options)

Q. 9 *ABCDEFGH* **is a hollow cube made of an insulator (figure) face** *ABCD* **has positive charge on it. Inside the cube, we have ionised hydrogen.**

The usual kinetic theory expression for pressure

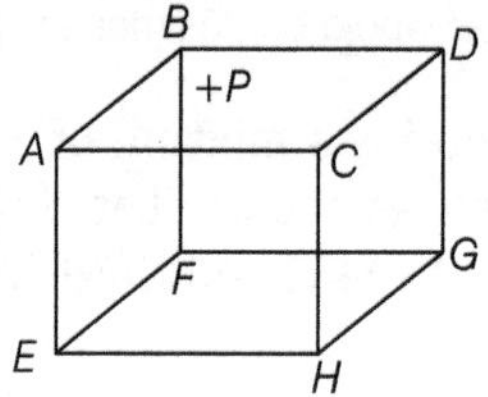

(a) will be valid

(b) will not be valid, since the ions would experience forces other than due to collisions with the walls

(c) will not be valid, since collisions with walls would not be elastic

(d) will not be valid because isotropy is lost

Thinking Process

As ionised hydrogen is present inside the cube, they are having charge. Now, due to presence of positive charge on the surface ABCD hydrogen ions would experience forces of electrostatic nature.

Ans. *(b, d)*

Due to presence of external positive charge on the face *ABCD*. The usual expression for pressure on the basis of kinetic theory will not be valid as ions would also experience electrostatic forces other than the forces due to collisions with the walls of the container. Due to presence of positive charge the isotropy is also lost.

Q. 10 Diatomic molecules like hydrogen have energies due to both translational as well as rotational motion. From the equation in kinetic theory $pV = \frac{2}{3}E$, E is

(a) the total energy per unit volume
(b) only the translational part of energy because rotational energy is very small compared to the translational energy
(c) only the translational part of the energy because during collisions with the wall pressure relates to change in linear momentum
(d) the translational part of the energy because rotational energies of molecules can be of either sign and its average over all the molecules is zero

Ans. *(c)* According to kinetic theory, we assume the walls only exert perpendicular forces on molecules. They do not exert any parallel force, hence there will not be any type of rotation present.

The wall produces only change in translational motion.

Hence, in the equation

$$pV = \frac{2}{3}E \qquad \begin{bmatrix} \text{where } P = \text{pressure} \\ V = \text{volume} \end{bmatrix}$$

E is representing only translational part of energy.

Q. 11 In a diatomic molecule, the rotational energy at a given temperature

(a) obeys Maxwell's distribution
(b) have the same value for all molecules
(c) equals the translational kinetic energy for each molecule
(d) is (2/3)rd the translational kinetic energy for each molecule

Ans. *(a, d)*

Consider a diatomic molecule as shown in the diagram.

The total energy associated with the molecule is

$$E = \frac{1}{2}mv_x^2 + \frac{1}{2}mv_y^2 + \frac{1}{2}mv_z^2 + \frac{1}{2}I_x\omega_x^2 + \frac{1}{2}I_y\omega_y^2$$

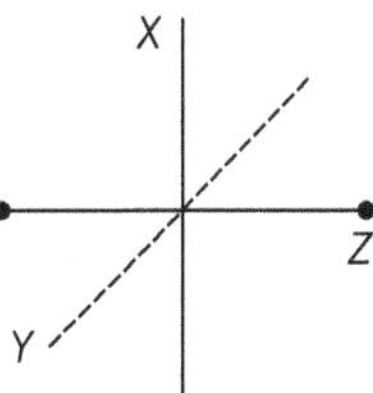

This above expression contains translational kinetic energy $\left(\frac{1}{2}mv^2\right)$ corresponding to velocity in each x, y and z-directions as well as rotational KE $\left(\frac{1}{2}I\omega^2\right)$ associated with axis of rotations x and y.

The number of independent terms in the above expression is 5.

As we can predict velocities of molecules by Maxwell's distribution, hence the above expression also obeys Maxwell's distribution.

$\because$ 2 rotational and 3 translational energies are associated with each molecule.

$\therefore$ Rotational energy at a given temperature is $\left(\frac{2}{3}\right)$rd of translational KE of each molecule.

Q. 12 Which of the following diagrams (figure) depicts ideal gas behaviour ?

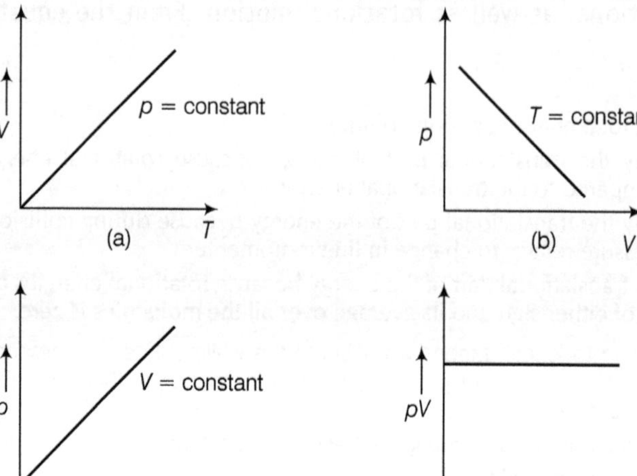

Ans ***(a, c)***

We know that ideal gas equation is

$$pV = nRT \quad ...(i)$$

(a) When pressure, $p =$ constant

From (i) volume $V \propto$ Temperature T

(b) When $T =$ constant

From (i) $pV =$ constant

So, the graph is rectangular hyperbola.

(c) When $V =$ constant.

From (i) $p \propto T$

So, the graph is straight line passes through the origin.

(d) From (i) $pV \propto T$

$\Rightarrow$ $$\frac{pV}{T} = \text{constant}$$

$\Rightarrow$ So, the graph hence, through origin.

So, (d) is not correct.

Q. 13 When an ideal gas is compressed adiabatically, its temperature rises the molecules on the average have more kinetic energy than before. The kinetic energy increases,

(a) because of collisions with moving parts of the wall only

(b) because of collisions with the entire wall

(c) because the molecules gets accelerated in their motion inside the volume

(d) because of redistribution of energy amongest the molecules

Thinking Process

The elastic collisions of the molecules with a moving part of two system increases their energy.

Ans. ***(a)*** When the gas is compressed adiabatically, the total work done on the gas increases its internal energy which in turn increase the KE of gas molecules and hence, the collisions between molecules also increases.

Very Short Answer Type Questions

Q. 14 Calculate the number of atoms in 39.4 g gold. Molar mass of gold is 197g $mole^{-1}$.

Ans. We know that,

$$\text{Molar mass} = \text{Mass of Avogadro's number of atoms (Molecules).}$$
$$= 6.023 \times 10^{23} \text{ atoms.}$$

Given, molar mass of gold = 197 g/mol

Now,

$\therefore$ 197 g of gold contains $= 6.023 \times 10^{23}$ atoms

$\therefore$ 1 g of gold contain $= \dfrac{6.023 \times 10^{23}}{197}$ atoms

$\therefore$ 39.4 g of gold contains $= \dfrac{6.023 \times 10^{23} \times 39.4}{197} \Rightarrow 1.20 \times 10^{23}$ atoms.

Q. 15 The volume of a given mass of a gas at 27°C, 1 atm is 100cc. What will be its volume at 327°C ?

Ans. We have to convert the given temperatures in kelvin .

If pressure of a given mass of the gas is kept constant, then

$$V \propto T$$

$$\Rightarrow \quad \frac{V}{T} = \text{constant} \qquad \begin{bmatrix} V = \text{Volume of gas} \\ T = \text{Temperature of gas} \end{bmatrix}$$

$$\Rightarrow \quad \frac{V_1}{T_1} = \frac{V_2}{T_2}$$

$$\Rightarrow \quad V_2 = V_1 \left(\frac{T_2}{T_1}\right)$$

$$T_1 = 273 + 27 = 300\,\text{K}$$
$$T_2 = 273 + 327 = 600\,\text{K}$$

But $\quad V_1 = 100\text{cc}$

$$V_2 = V_1 \left(\frac{600}{300}\right)$$

$$V_2 = 2V_1$$

$$\therefore \quad V_2 = 2 \times 100 = 200\,\text{cc}$$

Note *To apply ideal gas equation, we must convert the given temperature in kelvin.*

Q. 16 The molecules of a given mass of a gas have root mean square speeds of 100 ms^{-1} at 27°C and 1.00 atmospheric pressure. What will be the root mean square speeds of the molecules of the gas at 127°C and 2.0 atmospheric pressure?

Ans. We know that for a given mass of a gas

$$v_{rms} = \sqrt{\frac{3RT}{M}}$$

where, R is gas constant

T is temperature in kelvin

M is molar mass of the gas.

Clearly ,

$$v_{rms} \propto \sqrt{T}$$

As R, M are constants,

$$\frac{(v_{rms})_1}{(v_{rms})_2} = \sqrt{\frac{T_1}{T_2}}$$

Given,

$$(v_{rms})_1 = 100 \text{ m/s}$$
$$T_1 = 27°C = 27 + 273 = 300 \text{K}$$
$$T_2 = 127°C = 127 + 273 = 400 \text{K}$$

$\therefore$ From Eq. (i)

$$\frac{100}{(v_{rms})_2} = \sqrt{\frac{300}{400}} = \frac{\sqrt{3}}{2}$$

$$\Rightarrow \quad (v_{rms})_2 = \frac{2 \times 100}{\sqrt{3}} = \frac{200}{\sqrt{3}} \text{ m/s}$$

Q. 17 Two molecules of a gas have speeds of $9 \times 10^6 \text{ms}^{-1}$ and $1 \times 10^6 \text{ms}^{-1}$, respectively. What is the root mean square speed of these molecules.

Ans. For n-molecules, we know that

$$v_{rms} = \sqrt{\frac{v_1^2 + v_2^2 + v_3^2 + \ldots\ldots + v_n^2}{n}} \qquad [v_{rms} = \text{root mean square velocity}]$$

where $v_1, v_2, v_3 \ldots\ldots\ldots v_n$ are individual velocities of n-molecules of the gas.
For two molecules,

$$v_{rms} = \sqrt{\frac{v_1^2 + v_2^2}{2}} \qquad [v_1, v_2, v_3 \ldots\ldots\ldots v_n \text{ are individual velocity}]$$

Given,

$$v_1 = 9 \times 10^6 \text{m/s}$$

and

$$v_2 = 1 \times 10^6 \text{m/s}$$

$\therefore$

$$v_{rms} = \sqrt{\frac{(9 \times 10^6)^2 + (1 \times 10^6)^2}{2}}$$
$$= \sqrt{\frac{81 \times 10^{12} + 1 \times 10^{12}}{2}}$$
$$= \sqrt{\frac{(81 + 1) \times 10^{12}}{2}}$$
$$= \sqrt{\frac{82 \times 10^{12}}{2}}$$
$$= \sqrt{41} \times 10^6 \text{ m/s}$$

Q. 18 A gas mixture consists of 2.0 moles of oxygen and 4.0 moles of neon at temperature T. Neglecting all vibrational modes, calculate the total internal energy of the system. (Oxygen has two rotational modes.)

Thinking Process

To find exact value of total energy for a given molecule of a gas, we must know the number of degree of freedom associated with the molecules of the gas.

Ans. O_2 is a diatomic gas having 5 degrees of freedom.

Energy (total internal) per mole of the gas $= \frac{5}{2} RT$ $\qquad \left[\begin{array}{l} R = \text{Universal gas constant} \\ T = \text{temperature} \end{array}\right]$

For 2 moles of the gas total internal energy $= 2 \times \frac{5}{2} RT = 5RT$ $\qquad$ ...(i)

Neon (Ne) is a monoatomic gas having 3 degrees of freedom.

$\therefore$ Energy per mole $= \frac{3}{2} RT$

We have 4 moles of Ne.

Hence, $\quad \text{Energy} = 4 \times \frac{3}{2} RT = 6RT \quad$ ...(ii) [Using Eqs. (i) and (ii)]

$\therefore \quad \text{Total energy} = 5RT + 6RT = 11RT$

Q. 19 **Calculate the ratio of the mean free paths of the molecules of two gases having molecular diameters 1Å and 2Å. The gases may be considered under identical conditions of temperature, pressure and volume.**

Ans. Mean free path of a molecule is given by

$$l = \frac{1}{\sqrt{2} d^2 n}$$

where, n = number of molecules/ volume

d = diameter of the molecule

Now, we can write $l \propto \frac{1}{d^2}$

Given, $\quad d_1 = 1\text{ Å}, d_2 = 2\text{Å}$

As $\quad l_1 \propto \frac{1}{d_1^2}$ and $l_2 \propto \frac{1}{d_2^2}$

$\Rightarrow$ So, $\quad \frac{l_1}{l_2} = \left(\frac{d_2}{d_1}\right)^2 = \left(\frac{2}{1}\right)^2 = \frac{4}{1}$

Hence, $\quad l_1 : l_2 = 4 : 1$

Short Answer Type Questions

Q. 20 **The container shown in figure has two chambers, separated by a partition, of volumes $V_1 = 2.0$ L and $V_2 = 3.0$ L. The chambers contain $\mu_1 = 4.0$ and $\mu_2 = 5.0$ mole of a gas at pressures $p_1 = 1.00$ atm and $p_2 = 2.00$ atm. Calculate the pressure after the partition is removed and the mixture attains equilibrium.**

p_1, V_1 μ_1	p_2, V_2 μ_2

$V_1, \mu_1,$ p_1	V_2 $\mu_2,$ $p_2,$

Ans. Consider the diagram,

Given, $\quad V_1 = 2.0\text{L}, V_2 = 3.0\text{ L}$

$\mu_1 = 4.0\text{mol}, \mu_2 = 5.0\text{mol}$

$p_1 = 1.00\text{atm}, p_2 = 2.00\text{atm}$

For chamber 1, $p_1, V_1 = \mu_1 RT_1$

For chamber 2, $p_2, V_2 = \mu_2 RT_2$

When the partition is removed the gases get mixed without any loss of energy. The mixture now attains a common equilibrium pressure and the total volume of the system is sum of the volume of individual chambers V_1 and V_2.

So, $$\mu = \mu_1 + \mu_2, V = V_1 + V_2$$

From kinetic theory of gases,

For l mole $$pV = \frac{2}{3}E \quad \left[E = \text{translational kinetic energy}\right]$$

For μ_1 moles, $$p_1 V_1 = \frac{2}{3}\mu_1 E_1$$

For μ_2 moles, $$p_2 V_2 = \frac{2}{3}\mu_2 E_2$$

Total energy is $$(\mu_1 E_1 + \mu_2 E_2) = \frac{3}{2}(p_1 V_1 + p_2 V_2)$$

From the abvne relation, $$pV = \frac{2}{3}E_{\text{total}} = \frac{2}{3}\mu E_{\text{per mole}}$$

$$p(V_1 + V_2) = \frac{2}{3} \times \frac{3}{2}(p_1 V_1 + p_2 V_2)$$

$$p = \frac{p_1 V_1 + p_2 V_2}{V_1 + V_2}$$

$$= \left(\frac{1.00 \times 2.0 + 2.00 \times 3.0}{2.0 + 3.0}\right) \text{atm}$$

$$= \frac{8.0}{5.0} = 1.60 \text{atm}$$

Q. 21 A gas mixture consists of molecules of A, B and C with masses $m_A > m_B > m_C$. Rank the three types of molecules in decreasing order of (a) average KE (b) rms speeds.

Ans. (a) The average KE will be the same, as conditions of temperature and pressure are the same.

Now as, $$v_{\text{rms}} = \sqrt{\frac{3pV}{M}} = \sqrt{\frac{3RT}{M}}$$

$$= \sqrt{\frac{3RT}{mN}} = \sqrt{\frac{3kT}{m}}$$

where, M = molar mass of the gas

m = mass of each molecular of the gas,

R = gas constant

Clearly, $$v_{\text{rms}} \propto \sqrt{\frac{1}{m}}$$

(b) As k = Boltzmann constant

T = absolute temperature (same for all)

But $$m_A > m_B > m_C$$

$$(v_{\text{rms}})_A < (v_{\text{rms}})_B < (v_{\text{rms}})_C$$

$\therefore$ or $$(v_{\text{rms}})_C > (v_{\text{rms}})_B > (v_{\text{rms}})_A$$

Q. 22 **We have 0.5 g of hydrogen gas in a cubic chamber of size 3 cm kept at NTP. The gas in the chamber is compressed keeping the temperature constant till a final pressure of 100 atm. Is one justified in assuming the ideal gas law, in the final state? (Hydrogen molecules can be consider as spheres of radius 1 Å).**

Thinking Process

For justification of assuming the ideal gas law, the molecular volume and the volume occupied of the ideal gas is compared. If both matches, then law holds good otherwise not.

Ans. Assuming hydrogen molecules as spheres of radius 1 Å.

So, $r = 1\,\text{Å} =$ radius.

$$\text{The volume of hydrogen molecules} = \frac{4}{3}\pi r^3$$
$$= \frac{4}{3}(3.14)(10^{-10})^3$$
$$\approx 4 \times 10^{-30}\ \text{m}^3$$

$$\text{Number of moles of } H_2 = \frac{\text{Mass}}{\text{Molecular mass}}$$
$$= \frac{0.5}{2} = 0.25$$

$$\text{Molecules of } H_2 \text{ present} = \text{Number of moles of } H_2 \text{ present} \times 6.023 \times 10^{23}$$
$$= 0.25 \times 6.023 \times 10^{23}$$

$$\therefore \text{ Volume of molecules present} = \text{Molecules number} \times \text{volume of each molecule}$$
$$= 0.25 \times 6.023 \times 10^{23} \times 4 \times 10^{-30}$$
$$= 6.023 \times 10^{23} \times 10^{-30}$$
$$\approx 6 \times 10^{-7}\ \text{m}^3 \quad \text{.... (i)}$$

Now, if ideal gas law is considered to be constant.

$$p_i V_i = p_f V_f$$
$$V_f = \left(\frac{p_i}{p_f}\right) V_i = \left(\frac{1}{100}\right)(3 \times 10^{-2})^3$$
$$= \frac{27 \times 10^{-6}}{10^2}$$
$$= 2.7 \times 10^{-7}\ \text{m}^3 \quad \text{...(ii)}$$

Hence, on compression the volume of the gas is of the order of the molecular volume [form Eq.(i) and Eq.(ii)]. The intermolecular forces will play role and the gas will deviate from ideal gas behaviour.

Q. 23 **When air is pumped into a cycle tyre the volume and pressure of the air in the tyre both are increased. What about Boyle's law in this case?**

Ans. When air is pumped, more molecules are pumped and Boyle's law is stated for situation where number of molecules remains constant.

In this case, as the number of air molecules keep increasing. Hence, this is a case of variable mass. Boyle's law (and even Charle's law) is only applicable in situations, where number of gas molecules remains fixed.

Hence, in this case Boyle's law is not applicable.

Q. 24 **A balloon has 5.0 mole of helium at 7°C. Calculate**

(a) the number of atoms of helium in the balloon.

(b) the total internal energy of the system.

Thinking Process

Energy associated with a monoatomic molecule is $\frac{3}{2}kT$.

Ans. Given, number of moles of helium = 5

$$T = 7°C = 7 + 273 = 280K$$

(a) Hence, number of atoms (He is monoatomic)

$$= \text{Number of moles} \times \text{Avogadro's number}$$
$$= 5 \times 6.023 \times 10^{23}$$
$$= 30.015 \times 10^{23}$$
$$= 3.0 \times 10^{24} \text{ atoms}$$

(b) Now, average kinetic energy per molecule $= \frac{3}{2} k_B T$

Here, k_B = Boltzmann constant. (It has only 3 degrees of freedom)

$\therefore$ Total energy of all the atoms

$$= \text{Total internal energy}$$
$$= \frac{3}{2} k_b T \times \text{number of atoms}$$
$$= \frac{3}{2} \times 1.38 \times 10^{-23} \times 280 \times 3.0 \times 10^{24}$$
$$= 1.74 \times 10^4 \text{J}$$

Q. 25 **Calculate the number of degrees of freedom of molecules of hydrogen in 1 cc of hydrogen gas at NTP.**

Thinking Process

Total number of degrees of freedom in a thermodynamical system = number of degrees of freedom associated per molecule × number of molecules.

Ans. As given molecules are of hydrogen.

$\therefore$ Volume occupied by 1 mole

$$= 1 \text{ mole of the gas at NTP}$$
$$= 22400 \text{mL} = 22400 \text{ cc}$$

$\therefore$ Number of molecules in 1 cc of hydrogen

$$= \frac{6.023 \times 10^{23}}{22400} = 2.688 \times 10^{19}$$

H_2 is a diatomic gas, having a total of 5 degrees of freedom (3 translational + 2 rotational)

$\therefore$ Total degrees of freedom possessed by all the molecules

$$= 5 \times 2.688 \times 10^{19}$$
$$= 1.344 \times 10^{20}$$

Note *Any ideal gas has a molar volume of* 22400 mL (cc) at NTP.

Q. 26 An insulated container containing monoatomic gas of molar mass m is moving with a velocity v_o. If the container is suddenly stopped, find the change in temperature.

Thinking Process

As the container is suddenly stopped there is no time for exchange of heat in the process.

Ans. According to kinetic interpretation of temperature, absolute temperature of a given sample of a gas is proportional to the total translational kinetic energy of its molecules.

Hence, any change in absolute temperature of a gas will contribute to corresponding change in translational KE and *vice-versa*.

Assuming n = number of moles.

Given, m = molar mass of the gas.

When, the container stops, its total KE is transferred to gas molecules in the form of translational KE, thereby increasing the absolute temperature.

If ΔT = change in absolute temperature.

Then, KE of molecules due to velocity v_o, $\text{KE} = \frac{1}{2}(mn)v_0^2$ ...(i)

Increase in translational $\text{KE} = n\frac{3}{2}R(\Delta T)$ ...(ii)

According to kinetic theory Eqs. (i) and (ii) are equal

$$\Rightarrow \quad \frac{1}{2}(mn)v_0^2 = n\frac{3}{2}R(\Delta T)$$

$$(mn)v_0^2 = n3R(\Delta T)$$

$$\Rightarrow \quad \Delta T = \frac{(mn)v_0^2}{3nR}$$

$$\Rightarrow \quad \Delta T = \frac{mv_0^2}{3R}$$

Long Answer Type Questions

Q. 27 Explain why

(a) there is no atmosphere on moon

(b) there is fall in temperature with altitude

Ans. (a) The moon has small gravitational force (pull) and hence, the escape velocity is small. The value of escape velocity for the moon is 4.6 km/s.

As the moon is in the proximity of the earth as seen from the sun, the moon has the same amount of heat per unit area as that of the earth.

The air molecules have large range of speeds. Even though the rms speed of the air molecules is smaller than the escape velocity on the moon, a significant number of molecules have speed greater than escape velocity and they escape.

Now, rest of the molecules arrange the speed distribution for the equilibrium temperature. Again a significant number of molecules escape as their speed exceed escape speed. Hence, over a long time the moon has lost most of its atmosphere.

$$\text{At 300 K, } v_{rms} = \sqrt{\frac{3kT}{m}} = \sqrt{\frac{3\times 1.38\times 10^{-23}\times 300}{7.3\times 10^{-26}}} = 1.7 \text{ km/s}$$

v_{es} for moon = 4.6 km/s [v_{es} = escape velocity]

(b) As the molecules move higher; their potential energy increases and hence, kinetic energy decreases and hence, temperature reduces.
At greater height more volume is available and gas expands and hence, some cooling takes place.

Note *We should not relate temperature directly with potential energy. It is directly related with kinetic energy of the molecules.*

Q. 28 Consider an ideal gas with following distribution of speeds.

Speed (m/s)	% of molecules
200	10
400	20
600	40
800	20
1000	10

(a) Calculate v_{rms} and hence T. ($m = 3.0 \times 10^{-26}$ kg)

(b) If all the molecules with speed 1000 m/s escape from the system, calculate new v_{rms} and hence T.

Thinking Process

In this problem, it is shown that cooling takes place after evaporation.

Ans. (a) We know that $$v_{rms}^2 = \frac{\sum_i n_i v_i^2}{\sum n_i}$$

This is the rms speed for all molecules collectively.

Now, $$v_{rms} = \left(\frac{\sum_i n_i v_i^2}{\sum n_i} \right)^{\frac{1}{2}}$$

$$= \sqrt{\frac{n_1 v_1^2 + n_2 v_2^2 + n_3 v_3^2 + \ldots\ldots\ldots + n_n v_n^2}{n_1 + n_2 + n_3 + \ldots\ldots\ldots + n_n}}$$

$$= \sqrt{\frac{n_1 v_1^2 + n_2 v_2^2 + n_3 v_3^2 + n_4 v_4^2 + n_5 v_5^2}{n_1 + n_2 + n_3 + n_4 + n_5}}$$

$$= \sqrt{\frac{10 \times (200)^2 + 20 \times (400)^2 + 40 \times 600)^2 + 20 \times (800)^2 + 10 \times (1000)^2}{100}}$$

$$= \sqrt{1000 \times (4 + 32 + 144 + 128 + 100)}$$

$$= \sqrt{408 \times 1000} \approx 639 \text{ m/s.}$$

Now, according to kinetic theory of gasses

$$\frac{1}{2} m v_{rms}^2 = \frac{3}{2} k_B T$$ $\left[\begin{array}{l} K_B = \text{Boltzmann constant} \\ m = \text{mass of gaseous molecules} \end{array} \right]$

$$\therefore \quad T = \frac{1}{3} \frac{m v_{rms}^2}{k_B} = \frac{1}{3} \times \frac{3.0 \times 10^{-26} \times 4.08 \times 10^5}{1.38 \times 10^{-23}}$$

$$= 2.96 \times 10^2 \text{ K} = 296 \text{ K}$$

(b) If all the molecules with speed 1000 m/s escape, then

$$v_{rms}^2 = \frac{10 \times (200)^2 + 20 \times (400)^2 + 40 \times (600)^2 + 20 \times (800)^2}{90}$$

$$= \frac{10 \times 100^2 \times (1 \times 4 + 2 \times 16 + 4 \times 36 + 2 \times 64)}{90}$$

$$= 10000 \times \frac{308}{9} = 342 \times 1000 \text{ m}^2/\text{s}^2$$

$$v_{rms} = 584 \text{ m/s}$$

Again

$$T = \frac{1}{3} \frac{mv_{rms}^2}{k}$$

$$= \frac{1}{3} \times \frac{3 \times 10^{-26} \times 3.42 \times 10^5}{1.38 \times 10^{-23}}$$

$$= 2.478 \times 10^2$$

$$= 247.8 \approx 248 \text{K}$$

Note *After escaping of molecules with speed of 1000 m/s, the temperature in part (b) is 248 K whereas in part (a) before escaping of molecules the temperature was 296 K. Thus, evaporation facilitates cooling.*

Q. 29 **Ten small planes are flying at a speed of 150 km/h in total darkness in an air space that is $20 \times 20 \times 1.5$ km^3 in volume. You are in one of the planes, flying at random within this space with no way of knowing where the other planes are. On the average about how long a time will elapse between near collision with your plane. Assume for this rough computation that a saftey region around the plane can be approximated by a sphere of radius 10 m.**

Thinking Process

To solve this problem, we have to consider the relaxation time as well as mean free path.

Ans. The situation can be considered as the time of relaxation, based on kinetic theory of gases. Mean free path is the distance between two successive collisions, which we will consider here as the distance travelled by the plane before it just avoids the collision safe radius is equivalent to radius of the atom.

Hence, the required time

$$t = \frac{l}{v}, \; l = \text{mean free path} = \frac{1}{\sqrt{2}\pi d^2 n}, \; n = \text{number density} = \frac{N}{V}$$

$$n = \frac{\text{Number of aeroplanes(N)}}{\text{Volume (V)}}$$

$$= \frac{10}{20 \times 20 \times 1.5} = 0.0167 \text{ km}^{-3}$$

$$t = \frac{1}{\sqrt{2}\pi d^2 (N/V)} \times \frac{1}{v} \qquad [v = \text{velocity of aeroplane}]$$

By putting the given data,

$$t = \frac{1}{\sqrt{2} \times 3.14 \times (20)^2 \times 0.0167 \times 10^{-6} \times 150}$$

$$= \frac{10^6}{1776.25 \times 2.505}$$

$$= \frac{10^6}{4449.5} = 224.74 \text{h}$$

$$\approx 225 \text{h}$$

Q. 30 **A box of 1.00 m^3 is filled with nitrogen at 1.50 atm at 300 K. The box has a hole of an area 0.010 mm^2. How much time is required for the pressure to reduce by 0.10 atm, if the pressure outside is 1 atm.**

Ans. Given, volume of the box, $V = 1.00 m^3$

$$\text{Area} = a = 0.010\, mm^2$$
$$= 8.01 \times 10^{-6}\, m^2$$
$$= 10^{-8}\, m^2$$

N_2 gas
$p = 1.5$ min Hole
T
$p_{outside} = 1$ atm

Temperature outside = Temperature inside

Initial pressure inside the box = 1.50 atm.

Final pressure inside the box = 0.10 atm.

Assuming,

v_{ix} = Speed of nitrogen molecule inside the box along x-direction.

n_i = Number of molecules per unit volume in a time interval of ΔT, all the particles at a distance $(v_{ix}\Delta t)$ will collide the hole and the wall, the particle colliding along the hole will escape out reducing the pressure in the box.

Let area of the wall, number of particles colliding in time

$$\Delta t = \frac{1}{2} n_i (v_{ix} \Delta t) A$$

$\frac{1}{2}$ is the factor because all the particles along x-direction are behaving randomly. Hence, half of these are colliding against the walls on either side.

Inside the box, $v_{ix}^2 + v_{iy}^2 + v_{iz}^2 = v_{rms}^2$

$\therefore$ $$v_{ix}^2 = \frac{v_{rms}^2}{3} \qquad (\because v_{ix} = v_{iy} = v_{iz})$$

or $$\frac{1}{2} m v_{rms}^2 = \frac{3}{2} k_B T$$

$\left[\begin{array}{l} V_{rms} = \text{Root mean square velocity} \\ K_B = \text{Boltzmann constant} \\ T = \text{Temperature} \end{array}\right]$

$\Rightarrow$ $$v_{rms}^2 = \frac{3k_B T}{m}$$

$\Rightarrow$ $$v_{rms} = \sqrt{\frac{3k_B T}{m}}$$

[According to kinetic theory of gases]

Now, $$v_{ix}^2 = \frac{v_{rms}^2}{3} = \frac{1}{3} \times \frac{3k_B T}{m}$$

or $$v_{ix}^2 = \frac{k_B T}{m}$$

$\therefore$ Number of particles colliding in time

$$\Delta t = \frac{1}{2} n_i \sqrt{\frac{k_B T}{m}}\, \Delta t A$$

If particles collide along hole, they move out. Similarly, outer particles colliding along hole will move in.

If a = area of hole

Then, net particle flow in time $\Delta t = \frac{1}{2}(n_1 - n_2)\sqrt{\frac{k_B T}{m}}\, \Delta t a$

[Temperatures inside and outside the box are equal]

$$pV = \mu RT \Rightarrow \mu = \frac{pV}{RT}$$

Let n = number density of nitrogen $= \frac{\mu N_A}{V} = \frac{pN_A}{RT}$ $\left[\because \frac{\mu}{V} = \frac{p}{RT}\right]$

Let N_A = Avogardro's number

If after time τ pressure inside changes from p to p_1^{1}

$$\therefore \quad n_1' = \frac{vN_A}{RT}$$

Now, number of molecules gone out $= n_1V - n_1'V$

$$= \frac{1}{2}(n_1 - n_2)\sqrt{\frac{k_BT}{m}}\,\tau a$$

$$\therefore \quad \frac{p_1N_A}{RT}V - \frac{vN_A}{RT}V = \frac{1}{2}(p_1 - p_2)\frac{N_A}{RT}\sqrt{\frac{k_BT}{m}}\tau a$$

or
$$\frac{p_1N_A}{RT}V - \frac{vN_A}{RT}V = \frac{1}{2}(p_1 - p_2)\frac{N_A}{RT}\sqrt{\frac{k_BT}{m}}\,\tau a$$

$$\therefore \quad \tau = 2\left(\frac{p_1 - pv_1}{p_1 - p_2}\right)\frac{V}{a}\sqrt{\frac{m}{k_BT}}$$

Putting the values from the data given,

$$\tau = 2\left(\frac{1.5 - 1.4}{1.5 - 1.0}\right)\frac{1 \times 1.00}{0.01 \times 10^{-6}}\sqrt{\frac{46.7 \times 10^{-27}}{1.38 \times 10^{-23} \times 300}}$$

$$= 2\left(\frac{0.1}{0.5}\right)\frac{1}{10^{-8}}\sqrt{\frac{4.7}{1.38 \times 3} \times 10^{-6}}$$

$$= 2\left(\frac{1}{5}\right)1 \times 10^{8} \times 10^{-3} \times \sqrt{\frac{46.7}{4.14}} = \frac{2}{5} \times 10^{5}\sqrt{\frac{45.7}{4.14}}$$

$$= \frac{2}{5} \times 10^{5}\sqrt{11.28}$$

$$= \frac{2}{5} \times 3.358 \times 10^{5} = \frac{6.717}{5} \times 10^{5} = 1.343 \times 10^{5}\ \text{s}$$

Q. 31 Consider a rectangular block of wood moving with a velocity v_0 in a gas at temperature T and mass density ρ. Assume the velocity is along x-axis and the area of cross-section of the block perpendicular to v_0 is A. Show that the drag force on the block is $4rAv_0\sqrt{\frac{kT}{m}}$, where, m is the mass of the gas molecule.

Thinking Process

If a massive body is moving with respect to a lighter body with velocity $v + v_0$, then the lighter body suffers a change in momentum $2m(v + v_0)$ which is transferred to the heavier body.

Ans. Consider the diagram

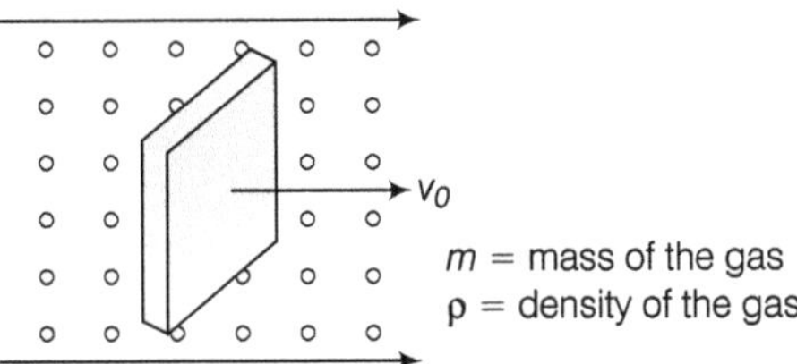

Let n = number of molecules per unit volume
v_{rms} = rms speed of the gas molecules
When block is moving with speed v_o, relative speed of molecules w.r.t. front face = $v + v_o$
Coming head on, momentum transferred to block per collision = $2m(v + v_o)$,
where, m = mass of molecule.

Number of collission in time $\Delta t = \frac{1}{2}(v + v_o)n\Delta tA$, where, A = area of cross-section of block
and factor of 1/2 appears due to particles moving towards block.
$\therefore$ Momentum transferred in time $\Delta t = m(v + v_0)^2 nA\Delta t$ from front surface.

Similarly, momentum transferred in time $\Delta t = m(v - v_0)^2 nA\Delta t$ (from back surface)

$\therefore$ Net force (drag force) $= mnA[(v + v_0)^2 - (v - v_0)^2]$ [from front]

$$= mnA(4vv_0) = (4mnAv)v_0$$

$$= (4\rho Av)v_0 \quad \text{... (i)}$$

where we have assumed $\rho = \frac{mn}{V} = \frac{M}{V}$

If v = velocity along x-axis

Then, we can write $KE = \frac{1}{2}mv^2 = \frac{1}{2}k_BT$

$\Rightarrow$ $v = \sqrt{\frac{k_BT}{m}}$

[K_B = Boltzmann constant
KE = Kinetic energy
T = Temperature]

$\therefore$ From Eq. (i), Drag force $= (4\rho Av)v_0 = 4\rho A\sqrt{\frac{k_BT}{m}}\, v_0$.

13

Oscillations

Multiple Choice Questions (MCQs)

Q. 1 The displacement of a particle is represented by the equation $y = 3\cos\left(\frac{\pi}{4} - 2\omega t\right)$. The motion of the particle is

(a) simple harmonic with period $2\pi/\omega$ (b) simple harmonic with period π/ω
(c) periodic but not simple harmonic (d) non- periodic

Ans. *(b)* Given, $y = 3\cos\left(\frac{\pi}{4} - 2\omega t\right)$

Velocity of the particle

$$v = \frac{dy}{dt} = \frac{d}{dt}\left[3\cos\left(\frac{\pi}{4} - 2\omega t\right)\right]$$

$$= 3(-2\,\omega)\left[-\sin\left(\frac{\pi}{4} - 2\omega t\right)\right]$$

$$= 6\omega\sin\left(\frac{\pi}{4} - 2\omega t\right)$$

$$\text{Acceleration, } a = \frac{dv}{dt} = \frac{d}{dt}\left[6\omega\sin\left(\frac{\pi}{4} - 2\omega t\right)\right]$$

$$= 6\omega \times (-2\omega)\cos\left(\frac{\pi}{4} - 2\omega t\right) = -12\omega^2\cos\left(\frac{\pi}{4} - 2\omega t\right)$$

$$= -4\,\omega^2\left[3\cos\left(\frac{\pi}{4} - 2\omega t\right)\right]$$

$$\Rightarrow \qquad a = -4\,\omega^2 y$$

$\Rightarrow$ As acceleration, $a \propto -y$

Hence, due to negative sign motion is SHM.

Clearly, from the equation

$$\omega' = 2\omega \qquad [\because \text{Standard equation } y = a\cos(\omega t + \phi)]$$

$$\Rightarrow \qquad \frac{2\pi}{T'} = 2\omega \Rightarrow T' = \frac{2\pi}{2\omega} = \frac{\pi}{\omega} \qquad \left[\text{and given equation } y = 3\cos\left(-2\omega t + \frac{\pi}{4}\right)\right]$$

So, motion is SHM with period $\frac{\pi}{\omega}$.

Q. 2 The displacement of a particle is represented by the equation $y = \sin^3 \omega t$. The motion is

(a) non-periodic
(b) periodic but not simple harmonic
(c) simple harmonic with period $2\pi/\omega$
(d) simple harmonic with period π/ω

Ans. *(b)* Given equation of motion is

$$y = \sin^3 \omega t$$

$$= (3\sin \omega t - 4\sin 3\omega t)/4 \qquad [\because \sin 3\theta = 3\sin\theta - 4\sin^3\theta]$$

$$\Rightarrow \quad \frac{dy}{dt} = \left[\frac{d}{dt}(3\sin\omega t) - \frac{d}{dt}(4\sin 3\omega t)\right]/4$$

$$\Rightarrow \quad 4\frac{dy}{dt} = 3\omega\cos\omega t - 4\times[3\omega\cos 3\omega t]$$

$$\Rightarrow \quad 4\times\frac{d^2y}{dt^2} = -3\omega^2\sin\omega t + 12\omega\sin 3\omega t$$

$$\Rightarrow \quad \frac{d^2y}{dt^2} = -\frac{3\omega^2\sin\omega t + 12\omega^2\sin 3\omega t}{4}$$

$\Rightarrow \frac{d^2y}{dt^2}$ is not proportional to y.

Hence, motion is not SHM.

As the expression is involving sine function, hence it will be periodic.

Q. 3 The relation between acceleration and displacement of four particles are given below

(a) $a_x = +2x$
(b) $a_x = +2x^2$
(c) $a_x = -2x^2$
(d) $a_x = -2x$

Which, one of the particle is exempting simple harmonic motion?

Ans. *(d)* For motion to be SHM acceleration of the particle must be proportional to negative of displacement.

i.e., $$a \propto -(y \text{ or } x)$$

We should be clear that y has to be linear.

Q. 4 Motion of an oscillating liquid column in a U-tube is

(a) periodic but not simple harmonic
(b) non-periodic
(c) simple harmonic and time period is independent of the density of the liquid
(d) simple harmonic and time period is directly proportional to the density of the liquid

Ans. *(c)* Consider the diagram in which a liquid column oscillates. In this case, restoring force acts on the liquid due to gravity. Acceleration of the liquid column, can be calculated in terms of restoring force.

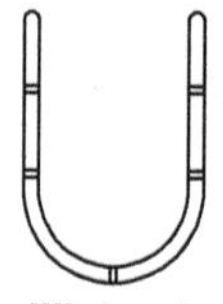

Equilibrium level

Restoring force f = Weight of liquid column of height $2y$

$\Rightarrow \quad f = -(A \times 2y \times \rho) \times g = -2A\rho g y \qquad [\because \eta = \rho v]$

$\Rightarrow f \propto -y \Rightarrow$ Motion is SHM with force constant $k = 2A\rho g$.

$\Rightarrow$ Time period $\quad T = 2\pi\sqrt{\dfrac{m}{k}} = 2\pi\sqrt{\dfrac{A \times 2h \times \rho}{2A\rho g}} = 2\pi\sqrt{\dfrac{h}{g}}$

$$T = 2\pi\sqrt{\frac{l}{g}}, \text{ where } l = h$$

Which is independent of the density of the liquid.

Q. 5 A particle is acted simultaneously by mutually perpendicular simple harmonic motion $x = a\cos\omega t$ and $y = a\sin\omega t$. The trajectory of motion of the particle will be

(a) an ellipse (b) a parabola (c) a circle (d) a straight line

Thinking Process

We have to find resultant-displacement by adding x and y-components. According to variation of x and y, trajectory will be predicted.

Ans. *(c)* Given,

$$x = a\cos\omega t \qquad \dots \text{(i)}$$

$$y = a\sin\omega t \qquad \dots \text{(ii)}$$

Squaring and adding Eqs. (i) and (ii),

$$x^2 + y^2 = a^2 \qquad (\cos^2\omega t + \sin^2\omega t)$$

$$= a^2 \Rightarrow x^2 + y^2 = a^2 \qquad [\because \cos^2\omega t + \sin^2\omega t = 1]$$

This is the equation. of a circle

Clearly, the locus is a circle of constant radius a.

Q. 6 The displacement of a particle varies with time according to the relation $y = a\sin\omega t + b\cos\omega t$.

(a) The motion is oscillatory but not SHM

(b) The motion is SHM with amplitude $a + b$

(c) The motion is SHM with amplitude $a^2 + b^2$

(d) The motion is SHM with amplitude $\sqrt{a^2 + b^2}$

Ans. *(d)* According to the question, the displacement

$$y = a\sin\omega t + b\cos\omega t$$

Let $\quad a = A\sin\phi$ and $b = A\cos\phi$

Now, $\quad a^2 + b^2 = A^2\sin^2\phi + A^2\cos^2\phi$

$$= A^2 \Rightarrow A = \sqrt{a^2 + b^2}$$

$$y = A\sin\phi . \sin\omega t + A\cos\phi . \cos\omega t$$

$$= A\sin(\omega t + \phi)$$

$$\frac{dy}{dt} = A\omega\cos(\omega t + \phi)$$

$$\frac{d^2y}{dt^2} = -A\omega^2\sin(\omega t + \phi) = -Ay\omega^2 = (-A\omega^2)y$$

$$\Rightarrow \quad \frac{d^2y}{dt^2} \propto (-y)$$

Hence, it is an equation of SHM with amplitude $A = \sqrt{a^2 + b^2}$.

Q. 7 Four pendulums A, B, C and D are suspended from the same

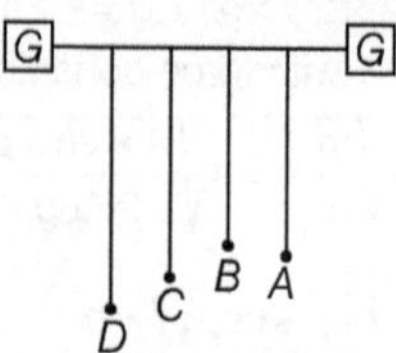

elastic support as shown in figure. A and C are of the same length, while B is smaller than A and D is larger than A. If A is given a transverse displacement,

(a) D will vibrate with maximum amplitude
(b) C will vibrate with maximum amplitude
(c) B will vibrate with maximum amplitude
(d) All the four will oscillate with equal amplitude

Ans. *(b)* According to the question, A is given a transverse displacement.

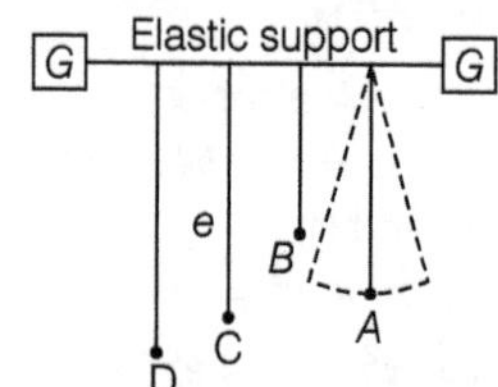

Through the elastic support the disturbance is transferred to all the pendulums.

A and C are having same length, hence they will be in resonance, because their time period of oscillation.

$$T = 2\pi\sqrt{\frac{l}{g}} \text{ and hence, frequency is same.}$$

So, amplitude of A and C will be maximum.

Note *In this problem, we have assumed that the support is perfectly elastic and there is no damping. Hence, oscillation is considered as undamped.*

Q. 8 Figure shows the circular motion of a particle. The radius of the circle, the period, sense of revolution and the initial position are indicated on the figure. The simple harmonic motion of the x-projection of the radius vector of the rotating particle P is

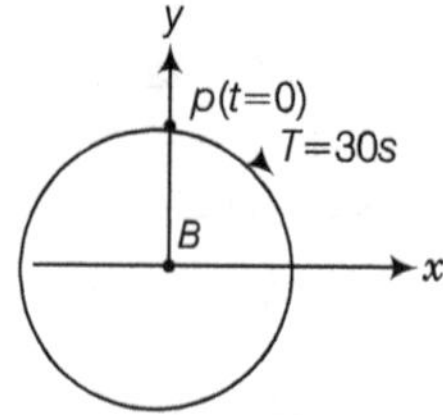

(a) $x(t) = B\sin\left(\frac{2\pi t}{30}\right)$
(b) $x(t) = B\cos\left(\frac{\pi t}{15}\right)$
(c) $x(t) = B\sin\left(\frac{\pi t}{15} + \frac{\pi}{2}\right)$
(d) $x(t) = B\cos\left(\frac{\pi t}{15} + \frac{\pi}{2}\right)$

Ans. *(a)* Let angular velocity of the particle executing circular motion is ω and when it is at Q makes and angle θ as shown in the diagram.

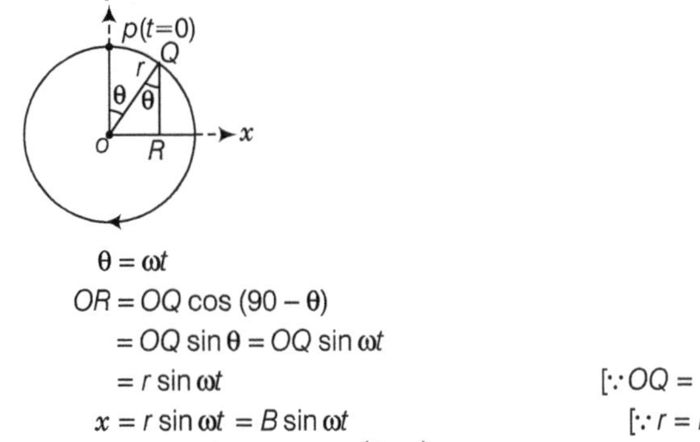

Clearly, $\theta = \omega t$

Now, we can write

$$OR = OQ \cos(90 - \theta)$$
$$= OQ \sin\theta = OQ \sin \omega t$$
$$= r \sin \omega t \quad [\because OQ = r]$$
$$\Rightarrow \quad x = r \sin \omega t = B \sin \omega t \quad [\because r = B]$$
$$= B \sin \frac{2\pi}{T} t = B \sin\left(\frac{2\pi}{30} t\right)$$

Clearly, this equation represents SHM.

Q. 9 The equation of motion of a particle is $x = a \cos(\alpha t)^2$. The motion is

(a) periodic but not oscillatory
(b) periodic and oscillatory
(c) oscillatory but not periodic
(d) neither periodic nor oscillatory

Ans. *(c)* As the given equation is

$$x = a \cos(\alpha t)^2$$

is a cosine function. Hence, it is an oscillatory motion.

Now, putting $t + T$ in place of t

$$x(t + T) = a \cos[\alpha(t + T)]^2 \quad [\because x(t) = a\cos(\alpha t)^2]$$
$$= a \cos[\alpha t^2 + \alpha T^2 + 2\alpha t T] \neq x(t)$$

where, T is supposed as period of the function $\omega(t)$.

Hence, it is not periodic.

Q. 10 A particle executing SHM has a maximum speed of 30 cm/s and a maximum acceleration of 60 cm/s^2. The period of oscillation is

(a) π sec
(b) $\frac{\pi}{2}$ sec
(c) 2π sec
(d) $\frac{\pi}{t}$ sec

Ans. *(a)* Let equation of an SHM is represented by $y = a \sin \omega t$

$$v = \frac{dy}{dt} = a\,\omega \cos \omega t$$
$$\Rightarrow \quad (v)_{max} = a\omega = 30 \quad \text{...(i)}$$
$$\text{Acceleration } (A) = \frac{dx^2}{dt^2} = -a\omega^2 \sin \omega t$$
$$A_{max} = \omega^2 a = 60 \quad \text{...(ii)}$$

Eqs. (i) and (ii), we get $\omega(\omega a) = 60 \Rightarrow \omega(30) = 60$

$$\Rightarrow \quad \omega = 2 \text{ rad / s}$$
$$\Rightarrow \quad \frac{2\pi}{T} = 2 \text{ rad/s} \Rightarrow T = \pi \text{ sec}$$

Multiple Choice Questions (More Than One Options)

Q. 11 When a mass m is connected individually to two springs S_1 and S_2, the oscillation frequencies are ν_1 and ν_2. If the same mass is attached to the two springs as shown in figure, the oscillation frequency would be

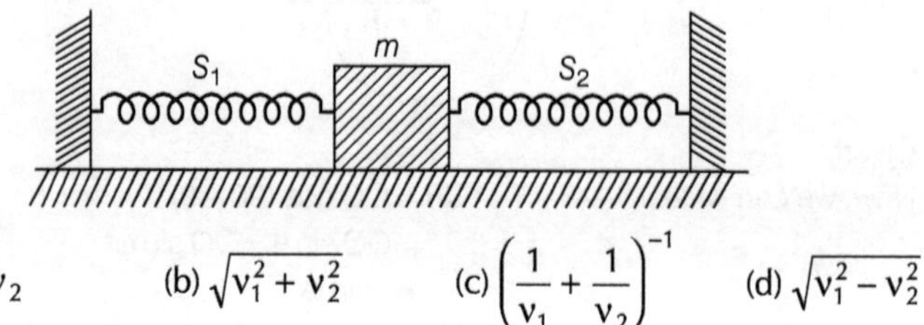

(a) $\nu_1 + \nu_2$ (b) $\sqrt{\nu_1^2 + \nu_2^2}$ (c) $\left(\frac{1}{\nu_1} + \frac{1}{\nu_2}\right)^{-1}$ (d) $\sqrt{\nu_1^2 - \nu_2^2}$

Thinking Process

To solve this question, we have to find equivalent spring constant of the system when mass is connected in between.

Ans. *(b)*

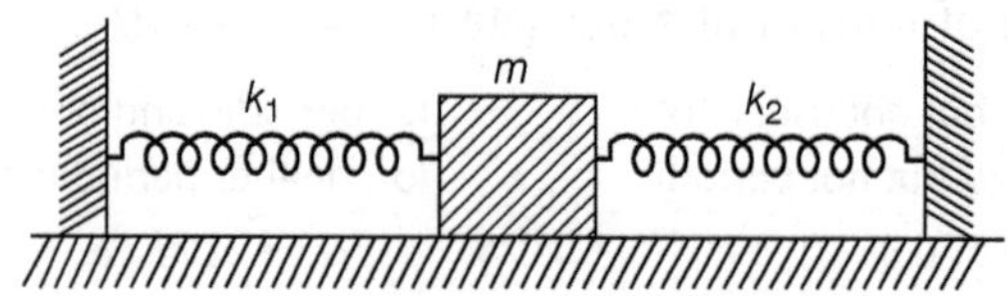

Consider the diagram, two springs can be considered as parallel.

Hence, k_{eq} = Equivalent spring constant

$$= k_1 + k_2$$

Time period of oscillation of the spring block- system

$$T = 2\pi\sqrt{\frac{m}{k_{eq}}} = 2\pi\sqrt{\frac{m}{k_1 + k_2}}$$

$$\Rightarrow \quad \nu = \frac{1}{T} = \frac{1}{2\pi} \times \sqrt{\frac{k_1 + k_2}{m}} \quad \text{...(i)}$$

= Equivalent oscillation frequency.

When the mass is connected to the two springs individually

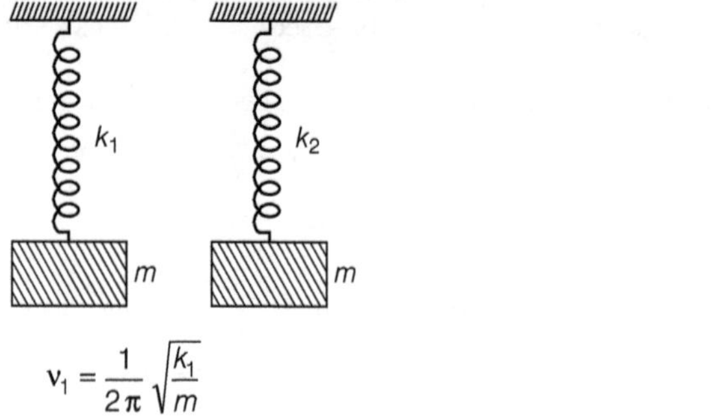

$$\nu_1 = \frac{1}{2\pi}\sqrt{\frac{k_1}{m}} \quad \text{...(ii)}$$

$$\nu_2 = \frac{1}{2\pi}\sqrt{\frac{k_2}{m}} \quad \text{...(iii)}$$

From Eqs. (i), (ii) and (iii),

$$\nu = \frac{1}{2\pi}\left[\frac{k_1}{m} + \frac{k_2}{m}\right]^{1/2} \quad \text{[from Eq. (i)]}$$

$$= \frac{1}{2\pi}\left[\frac{4\pi^2 \nu_1^2}{1} + \frac{4\pi^2 \nu_2^2}{1}\right]^{1/2}$$

$$\left[\because \text{from Eq. (ii)} \frac{k_1}{m} = 4\pi^2\nu_1^2 \text{ and from Eq. (iii), } \frac{k_2}{m} = 4\pi^2\nu_2^2\right]$$

$$= \frac{2\pi}{2\pi}[\nu_1^2 + \nu_2^2]^{1/2} \Rightarrow \nu = \sqrt{\nu_1^2 + \nu_2^2}$$

Note *Do not confuse with parallel and series combinations of springs.*

Q. 12 The rotation of earth about its axis is

(a) periodic motion

(b) simple harmonic motion

(c) periodic but not simple harmonic motion

(d) non-periodic motion

Ans. *(a, c)*

The rotation of earth about its axis is periodic because it repeats after a regular interval of time.

The rotation of earth is obviously not a to and fro type of motion about a fixed point, hence its motion is not SHM.

Q. 13 Motion of a ball bearing inside a smooth curved bowl, when released from a point slightly above the lower point is

(a) simple harmonic motion (b) non-periodic motion

(c) periodic motion (d) periodic but not SHM

Ans. *(a, c)*

Consider the motion of the ball inside a smooth curved bowl.

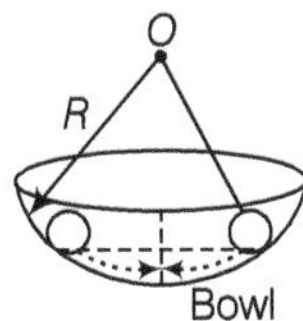

For small angular displacement or slightly released motion, it can be considered as angular SHM.

When the ball is at an angle of θ the restoring force $(g \sin\theta)\, m$ acts as shown.

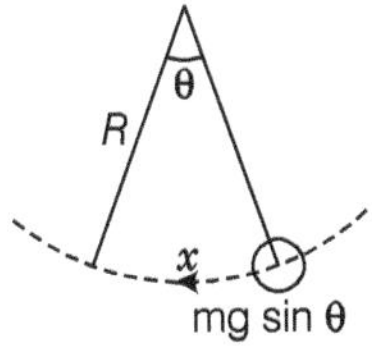

$\because \quad ma = mg\sin\theta$

$\Rightarrow \quad a = g\sin\theta$

$\Rightarrow \quad \dfrac{d^2x}{dt^2} = -g\sin\theta = -g \times \dfrac{x}{R} \quad [\because \sin\theta \approx \theta = x/R]$

Hence ,motion is SHM

$$\Rightarrow \qquad d2x/dt^2 \propto (-x) \qquad (\because a \propto -x)$$

$$\Rightarrow \qquad \omega = \sqrt{g/R}$$

$$\text{Time period } T = \frac{2\pi}{\omega} = 2\pi\sqrt{\frac{R}{g}}.$$

As motion is SHM, hence it must be periodic.

Q. 14 Displacement *versus* time curve for a particle executing SHM is shown in figure. Choose the correct statements.

(a) Phase of the oscillator is same at $t = 0$ s and $t = 2$ s

(b) Phase of the oscillator is same at $t = 2$ s and $t = 6$ s

(c) Phase of the oscillator is same at $t = 1$ s and $t = 7$ s

(d) Phase of the oscillator is same at $t = 1$ s and $t = 5$ s

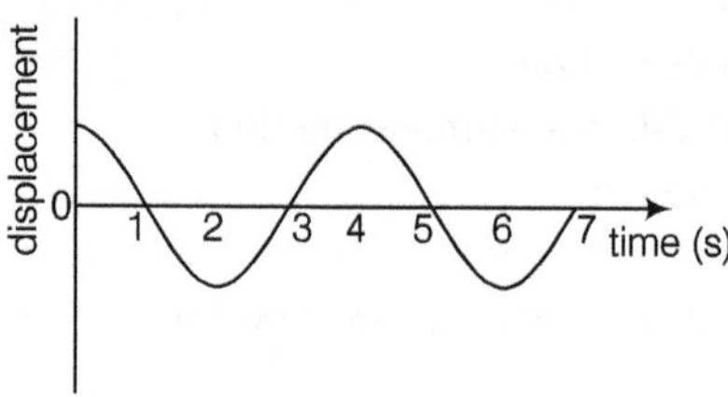

Ans. *(b, d)*

It is clear from the curve that points corresponding to $t = 2$ s and $t = 6$ s are separated by a distance belongs to one time period. Hence, these points must be in same phase.

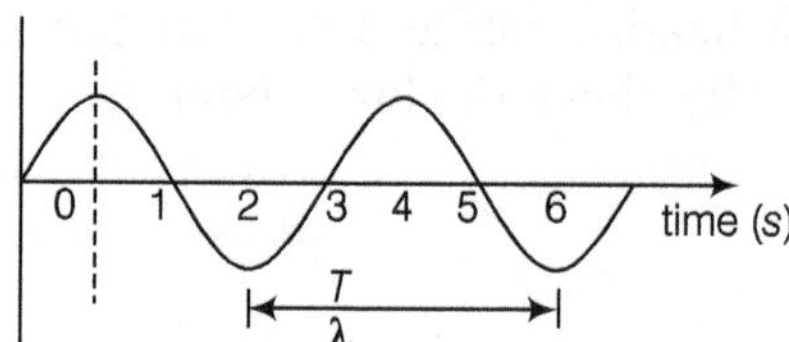

Similarly, points belong to $t = 1$ s and $t = 5$ s are at separation of one time period, hence must be in phase.

Q. 15 Which of the following statements is/are true for a simple harmonic oscillator ?

(a) Force acting is directly proportional to displacement from the mean position and opposite to it

(b) Motion is periodic

(c) Acceleration of the oscillator is constant

(d) The velocity is periodic

Thinking Process

We have to write equation for the SHM and then find out velocity as well as acceleration corresponding to the displacement.

Ans. *(a, b, d)*

Let the equation for the SHM is $x = a \sin \omega t$.

Clearly, it is a periodic motion because it involves sine function.

$$\text{Velocity } v = \frac{dx}{dt} = \frac{d}{dt}(a\sin\omega t) = a\,\omega \cos \omega t$$

Velocity is also periodic because of cosine function.

Acceleration, $A = \frac{dv}{dt} = \frac{d^2x}{dt^2} = -a\,\omega^2 \sin \omega t$

[$\because$ Acceleration is a sine function, hence cannot be constant]

$= -(\omega^2 a) \sin\omega t = -\omega^2 x$

Force, $F = \text{mass} \times \text{acceleration}$

$= mA = -m\omega^2 x$

Hence, force acting is directly proportional to displacement from the mean position and opposite to it.

Q. 16 **The displacement-time graph of a particle executing SHM is shown in figure. Which of the following statement is/are true ?**

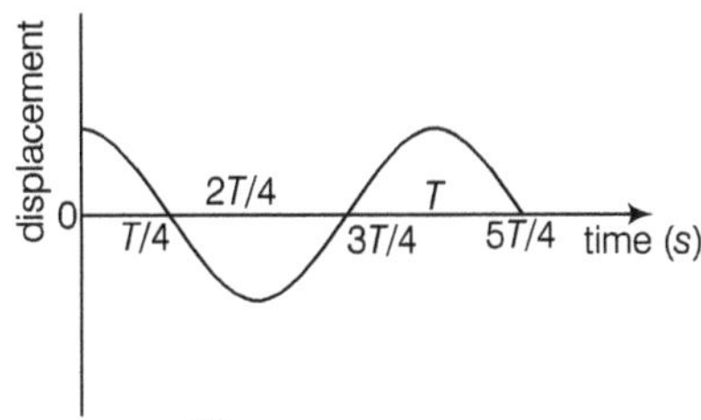

(a) The force is zero at $t = \frac{3T}{4}$

(b) The acceleration is maximum at $t = \frac{4T}{4}$

(c) The velocity is maximum at $t = \frac{T}{4}$

(d) The PE is equal to KE of oscillation at $t = \frac{T}{2}$

Ans. *(a, b, c)*

Consider the diagram

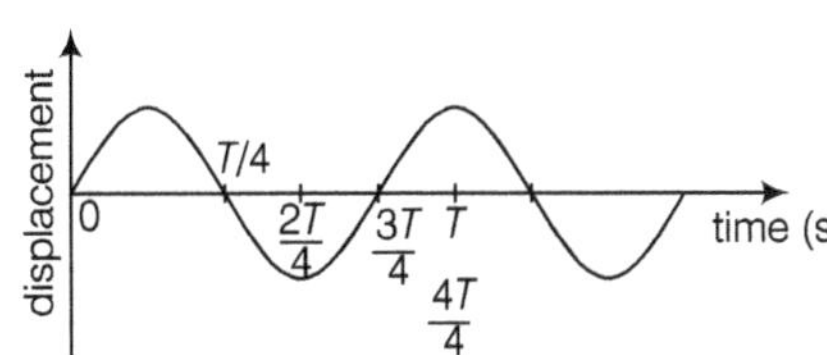

From the given diagram; it is clear that

(a) At $t = \frac{3T}{4}$, the displacement of the particle is zero. Hence, the particle executing SHM will be at mean position *i.e.*, $x = 0$. So, acceleration is zero and force is also zero.

(b) At $t = \frac{4T}{4}$, displacement is maximum *i.e.*, extreme position, so acceleration is maximum.

(c) At $t = \frac{T}{4}$, corresponds to mean position, so velocity will be maximum at this position.

(d) At $t = \frac{2T}{4} = \frac{T}{2}$, corresponds to extreme position, so KE = 0 and PE = maximum.

Q. 17 **A body is performing SHM, then its**

(a) average total energy per cycle is equal to its maximum kinetic energy

(b) average kinetic energy per cycle is equal to half of its maximum kinetic energy

(c) mean velocity over a complete cycle is equal to $\frac{2}{\pi}$ times of its maximum velocity

(d) root mean square velocity is $\frac{1}{\sqrt{2}}$ times of its maximum velocity

Ans. *(a, b, d)*

Let the equation of a SHM is represented as $x = a \sin \omega t$

Assume mass of the body is m.

(a) Total mechanical energy of the body at any time t is

$$E = \frac{1}{2} m \omega^2 a^2 \quad \text{...(i)}$$

Kinetic energy at any instant t is

$$K = \frac{1}{2} m v^2 = \frac{1}{2} m \left[\frac{dx}{dt}\right]^2 \quad \left[\because v = \frac{dx}{dt}\right]$$

$$= \frac{1}{2} m \omega^2 a^2 \cos^2 \omega t \quad [\because x = a \sin \omega t]$$

$$\Rightarrow \quad K_{max} = \frac{1}{2} m\omega^2 a^2 = E \quad [\because \text{for } k_{max}, \cos \omega t = 1] \text{ ...(ii)}$$

(b) KE at any instant t is

$$K = \frac{1}{2} m \omega^2 a^2 \cos^2 \omega t$$

$$(K_{av}) \text{ for a cycle} = \frac{1}{2} m \omega^2 a^2 [(\cos^2 \omega t)_{av}] \text{ for a cycle}$$

$$= \frac{1}{2} m \omega^2 a^2 \left[\frac{0+1}{2}\right]$$

$$= \frac{1}{4} m \omega^2 a^2 = \frac{K_{max}}{2} \quad \text{[from Eq. (ii)]}$$

(c) Velocity $= v = \frac{dx}{dt} = a \omega \cos \omega t$

$$v_{mean} = \frac{v_{max} + v_{min}}{2}$$

$$= \frac{a\omega + (-a\omega)}{2} = 0 \quad \text{[For a complete cycle]}$$

$$v_{max} \neq v_{mean}$$

(d) $v_{rms} = \sqrt{\frac{v_1^2 + v_2^2}{2}} = \sqrt{\frac{0 + a^2 \omega^2}{2}} = \frac{a\omega}{\sqrt{2}}$

$$\Rightarrow \quad v_{rms} = \frac{v_{max}}{\sqrt{2}}$$

Q. 18 **A particle is in linear simple harmonic motion between two points. *A* and *B*, 10 cm apart (figure.) take the direction from *A* to *B* as the positive direction and choose the correct statements.**

A O C B

$$AO = OB = 5\text{ cm}$$
$$BC = 8\text{ cm}$$

(a) The sign of velocity, acceleration and force on the particle when it is 3 cm away from *A* going towards *B* are positive

(b) The sign of velocity of the particle at *C* going towards *B* is negative

(c) The sign of velocity, acceleration and force on the particle when it is 4 cm away from *B* going towards *A* are negative

(d) The sign of acceleration and force on the particle when it is at points *B* is negative

Ans. *(a, c, d)*

Consider the diagram.

$u=0$ $v=$positive $v=0$

B O C A

(a) When the particle is 3cm away from *A* going towards *B*, velocity is towards *AB* *i.e.*, positive.

In SHM, acceleration is always towards mean position (*O*) in this case.

Hence, it is positive.

(b) When the particle is at *C*, velocity is towards *B* hence positive.

(c) When the particle is 4 cm away from *B* going towards *A* velocity is negative and acceleration is towards mean position (*O*) hence negative.

(d) Acceleration is always towards mean position (*O*). When the particle is at *B* acceleration and force are towards *BA* that is negative.

Very Short Answer Type Questions

Q. 19 **Displacement *versus* time curve for a particle executing SHM is shown in figure. Identify the points marked at which (i) velocity of the oscillator is zero, (ii) speed of the oscillator is maximum.**

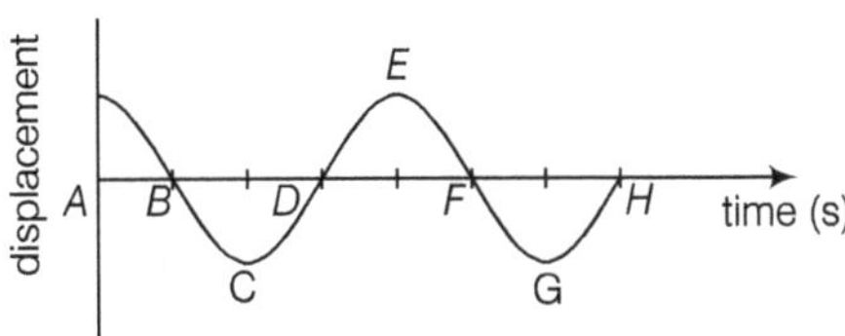

Ans. In SHM *y-t* graph, zero displacement values correspond to mean position; where velocity of the oscillator is maximum.

Whereas the crest and troughs represent extreme positions, where displacement is maximum and velocity of the oscillator is minimum and is zero. Hence,

(a) *A*, *C*, *E*, *G* are either crest or trough having zero velocity.

(b) speed is maximum at mean positions represented by *B*, *D*, *F*, *H* points.

Q. 20 Two identical springs of spring constant k are attached to a block of mass m and to fixed supports as shown in figure. When the mass is displaced from equilibrium position by a distance x towards right, find the restoring force.

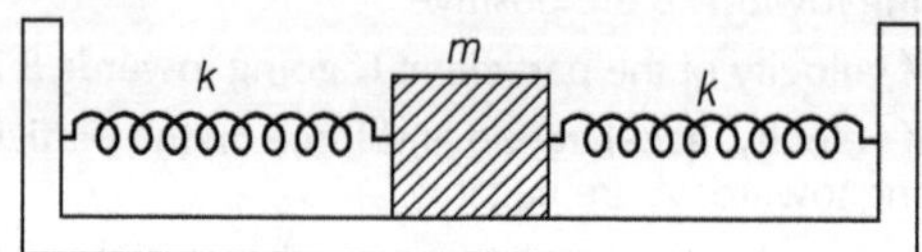

Ans. Consider the diagram in which the block is displaced right through x.

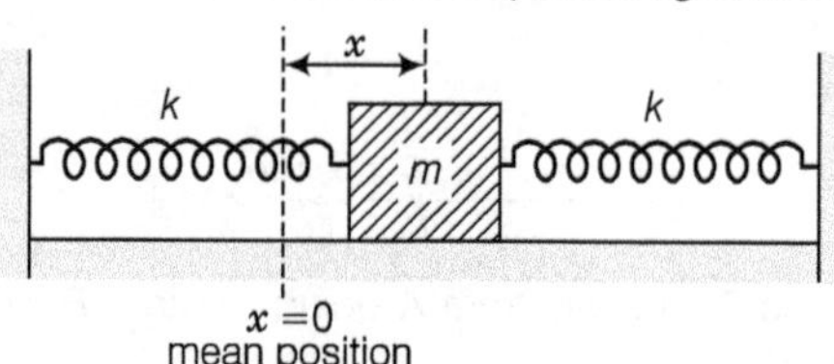

The right spring gets compressed by x developing a restoring force kx towards left on the block. The left spring is stretched by an amount x developing a restoring force kx towards left on the block as gven in the free body diagram of the block.

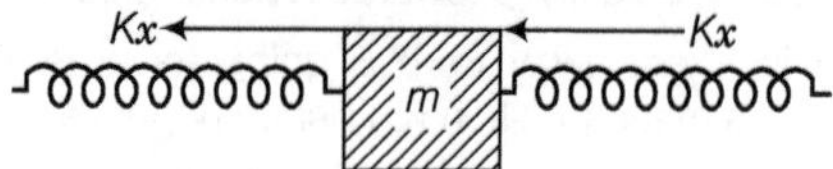

Hence, total force (restoring) $= (kx + kx)$ [$\because$ Both forces are in same direction]

$= 2kx$ towards left

Q. 21 What are the two basic characteristics of a simple harmonic motion?

Ans. *The two basic characteristics of a simple harmonic motion*

(i) Acceleration is directly proportional to displacement.

(ii) The direction of acceleration is always towards the mean position, that is opposite to displacement.

Q. 22 When will the motion of a simple pendulum be simple harmonic?

Ans. Consider the diagram of a simple pendulum.

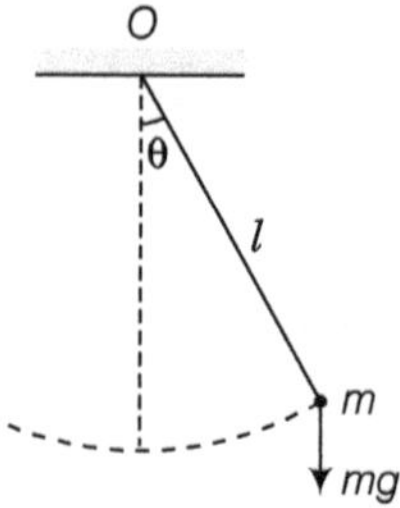

The bob is displaced through an angle θ shown.
The restoring torque about the fixed point O is

$$\tau = -mg\sin\theta$$

If θ is small angle in radians, then $\sin\theta \approx \theta$

$$\Rightarrow \quad \tau \approx -mg\,\theta \Rightarrow \tau \propto (-\theta)$$

Hence, motion of a simple pendulum is SHM for small angle of oscillations.

Q. 23 What is the ratio of maximum acceleration to the maximum velocity of a simple harmonic oscillator?

Thinking Process

We have to find velocity by differentiating the equation representing displacement and acceleration by differentiating the equation relating velocity and time.

Ans. Let $x = A\sin\omega t$ is the displacement function of SHM.

Velocity, $$v = \frac{dx}{dt} = A\omega\cos\omega t$$

$$v_{max} = A\omega|\cos\omega t|_{max}$$
$$= A\omega \times 1 = \omega A \qquad [\because |\cos\omega t|_{max} = 1] \quad \ldots\text{(i)}$$

Acceleration, $$a = \frac{dv}{dt} = -\omega A \cdot \omega\sin\omega t$$
$$= -\omega^2 A\sin\omega t$$
$$|a_{max}| = |(-\omega^2 A)(+1)| \qquad [\because (\sin\omega t)_{max} = 1]$$
$$|a_{max}| = \omega^2 A \quad \ldots\text{(ii)}$$

From Eqs. (i) and (ii), we get

$$\frac{v_{max}}{a_{max}} = \frac{\omega A}{\omega^2 A} = \frac{1}{\omega}$$

$$\Rightarrow \quad \frac{a_{max}}{v_{max}} = \omega$$

Q. 24 What is the ratio between the distance travelled by the oscillator in one time period and amplitude?

Ans. The diagram represents

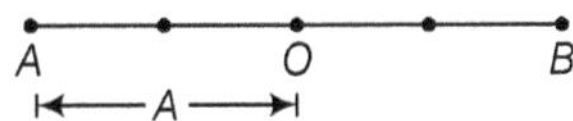

the motion of a particle executing SHM between A and B.
Total distance travelled while it goes from A to B and returns to A is

$$= AO + OB + BO + OA$$
$$= A + A + A + A = 4A \qquad [\because OA = A]$$

Amplitude $= OA = A$

Hence, ratio of distance and amplitude $= \dfrac{4A}{A} = 4$

Q. 25 **In figure, what will be the sign of the velocity of the point P', which is the projection of the velocity of the reference particle P. P is moving in a circle of radius R in anti-clockwise direction.**

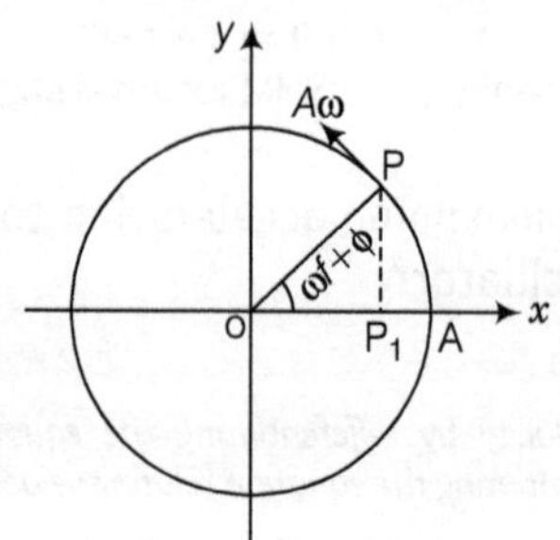

Ans. As the particle on reference circle moves in anti-iclockwise direction. The projection will move from P' to O towards left.

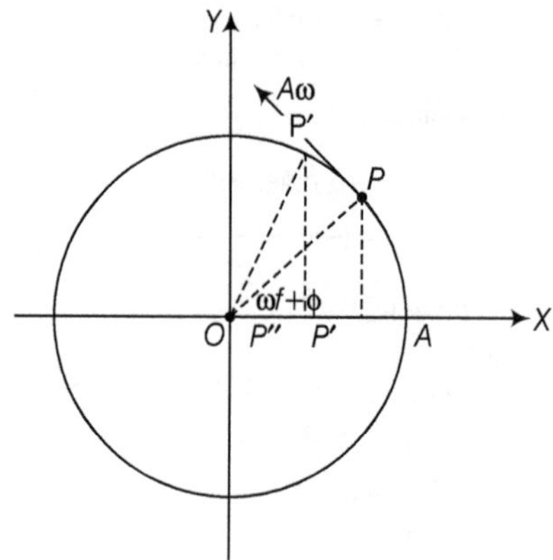

Hence, in the position shown the velocity is directed from $P' \rightarrow P''$ *i.e.*, from right to left, hence sign is negative.

Q. 26 **Show that for a particle executing SHM, velocity and displacement have a phase difference of $\pi/2$.**

Ans. Let us assume the displacement function of SHM

$$x = a\cos\omega t$$

where, a = amplitude of motion

$$\text{velocity } v = \frac{dx}{dt}$$

or $$\frac{dx}{dt} = a(-\sin\omega t)\omega = -\omega\, a\sin\omega t$$

or $$v = -\omega\, a\sin\omega t$$

$$= \omega\, a\cos\left(\frac{\pi}{2} + \omega t\right) \qquad \left[\because \sin\omega t = -\cos\left(\frac{\pi}{2} + \omega t\right)\right]$$

Now, phase of displacement $= \omega t$

$$\text{Phase of velocity} = \frac{\pi}{2} + \omega t$$

$\therefore$ Difference in phase of velocity to that of phase of displacement

$$= \frac{\pi}{2} + \omega t - \omega t = \frac{\pi}{2}$$

Q. 27 Draw a graph to show the variation of PE, KE and total energy of a simple harmonic oscillator with displacement.

Ans. Potential energy (PE) of a simple harmonic oscillator is

$$= \frac{1}{2}kx^2 = \frac{1}{2}m\omega^2x^2 \quad \text{...(i)}$$

where, k = force constant = $m\omega^2$

When, PE is plotted against displacement x, we will obtain a parabola.

When $x = 0$, PE = 0

When $x = \pm A$, PE = maximum

$$= \frac{1}{2}m\omega^2A^2$$

KE of a simple harmonic oscillator $= \frac{1}{2}mv^2$ $\quad [\because v = \omega\sqrt{A^2 - x^2}]$

$$= \frac{1}{2}m\left[\omega\sqrt{A^2 - x^2}\right]^2$$

$$= \frac{1}{2}m\omega^2(A^2 - x^2) \quad \text{...(ii)}$$

This is also parabola, if plot KE against displacement x.

i.e., KE = 0 at $x = \pm A$

and KE $= \frac{1}{2}m\omega^2A^2$ at $x = 0$

Now, total energy of the simple harmonic oscillator = PE + KE [using Eqs. (i) and (ii)]

$$= \frac{1}{2}m\omega^2x^2 + \frac{1}{2}m\omega^2(A^2 - x^2)$$

$$= \frac{1}{2}m\omega^2x^2 + \frac{1}{2}m\omega^2A^2 - \frac{1}{2}m\omega^2x^2$$

$$\text{TE} = \frac{1}{2}m\omega^2A^2$$

Which is constant and does not depend on x.

Plotting under the above guidelines KE, PE and TE *versus* displacement x-graph as follows

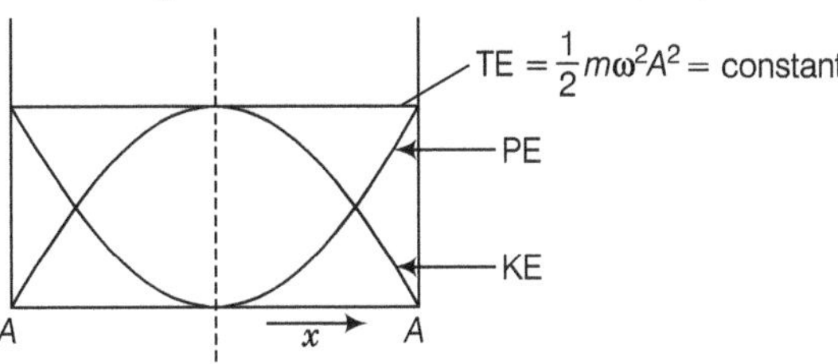

Q. 28 The length of a second's pendulum on the surface of earth is 1 m. What will be the length of a second's pendulum on the moon?

Ans. A second's pendulum means a simple pendulum having time period $T = 2$ s.

For a simple pendulum, $T = 2\pi\sqrt{\frac{l}{g}}$

where, l = length of the pendulum and

g = acceleration due to gravity on surface of the earth.

$$T_e = 2\pi\sqrt{\frac{l_e}{g_e}} \quad \text{...(i)}$$

On the surface of the moon, $T_m = 2\pi\sqrt{\frac{l_m}{g_m}}$ ...(ii)

$\therefore \quad \frac{T_e}{T_m} = \frac{2\pi}{2\pi}\sqrt{\frac{l_e}{g_e}} \times \sqrt{\frac{g_m}{l_m}}$

$T_e = T_m$ to maintain the second's pendulum time period.

$\therefore \quad 1 = \sqrt{\frac{l_e}{l_m} \times \frac{g_m}{g_e}}$ ...(iii)

But the acceleration due to gravity at moon is 1/6 of the acceleration due to gravity at earth, *i.e.*, $g_m = \frac{g_e}{6}$

Squaring Eq. (iii) and putting this value,

$$1 = \frac{l_e}{l_m} \times \frac{g_e/6}{g_e} = \frac{l_e}{l_m} \times \frac{1}{6}$$

$$\Rightarrow \quad \frac{l_e}{6l_m} = 1 \Rightarrow 6l_m = l_e$$

$$\Rightarrow \quad l_m = \frac{1}{6}l_e = \frac{1}{6} \times 1 = \frac{1}{6}\text{ m}$$

Short Answer Type Questions

Q. 29 Find the time period of mass M when displaced from its equilibrium position and then released for the system shown in figure.

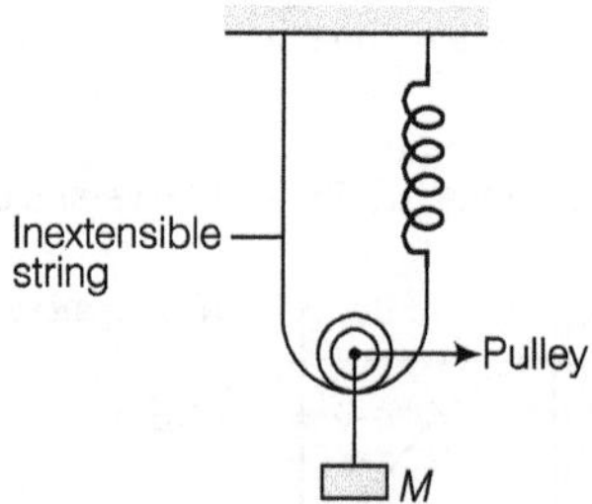

Thinking Process

To predict the nature of the motion, we have to displace the mass slightly and find the acceleration due to the restoring force.

Ans. For the calculation purpose, in this situation we will neglect gravity because it is constant throughout and will not effect the net restoring force.

Let in the equilibrium position, the spring has extended by an amount x_0.

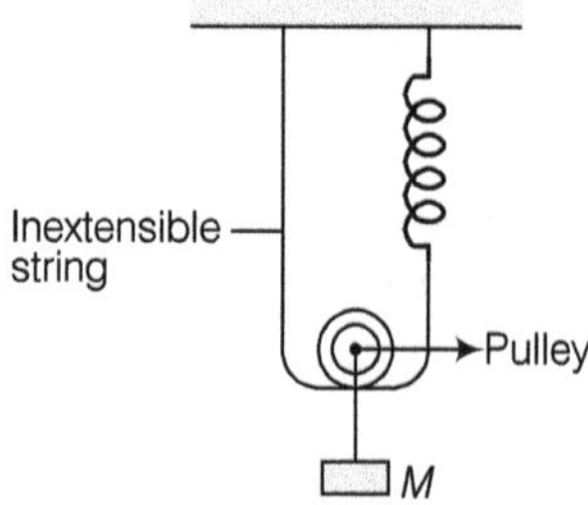

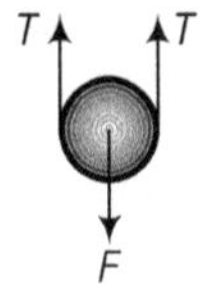

Now, if the mass is given a further displacement downwards by an amount x. The string and spring both should increase in length by x.

But, string is inextensible, hence the spring alone will contribute the total extension $x + x = 2x$, to lower the mass down by x from initial equilibrium mean position x_0. So, net extension in the spring $(= 2x + x_0)$.

Now force on the mass before bulling (in the x_0 extension case)

$$F = 2T$$

But $T = kx_0$ [where k is spring constant]

$\therefore$ $F = 2kx_0$ ...(i)

When the mass is lowered down further by x,

$$F' = 2T'$$

But new spring length $= (2x + x_0)$

$\therefore$ $F' = 2k(2x + x_0)$ ...(ii)

Restoring force on the system.

$$F_{restoring} = -[F' - F]$$

Using Eqs. (i) and (ii), we get

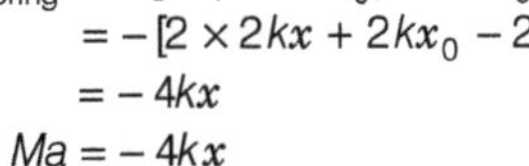

$$F_{restoring} = -[2k(2x + x_0) - 2kx_0]$$
$$= -[2 \times 2kx + 2kx_0 - 2kx_0]$$
$$= -4kx$$

or $Ma = -4kx$

where, a = acceleration (As, $F = ma$)

$\Rightarrow$ $a = -\left(\dfrac{4k}{M}\right)x$

k, M being constant.

$\therefore$ $a \propto -x$

Hence, motion is SHM.

Comparing the above acceleration expression with standard SHM equation $a = -\omega^2 x$, we get

$$\omega^2 = \frac{4k}{M} \Rightarrow \omega = \sqrt{\frac{4k}{M}}$$

$\therefore$ Time period $T = \dfrac{2\pi}{\omega} = \dfrac{2\pi}{\sqrt{\dfrac{4k}{M}}} = 2\pi\sqrt{\dfrac{M}{4k}}$

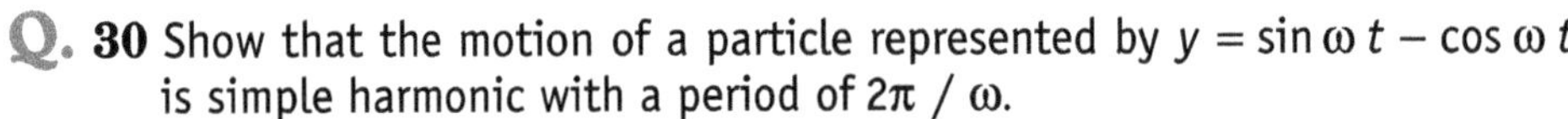

Q. 30 Show that the motion of a particle represented by $y = \sin \omega t - \cos \omega t$ is simple harmonic with a period of $2\pi / \omega$.

Ans. We have to convert the given combination of two harmonic functions to a single harmonic (sine or cosine) function.

Given, displacement function $y = \sin\omega t - \cos\omega t$

$$= \sqrt{2}\left(\frac{1}{\sqrt{2}} \cdot \sin\omega t - \frac{1}{\sqrt{2}} \cdot \cos\omega t\right)$$
$$= \sqrt{2}\left[\cos\left(\frac{\pi}{4}\right) \cdot \sin\omega t - \sin\left(\frac{\pi}{4}\right) \cdot \cos\omega t\right]$$
$$= \sqrt{2}\left[\sin\left(\omega t - \frac{\pi}{4}\right)\right] = \sqrt{2}\left[\sin\left(\omega t - \frac{\pi}{4}\right)\right]$$

Comparing with standard equation

$y = a\sin(\omega t + \phi)$, we get $= \omega = \dfrac{2\pi}{T} \Rightarrow T = \dfrac{2\pi}{\omega}$

Clearly, the function represents SHM with a period $T = \dfrac{2\pi}{\omega}$.

Q. 31 Find the displacement of a simple harmonic oscillator at which its PE is half of the maximum energy of the oscillator.

Ans. Let us assume that the required displacement be x.

$\therefore$ Potential energy of the simple harmonic oscillator $= \frac{1}{2}kx^2$

where, $k =$ force constant $= m\omega^2$

$$\therefore \quad PE = \frac{1}{2}m\omega^2 x^2 \quad \ldots(i)$$

Maximum energy of the oscillator

$$TE = \frac{1}{2}m\omega^2 A^2 \quad [\because x_{max} = A] \ldots(ii)$$

where, $A =$ amplitude of motion

Given, $PE = \frac{1}{2}TE$

$$\Rightarrow \quad \frac{1}{2}m\omega^2 x^2 = \frac{1}{2}\left[\frac{1}{2}m\omega^2 A^2\right]$$

$$\Rightarrow \quad x^2 = \frac{A^2}{2}$$

$$\text{or} \quad x = \sqrt{\frac{A^2}{2}} = \pm \frac{A}{\sqrt{2}}$$

Sign $\pm$ indicates either side of mean position.

Q. 32 A body of mass m is situated in a potential field $U(x) = U_0\,(1 - \cos\alpha x)$ when, U_0 and α are constants. Find the time period of small oscillations.

Ans. Given potential energy associated with the field

$$U(x) = U_0\,(1 - \cos\alpha x) \quad \ldots\ldots (i)$$

Now, $$\text{force } F = -\frac{dU(x)}{dx}$$

[$\because$ for conservatine force f, we can write $f = \frac{-du}{dx}$]

[We have assumed the field to be conservative]

$$F = -\frac{d}{dx}(U_0 - U_0\cos\alpha x) = -U_0\,\alpha\sin\alpha x$$

$$F = -U_0\,\alpha^2 x \quad \ldots (ii)$$

[$\because$ for small oscillations αx is small, $\sin\alpha x \approx \alpha x$]

$$\Rightarrow \quad F \propto (-x)$$

As, U_0, α being constant.

$\therefore$ Motion is SHM for small oscillations.

Standard equation for SHM $$F = -m\omega^2 x \quad \ldots(iii)$$

Comparing Eqs. (ii) and (iii), we get

$$m\omega^2 = U_0\alpha^2$$

$$\omega^2 = \frac{U_0\alpha^2}{m} \text{ or } \omega = \sqrt{\frac{U_0\alpha^2}{m}}$$

$$\therefore \quad \text{Time period } T = \frac{2\pi}{\omega} = 2\pi\sqrt{\frac{m}{U_0\alpha^2}}$$

Note *The motion is SHM only for small oscillations and hence, the time period is valid only in case of small oscillations.*

Q. 33 **A mass of 2 kg is attached to the spring of spring constant 50 Nm^{-1}. The block is pulled to a distance of 5 cm from its equilibrium position at $x = 0$ on a horizontal frictionless surface from rest at $t = 0$. Write the expression for its displacement at anytime t.**

Thinking Process

The spring- block system will perform SHM about the mean position with an amplitude of 5cm.

Ans. Consider the diagram of the spring block system. It is a SHM with amplitude of 5cm about the mean position shown.

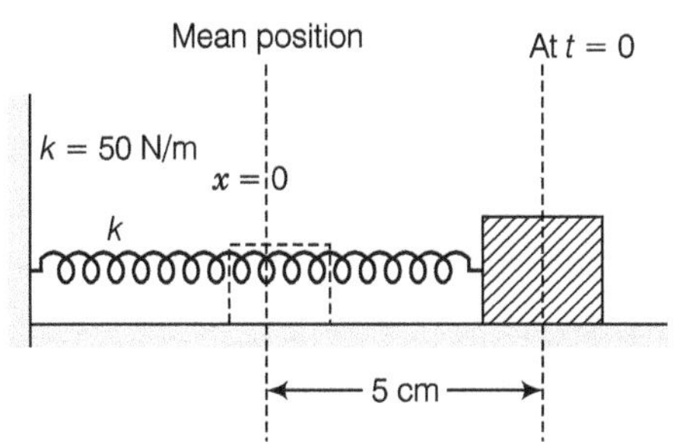

Given, spring constant $k = 50$ N/m

m = mass attached = 2 kg

$\therefore$ Angular frequency $\omega = \sqrt{\frac{k}{m}} = \sqrt{\frac{50}{2}} = \sqrt{25} = 5$ rad/s

Assuming the displacement function

$$y(t) = A\sin(\omega t + \phi)$$

where, ϕ = initial phase

But given at $t = 0$, $y(t) = +A$

$$y(0) = +A = A\sin(\omega \times 0 + \phi)$$

or $\sin\phi = 1 \Rightarrow \phi = \frac{\pi}{2}$

$\therefore$ The desired equation is $y(t) = A\sin\left(\omega t + \frac{\pi}{2}\right) = A\cos\omega t$

Putting $A = 5$ cm, $\omega = 5$ rad/s

we get, $y(t) = 5\sin 5t$

where, t is in second and y is in centimetre.

Q. 34 **Consider a pair of identical pendulums, which oscillate with equal amplitude independently such that when one pendulum is at its extreme position making an angle of 2° to the right with the vertical, the other pendulum makes an angle of 1° to the left of the vertical. What is the phase difference between the pendulums?**

Ans. Consider the situations shown in the diagram (i) and (ii)

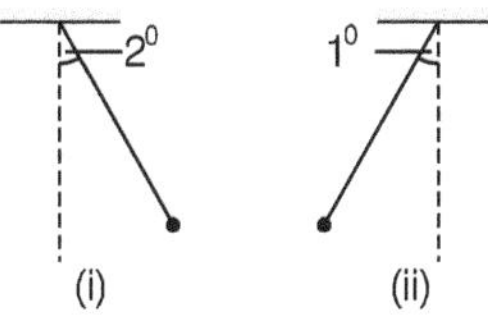

Assuming the two pendulums follow the following functions of their angular displacements

$$\theta_1 = \theta_0 \sin(\omega t + \phi_1) \quad \text{...(i)}$$

and

$$\theta_2 = \theta_0 \sin(\omega t + \phi_2) \quad \text{...(ii)}$$

As it is given that amplitude and time period being equal but phases being different.

Now, for first pendulum at any time t

$$\theta_1 = +\theta_0 \quad \text{[Right extreme]}$$

From Eq. (i), we get

$$\Rightarrow \quad \theta_0 = \theta_0 \sin(\omega t + \phi_1) \text{ or } 1 = \sin(\omega t + \phi_1)$$

$$\Rightarrow \quad \sin\frac{\pi}{2} = \sin(\omega t + \phi_1)$$

or

$$(\omega t + \phi_1) = \frac{\pi}{2} \quad \text{...(iii)}$$

Similarly, at the same instant t for pendulum second, we have

$$\theta_2 = -\frac{\theta_0}{2}$$

where $\theta_0 = 2°$ is the angular amplitude of first pendulum. For the second pendulum, the angular displacement is one degree ,therefore $\theta_2 = \frac{\theta_0}{2}$ and negative sign is taken to show for being left to mean position.

From Eq. (ii), then

$$-\frac{\theta_0}{2} = \theta_0 \sin(\omega t + \phi_2)$$

$$\Rightarrow \quad \sin(\omega t + \phi_2) = -\frac{1}{2} \Rightarrow (\omega t + \phi_2) = -\frac{\pi}{6} \text{ or } \frac{7\pi}{6}$$

or

$$(\omega t + \phi_2) = -\frac{\pi}{6} \text{ or } \frac{7\pi}{6} \quad \text{...(iv)}$$

From Eqs. (iv) and (iii), the difference in phases

$$(\omega t + \phi_2) - (\omega t + \phi_1) = \frac{7\pi}{6} - \frac{\pi}{2} = \frac{7\pi - 3\pi}{6} = \frac{4\pi}{6}$$

or

$$(\phi_2 - \phi_1) = \frac{4\pi}{6} = \frac{2\pi}{3} = 120°$$

Long Answer Type Questions

Q. 35 A person normally weighing 50 kg stands on a massless platform which oscillates up and down harmonically at a frequency of 2.0 s^{-1} and an amplitude 5.0 cm. A weighing machine on the platform gives the persons weight against time.

(a) Will there be any change in weight of the body, during the oscillation?

(b) If answer to part (a) is yes, what will be the maximum and minimum reading in the machine and at which position?

Ans. In this case acceleration is variable. In accelerated motion, weight of body depends on the magnitude and direction of acceleration for upward or downward motion.

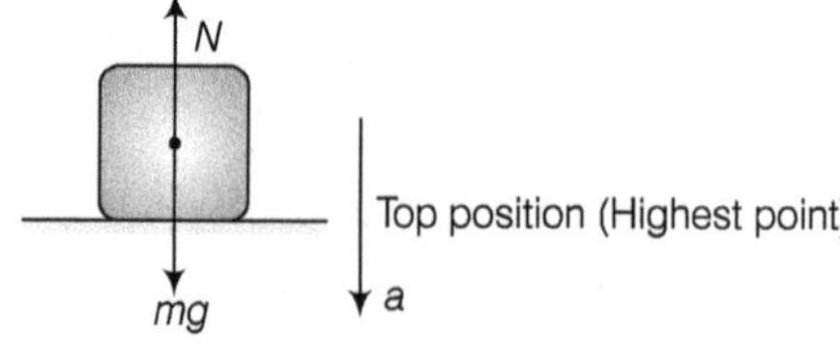

(a) Hence, the weight of the body changes during oscillations

(b) Considering the situation in two extreme positions, as their acceleration is maximum in magnitude.

we have, $mg - N = ma$

$\because$ At the highest point, the platform is accelerating downward.

$\Rightarrow \quad N = mg - ma$

But $\quad a = \omega^2 A$ [in magnitude]

$\therefore \quad N = mg - m\omega^2 A$

where, $\quad A =$ amplitude of motion.

Given, $\quad m = 50\,\text{kg}$, frequency $\nu = 2\ \text{s}^{-1}$

$\therefore \quad \omega = 2\pi\nu = 4\pi\ \text{rad/s}$

$A = 5\,\text{cm} = 5 \times 10^{-2}\ \text{m}$

$$\therefore \quad N = 50 \times 9.8 - 50 \times (4\pi)^2 \times 5 \times 10^{-2}$$
$$= 50[9.8 - 16\pi^2 \times 5 \times 10^{-2}]$$
$$= 50[9.8 - 7.89]$$
$$= 50 \times 1.91$$
$$= 95.5\,\text{N}$$

When the platform is at the lowest position of its oscillation,

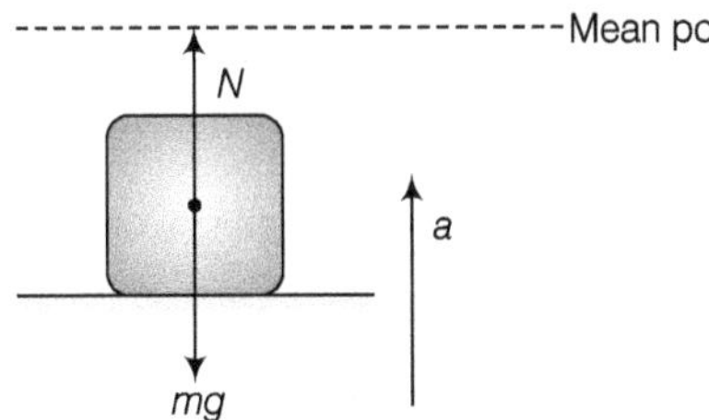

It is accelerating towards mean position that is vertically upwards.

Writing equation of motion

$$N - mg = ma = m\omega^2 A$$

or $\quad N = mg + m\omega^2 A$

$$= m[g + \omega^2 A]$$

Putting the data $\quad N = 50[9.8 + (4\pi)^2 \times 5 \times 10^{-2}]$

$$= 50[9.8 + (12.56)^2 \times 5 \times 10^{-2}]$$
$$= 50\,[9.8 + 7.88]$$
$$= 50 \times 17.68 = 884\,\text{N}$$

Now, the machine reads the normal reaction. It is clear that

maximum weight = 884 N (at lowest point)

minimum weight = 95.5 N (at top point)

Q. 36 A body of mass m is attached to one end of a massless spring which is suspended vertically from a fixed point. The mass is held in hand, so that the spring is neither stretched nor compressed. Suddenly, the support of the hand is removed. The lowest position attained by the mass during oscillation is 4 cm below the point, where it was held in hand.

(a) What is the amplitude of oscillation?

(b) Find the frequency of oscillation?

Thinking Process

When we have given the support of hand, net force = 0 and when it is released, all of its PE will convert into KE.

Ans. (a) When the support of the hand is removed, the body oscillates about a mean position.

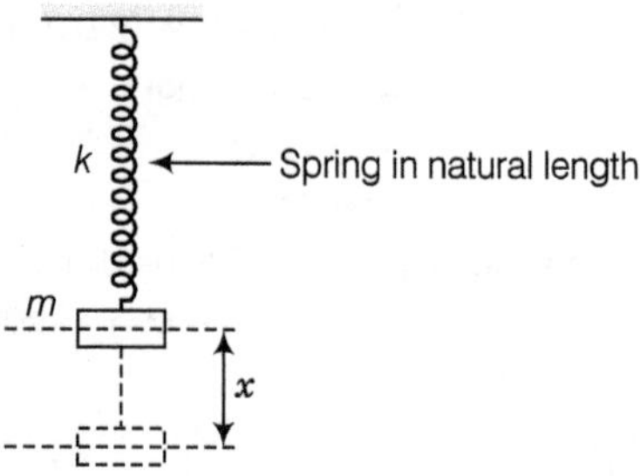

Suppose x is the maximum extension in the spring when it reaches the lowest point in oscillation.

Loss in PE of the block = mgx ...(i)

where, m = mass of the block

Gain in elastic potential energy of the spring

$$= \frac{1}{2}kx^2 \quad \text{...(ii)}$$

As the two are equal, conserving the mechanical energy,

we get, $$mgx = \frac{1}{2}kx^2 \text{ or } x = \frac{2mg}{k} \quad \text{...(iii)}$$

Now, the mean position of oscillation will be, when the block is balanced by the spring.

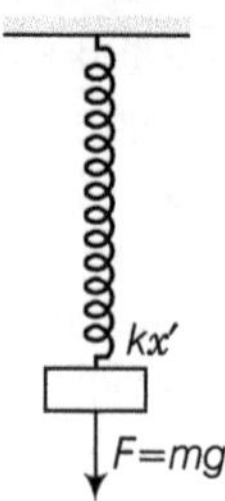

If x' is the extension in that case, then

$$F = +kx'$$

But $$F = mg$$

$\Rightarrow$ $$mg = +kx'$$

or $$x' = \frac{mg}{k} \quad \text{...(iv)}$$

Dividing Eq. (iii) by Eq. (iv),

$$\frac{x}{x'} = \frac{2mg}{k} / \frac{mg}{k} = 2$$

$\Rightarrow$ $$x = 2x'$$

But given $x = 4$ cm (maximum extension from the unstretched position)

$\therefore$ $$2x' = 4$$

$\therefore$ $$x' = \frac{4}{2} = 2 \text{ cm}$$

But the displacement of mass from the mean position to the position when spring attains its natural length is equal to amplitude of the oscillation.

$\therefore$ $$A = x' = 2 \text{ cm}$$

where, A = amplitude of the motion.

(b) Time period of the oscillating system depends on mass spring constant given by

$$T = 2\pi\sqrt{\frac{m}{k}}$$

It does not depend on the amplitude.

But from Eq. (iii),

$$\frac{2mg}{k} = x \quad \text{(maximum extension)}$$

$$\frac{2mg}{k} = 4 \text{ cm} = 4 \times 10^{-2} \text{ m}$$

$\therefore$ $$\frac{m}{k} = \frac{4 \times 10^{-2}}{2g} = \frac{2 \times 10^{-2}}{g}$$

$\therefore$ $$\frac{k}{m} = \frac{g}{2 \times 10^{-2}}$$

and $$\nu = \text{frequency} = \frac{1}{T} = \frac{1}{2\pi}\sqrt{\frac{k}{m}}$$

$\therefore$ $$\nu = \frac{1}{2 \times 3.14}\sqrt{\frac{g}{2 \times 10^{-2}}}$$

$$= \frac{1}{2 \times 3.14}\sqrt{\frac{4.9}{10^{-2}}} = \frac{1}{6.28} \times \sqrt{4.9 \times 100}$$

$$= \frac{10}{6.28} \times 2.21 = 3.51 \text{ Hz.}$$

Note *The block during oscillation cannot go above the position it was released, as it is given that there is no velocity in the upward direction either by the system or external agent.*

Q. 37 A cylindrical log of wood of height h and area of cross-section A floats in water. It is pressed and then released. Show that the log would execute SHM with a time period.

$$T = 2\pi\sqrt{\frac{m}{A\rho g}}$$

where, m is mass of the body and ρ is density of the liquid.

Thinking Process

To find the time period for the SHM displace the log from equilibrium position by a small displacement and then find the restoring force.

Ans. Consider the diagram.

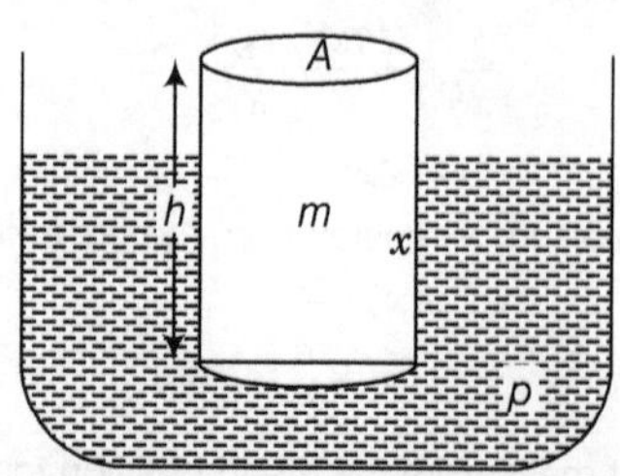

Let the log be pressed and let the vertical displacement at the equilibrium position be x_0.
At equilibrium,

$$mg = \text{buoyant force} = (\rho A x_0)g \qquad [\because m = V\rho = (Ax_0)\rho]$$

When it is displaced by a further displacement x, the buoyant force is $A(x_0 + x)\rho g$

$\therefore$ $$\text{Net restoring force} = \text{Buoyant force} - \text{Weight}$$
$$= A(x_0 + x)\rho g - mg$$
$$= (A\rho g)x \qquad [\because mg = \rho A x_0 g]$$

As displacement x is downward and restoring force is upward,
we can write

$$F_{\text{restoring}} = -(A\rho g)x$$
$$= -kx$$

where $$k = \text{constant} = A\rho g$$

So, the motion is SHM $(\because F \propto -x)$

Now, $$\text{Acceleration } a = \frac{F_{\text{restoring}}}{m} = -\frac{k}{m}x$$

Comparing with $$a = -\omega^2 x$$

$\Rightarrow$ $$\omega^2 = \frac{k}{m} \Rightarrow \omega = \sqrt{\frac{k}{m}}$$

$\Rightarrow$ $$\frac{2\pi}{T} = \sqrt{\frac{k}{m}} \Rightarrow T = 2\pi\sqrt{\frac{m}{k}}$$

$\Rightarrow$ $$T = 2\pi\sqrt{\frac{m}{A\rho g}}$$

Q. 38 One end of a V-tube containing mercury is connected to a suction pump and the other end to atmosphere. The two arms of the tube are inclined to horizontal at an angle of 45° each. A small pressure difference is created between two columns when the suction pump is removed. Will the column of mercury in V-tube execute simple harmonic motion? Neglect capillary and viscous forces. Find the time period of oscillation.

Ans. Consider the diagram shown below

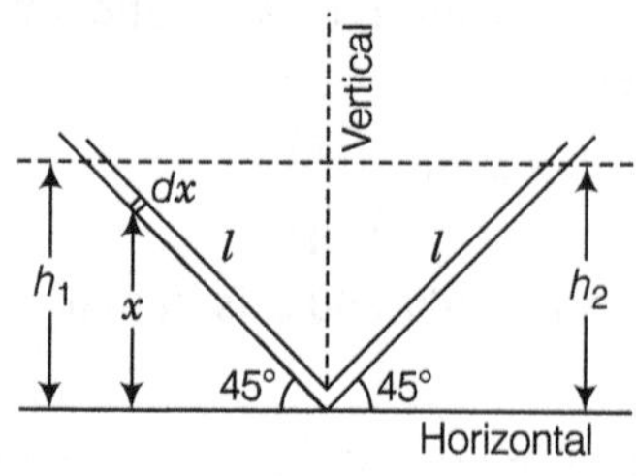

Let us consider an infinitesimal liquid column of length dx at a height x from the horizontal line.

If ρ = density of the liquid

A = cross-sectional area of V-tube

PE of element dx will be given as

$$PE = dmgx = (A\rho dx)gx \qquad [\because dm = \rho V = \rho A dx]$$

where $A\rho dx = dm$ = mass of element dx

$\therefore$ Total PE of the left column

$$= \int_0^{h_1} A\rho g x dx$$

$$= A\rho g \int_0^{h_1} x\, dx$$

$$= A\rho g \left|\frac{x^2}{2}\right|_0^{h_1} = A\rho g \frac{h_1^2}{2}$$

But, $h_1 = l \sin 45°$

$$\therefore \quad PE = \frac{A\rho g}{2} l^2 \sin^2 45° \qquad \ldots(i)$$

In a similar way,

$$\text{PE of right column} = \frac{A\rho g}{2} l^2 \sin^2 45° \qquad \ldots(ii)$$

$$\text{Total PE} = \frac{A\rho g}{2} l^2 \sin^2 45° + \frac{A\rho g}{2} l^2 \sin^2 45°$$

$$= 2 \times \frac{1}{2} A\rho g l^2 \left(\frac{1}{\sqrt{2}}\right)^2 = \frac{A\rho g l^2}{2} \qquad \ldots(iii)$$

If due to pressure difference created y element of left side moves on the right side, then

liquid present in the left arm = $l - y$

liquid present in the right arm = $l + y$

$$\therefore \quad \text{Total PE} = A\rho g (l - y)^2 \sin^2 45° + A\rho g (l + y)^2 \sin^2 45°$$

$$\text{Changes in PE} = (PE)_{final} - (PE)_{initial}$$

or

$$\Delta PE = \frac{A\rho g}{2} [(l - y)^2 + (l + y)^2 - l^2]$$

$$= \frac{A\rho g}{2} [l^2 + y^2 - 2ly + l^2 + y^2 + 2ly - l^2]$$

$$= \frac{A\rho g}{2} [2(l^2 + y^2)]$$

$$= A\rho g (l^2 + y^2) \qquad \ldots(iv)$$

If v is the change in velocity of the total liquid column, then change in KE

$$\Delta KE = \frac{1}{2} m v^2$$

But $m = A\rho(2l)$

$$\therefore \quad \Delta KE = \frac{1}{2} A\rho 2 l v^2 = A\rho l v^2 \qquad \ldots(v)$$

From Eqs. (iv) and (v),

$$\Delta PE + \Delta KE = A\rho g (l^2 + y^2) + A\rho l v^2 \qquad \ldots(vi)$$

System being conservative.

$\therefore$ Change in total energy = 0

From Eq. (vi),

$$A\rho g (l^2 + y^2) + A\rho l v^2 = 0$$

Differentiating both sides with respect to time (t), we get

$$A\rho g\left[0 + 2y\frac{dy}{dt}\right] + A\rho l(2v)\frac{dv}{dt} = 0$$

But, $\frac{dy}{dt} = v$ and $\frac{dv}{dt} = a$ [acceleration]

$\Rightarrow$ $A\rho g(2yv) + A\rho l(2v)a = 0$

$\Rightarrow$ $(gy + la)2A\rho v = 0$

$2A\rho v =$ constant and $2A\rho v \neq 0$

$\therefore$ $la + gy = 0$

$$a + \left(\frac{g}{l}\right)y = 0$$

or $\frac{d^2y}{dt^2} + \left(\frac{g}{l}\right)y = 0$

This is the standard differential equation for SHM of the form

$$\frac{d^2y}{dt^2} + \omega^2 y = 0$$

$\therefore$ $\omega = \sqrt{\frac{g}{l}}$

$\therefore$ $T = \frac{2\pi}{\omega} = 2\pi\sqrt{\frac{l}{g}}$

Q. 39 A tunnel is dug through the centre of the earth. Show that a body of mass *m* when dropped from rest from one end of the tunnel will execute simple harmonic motion.

Ans. Consider the situation shown in the diagram.

The gravitational force on the particle at a distance r from the centre of the earth arises entirely from that portion of matter of the earth in shells internal to the position of the particle. The external shells exert no force on the particle.

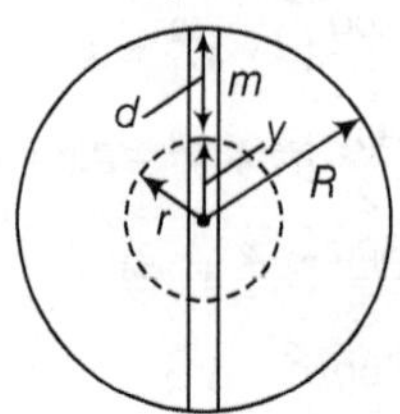

More clearly,

let g' be the acceleration at P.

So, $g' = g\left(1 - \frac{d}{R}\right) = g\left(\frac{R-d}{R}\right)$

From figure, $R - d = y$

$\Rightarrow$ $g' = g\frac{y}{R},$

Force on body at p, $F = -mg' = \frac{-mg}{R}y$ ...(i)

$\Rightarrow$ $F \propto -y$ [where, y is distance from the centre]

So, motion is SHM.

For time period, we can write Eq. (i)

As
$$ma = -\frac{Mg}{R}y \Rightarrow a = -\frac{g}{R}y$$

Comparing with $a = -\omega^2 y$

$$\omega^2 = \frac{g}{R}$$

$\Rightarrow$
$$\left(\frac{2\pi}{T}\right) = \frac{g}{R} \Rightarrow T = 2\pi\sqrt{\frac{R}{g}}$$

Q. 40 A simple pendulum of time period 1s and length l is hung from a fixed support at O. Such that the bob is at a distance H vertically above A on the ground (figure) the amplitude is θ_0 the string snaps at $\theta = \theta_0 / 2$. Find the time taken by the bob to hit the ground. Also find distance from A where bob hits the ground. Assume θ_0 to be small, so that $\sin\theta_0 \simeq \theta_0$ and $\cos\theta_0 \simeq 1$.

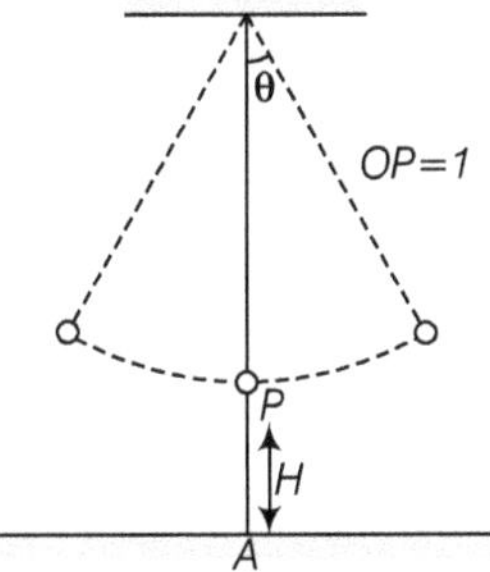

Thinking Process

We have to consider $\theta = \theta_0$ as reference point that is when $\theta = \theta_0$ the time will be considered as $t = 0$. Then, equation of rectilinear motion will be applied.

Ans. Consider the diagram.

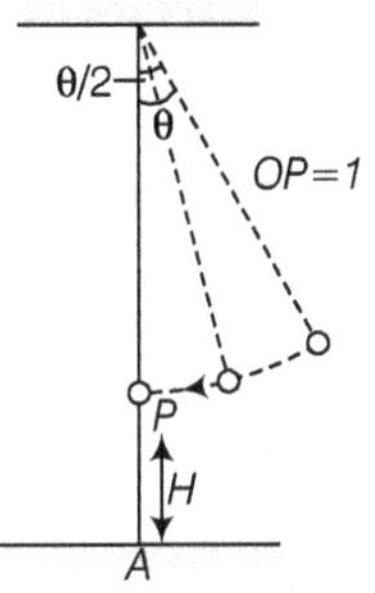

Let us assume $t = 0$ when $\theta = \theta_0$, then $\theta = \theta_0 \cos\omega t$

Given a seconds pendulum $\omega = 2\pi \Rightarrow \theta = \theta_0 \cos 2\pi t$ ......(i)

At time t_1 let $\theta = \theta_0 / 2$

$\therefore$
$$\cos 2\pi t_1 = 1/2 \Rightarrow t_1 = \frac{1}{6} \qquad \left[\because \cos 2\pi t_1 = \cos\frac{\pi}{3} \Rightarrow 2\pi t_1 = \frac{\pi}{3}\right]$$

$$\frac{d\theta}{dt} = -(\theta_0 \, 2\pi)\sin 2\pi t \qquad \text{[from Eq. (i)]}$$

At $$t = t_1 = \frac{1}{6}$$

$$\frac{d\theta}{dt} = -\theta_0\, 2\pi \sin\frac{2\pi}{6} = -\sqrt{3}\,\pi\,\theta_0$$

Negative sign shows that it is going left.

Thus, the linear velocity is

$$u = -\sqrt{3}\pi\theta_0 l \text{ perpendicular to the string.}$$

The vertical component is

$$u_y = -\sqrt{3}\pi\theta_0 l \sin(\theta_0/2)$$

and the horizontal component is

$$u_x = -\sqrt{3}\pi\theta_0 l \cos(\theta_0/2)$$

At the time it snaps, the vertical height is

$$H' = H + l(1 - \cos(\theta_0/2)) \qquad \text{... (ii)}$$

Let the time required for fall be t, then

$$H' = u_y t + (1/2)gt^2 \qquad \text{(notice } g \text{ also in the negative direction)}$$

or $$\frac{1}{2}gt^2 + \sqrt{3}\pi\theta_0 l \sin\frac{\theta_0}{2}t - H' = 0$$

$$\therefore \quad t = \frac{-\sqrt{3}\pi\theta_0\, l\sin\frac{\theta_0}{2} \pm \sqrt{3\pi^2\theta_0^2 l^2 \sin^2\frac{\theta_0}{2} + 2gH'}}{g}$$

$$= \frac{-\sqrt{3}\pi l\frac{\theta_0^2}{2} \pm \sqrt{3\pi^2\left(\frac{\theta_0}{4}^4\right)l^2 + 2gH'}}{g} \qquad \left[\because \sin\frac{\theta_0}{2} \simeq \frac{\theta_0}{2} \text{ for small angle}\right]$$

Given that θ_0 is small, hence neglecting terms of order θ_0^2 and higher

$$t = \sqrt{\frac{2H'}{g}} \qquad \text{[from Eq. (iii)]}$$

Now, $$H' \approx H + l(1-1) \qquad [\therefore \cos\theta_0/2 \approx 1]$$

$$= H \qquad \text{[from Eq. (ii)]}$$

$$\Rightarrow \quad t = \sqrt{\frac{2H}{g}}$$

The distance travelled in the x-direction is $u_x t$ to the left of where the bob is snapped

$$X = Uxt = \sqrt{3}\,\pi\theta_0 l \,Cos\left(\frac{\theta_0}{2}\right)\sqrt{\frac{2H}{g}} s$$

As θ_0 is small $\Rightarrow \cos\left(\frac{\theta_0}{2}\right) \approx 1$

$$X = \sqrt{3}\,\pi\,\theta_0 l\sqrt{\frac{2H}{g}} = \sqrt{\frac{6H}{g}}\,\theta_0 l\pi$$

At the time of snapping, the bob was at a horizontal distance of $l\sin(\theta_0/2) \approx l\frac{\theta_0}{2}$ from A.

Thus, the distance of bob from A where it meets the ground is

$$= \frac{l\theta_0}{2} - X = \frac{l\theta_0}{2} - \sqrt{\frac{6H}{g}}\,\theta_0 l\pi$$

$$= \theta_0 l\left(\frac{1}{2} - \pi\sqrt{\frac{6H}{g}}\right)$$

14

Waves

Multiple Choice Questions (MCQs)

Q. 1 Water waves produced by a motorboat sailing in water are

(a) neither longitudinal nor transverse
(b) both longitudinal and transverse
(c) only longitudinal
(d) only transverse

Ans. *(b)* Water waves produced by a motorboat sailing in water are both longitudinal and transverse, because the waves, produce transverse as well as lateral vibrations in the particles of the medium.

Q. 2 Sound waves of wavelength λ travelling in a medium with a speed of v m/s enter into another medium where its speed in $2v$ m/s. Wavelength of sound waves in the second medium is

(a) λ (b) $\frac{\lambda}{2}$ (c) 2λ (d) 4λ

Ans. *(c)* Let the frequency in the first medium is ν and in the second medium is ν'.

Frequency remains same in both the medium

So, $$\nu = \nu' \Rightarrow \frac{v}{\lambda} = \frac{v'}{\lambda'}$$

$$\Rightarrow \quad \lambda' = \left(\frac{v'}{v}\right)\lambda$$

λ and λ', v and v' are wavelengths and speeds in first and second medium respectively.

So, $$\lambda' = \left(\frac{2v}{v}\right)\lambda = 2\lambda$$

Q. 3 Speed of sound wave in air

(a) is independent of temperature
(b) increases with pressure
(c) increases with increase in humidity
(d) decreases with increase in humidity

Ans. *(c)* Due to presence of moisture density of air decreases.

We know that speed of sound in air is given by $v = \sqrt{\frac{\gamma p}{\rho}}$

For air γ and p are constants.

$$v \propto \frac{1}{\sqrt{\rho}}, \text{ where } \rho \text{ is density of air.}$$

$$\frac{v_2}{v_1} = \sqrt{\frac{\rho_2}{\rho_1}}$$

where ρ_1 is density of dry air and ρ_2 is density of moist air.

As $\rho_2 < \rho_1 = \frac{v_2}{v_1} > 1 \Rightarrow v_2 > v_1$

Hence, speed of sound wave in air increases with increase in humidity.

Q. 4 Change in temperature of the medium changes

(a) frequency of sound waves

(b) amplitude of sound waves

(c) wavelength of sound waves

(d) loudness of sound waves

Ans. *(c)* Speed of sound wave in a medium $v \propto \sqrt{T}$ (where T is temperature of the medium)

Clearly, when temperature changes speed also changes.

As, $v = \nu\lambda$

where ν is frequency and λ is wavelength.

Frequency (ν) remains fixed

$\Rightarrow$ $v \propto \lambda$ or $\lambda \propto v$

As does not change, so wavelength (λ) changes.

Q. 5 With propagation of longitudinal waves through a medium, the quantity transmitted is

(a) matter
(b) energy
(c) energy and matter
(d) energy, matter and momentum

Ans. *(b)* Propagation of longitudinal waves through a medium leads to transmission of energy through the medium without matter being transmitted.

There is no movement of matter (mass) and hence momentum.

Q. 6 Which of the following statements are true for wave motion?

(a) Mechanical transverse waves can propagate through all mediums

(b) Longitudinal waves can propagate through solids only

(c) Mechanical transverse waves can propagate through solids only

(d) Longitudinal waves can propagate through vacuum

Ans. *(c)* When mechanical transverse wave propagates through a medium, the constituent of the medium oscillate perpendicular to wave motion causing change in shape. That is each, element of the medium is subjected to shearing stress. Solids and strings have shear modulus, that is why, sustain shearing stress.

Fluids have no shape of, their own, they yield to shearing stress. This is why transverse waves are possible in solids and strings but not in fluids.

Q. 7 A sound wave is passing through air column in the form of compression and rarefaction. In consecutive compressions and rarefactions,

(a) density remains constant

(b) Boyle's law is obeyed

(c) bulk modulus of air oscillates

(d) there is no transfer of heat

Ans. *(d)* (a) Due to compression and rarefactions density of the medium (air) changes. At compressed regions density is maximum and at rarefactions density is minimum

(b) As density is changing, so Boyle's law is not obeyed

(c) Bulk modulus remains same

(d) The time of compression and rarefaction is too small *i.e.*, we can assume adiabatic process and hence no transfer of heat

Q. 8 Equation of a plane progressive wave is given by $y = 0.6 \sin 2\pi\left(t - \frac{x}{2}\right)$. On reflection from a denser medium its amplitude becomes $\frac{2}{3}$ of the amplitude of the incident wave. The equation of the reflected wave is

(a) $y = 0.6 \sin 2\pi\left(t + \frac{x}{2}\right)$

(b) $y = -0.4 \sin 2\pi\left(t + \frac{x}{2}\right)$

(c) $y = 0.4 \sin 2\pi\left(t + \frac{x}{2}\right)$

(d) $y = -0.4 \sin 2\pi\left(t - \frac{x}{2}\right)$

Thinking Process

Due to reflection from a denser medium there is a phase change of 180° in the reflected wave.

Ans. *(b)* Amplitude of reflected wave

$$A_r = \frac{2}{3} \times A_i = \frac{2}{3} \times 0.6 = 0.4 \text{ units}$$

Given equation of incident wave

$$y_i = 0.6 \sin 2\pi\left(t - \frac{x}{2}\right)$$

Equation of reflected wave is

$$y_r = A_r \sin 2\pi\left(t + \frac{x}{2} + \pi\right)$$

[$\because$ At denser medium, phase changes by π]

The positive sign is due to reversal of direction of propagation

So, $$y_r = -0.4 \sin 2\pi\left(t + \frac{x}{2}\right)$$ [$\because \sin(\pi + \theta) = -\sin\theta$]

Q. 9 **A string of mass 2.5 kg is under tension of 200 N. The length of the stretched string is 20.0 m. If the transverse jerk is struck at one end of the string, the disturbance will reach the other end in**

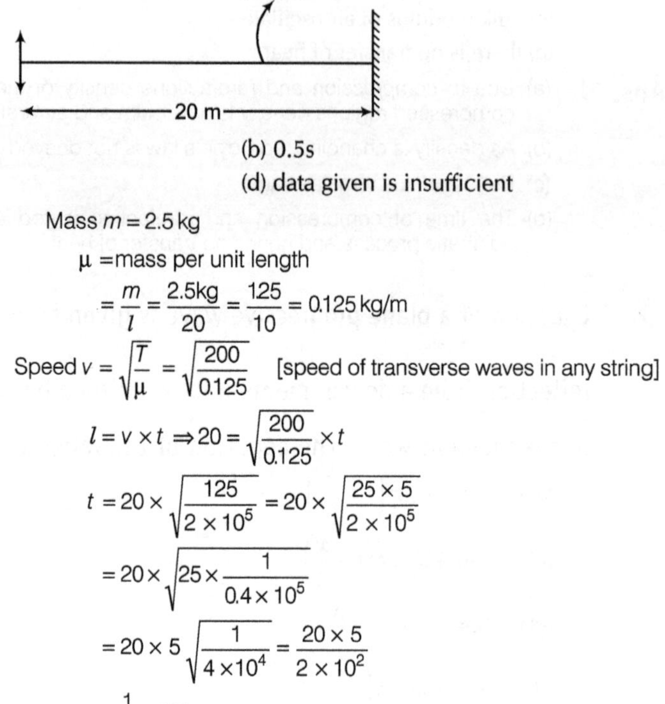

(a) 1s
(b) 0.5s
(c) 2s
(d) data given is insufficient

Ans. *(b)* Mass $m = 2.5$ kg

μ = mass per unit length

$$= \frac{m}{l} = \frac{2.5\text{kg}}{20} = \frac{125}{10} = 0.125 \text{ kg/m}$$

$$\text{Speed } v = \sqrt{\frac{T}{\mu}} = \sqrt{\frac{200}{0.125}} \quad \text{[speed of transverse waves in any string]}$$

$$l = v \times t \Rightarrow 20 = \sqrt{\frac{200}{0.125}} \times t$$

$$\Rightarrow \quad t = 20 \times \sqrt{\frac{125}{2 \times 10^5}} = 20 \times \sqrt{\frac{25 \times 5}{2 \times 10^5}}$$

$$= 20 \times \sqrt{25 \times \frac{1}{0.4 \times 10^5}}$$

$$= 20 \times 5\sqrt{\frac{1}{4 \times 10^4}} = \frac{20 \times 5}{2 \times 10^2}$$

$$= \frac{1}{2} = 0.5$$

Q. 10 **A train whistling at constant frequency is moving towards a station at a constant speed v. The train goes past a stationary observer on the station. The frequency n' of the sound as heard by the observer is plotted as a function of time t (figure). Identify the expected curve.**

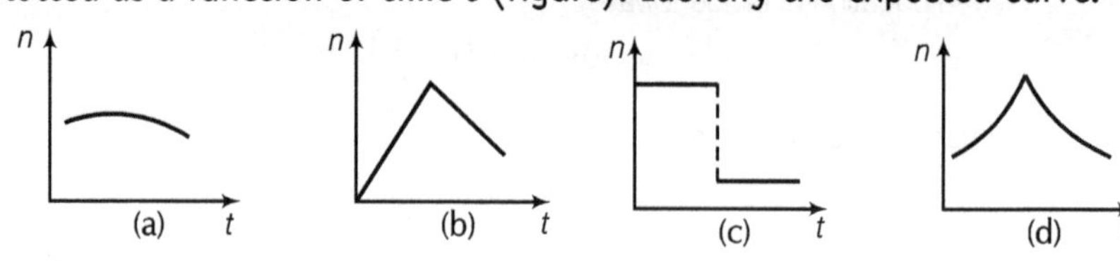

Thinking Process

The observed frequency is apparent frequency due to Doppler shift.

Ans. *(c)* Let the original frequency of the source is n_0.

Let the speed of sound wave in the medium is v.

As observer is stationary

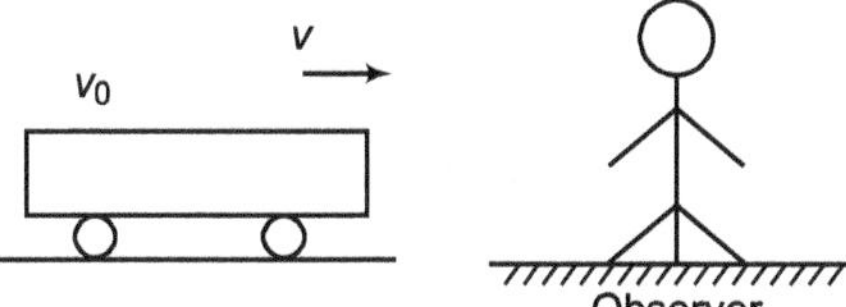

Apparent frequency $n_a = \left(\frac{v}{v - v_s}\right) n_o$ [when train is approaching]

$$= \left(\frac{v}{v - v_s}\right) n_o = n_a > n_o$$

When the train is going away from the observer

Apparent frequency $n_a = \left(\frac{v}{v + v_s}\right) n_o = n_a < n_o$

Hence, the expected curve is (c).

Multiple Choice Questions (More Than One Options)

Q. 11 A transverse harmonic wave on a string is described by

$$y(x, t) = 3.0 \sin\left(36t + 0.018x + \frac{\pi}{4}\right)$$

where x and y are in cm and t is in sec. The positive direction of x is from left to right.

(a) the wave is travelling from right to left
(b) the speed of the wave is 20 m/s
(c) frequency of the wave is 5.7 Hz
(d) the least distance between two successive crests in the wave is 2.5 cm

Thinking Process

To find the characteristic parameters associated with a wave, compare the given equation of the wave with a standard equation.

Ans. *(a, b, c)*

Given equation is $y(x, t) = 3.0\sin\left(36t + 0.018x + \frac{\pi}{4}\right)$

Compare the equation with the standard form.

$$y = a\sin(\omega t + kx + \phi)$$

(a) As the equation involves positive sign with x ,hence the wave is travelling from right to left. Hence, option (a) is correct.

(b) Given, $\omega = 36 \Rightarrow 2\pi\nu = 36$

$\Rightarrow$ $\nu = \text{frequency} = \frac{36}{2\pi} = \frac{18}{\pi}$

$$k = 0.018 \Rightarrow \frac{2\pi}{\lambda} = 0.018$$

$$\Rightarrow \quad \frac{2\pi\nu}{\nu\lambda} = 0.018 \Rightarrow \frac{\omega}{v} = 0.018 \qquad [\because 2\pi\nu = \omega \text{ and } \nu\lambda = v]$$

$$\Rightarrow \quad \frac{36}{v} = 0.018 = \frac{18}{1000}$$

$$\Rightarrow \quad v = 2000 \text{ cm/s} = 20 \text{ m/s}$$

(c) $2\pi\nu = 36$

$$\Rightarrow \quad \nu = \frac{36}{2\pi}\text{Hz} = \frac{18}{\pi} = 5.7\text{Hz}$$

(d) $\frac{2\pi}{\lambda} = 0.018$

$$\Rightarrow \quad \lambda = \frac{2\pi}{0.018}\text{cm}$$

$$= \frac{2000\pi}{18}\text{cm} = \frac{20\pi}{18}\text{m} = 3.48 \text{ cm}$$

Hence, least distance between two successive crests = λ = 3.48 m.

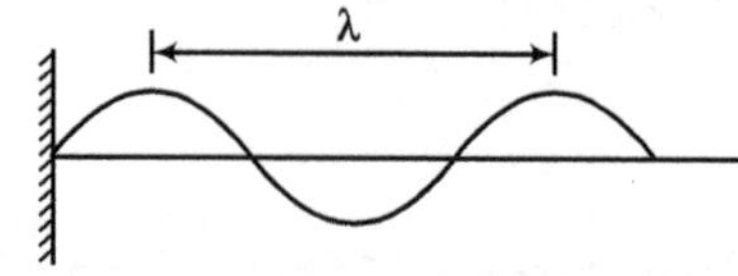

Q. 12 The displacement of a string is given by

$$y(x, t) = 0.06\sin\left(\frac{2\pi x}{3}\right)\cos(120\pi t)$$

where x and y are in metre and t in second. The length of the string is 1.5 m and its mass is 3.0×10^{-2} kg.

(a) It represents a progressive wave of frequency 60 Hz

(b) It represents a stationary wave of frequency 60 Hz

(c) It is the result superposition of two waves of wavelength 3 m, frequency 60 Hz each travelling with a speed of 180 m/s in opposite direction

(d) Amplitude of this wave is constant

Ans. *(b, c)*

Given equation is $\quad y(x, t) = 0.06\sin\left(\frac{2\pi x}{3}\right)\cos(120\pi t)$

(a) Comparing with a standard equation of stationary wave

$$y(x, t) = a\sin(kx)\cos(\omega t)$$

Clearly, the given equation belongs to stationary wave. Hence, option (a) is not correct.

(b) By comparing,

$$\omega = 120\pi$$

$$\Rightarrow \quad 2\pi f = 120\pi \Rightarrow f = 60\text{Hz}$$

(c) $k = \frac{2\pi}{3} = \frac{2\pi}{\lambda}$

$$\Rightarrow \quad \lambda = \text{wavelength} = 3\text{m}$$

$$\text{Frequency} = f = 60\text{Hz}$$

$$\text{Speed} = v = f\lambda = (60\text{ Hz})(3\text{m}) = 180 \text{ m/s}$$

(d) Since in stationary wave, all particles of the medium execute SHM with varying amplitude `nodes.

Q. 13 Speed of sound wave in a fluid depends upon

(a) directly on density of the medium
(b) square of Bulk modulus of the medium
(c) inversly on the square root of density
(d) directly on the square root of bulk modulus of the medium

Ans. *(c, d)*

Speed of sound waves in a fluid is given by

$v = \sqrt{\frac{B}{\rho}}$, where B is Bulk modulus and ρ is density of the medium.

Clearly, $v \propto \frac{1}{\sqrt{\rho}}$ [$\because$ for any fluid, B=constant]

and $v \propto \sqrt{B}$ [$\because$ for medium, ρ= constant]

Q. 14 During propagation of a plane progressive mechanical wave,

(a) all the particles are vibrating in the same phase
(b) amplitude of all the particles is equal
(c) particles of the medium executes SHM
(d) wave velocity depends upon the nature of the medium

Ans. *(b, c, d)*

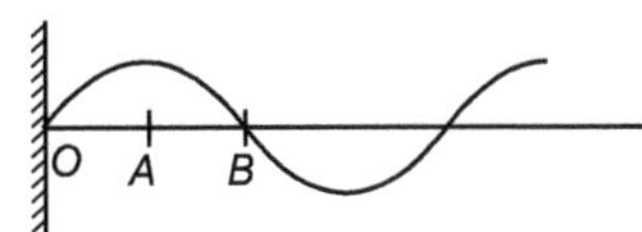

During propagation of a plane progressive mechanical wave, like shown in the diagram, amplitude of all the particles is equal.

(i) Clearly, the particles O, A and B are having different phase.
(ii) Particles of the wave shown in the figure are having up and down SHM.
(iii) For a progressive wave propagating in a fluid .

$$\text{Speed} = v = \sqrt{\frac{B}{\rho}}$$

Hence, $v \propto \sqrt{\frac{1}{\rho}}$ [$\because B$ is constant]

As ρ depends upon nature of the medium, hence v also depends upon the nature of the medium.

Q. 15 The transverse displacement of a string (clamped at its both ends) is given by $y\ (x,t) = 0.06\sin\left(\frac{2\pi x}{3}\right)\cos(120\pi t)$.

All the points on the string between two consecutive nodes vibrate with

(a) same frequency
(b) same phase
(c) same energy
(d) different amplitude

Ans. *(a, b, d)*

Given equation is $y(x,t) = 0.06\sin\left(\frac{2\pi}{3}x\right)\cos(120\pi t)$

Comparing with standard equation of stationary wave

$$y(x,t) = a\sin(kx)\cos(\omega t)$$

It is represented by diagram.
where N denotes nodes and A denotes antinodes.

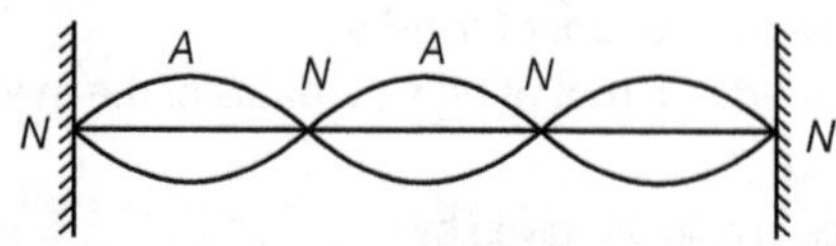

(a) Clearly, frequency is common for all the points.
(b) Consider all the particles between two nodes they are having same phase of $(120\pi t)$ at a given time.
(c) and (d) But are having different amplitudes of $0.06\sin\left(\frac{2\pi}{3}x\right)$ and because of different amplitudes they are having different energies.

Q. 16 **A train, standing in a station yard, blows a whistle of frequency 400 Hz in still air. The wind starts blowing in the direction from the yard to the station with a speed of 10 m/s. Given that the speed of sound in still air is 340 m/s. Then**

(a) the frequency of sound as heard by an observer standing on the platform is 400 Hz
(b) the speed of sound for the observer standing on the platform is 350 m/s
(c) the frequency of sound as heard by the observer standing on the platform will increase
(d) the frequency of sound as heard by the observer standing on the platform will decrease

Thinking Process

When the wind is blowing in the same direction as that of sound wave then net speed of the wave is sum of speed of sound wave and speed of the wind.

Ans. *(a, b)*

Given, $\nu_0 = 400\text{ Hz}, v = 340\text{ m/s}$
Speed of wind $v_w = 10\text{ m/s}$

(a) As both source and observer are stationary, hence frequency observed will be same as natural frequency $\nu_0 = 400\text{ Hz}$
(b) The speed of sound $v = v + v_w$

$$= 340 + 10 = 350\text{ m/s}$$

(c) and (d) There will be no effect on frequency,because there is no relative motion between source and observer hence (c),(d) are incorrect.

Q. 17 **Which of the following statement are true for a stationary waves?**

(a) Every particle has a fixed amplitude which is different from the amplitude of its nearest particle
(b) All the particles cross their mean position at the same time
(c) All the particles are oscillating with same amplitude
(d) There is no net transfer of energy across any plane
(e) There are some particles which are always at rest

Ans. *(a, b, d, e)*

Consider the equation of a stationary wave $y = a\sin(kx)\cos\omega t$

(a) clearly every particle at x will have amplitude $= a\sin kx$ = fixed

(b) for mean position $y = 0$

$$\Rightarrow \quad \cos\omega t = 0$$

$$\Rightarrow \quad \omega t = (2n-1)\frac{\pi}{2}$$

Hence, for a fixed value of n, all particles are having same value of

$$\text{time } t = (2n-1)\frac{\pi}{2\omega} \qquad [\because \omega = \text{constant}]$$

(c) amplitude of all the particles are $a\sin(kx)$ which is different for different particles at different values of x

(d) the energy is a stationary wave is confined between two nodes

(e) particles at different nodes are always at rest.

Very Short Answer Type Questions

Q. 18 **A sonometer wire is vibrating in resonance with a tuning fork. Keeping the tension applied same, the length of the wire is doubled. Under what conditions would the tuning fork still be is resonance with the wire?**

Ans. Wire of twice the length vibrates in its second harmonic. Thus, if the tuning fork resonates at L, it will resonate at $2L$. This can be explained as below

The sonometer frequency is given by

$$\nu = \frac{n}{2L}\sqrt{\frac{T}{m}} \qquad (n = \text{number of loops})$$

Now, as it vibrates with length L, we assume $\nu = \nu_1$

$$n = n_1$$

$$\therefore \quad \nu_1 = \frac{n_1}{2L}\sqrt{\frac{T}{m}} \qquad \ldots(\text{i})$$

When length is doubled, then

$$\nu_2 = \frac{n_2}{2 \times 2L}\sqrt{\frac{T}{m}} \qquad \ldots(\text{ii})$$

Dividing Eq. (i) by Eq. (ii), we get

$$\frac{\nu_1}{\nu_2} = \frac{n_1}{n_2} \times 2$$

To keep the resonance

$$\frac{\nu_1}{\nu_2} = 1 = \frac{n_1}{n_2} \times 2$$

$$\Rightarrow \quad n_2 = 2n_1$$

Hence, when the wire is doubled the number of loops also get doubled to produce the resonance. That is it resonates in second harmonic.

Q. 19 An organ pipe of length L open at both ends is found to vibrate in its first harmonic when sounded with a tuning fork of 480 Hz. What should be the length of a pipe closed at one end, so that it also vibrates in its first harmonic with the same tuning fork?

Thinking Process

We should not confuse between pressure wave and displacement wave. By considering any type of wave outcome will be same.

Ans. Consider the situation shown in the diagram

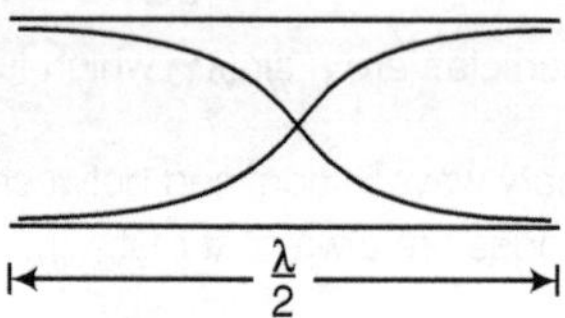

As the organ pipe is open at both ends, hence for first harmonic

$$l = \frac{\lambda}{2}$$

$\Rightarrow$ $$\lambda = 2l \Rightarrow \frac{c}{\nu} = 2l \Rightarrow \nu = \frac{c}{2l}$$

where c is speed of the sound wave in air.

For pipe closed at one end

$$\nu' = \frac{c}{4L'}$$

c for first harmonic

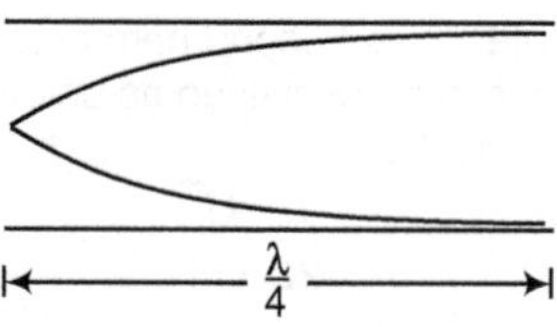

Hence, $$\nu = \nu' \quad \text{[for resonance with same tuning fork]}$$

$\Rightarrow$ $$\frac{c}{2L} = \frac{c}{4L'} \quad [\because \text{ speed remains constant}]$$

$\Rightarrow$ $$\frac{L'}{L} = \frac{2}{4} = \frac{1}{2} \Rightarrow L' = \frac{L}{2}$$

Q. 20 A tuning fork A, marked 512 Hz, produces 5 beats per second, where sounded with another unmarked tuning fork B. If B is loaded with wax the number of beats is again 5 per second. What is the frequency of the tuning fork B when not loaded?

Ans. Frequency of tuning fork A,

$$\nu_A = 512 \text{ Hz}$$

Probable frequency of tuning fork B,

$$\nu_B = \nu_A \pm 5 = 512 \pm 5 = 517 \text{ or } 507\text{Hz}$$

when B is loaded, its frequency reduces.

If it is 517 Hz, it might reduced to 507 Hz given again a beat of 5 Hz.

If it is 507 Hz, reduction will always increase the beat frequency, hence $\nu_B = 517$ Hz

Note *For production of beats frequencies of the two tuning forks must be nearly equal i.e., slight difference in frequencies.*

Q. 21 The displacement of an elastic wave is given by the function $y = 3\sin\omega t + 4\cos\omega t$, where y is in cm and t is in second. Calculate the resultant amplitude.

Ans. Given, displacement of an elastic wave $y = 3\sin\omega t + 4\cos\omega t$

Assume, $$3 = a\cos\phi \quad \ldots(i)$$
$$4 = a\sin\phi \quad \ldots(ii)$$

On dividing Eq. (ii) by Eq. (i)

$$\tan\phi = \frac{4}{3} \Rightarrow \phi = \tan^{-1}(4/3)$$

Also, $$a^2\cos^2\phi + a^2\sin^2\phi = 3^2 + 4^2$$

$\Rightarrow$ $$a^2(\cos^2\phi + \sin^2\phi) = 25$$
$$a^2 \cdot 1 = 25 \Rightarrow a = 5$$

Hence, $$Y = 5\cos\phi\sin\omega t + 5\sin\phi\cos\omega t$$
$$= 5[\cos\phi\sin\omega t + \sin\phi\cos\omega t] = 5\sin(\omega t + \phi)$$

where $$\phi = \tan^{-1}(4/3)$$

Hence, amplitude = 5 cm

Q. 22 A sitar wire is replaced by another wire of same length and material but of three times the earlier radius. If the tension in the wire remains the same, by what factor will the frequency change?

Thinking Process

In a sitar wire, the vibration is assumed to be similar as a wire fixed at both ends.

Ans. Frequency of vibrations produced by a stretched wire

$$\nu = \frac{n}{2l}\sqrt{\frac{T}{\mu}}$$

Mass per unit length $$\mu = \frac{\text{Mass}}{\text{Length}} = \frac{\pi r^2 l\rho}{l} = \pi r^2\rho \quad [\because M = V\rho = Al\rho = \pi r^2 l\rho]$$

$\therefore$ $$\nu = \frac{n}{2l}\sqrt{\frac{T}{\pi r^2\rho}} \Rightarrow \nu \propto \sqrt{\frac{1}{r^2}}$$
$$\nu \propto \frac{1}{r}$$

Hence, when radius is tripled, v will be $\frac{1}{3}$rd of previous value.

Q. 23 At what temperatures (in °C) will the speed of sound in air be 3 times its value at 0°C?

Ans. We know that speed of sound in air $v \propto \sqrt{T}$

$\therefore$ $$\frac{v_T}{v_0} = \sqrt{\frac{T_T}{T_0}} = \sqrt{\frac{T_T}{273}} \quad \text{[where } T \text{ is in kelvin]}$$

But $$\frac{v_T}{v_0} = \frac{3}{1} \quad [\because \text{speed becomes three times}]$$

$\therefore$ $$\frac{3}{1} = \sqrt{\frac{T_T}{T_0}} \Rightarrow \frac{T_T}{273} = 9$$

$\therefore$ $$T_T = 273 \times 9 = 2457\text{ K}$$
$$= 2457 - 273 = 2184°\text{C}$$

Q. 24 **When two waves of almost equal frequencies n_1 and n_2 reach at a point simultaneously, what is the time interval between successive maxima?**

Thinking Process

When two waves of almost equal frequencies interfere, they are producing beats.

Ans. Let, $n_1 > n_2$

Beat frequency $\nu_b = n_1 - n_2$

$\therefore$ Time period of beats $= T_b = \dfrac{1}{\nu_b} = \dfrac{1}{n_1 - n_2}$

Short Answer Type Questions

Q. 25 **A steel wire has a length of 12 m and a mass of 2.10 kg. What will be the speed of a transverse wave on this wire when a tension of 2.06×10^4 N is applied?**

Ans. Given, length of the wire

$$l = 12 \text{ m}$$

Mass of wire $m = 2.10 \text{ kg}$

Tension $T = 2.06 \times 10^4 \text{ N}$

Speed of transverse wave $v = \sqrt{\dfrac{T}{\mu}}$ [where μ = mass per unit length]

$$= \sqrt{\frac{2.06 \times 10^4}{\left(\frac{2.10}{12}\right)}} = \sqrt{\frac{2.06 \times 12 \times 10^4}{2.10}} = 343 \text{ m/s}$$

Q. 26 **A pipe 20 cm long is closed at one end. Which harmonic mode of the pipe is resonantly excited by a source of 1237.5 Hz? (sound velocity in air $= 330 \text{ ms}^{-1}$)**

Ans. Length of pipe

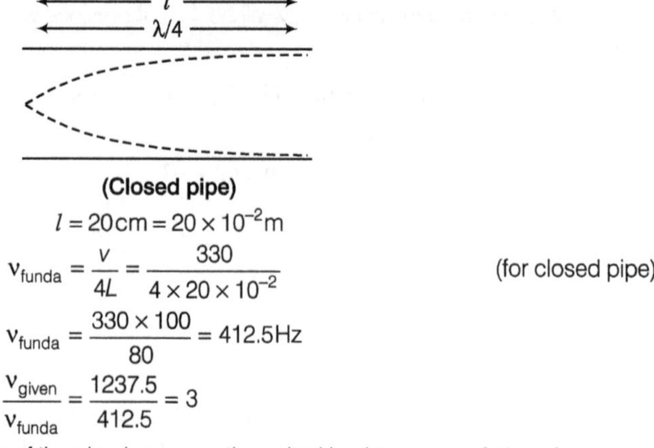

(Closed pipe)

$$l = 20 \text{cm} = 20 \times 10^{-2} \text{m}$$

$$\nu_{funda} = \frac{v}{4L} = \frac{330}{4 \times 20 \times 10^{-2}} \quad \text{(for closed pipe)}$$

$$\nu_{funda} = \frac{330 \times 100}{80} = 412.5 \text{Hz}$$

$$\frac{\nu_{given}}{\nu_{funda}} = \frac{1237.5}{412.5} = 3$$

Hence, 3rd harmonic node of the pipe is resonantly excited by the source of given frequency.

Q. 27 **A train standing at the outer signal of a railway station blows a whistle of frequency 400 Hz still air. The train begins to move with a speed of 10 ms^{-1} towards the platform. What is the frequency of the sound for an observer standing on the platform? (sound velocity in air = 330 ms^{-1})**

Ans. As the source (train) is moving towards the observer (platform) hence apparent frequency observed is more than the natural frequency.

Frequency of whistle $\nu = 400\,\text{Hz}$

Speed of train $v_t = 10\,\text{m/s}$

Velocity of sound in air $v = 330\,\text{m/s}$

Apparent frequency when source is moving $\nu_{app} = \left(\frac{v}{v - v_t}\right)\nu$

$$= \left(\frac{330}{330 - 10}\right)400$$

$$\Rightarrow \quad \nu_{app} = \frac{330}{320} \times 400 = 412.5\,\text{Hz}$$

Q. 28 **The wave pattern on a stretched string is shown in figure. Interpret what kind of wave this is and find its wavelength.**

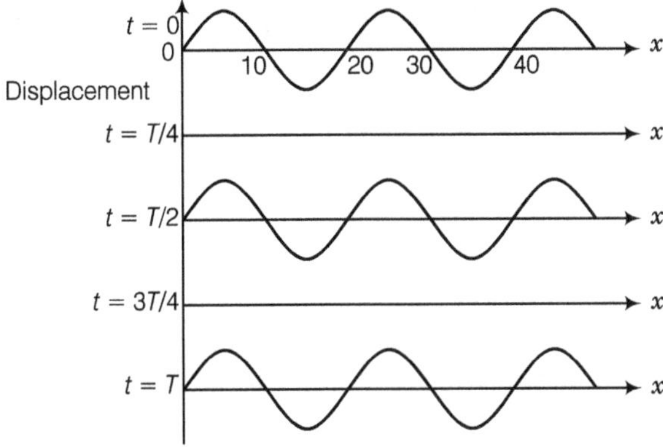

Ans. We have to observe the displacement and position of different points, then accordingly nature of two wave is decided.

Points on positions $x = 10, 20, 30, 40$ never move, always at mean position with respect to time. These are forming nodes which characterise a stationary wave.

$\because$ Distance between two successive nodes $= \frac{\lambda}{2}$

$$\Rightarrow \quad \lambda = 2 \times (\text{node to node distance})$$

$$= 2 \times (20 - 10)$$

$$= 2 \times 10 = 20\ \text{cm}$$

Q. 29 **The pattern of standing waves formed on a stretched string at two instants of time are shown in figure. The velocity of two waves superimposing to form stationary waves is 360 ms^{-1} and their frequencies are 256 Hz.**

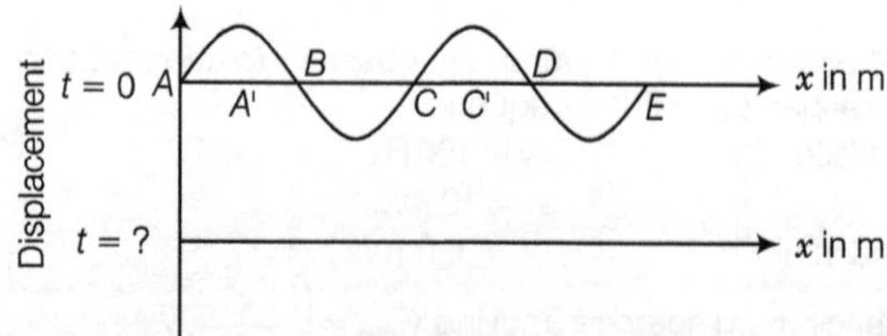

(a) Calculate the time at which the second curve is plotted.

(b) Mark nodes and antinodes on the curve.

(c) Calculate the distance between A' and C'.

Ans. Given, frequency of the wave $\nu = 256$ Hz

Time period $$T = \frac{1}{\nu} = \frac{1}{256} \text{ s} = 3.9 \times 10^{-3} \text{ s}$$

(a) Time taken to pass through mean position is

$$t = \frac{T}{4} = \frac{1}{40} = \frac{3.9 \times 10^{-3}}{4} \text{ s} = 9.8 \times 10^{-4} \text{ s}$$

(b) Nodes are A, B, C, D, E (*i.e.*, zero displacement)

Antinodes are A', C' (*i.e.*, maximum displacement)

(c) It is clear from the diagram A' and C' are consecutive antinodes, hence separation = wavelength (λ)

$$= \frac{v}{\nu} = \frac{360}{256} = 1.41 \text{ m} \qquad [\because v = \nu\lambda]$$

Q. 30 **A tuning fork vibrating with a frequency of 512 Hz is kept close to the open end of a tube filled with water (figure). The water level in the tube is gradually lowered. When the water level is 17 cm below the open end, maximum intensity of sound is heard. If the room temperature is 20°C, calculate**

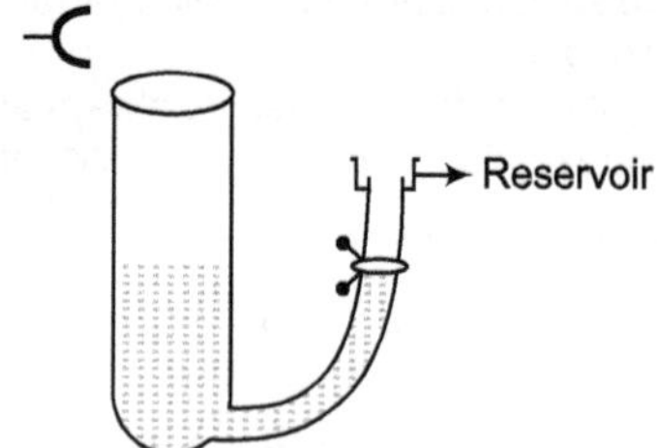

(a) speed of sound in air at room temperature.

(b) speed of sound in air at 0°C.

(c) if the water in the tube is replaced with mercury, will there be any difference in your observations?

Thinking Process

The pipe partially filled with water, acts as closed organ pipe. According to this, we will find associated frequencies.

Ans. Consider the diagram frequency of tuning fork $\nu = 512$ Hz.

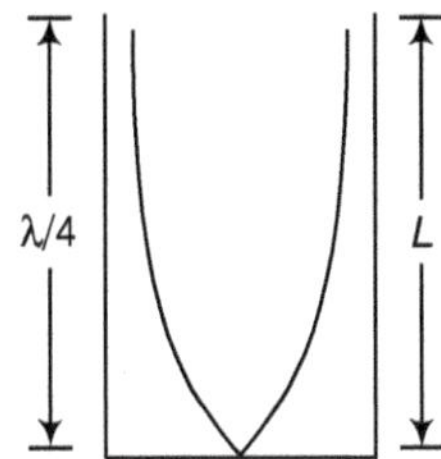

For observation of first maxima of intensity

(a) $L = \frac{\lambda}{4} \Rightarrow \lambda = 4L$ [for closed pipe]

$$v = \nu\lambda = 512 \times 4 \times 17 \times 10^{-2}$$
$$= 348.16 \text{m/s}$$

(b) We know that $v \propto \sqrt{T}$

where temperature (T) is in kelvin.

$$\frac{v_{20}}{v_0} = \sqrt{\frac{273+20}{273+0}} = \sqrt{\frac{293}{273}}$$

$$\frac{v_{20}}{v_0} = \sqrt{1.073} = 1.03$$

$$v_0 = \frac{v_{20}}{1.03} = \frac{348.16}{1.03} = 338 \text{ m/s}$$

(c) Resonance will be observed at 17 cm length of air column, only intensity of sound heard may be greater due to more complete reflection of the sound waves at the mercury surface because mercury is more denser than water.

Q. 31 Show that when a string fixed at its two ends vibrates in 1 loop, 2 loops, 3 loops and 4 loops, the frequencies are in the ratio 1 : 2 : 3 : 4.

Ans. Let, there are n number of loops in the string.

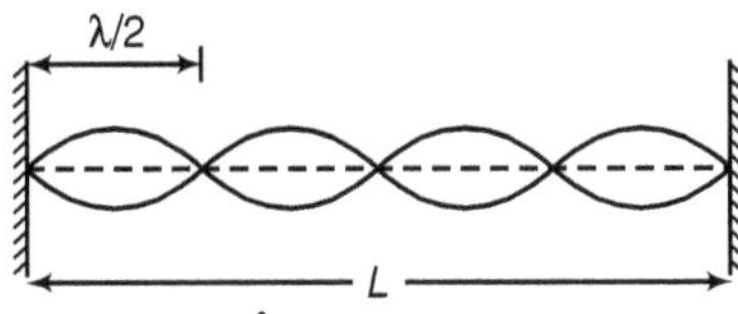

Length corresponding each loop is $\frac{\lambda}{2}$.

Now, we can write

$$L = \frac{n\lambda}{2} \Rightarrow \lambda = \frac{2L}{n} \quad \text{[for } n \text{ loops]}$$

$$\Rightarrow \quad \frac{v}{\nu} = \frac{2L}{n} \Rightarrow \quad [\because v = \nu\lambda]$$

$$\Rightarrow \quad \nu = \frac{n}{2L}v = \frac{n}{2L}\sqrt{\frac{T}{\mu}} \quad [\because \text{velocity of transverse waves} = \sqrt{T/\mu}]$$

$\Rightarrow \nu \propto n$ [∵ length and speed are constants]

So, $\nu_1 : \nu_2 : \nu_3 : \nu_4 = n_1 : n_2 : n_3 : n_4$

$= 1 : 2 : 3 : 4$

Long Answer Type Questions

Q. 32 **The earth has a radius of 6400 km. The inner core of 1000 km radius is solid. Outside it, there is a region from 1000 km to a radius of 3500 km which is in molten state. Then again from 3500 km to 6400 km the earth is solid. Only longitudinal (*P*) waves can travel inside a liquid.**

Assume that the *P* wave has a speed of 8 km s^{-1} in solid parts and of 5 km s^{-1} in liquid parts of the earth. An earthquake occurs at some place close to the surface of the earth. Calculate the time after which it will be recorded in a seismometer at a diametrically opposite point on the earth, if wave travels along diameter?

Ans. Speed of wave in solid = 8 km/s

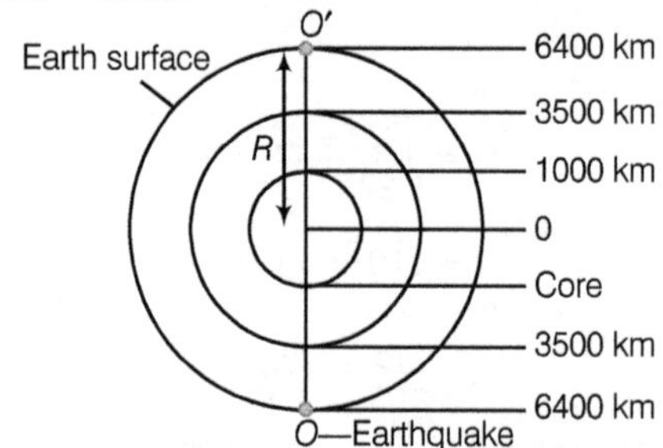

Speed of wave in liquid = 5 km/s

$$\text{Required time} = \left[\frac{1000-0}{8} + \frac{3500-1000}{5} + \frac{6400-3500}{8}\right] \times 2 \qquad [\because \text{diameter} = \text{radius} \times 2]$$

$$= \left[\frac{1000}{8} + \frac{2500}{5} + \frac{2900}{8}\right] \times 2 \qquad \left[\text{time} = \frac{\text{dis tance}}{\text{speed}}\right]$$

$$= [125 + 500 + 362.5] \times 2 = 1975$$

As we are considering at diametrically opposite point, hence there is a multiplication of 2.

Q. 33 **If c is rms speed of molecules in a gas and *v* is the speed of sound waves in the gas, show that *c/v* is constant and independent of temperature for all diatomic gases.**

Ans. We know that rms speed of molecules of a gas

$$c = \sqrt{\frac{3p}{\rho}} = \sqrt{\frac{3RT}{M}} \qquad \ldots\text{(i)}$$

where M = molar mass of the gas.

$$\text{Speed of sound wave in gas } v = \sqrt{\frac{\gamma p}{\rho}} = \sqrt{\frac{\gamma RT}{M}} \qquad \ldots\text{(ii)}$$

On dividing Eq. (i) by Eq. (ii), we get

$$\frac{c}{v} = \sqrt{\frac{3RT}{M} \times \frac{M}{\gamma RT}} \Rightarrow \frac{c}{v} = \sqrt{\frac{3}{\gamma}}$$

where γ = adiabatic constant for diatomic gas

$$\gamma = \frac{7}{5} \qquad \left[\text{since } \gamma = \frac{C_p}{C_V}\right]$$

Hence, $\frac{c}{v}$ = constant

Q. 34 Given below are some functions of x and t to represent the displacement of an elastic wave.

(i) $y = 5\cos(4x)\sin(20t)$

(ii) $y = 4\sin(5x - t/2) + 3\cos(5x - t/2)$

(iii) $y = 10\cos[(252 - 250)\pi t] \cos[(252 + 250)\pi t]$

(iv) $y = 100\cos(100\pi t + 0.5x)$

State which of these represent

(a) a travelling wave along– x-direction
(b) a stationary wave
(c) beats
(d) a travelling wave along– x-direction

Given reasons for your answers.

Thinking Process

To predict the nature of wave we have to compare with standard equations.

Ans. (a) The equation $y = 100\cos(100\pi t + 0.5x)$ is representing a travelling wave along x-direction.

(b) The equation $y = 5\cos(4x)\sin(20t)$ represents a stationary wave, because it contains sin, cos terms *i.e.*, combination of two progressive waves

(c) As the equation $y = 10\cos[(252 - 250)\pi t] \cdot \cos[(252 + 250)\pi t]$ involving sum and difference of two near by frequencies 252 and 250 have this equation represents beats formation.

(d) As the equation $y = 4\sin(5x - t/2) + 3\cos(5x - t/2)$ involves negative sign with x, have if represents a travelling wave along x-direction.

Note *We must not confuse with sign connected with x and direction of propagation of wave. It is just reversed, positive sign with x shown propagation of the wave in negative x-direction and vice-versa.*

Q. 35 In the given progressive wave $y = 5\sin(100\pi t - 0.4\pi x)$ where y and x are in metre, t is in second. What is the

(a) amplitude?
(b) wavelength?
(c) frequency?
(d) wave velocity?
(e) particle velocity amplitude?

Ans. Standard equation of a progressive wave is given by

$$y = a\sin(\omega t - kx + \phi)$$

This is travelling along positive x-direction.

Given equation is $y = 5\sin(100\pi t - 0.4\pi x)$

Comparing with the standard equation

(a) Amplitude = 5m

(b) $k = \dfrac{2\pi}{\lambda} = 0.4\pi$

$$\therefore \quad \text{Wavelength } \lambda = \frac{2\pi}{k} = \frac{2\pi}{0.4\pi} = \frac{20}{4} = 5\text{m}$$

(c) $\omega = 100\pi$

$$\omega = 2\pi\nu = 100\pi$$

$$\therefore \quad \text{Frequency } \nu = \frac{100\pi}{2\pi} = 50\,\text{Hz}$$

(d) Wave velocity $v = \frac{\omega}{k}$, where k is wave number and $k = \frac{2\pi}{\lambda}$.

$$= \frac{100\pi}{0.4\pi} = \frac{1000}{4}$$
$$= 250 \text{ m/s}$$

(e)
$$y = 5\sin(100\pi t - 0.4\pi x) \quad \ldots\text{(i)}$$
$$\frac{dy}{dt} = \text{particle velocity}$$

From Eq. (i),

$$\frac{dy}{dt} = 5(100\pi)\cos[100\pi t - 0.4\pi x]$$

For particle velocity amplitude $\left(\frac{dy}{dt}\right)_{max}$

Which will be for $\{\cos[100\pi t - 0.4\pi x]\}_{max} = 1$

$\therefore$ Particle velocity amplitude

$$= \left(\frac{dy}{dt}\right)_{max} = 5(100\pi) \times 1$$
$$= 500\,\pi \text{ m/s}$$

Q. 36 For the harmonic travelling wave $y = 2\cos 2\pi(10t - 0.0080x + 3.5)$ where x and y are in cm and t is in second. What is the phase difference between the oscillatory motion at two points separated by a distance of

(a) 4 m

(b) 0.5 m

(c) $\frac{\lambda}{2}$

(d) $\frac{3\lambda}{4}$ (at a given instant of time)

(e) What is the phase difference between the oscillation of a particle located at $x = 100$ cm, at $t = T$ sec and $t = 5$?

Ans. Given, wave functions are

$$y = 2\cos 2\pi(10t - 0.0080x + 3.5)$$
$$= 2\cos(20\pi t - 0.016\pi x + 7\pi)$$

Now, standard equation of a travelling wave can be written as

$$y = a\cos(\omega t - kx + \phi)$$

On comparing with above equation, we get

$$a = 2 \text{ cm}$$
$$\omega = 20\pi \text{ rad/s}$$
$$k = 0.016\pi$$

Path difference = 4 cm

(a) Phase difference $\Delta\phi = \frac{2\pi}{\lambda} \times$ Path difference

$$\therefore \quad \Delta\phi = 0.016\pi \times 4 \times 100 \quad \left(\because \frac{2\pi}{\lambda} = k\right)$$
$$= 6.4\pi \text{ rad}$$

(b) $\Delta\phi = \frac{2\pi}{\lambda} \times (0.5 \times 100)$ [$\because$ Path difference = 0.5 m]

$$= 0.016\pi \times 0.5 \times 100$$
$$= 0.8\pi \text{ rad}$$

(c) $\Delta\phi = \frac{2\pi}{\lambda} \times \left(\frac{\lambda}{2}\right) = \pi$ rad [$\because$ Path difference = $\lambda/2$]

(d) $\Delta\phi = \frac{2\pi}{\lambda} \times \frac{3\lambda}{4} = \frac{3\pi}{2}$ rad

(e) $T = \frac{2\pi}{\omega} = \frac{2\pi}{20\pi} = \frac{1}{10}$ s

$\therefore$ At $x = 100$ cm,

$$t = T$$
$$\phi_1 = 20\pi T - 0.016\pi(100) + 7\pi$$
$$= 20\pi\left(\frac{1}{10}\right) - 1.6\pi + 7\pi = 2\pi - 1.6\pi + 7\pi \quad \text{...(i)}$$

Again, at $x = 100$ cm, $t = 5$s

$$\phi_2 = 20\pi(5) - 0.016\pi(100) + 7\pi$$
$$= 100\pi - (0.016 \times 100)\pi + 7\pi$$
$$= 100\pi - 1.6\pi + 7\pi \quad \text{...(ii)}$$

$\therefore$ From Eqs. (i) and (ii), we get

$\Delta\phi$ = phase difference = $\phi_2 - \phi_1$

$$= (100\pi - 1.6\pi + 7\pi) - (2\pi - 1.6\pi + 7\pi)$$
$$= 100\pi - 2\pi = 98\pi \text{ rad}$$

Ingram Content Group UK Ltd.
Milton Keynes UK
UKHW021810060423
419751UK00006B/305